The Poetics of
Primitive Accumulation

# The Poetics of
# Primitive Accumulation

*English Renaissance Culture
and the Genealogy of Capital*

RICHARD HALPERN

*Cornell University Press*

Ithaca and London

First published 1991 by Cornell University Press.

International Standard Book Number 0–8014–2539–5 (cloth)
International Standard Book Number 0–8014–9772–8 (paper)
Library of Congress Catalog Card Number 90–55757
Printed in the United States of America
*Librarians: Library of Congress cataloging information
appears on the last page of the book.*

♾ The paper in this book meets the minimum requirements
of the American National Standard for Information Sciences—
Permanence of Paper for Printed Library Materials, ANSI Z39.48–1984.

# Contents

# Acknowledgments

An earlier version of Chapter 3 appeared as "John Skelton and the Poetics of Primitive Accumulation" in *Literary Theory/Renaissance Texts*, ed. Patricia Parker and David Quint (Baltimore: Johns Hopkins University Press, 1986). I thank the Johns Hopkins University Press for permission to reprint it here.

Friends and colleagues have aided and encouraged me at various points in this project. I especially thank Jeffrey Nunokawa, Lawrence Manley, James Holstun, Walter Cohen, and Thomas Greene. Richard Burt and Arthur Marotti, who read the manuscript for Cornell University Press, offered helpful and exacting appraisals. Both the style and substance of this book were improved by Judith Bailey's fine editing. For friendship, aid, and support during the rather drawn-out process of writing this book, four persons singled themselves out. Margaret Ferguson taught me how to read Renaissance texts; her counsel and friendship mean more to me than she can know. Joseph Loewenstein often placed his considerable erudition and intelligence at my service and saved me from embarrassing blunders more than once. Christopher Kendrick corrected everything from my spelling to my episteme. I thank him as well for maintaining a nourishing intellectual dialogue with me over many years and often several thousand miles. Rhonda Garelick read every chapter at every stage of completion. In many respects she has been my most loyal and most demanding critic, and she has sustained me in a hundred ways besides.

R. H.

The Poetics of
Primitive Accumulation

# Marxism, New Historicism, and the Renaissance

This book attempts to inscribe the English literary Renaissance within the prehistory of capital. It takes its place within the various attempts at historical renarration at work in Renaissance studies today, but it employs a narrative and a set of concepts derived mainly from the realm of Marxist theory. More specifically, it situates certain aspects of Renaissance culture within the transition from feudalism to capitalism, conceived of as both economic and social modes of production.

To delimit what might otherwise be an unwieldy and impossibly ambitious topic I have chosen to focus my narrative on a process Marx dubbed "primitive accumulation." Marx's term denotes the various means by which fractions of the late feudal producing classes, including peasants and some small artisans, were dispossessed or otherwise deprived of the means of economic production by which they sustained themselves and thus became available for employment as landless or "free" laborers. Marx introduces the concept of primitive accumulation at the end of volume 1 of *Capital* in order to provide what he calls a "prehistory" of capitalism. In his historical exposition he focuses on violent and often state-supported methods, such as enclosure of agricultural land or the dissolution of monasteries, by means of which significant numbers of persons were converted into free laborers during the sixteenth and seventeenth centuries. Such matters may well seem both socially and conceptually distant from the literary realm. My interest in Marx's narrative has less to do with the materials it can provide for topical readings than with the way in which it highlights the distinctiveness of a Marxist narrative of transition.

But it is precisely this narrative and its theoretical assumptions, more than the historical data it mobilizes in its support, that will likely provoke resistance today. Putting aside the "practical" critique of neo-Stalinism and its theoretical underpinnings, now well under way in (what was formerly) the Eastern bloc, there is still a general assumption among both new historicists and poststructuralists that the "metanarrative" of Marxism is a hopeless antique.[1] To invoke "modes of production" is to come perilously close to an array of conceptions that, in this post-Foucauldian climate, have given Marxism the aura of metaphysics: conceptions such as economic determinism and the base-superstructure model of society. It is to raise the specter of a totalizing mode of analysis, one that would reduce multiple histories to the *grand récit* of History (its capital H evidently borrowed from "Hegel"). It is, finally, to abandon the narrative richness of anecdote for the gray abstractions of theory.

A full-scale defense of a Marxist hermeneutics obviously falls beyond the scope of this book. Such defenses have already been made by theorists of considerable power—most persuasively, to my mind, by Louis Althusser and Fredric Jameson.[2] It is not my intention, in any case, to deny the validity of some of the questions and objections raised against Marxism. Given a generally and increasingly hostile climate, however, I think it prudent, by way of introduction to this book, to state what I think Marxism still has to offer that other varieties of historical and political criticism do not. In so doing I hope also to set forth the principles that, sometimes only implicitly, unite the following chapters.

Instead of defending against Foucauldian and new-historical critique, launching a counterattack against them, or "subsuming" these movements within a Marxist project, I prefer to begin by arguing the *complementarity* of Marxist and non-Marxist approaches. This I do somewhat polemically by isolating regions and models of power which are accessible to Marxist but not to Foucauldian or new-historical analysis.

Because the new historicism shuns overt allegiance to any single authorizing model (for example, Marx or Foucault), because it draws its inspiration from a variety of disciplines including social history and anthropology, and because its leading practitioners tend to resist both incorporation into a movement and, sometimes, the name "new historicism" itself, one must be careful in ascribing one particular model of power to all its exponents and productions.[3] In the case of Renaissance new historicism, it nevertheless seems safe to say that the predominant model of power is sovereignty, and that power is therefore given a juridico-political coding. Much of the significant work of new historicism has concentrated on the institutions of monarchy and the court—a reasonable strategy given the centrality of the monarch to both political power and cultural production.[4] This orientation naturally enough leads to a focus on those mechanisms of power which radiate out from political sovereignty: censorship, punishment, surveillance, and above all spectacle. The power of sovereignty works primarily by making itself *visible*; it promulgates and extends itself through public progresses, entertainments, and propaganda, on the one hand, and overt force or threats of force, on the other. Its cultural manifestation as spectacle thus corresponds to its manner of juridico-political coding, which quite openly proclaims its rule through declarations of unique customary right, the executive power of proclamation, and so forth. The privilege of kingship does not try to conceal itself; it is explicitly inscribed in law, in the structure of the state, and in royal spectacle—all of which declare an essential and patent inequality of power in the relation between monarch and subject. Some more recent new-historical work has shifted its gaze from the dazzling sight of the king, but a kind of afterimage persists in its *model* of power, which is still predominantly juridico-political, and therefore focuses on relations of force or sovereignty (more or less subtle) between unequal, hierarchical subjects: husband and wife, father and child, master and servant, colonizer and colonized.

The predominance of this model in new-historical studies simply reflects its predominance in Renaissance society itself. But it is not, and does not claim to be, theoretically or historically exhaustive. An important instance of social power that eludes politico-juridical coding occupies the very heart of Marx's theoretical inquiry in *Capital*: the method of extracting surplus value, which distinguishes capitalism from all prior modes of production. By definition, class societies require mechanisms for transferring labor (or the value produced by it) from the direct producers to the ruling groups. But in the capitalist mode of production such extraction occurs entirely within the economic mechanism itself, without the need for direct political or legal coercion. As a result, capital operates a historically unprecedented form of social power which is opaque to analysis by models derived from the political, legal, or even (it turns out) economic sphere, if the economic is conceived of merely as a sphere of exchange. The early chapters of *Capital*, which examine the exchange or circulation of commodities, systematize the theoretical concepts and field of classical political economy, and in so doing, they render the origin of economic profit increasingly fugitive, ultimately driving it in part from the sphere of economic circulation. Even the buying and selling of labor power (which for Marx will ultimately constitute the "secret" of surplus value) is represented as being as free and equal as any other exchange of commodities:

> The sphere of circulation or commodity exchange, within whose boundaries the sale and purchase of labour-power goes on, is in fact a very Eden of the innate rights of man. It is the exclusive realm of Freedom, Equality, Property, and Bentham. Freedom, because both buyer and seller of a commodity, let us say of labour-power, are determined only by their own free will. They contract as free persons, who are equal before the law. Their contract is the final result in which their joint will finds a common legal expression. Equality, because each enters into relation with the other, as with a simple owner of commodities, and they exchange equivalent for equivalent. Property, because each disposes only of what is his own. And Bentham, because each looks only to his own advantage.[5]

Marx's sarcasm reveals his contempt for the ideology of political economy; it should not, nevertheless, be taken to suggest that the "Eden" he describes is entirely an illusion. If the marketplace represents for him a debasement (or rather, a debased fulfillment) of the ideals of the Enlightenment, if the bourgeois revolutions find their struggles for politico-juridical equality and against monarchical privilege reduced to commercial contract law, it nevertheless remains true that as buyers and sellers of commodities, labor and capital *are* formally free and equal. No direct compulsion, force, or hierarchic obligation—in short, no sovereignty—clouds the social transparency of the labor contract. If this contract nevertheless ensures the economic dominance of one party or class over the other, this is not because a moment of juridico-political force has intervened. Labor power, it turns out, is unique among commodities because its "consumption" by the purchaser produces more value than it cost him; but in consuming this commodity he acts as all other purchasers do, and he has paid for it as fully. Thus the moment of "power" or coercion remains fugitive or latent even when we step into the factory or site of production, for whereas industry has a visibly disciplinary character, neither physical nor mind-forged manacles tie workers to their machines. It is true that they will starve if they do *not* agree to a wage-labor contract, since no other means of support is available, but "necessity" of one sort or another determines the purchase and sale of all commodities. Capital replaces the visible or patent form of sovereign political power with an invisible and resolutely *latent* form of economic domination.[6]

Clearly, Marx's analysis of capital provides an influential model for Michel Foucault's investigations into the *technologies* of social power. Like Marx, Foucault is interested in the social regimes that succeed sovereignty and its "juridico-discursive" coding.[7] For Foucault, capital offers a sometimes explicit, sometimes implicit model for mechanisms of power which are latent rather than patent, and invisible rather than spectacular;[8] mechanisms that aim not at restricting or immobilizing (as does the law) but at "proliferating, innovating, annexing, creating" and at "expanding at an increasing rate";[9] "mechanisms of power which, instead of proceeding by deduction, are integrated into the productive efficiency of the apparatuses from within, into the growth of this efficiency and into the use of what it produces."[10] When Foucault contrasts the "old principle of 'levying violence,' which governed the economy of power," to the "principle of 'mildness-production-profit,'" which governs the economy of discipline, it is clear that a more classical and restricted notion of economic transition inspires this more general one. Foucault quite directly aligns the "old" principle of "levying violence" with precapitalist modes of economic extraction: "levying on money or products by royal, seigneurial, ecclesiastical taxation; levying on men and time by *corvées* or press-ganging, by locking up or banishing vagabonds."[11] Similarly, the principle of "mildness-production-profit" corresponds to capitalist modes of producing and extracting surplus value.

At one point in *Discipline and Punish*, Foucault explicitly coordinates his historical project with Marx's history of the transition to capitalism:

If the economic take-off of the West began with the techniques that made possible the accumulation of capital, it might perhaps be said that the methods for administering the accumulation of men [in schools, workshops, barracks, etc.] made possible a political take-off in relation to the traditional, ritual, costly, violent forms of power, which soon fell into disuse and were superseded by a subtle, calculated technology of subjection. In fact, the two processes—the accumulation of men and the accumulation of capital—cannot be separated; it would not have been possible to solve the problem of the accumulation of men without the growth of an apparatus of production capable of both sustaining them and using them; conversely, the techniques that made the cumulative multiplicity of men useful accelerated the accumulation of capital. At a less general level, the technological mutation of the apparatus of production, the division of labour and the elaboration of the disciplinary techniques sustained an ensemble of very close relations. . . . Each makes the other possible and necessary; each provides a model for the other.[12]

Obviously, there are limits to this apparent harmony of approach; Foucault's work is often deeply subversive of Marxist assumptions. Yet a tense and mutually critical complementarity is possible, and has been persuasively urged by some Marxist critics.[13]

The first part of my book takes up Foucault's suggestion that the histories of discipline and capital might supplement each other. My first chapter examines literary style and culture in the disciplinary context of the Tudor schools. Although the specific techniques and models of discipline differ in important ways from those Foucault locates in the eighteenth and nineteenth centuries (and, indeed, bear a closer kinship to Louis Althusser's concept of ideological "interpellation"), my project is generally congruent with Foucault's in that I locate a model for pedagogical authority other than sovereignty, and a mechanism of ideological training that bears a close affinity to Foucault's principle of "mildness-production-profit." The second chapter then outlines a Marxist model of the transition to capitalism and investigates the ways in which the disciplinary and literary training of the Tudor schools inhabits this socioeconomic transformation. Thus, in my preliminary, institutional analysis of Renaissance literary culture, I interweave two histories: of the "primitive" accumulation of capital, and of the "primitive" accumulation of men.[14]

For all the working or provisional complementarity between Marxist and Foucauldian approaches, however, there are important differences to be discerned. Some that are especially pertinent to this book derive from the Althusserian concept of relative autonomy and its implications for a theory of the capitalist state. For Althusser, relative autonomy signifies that each level or instance of a social formation—political, ideological, cultural, economic, etc.—possesses its own characteristic structures, temporalities, and effectivity. These instances react on one another in a complexly overdetermining manner, and as a result, social formations cannot be conceived of as "expressive totalities" in which everything directly reflects an economic base.[15]

Nicos Poulantzas puts this Althusserian conception to interesting use in expounding a theory of the capitalist state. Poulantzas's theory is founded on the uniquely distinct autonomy of the political from the economic which marks the capitalist mode of production. Because capital can extract surplus value "on its own" (that is, without direct political or juridical coercion), the capitalist state is not obligated to intervene directly in the economic mechanism or in the process of surplus extraction. In order to secure class rule, then, the state generally need neither engage in direct political domination nor determine its subjects as agents of production; it need only maintain the global equilibrium of the system and safeguard those forms of juridical cohesion and equality which underwrite the sale and purchase of labor power.[16] By addressing its subjects as the abstractly equal "citizens" of a nation-state, Poulantzas argues, the capitalist state both obscures from these subjects their own class identities and safeguards the economic mechanism of capital. As a result, the liberal capitalist state secures class domination by the paradoxical means of promoting political and legal equality; and it does so not as the conspiratorial instrument of the ruling classes but by means of a genuine (if relative) autonomy even from the immediate political or economic interests of those classes.[17]

The Marxist notion of relative autonomy, as instanced in Poulantzas's theory of the capitalist state, has several important consequences for cultural studies. First of all, it extends "latent," fugitive, or nonsovereign forms of power even to the juridico-political mechanisms of the state itself. For the capitalist state secures and reproduces political dominion precisely by *not* exercising violence or class power, save in exceptional instances, and by limiting the right of others to do so. If this is a form of power, it nevertheless lacks points of application or surfaces of transmission. Class domination is still secured, but through an indirect and dislocated mechanism: domination is "recouped" elsewhere (in the economic), almost accidentally and not through any mechanism recognizable as sovereign "power."

At the same time, the concept of relative autonomy also distinguishes a Marxist from a Foucauldian mode of analysis. Foucault abandons the model of sovereignty in part to free his concept of power from any origin in a governing subjectivity. Power, that is, cannot be theorized as originating in the "choices or decisions of an individual subject" (a sovereign subject); yet it is "imbued, through and through, with calculation: there is no power that is exercised without a series of aims and objectives." Hence, "power relationships are both intentional and non-subjective."[18] In rejecting a juridico-discursive coding of power, then, Foucault adopts what might be called a strategic-instrumentalist coding, in which technologies of power serve, if not subjects exactly, then at least strategic intentionalities that operate *like* subjects in some ways. In so doing, however, he saddles his analytical method with certain functionalist assumptions. The so-called antirepressive hypothesis, for example, defines a circuit in which the "perverse implantation" of sexuality is directly recouped as knowledge-power.[19] No matter how mobile or interrupted, this discursive apparatus loops back into itself so as to form a strategic instrument of social control—which is why Foucault's conception of power often takes on a seemingly conspiratorial mien. This functionalist totality, imbued with many of the characteristics or effects of consciousness even while it is denied any origin in subjectivity, may be Foucault's own metaphysical counterpart to the Marxist notion of society as a structural totality. The strategic-instrumentalist aspect of his method has flourished, moreover, in new-historical studies of the Renaissance, which frequently argue that some dominant institution strategically "provokes" subversion so as to recontain it all the better.[20]

Nothing, of course, is intrinsically wrong with such an approach; my analysis of Tudor schooling in Chapter 1 argues for just such a strategic intentionality. Only this ought not be made into a necessary or untranscendable precondition for analysis, and its consequences ought to be recognized. A Marxist theory of relative autonomy, by contrast, frees one from the Foucauldian axiom that "power is everywhere" as well as from the tracing of closed strategic-discursive loops. It enables one to maintain that even if a cultural discourse is *not* directly inscribed in power—that is to say, even if it does not form part of a "strategic" formation—it may nevertheless generate effects of domination or, for that matter, subversion by means of its (nonstrategic and purely structural) relation to other, relatively autonomous areas of the social formation. Althusserian Marxism, in other words, understands history as a "process without a subject," meaning not only individual subjects but also institutional or collective ones, including classes. And it allows that pertinent political effects may arise from *purely con-*

*junctural* formations, even if these are not "strategic." Many of the ideological effects of Tudor schooling which I discuss in my second chapter (especially the last section) fall under this category.

Of course, my claims for Marxism have centered on its value for understanding a specifically *capitalist* social formation and, indeed, a mature or liberal one, in which "fugitive" or latent modes of power predominate. Since the Renaissance predates not only this liberal phase but, as I shall later maintain, all but the most nascent forms of capitalist production, it might reasonably be objected that my arguments thus far are irrelevant to the subject matter of this book. Indeed, primitive accumulation as it is described by Marx entails applications of class power far cruder and more direct than those that tend to attract the interest of new historicists. Why, then, should the subtler logics of surplus value or relative autonomy be brought into play here?

One answer is that certain early forms of capital—in particular, merchant's capital—were already firmly entrenched by the beginning of the sixteenth century. Another is that certain political, legal, or cultural domains were able to anticipate those of a capitalist formation even in advance of capitalism *as such*. Poulantzas argues a strong version of this thesis in his treatment of the absolutist state, which he regards as actively creating the preconditions for capitalist production. Its ability to do so is predicated, however, on the fact that absolutism *already* possesses the specific autonomy characteristic of the capitalist state, even though, Poulantzas says, "the theoretical presuppositions of this autonomy (the separation of the direct producer from the means of production) are not yet actually realized." Indeed, "the relative autonomy of the absolutist state relative both to the economic instance and to the field of the class struggle . . . was precisely what allowed it to function in favour of primary accumulation of capital."[21]

Some readers have found Poulantzas's reasoning to be circular, but his specific claims have some merit. Tudor absolutism certainly *claimed* a relative autonomy whenever it cast itself as acting either in its own interest or in those of the commonwealth, rather than on behalf of a particular class. And in fact its relations with the landed nobility were not such as to suggest that it was in any simple sense the political instrument of that class.[22] Poulantzas, further, is correct to suggest that the state's ability to promote the primitive accumulation of capital (for instance, in appropriating and then selling monastic lands—a direct assault on a fraction of the feudal landowning class) depended on its relative autonomy. Thus, even in its crudest exercises of power the Tudor state anticipated in certain respects the characteristics of the capitalist state. It did so as well in its conversion of feudal ties to strictly political ties and in the consequent propensity of its official language to speak of abstract "subjects" of the realm, with implications of formal juridico-political equality. This language did not replace the older vocabulary of estates and classes, but it signified a newly constituted autonomy of the state with respect to them. In all these ways and others (for example, its claim to a legitimate monopoly on the use of force), the abolutist state anticipated the forms of a more advanced capitalist state and thus created many of the juridical, political, and even economic presuppositions of capital.

Poulantzas's theory of absolutism has been criticized as teleological and circular for seeming to depict the absolutist state as a kind of scouting party sent out to colonize the late feudal polity on behalf of a capitalism that does not yet exist. (I shall take up this issue in Chapter 2). At the very least, the fact that the politico-juridical "superstructure" of capitalism seems to predate capital itself might be taken to argue for an absolute rather than a merely relative autonomy of the political from the economic, thus negating the Althusserian belief that the economy always exerts "determination in the last instance" over the whole of a social formation.

Such objections locate, if not a theoretical contradiction, at least a silence concerning the origins of absolutism. Poulantzas analyzes the absolutist state from the point of view of its role in creating the preconditions for capital, but he is vague about what enabled it to play this role, to assume a position of relative autonomy with respect to the social classes of the late feudal polity, and so on.[23] In other words, Poulantzas locates absolutism in a prehistory of capital rather than in the late feudal formation that served as its point of origin.

In this respect Poulantzas's account of absolutism is congruent—both in its emphases and in its silences or absences—with Marx's account of primitive accumulation. For as I argue in my second chapter, Marx offers an *economic* prehistory of capital rather than a history of the transition to capitalism, and thus Poulantzas's account of absolutism may justly be regarded as an extension of this project to the politico-juridical realm. What we have here is a genealogy of elements—political, legal, economic, cultural—which will later combine into or contribute to a capitalist social formation, yet are not in any sense embryonic forms of capitalism. This narration from the perspective of the future is not only *not* teleological but, as I maintain later, a defense against teleology, as well as against other "metaphysical" remnants that Marxist history is often accused of harboring. The shift to a genealogical mode of analysis in both Marx and Poulantzas signals the difficulty of fully theorizing a transitional process, if by this one means arguing for its theoretical ineluctability. Yet to have "succeeded" in such a project would have been to impose an iron grid of necessity on history. The determinism for which Marxism can legitimately argue is more modest; it agrees with the etymological sense of the word as a limit on the field of the possible rather than an irresistible compulsion in any one direction. The presence of a genealogical discourse within a narrative of transition is not a mere failure to achieve theoretical closure or completeness, then, but the sign of a certain lack within theory when it confronts the concrete of history.

Disrupting both the internal coherence of theory and its complete adequation with the concrete-real, this lack has served some as an excuse to abandon Marxist theory entirely. Might not such theoretical difficulties point to a more fundamental and indeed incurable flaw within the entire machinery of periodization and transition? Why not abandon even the concept of *relative* autonomy, which still assumes a social totality? Why not simply substitute Foucauldian genealogy for the cumbersome Marxist concept of transition?

To answer these questions it will suffice to examine the results of Foucault's own "break" with Marxism. If *Discipline and Punish* left open the possibility of a *rapprochement* with Marxist history, *The History of Sexuality* opens by rejecting any such entanglements. In his initial assault on the "repressive hypothesis," Foucault remarks:

This discourse on modern sexual repression holds up well, owing no doubt to how easy it is to uphold. A solemn historical and political guarantee protects it. By placing the advent of the age of repression in the seventeenth century, after hundreds of years of open spaces and free expression, one adjusts it to coincide with the development of capitalism: it becomes an integral part of the bourgeois order. The minor chronicle of sex and its trials is transposed into the ceremonious history of the modes of production; its trifling aspect fades from view. A principle of explanation emerges after the fact: if sex was so rigorously repressed, this is because it is incompatible with a general and intensive work imperative.

In rejecting this system of explanation, Foucault suggests that it is Marxism's hypotheses that are "repressive." By subordinating sexuality to economy and assigning it a superstructural place in the social totality, Marxism forces the history of sexuality (like everything else) to fit the contours of the history of modes of production. Overturning the repressive hypothesis thus mean rejecting Marxism as well, and correlating sexuality instead with multiple, shifting domains of discourse.

Having freed sexuality from capital, however, Foucault paradoxically reconstitutes it *as* capital, or rather, invests it with the formal logic of capital. Hence sexuality is "proliferating, innovating, annexing, creating," and has been "expanding at an increasing rate since the seventeenth century."[24] Nor are these characteristics limited to the restricted domain of sexuality as "bio-power," where it feeds back into the economic mechanism; rather, they characterize sexuality in all its discursive fields and all its operations of power. Sexuality need not be constrained by an external "law of capital" because it already manifests this as its own, immanent law. Foucault, in effect, dismantles Marxism a system of metonymies only to rebuild it as a constellation of metaphor. Capital does not subordinate other social instances to itself but finds itself already replicated throughout the social formation, as if it were the god of some Leibnitzian universe. Or perhaps it is itself just one such replication in a larger discursive field. In any case, despite its theoretical aim of preserving heterogeneity, in practice Foucault's insistence on absolute rather than relative autonomy ends up homogenizing the social field. As a result Foucault cannot really theorize the conditions under which regimes of power replace each other and is forced to adopt the relatively abstract expedient of Nietzschean genealogy.

Despite these shortcomings, however, Foucault is still willing to tackle the issue of epochal transitions head on. Renaissance new historicism tends to abjure such questions entirely, situating itself within a realm of the "early modern" which is somehow always-already-there yet always still in progress. Local, institutional transactions are analyzed without asking what global conditions, if any, serve as their condition of possibility. "Modernity" is simply assumed as the ever-receding and unexamined horizon of analysis. If

Foucault's version of genealogy renders questions of epochal transition excessively abstract, the new historicism dissolves them
into empiricisms or pragmatisms. In this study I have tried, instead, to maintain theoretical and genealogical narratives in a
state of creative tension. Marx's prehistory of capital provides a
model for how theoretical discourse can absorb a genealogical narrative without simply fragmenting.

My project in this book is to locate those regions within English
Renaissance culture where the elements of a specifically capitalist
culture begin to emerge in nascent or anticipatory forms from
within the context of a late feudal society. Their emergence in advance of capital itself is made possible by the relative autonomy of
culture. Yet to state this is not to ignore more direct and ordinary
relations of social causality or influence, nor is it to deny that
these anticipatory regions exert in their turn a powerful and complex counterinfluence on the dominant social order. It is simply to
indicate that as part of a larger prehistory of capital, my own book
tends to lean forward in certain respects. Sometimes this stance
necessitates pushing the boundaries of narration a bit beyond the
Renaissance proper, as when in Chapter 2 I connect elements of
humanist theory and pedagogy with the later birth of political
economy. Sometimes it requires me to locate how these anticipatory regions disrupt the ideological closure or coherence of an
older mode of discourse, as I do in my chapter on More's *Utopia*,
which shows how the economic logic of capital tends to dislocate
the juridico-political order of the Utopian polity. Sometimes it
calls for locating vectors of historical development within literary
works, such as in the *Lear* chapter, which traces Shakespeare's reaction to nascent and unprecedented modes of class conflict and
competition. I call this book *The Poetics of Primitive Accumulation* not to oblige myself to refer repeatedly to a specifically economic narrative but to mobilize the genealogical force of this
narrative and to articulate it with other areas of the social formation—political, cultural, ideological.[25]

Nevertheless, it is the specificity of the economic that makes it
valuable both as an intermittent topical focus and as the source for
a different model of social power. If this book departs from the
loose boundaries of new-historical practice, it does so in part by its
inclination toward the economic and away from the political
(though this is *only* an inclination). The thread that ties all these
chapters together is the assumption that the rhetorical and literary
culture of the Renaissance can be usefully situated within, if not

quite "explained" by, the transition from feudalism to capitalism. To advance this thesis is also to claim that economic modes of production are crucial categories for an understanding of historical (and hence cultural) process. It is not to impute to them a mysterious omnipotence that installs them at the heart of all historical phenomena, but it is to grant them a specific and powerful materiality that is worthy of notice.

If there is a polemical point here, it is that the new historicism has tended to avoid the materiality of the economic in order to focus on political or sovereign models of power. Yet it is not quite true to suggest that the economic has been entirely ignored. The more recent work of Stephen Greenblatt, in particular, has tended to invoke a model of economic circulation (or "negotiation") and to understand cultural production as a process of inter- or ex-change among different levels or regions of the social edifice. He has recently gone so far as to employ the term *capitalism* to designate our sociocultural formation, and if he still expresses a noticeable hostility toward Marxist theory, his work nevertheless employs a conceptual vocabulary that increasingly suggests a (still antagonistic) compromise of sorts.[26]

On the other hand, to argue that *everything* is an economy, to figure all of culture as an expanded or general process of circulation, risks obliterating the specificity of the economic just as fully as did the early new-historical avoidance of it. If it is not to become trapped by a sort of specious metaphor, any theory of symbolic capital (of which Greenblatt's "poetics of culture" forms one version) cannot overhastily absorb or cancel the concept of capital as it is understood in a strictly (or restrictedly) economic sense. It is to Greenblatt's credit that he does *not* reduce circulation or exchange to merely figural status; on the contrary, his insistence on a semipermeable boundary between economic and cultural spheres ends up producing something that looks not entirely unlike a Marxist concept of relative autonomy. I would only want to add that the boundaries between economic and noneconomic regions are not merely imperfectly permeable but also asymmetrically so and that capital in the restricted sense defines the conditions under which other kinds of cultural material or "energy" can enter its domain. Lawrence Stone's book *The Crisis of the Aristocracy* can, in this context, be reread as an argument for the dominance of economic over symbolic capital.[27] For the economic changes that began to favor the gentry over the aristocracy not only set limits to the extent of aristocratic expense or display; they also interrupted the circuit through which these older forms of symbolic capital could be reconverted into liquid wealth, while creating entirely new domains of cultural capital (literacy, education, and others). If the economic and the cultural reveal a mutual determination here, it is nevertheless clear that the economic plays the leading role, both in "funding" a symbolic economy and in specifying what can and cannot enter its circuits of exchange. To say that a ruling class secures its dominance through symbolic as well as material means should not, then, be taken to impute a perfect equivalence between these.

The limits to a symbolic economy form an explicit focus for my reading of *King Lear*. They also determine my decision in the first and second chapters to analyze Tudor education not as a form of cultural capital but as a form of ideological training and to treat it less as a directly convertible means of enrichment for the rising classes than as a relatively autonomous process that nevertheless has pertinent (but merely conjunctural) effects on economic class divisions.

On the other hand, in my choice of post-Marxist theorists (Bataille, Deleuze and Guattari, the early Baudrillard) I have focused on those figures who try to expand the boundaries of Marxist political economy while still respecting them and who therefore open up lines of connection with other cultural areas without simply erasing distinctions. As I have argued, I think that Foucault can be assimilated to this group as well and that his indebtedness to Marxism is, though often more covert, yet no less direct.[28] Ultimately, all these theorists are connected here by their relation to Marxist political economy, which provides the theoretical center of this book and which radiates out, more or less directly, into each of its chapters.

# PART ONE

# CHAPTER ONE

# A Mint of Phrases:
# Ideology and Style Production
# in Tudor England

Looking back somewhat sourly on the culture of the sixteenth century, Francis Bacon wrote that it was marked by

> an affectionate study of eloquence and copie of speech, which then began to flourish. This grew speedily to an excess; for men began to hunt more after words than matter; and more after the choiceness of the phrase, and the round and clean composition of the sentence, and the sweet falling of the clauses, and the varying and illustration of their works with tropes and figures, than after the weight of matter, worth of subject, soundness of argument, life of invention, or depth of judgement. . . . Then did Car of Cambridge, and Ascham, with their lectures and writings, almost deify Cicero and Demosthenes, and allure all young men that were studious unto that delicate and polished kind of learning. . . . In sum, the whole inclination and bent of those times was rather towards copie than weight.[1]

What concerns Bacon here is not an imbalance within literary style but the proliferation of stylistic elegance throughout all of serious discourse. Paradoxically, the very autonomy of style allows it to colonize and dominate all other discursive functions; and as if to illustrate this peril, Bacon's own language falls temporarily under the spell of style, succumbing to a delight in the "round and clear composition of the sentence, and the sweet falling of the clauses." This sudden access of eloquence is not a return of the repressed, however, but a witty tribute to the lures of a humanist tradition from which Bacon only halfheartedly tried to extricate himself.

In assailing what one critic has called the "stylistic explosion" of the sixteenth century,[2] Bacon questions the values of the English literary Renaissance itself. Ciceronianism was only one small part of this movement, but more than any other it came to represent a mysterious addiction to style. Gabriel Harvey famously described his own bout with Ciceronianism in the confessional manner of a recovering alcoholic:

> I valued words more than content, language more than thought, the one art of speaking more than the thousand subjects of knowledge; I preferred the mere style of Marcus Tully to all the postulates of philosophers and mathematicians; I believed that the bone and sinew of imitation lay in my ability to choose as many brilliant and elegant words as possible, to reduce them into order, and to connect them together in a rhythmical period.[3]

Both Bacon and Harvey attribute this addiction to style to the influence of humanism in the universities; thus what begins as a textual imbalance is revealed to be an institutional and cultural one.[4]

Bacon's criticisms focus on the universities, but humanists from Erasmus to Roger Ascham to Richard Mulcaster devoted their pedagogical writings mostly to issues of primary and secondary schooling. It was in the Tudor and early Stuart grammar schools that the humanist program achieved its widest social and cultural influence; and it was there too that an education in classical letters and style was most rigorously pursued. "In our *grammer* schooles we professe the tongues nay rather the entraunce of tongues," wrote Mulcaster in his *Positions* (1581).[5] In *A Consolation for our Grammar Schooles* (London, 1622), John Brinsley included a section titled "Contents in Generall of Such Things as may (by Gods blessing) be easily effected in our ordinarie Grammar schooles." Of the 34 goals listed, 32 have to do with classical style, rhetoric, and language; one (number 25) with making use of the "matter" of these authors; and one (number 31) with religious instruction. Such a curriculum made some sense as preparation for the universities, but more often the grammar schools represented the limits of formal education—something Mulcaster worried about in print: "And what if some will never proceede any further, but rest in those pleasaunt kinde of writers, which delite most in gaing [gaying] of their language as poetes, histories, discourses, and such, as wil be counted generall men?"[6] The question was not an idle one since entrance to the universities was restricted but the number of grammar schools had long been rising.[7] The "excessive" delight in style which Bacon attributed to sixteenth-century texts was thus in some sense merely the expression of an instituted curriculum; the autonomy of style from content and of word from thing reflected a mysteriously "autonomous" force within the pedagogical apparatus that cultivated textual production.

But why did Tudor society spend so much of its resources on a pedagogical apparatus—the grammar school—devoted largely to the "gaying" of language? Classic studies such as T. W. Baldwin's *William Shakspere's Small Latine and Lesse Greeke* (1944) and Donald Clark's *John Milton at St. Paul's School* (1948) have demonstrated the formative influence of grammar school curricula on some of the great writers of the English Renaissance. Yet Baldwin and Clark found the dominance of such a program surprisingly unproblematic. Figures such as Shakespeare and Milton were, after all, only the exotic effluvia of a system whose central purpose was presumably not to train poets and playwrights. A strange and implicit circularity inhabits these curricular studies of the Tudor grammar schools; it is as if the *Geist* of the Renaissance, writing history in the future anterior, simply produced the perfect institutional apparatus for its own development. Yet the extraordinary thing is that the Tudor educational system was so well adapted to training poets, playwrights, and pamphleteers—or, to put it differently, that the great writers and stylists of the age were precisely those who most fully mastered and internalized this system, who followed, to prodigious lengths, the cultural trajectory it imparted to them. Once we step outside of a literary context, however, it is no longer obvious why Tudor society would allocate a substantial part of its resources to an educational program that so heavily emphasized the teaching of classical rhetoric, letters, and style. One no longer wishes to identify the Renaissance with humanism, of course, but humanist schooling comes closest to representing what might seem an organized, strategic "investment" in a literary Renaissance. Who, if anyone, decided to "have" a Renaissance? And who paid for it?

## Humanism, Rhetoric, and the Ideological Production of the Subject

While the form of these questions is somewhat facetious, they nevertheless pose a real problem, one that becomes all the more puzzling if we take it as axiomatic that the primary function of schooling is to reproduce the dominant social order. This idea, which has informed recent work, was current even in the early modern period.[8] In the words of a seventeenth-century educator, "'Tis plain, that the scholastic state lays the groundwork and foundation for the other three states, *viz.* economical, ecclesiastical and political."[9] Even allowing for rhetorical exaggeration we can see in this statement a growing sense of the importance of the school as a means of social reproduction.

Desire to maintain the ecclesiastical and political "states" certainly influenced the crown's role in Tudor education. The authorized primer issued by Henry VIII in 1545 announced that, along with reading, it would teach "the better bringing up of youth in the knowledge of their duty toward God, their prince, and all others in their degree."[10] In the 1530s Erasmian humanism got an important boost from Henry VIII's quarrel with the canon lawyers, when the need for a curricular substitute for scholasticism helped to install humanism at Oxford and Cambridge.[11] Yet even from this perspective the success of the humanist program seems peculiar, for its emphasis on the classical canon tended to displace Christian training. To be sure, many classical authors were felt to be ethically improving (even if some held republicanist political views), but this relative movement from religious to ethical ideology may seem striking at a time when the state was embroiled in religious controversies of considerable import.[12] As we shall see, moreover, the humanist program of style production tended to neutralize textual content, to the detriment of older schemes of social legitimation. If grammar schools served an ideological function, then, this cannot be understood in a crudely functionalist way as mere religious or political propaganda.

Maintenance of the economic "state," as well as of the political and ecclesiastical, seems also to have played a role in Tudor education, at least judging by those who funded the building and support of schools. The state and the landed aristocracy (especially the courtier fraction) had a significant part, but merchant's capital played the leading role; thus various elements of the late feudal ruling class saw some reason or reasons to invest a good deal of money in the building of schools.[13]

Merchant's capital, supplied in part by individuals and in part by trade guilds (the Mercers and the Merchant Tailors of London are conspicuous examples), funded schooling for various reasons, including cultural prestige, conspicuous philanthropic expense, and the (slightly exaggerated) belief that literacy contributed to social mobility. Richard Mulcaster was cynical but largely just: "These people by their generall trades, will make thousandes poore: and for giving one penie to any one poore of those many thousands will be counted charitable. They will give a scholer some petie poore exhibition to seeme to be religious, and under a sclender veale of counterfeit liberalitie, hide the spoil of the ransaked povertie."[14] Mulcaster depicts such charity in a purely conspiratorial light (common enough when discussing merchants, who were frequently accused of economic conspiracy), but it probably worked to mystify the givers as well as others.

Merchants funded schools as well "for practical business purposes—to supply literate apprentices for the growing range of skilled occupations on which commercial enterprise depended: book-keeping, surveying, cartography, navigation, ship-building, and so forth."[15] Free schools, designed for the lower classes, were touted as good preparation for apprenticeship and labor. One exponent claimed that they brought "improvement of mind, the fruits of discipline, not to be despised. A learned slave would sell for more. A youth brought up at school will be taken apprentice with less money than one illiterate. The broken colt, tamed heifer, polished diamond, known instances. Nay, ground reclaimed by culture will let at higher rent."[16] Schools were thus an economically productive investment, providing both the discipline and the technical skills necessary for the reproduction of merchant's capital.

The only problem here is that *grammar* schools were spectacularly unsuited to technical training. Arithmetic and the reading and writing of English, which *were* necessary for the skilled trades, were supposed to be taught in the so-called petty schools. Not only did the curricula of the grammar schools tend not to broaden this kind of training, but because of their almost exclusive focus on the classical tongues, students sometimes forgot how to read English, and many were incapable of reading numbers, even well enough to use an index or to find biblical quotations, by the time they graduated.[17] (This is not to suggest that the schools were always successful at teaching Latin either.) Nor was a knowledge of classical Latin widely useful to the landed and merchant classes themselves, though it was helpful in a number of professions including the law and the ministry. Thus, the curricula of the grammar schools were at best adequately, though by no means brilliantly, suited to the practical needs of the ruling classes, while they were totally unsuited to training in most of the humbler trades.

Neither can it be said that the humanist curriculum accurately reflected the "world views" of the classes that financed it. In the seventeenth century, when the merchant classes stopped simply funding education and began asking that it represent their own interests and needs, they tended to deplore the training of "empty Nominalists and verbalists only" and wished that students might "henceforth bee *realists* and *materialists*: to know the verie things and matters themselvs, and yet onely such matters as may best further a man for the sufficient doing of all duties and works perteining to his own profession & person."[18]

Clearly we must discount any reductive economic functionalism in trying to understand Tudor schooling. Grammar schools, in particular, seem to have been miracles of impracticality when judged as means of vocational training. In a letter to James I, Bacon even urged against funding more such schools, claiming that they produced a lack "both of servants for husbandry and of apprentices for trade" and an excess of "persons [who] will be bred unfit for other vocations, and unprofitable for that in which they were bred up, which fill the realm full of indigent, idle and wanton people."[19]

If it is true, then, that the "scholastic state lays the groundwork and foundation for the other three states," we have still to discover a convincing way in which grammar schools and their humanist curricula contributed to this work. As we have seen, the assumption of a direct or unmediated intervention in the economic, political, and religious spheres poses certain problems. Another, more promising approach might begin by viewing education not as it interacts directly with other social areas but as it constitutes a mechanism of class distinction on its own. Appropriating the more elite schools and curricula, it has been argued, gave a cultural coherence to the ruling groups. The gentry "all had the same sort of classical education and common ties with the same few educational institutions imparting the same elitist social values. The dichotomy between liberal and mechanical arts became the most striking feature of the educational system: Latin and Greek were subjects for gentlemen, merely useful or practical subjects were for tradesmen and artificers."[20] There was, to be sure, considerable social stratification among the Tudor schools. Grammar schools and universities were largely the preserves of the gentry, merchant, and professional classes; poorer students made do with the petty schools, which taught English reading and writing and some basic arithmetic. The working classes were largely excluded from the Tudor schools, though scholarships and free schools were available for some.[21] Latinity was thus indeed a mark of gentility and hence a support for class distinctions, but to treat it simply as an ornament or class *marker* is to place it in an exteriorized and abstract relation to the process of social reproduction. Rhetorical education was not something that merely signified an already existing class system; the "appropriation thesis" overlooks the ways in which it intervened in the system itself, transforming both the ruling groups and the very nature of class distinction.

The exclusionary character of Tudor schooling was compromised, or at least complicated, by being far from absolute. Elite academies such as Eton, Westminster, St. Paul's, and the Merchant Tailors' School attracted the most renowned teachers and the most affluent students, but humanist training, sometimes of good quality, was also available in humbler village schools. More important than the de facto exclusion of poorer students from Tudor schools was the quite explicit suppression of popular *culture* within humanist pedagogy.[22] Education by means of a classical curriculum was designed in part to alienate youth from more spontaneous forms of popular learning. Thus Erasmus insisted that "a boy [may] learn a pretty story from the ancient poets, or a memorable tale from history, just as readily as the stupid and vulgar ballad, or the old wives' fairy rubbish such as most children are steeped in nowadays by nurses and serving women." Erasmus and the other humanists were openly hostile to narrative forms of popular culture such as "ridiculous riddles, stories of dreams, of ghosts, witches, fairies, demons; of foolish tales drawn from popular annals."[23] Tudor education sought to inoculate students of whatever class against infection from a popular milieu. The statutes of St. Bee's Grammar School (1584) stipulated that "the schoolmaster shall not suffer his scholars to have any lewd or superstitious books or ballads among them."[24]

At the same time, moreover, humanism also sought to reform the behavior of the ruling groups. Erasmus hoped to cure the "over-feeding, late hours, and unsuitable dressing which are the common indulgences allowed to children in the [upper] classes about whom I am here concerned."[25] Richard Mulcaster held that both rich and poor students ought to be reformed after a third model: "The midle sort of parentes which neither welter in to much wealth, nor wrastle with to much want, seemeth fitteth [*sic*] of all, if the childrens capacitie be aunswerable to their parentes state and qualitie: which must be the levell for the fattest to fall downe to, and the leanest to leape up to, to bring forth that student, which must serve his countrey best."[26] The schools' exclusionary function was thus complemented by a hegemonic one in which the behavioral disposition of the "middle sort" was imposed on a relatively broad array of classes. In this second function the school neither signified an already-existing class system nor simply reproduced it; it helped reform both the ruling and the subaltern classes along the lines of a proto-bourgeois model. It is here that the school began to play a genuinely transitional role, even while its exclusionary function still worked to reproduce traditional lines of class distinction.

As transformative or transitional institutions, Tudor schools instilled a new disciplinary economy in their subjects. "More than any other contemporary institution," writes the historian Keith Thomas, "the school was dominated by the hourglass, the clock, and the bell. Schooling was meant to teach application and self-control, sitting still for hours at a time being in itself justified as a valuable preparation for the renunciation upon which later success depended."[27] The ideological function of Tudor schooling must, then, be understood to include not only the transmission of doctrines or governing representations but also the imposition of certain productive and disciplinary practices. The schools hammered in ideological content and also laid down economies of recreation and labor, punishment and reward. They thus participated in the disciplinary "accumulation of men" which, according to Foucault, complemented and reinforced the accumulation of capital. This "discipline," however, was not of the kind that Foucault describes for the classical period: it was not methodical, compartmentalized, and analytical.[28] Rather, the Tudor pedagogue often exercised a sovereign, sometimes unpredictable form of violence. In many cases, noted Erasmus, "the school is, in effect, a torture-chamber; blows and shouts, sobs and howls fill the air." He describes one case in which "hanging the luckless child up by the arms and flogging him as he hung until the brutal master was too tired to go on, was the least disgusting part of the punishment."[29] The tortures of the Tudor schoolroom—sadistic, arbitrary, sometimes explicitly sexual—clearly worked as a political ritual, in which the pedagogue both assumed and reinforced the sovereign authority of the monarch or magistrate. "For the *rod* may no more be spared in schooles, then the *sworde* may in the *Princes* hand," wrote Mulcaster, adding that "by the *rod* I mean *correction* and *awe.*"[30] This petty tyranny did not always go unchallenged, and students in the early modern period devised forms of collective resistance—sometimes openly insurrectional—to oppose excessive punishment.[31]

It goes without saying that the enforcement of a monarchical regime was also the enforcement of a patriarchal one, and that Tudor schooling was designed to produce gendered as well as political subjects. Young girls were occasionally found in public elementary schools, but grammar schools were reserved exclusively for adolescent boys (and sometimes grown men) along with their male schoolmasters and ushers. Erasmus's complaint about the "old wives' fairy rubbish" suggests that formal schooling was intended to rescue elite male children from the contaminating effects of both a popular milieu and a feminine one. Training in Latin separated young males from the "mother tongue" and introduced them to an exclusively male realm of culture. Walter Ong has argued persuasively that Renaissance training in classical Latin constituted a "male puberty rite" presided over by the ritualized violence of the schoolmaster's rod.[32]

One of the few Tudor pedagogues to defend in print the necessity of beatings was Richard Mulcaster, who viewed the rod not only as an indispensable instrument for controlling groups but also as a means of testing the social and political dispositions of students. Asking "what wit is fittest for learning in a monarchie," he concludes:

> The child therefore is likest to prove in further yeares, the fittest for learning in a *monarchie*, which in his tender age sheweth himselfe obedient to schole orders, and either will not lightly offend, or if he do, will take his punishment gently: without either much repyning, or great stomacking. In behaviour towardes his companions he is gentle and curteous, not wrangling, not quarrelling and complaining. . . . At home we will be . . . obsequious to parentes, . . . courteous among servantes, . . . dutiefull toward all, with whom he hath to deale.[33]

For Mulcaster, the ability to endure punishment "gently" signifies a global disposition that will manifest itself in all social and political relations: with parents, companions, servants, and monarchs. It is not a specific hierarchical position that is inculcated here but rather a style of negotiating multiple hierarchical relations with superiors, inferiors, and equals. Schooling imbues all such relations with a style of restraint—Mulcaster calls it "courtesy" or "gentleness"—which bears a specific class character but attempts to extend itself throughout the social body.

It is in relation to—indeed, in reaction to—this sovereign or political model of discipline that the importance of humanist curricula and pedagogy can begin to be assessed. Humanism's most decisive innovation was the injection of *rhetoric* into pedagogy, not only as a principal subject of instruction but also as a way of reshaping the pedagogical process itself. The sixteenth century introduced "for the first time . . . an approach to education which combined ideological content with persuasion rather than with legal compulsion."[34] Humanist rhetorical education tried to evolve a mode of indoctrination based on hegemony and consent rather than force and coercion; it aimed to produce an active embrace of ideology rather than a passive acceptance. Thus humanist polemics abjured violent pedagogy in favor of a gentler method that would elicit pleasure rather than inflict pain. The preface to Ascham's *Scholemaster* (1570) expressed the hope that "the Scholehouse should be in deede, as it is called by name, the house of playe and pleasure, and not of feare and bondage."[35] Even Mulcaster, while defending the necessity of beatings, sensed their incompatibility with the otherwise peaceable disposition toward hierarchy that he hoped to instill in students: "For gentlenesse and curtesie towarde children," he conceded, "I do thinke it more needefull than beating, and ever to be wished."[36] The Spaniard Juan Luis Vives, who came to the English court with Catherine of Aragon, advised that the more tedious kinds of learning and drill should be enlivened with "jokes, witty and pleasant stories, lively historical narratives, with proverbs, apophthegms, and with acute short precepts, sometimes lively, sometimes grave"—in brief, with all the elocutionary tricks of the *orator*.[37]

But the normal relations of rhetoric and authority are decisively reversed here, for the techniques of oratorical persuasion are directed at an audience that is neither sovereign nor even independent but rather subject to the authority of the pedagogue. Thus pedagogical rhetoric incorporates a new element: the suspension of sovereignty. This suspension does not cancel the power to punish but delineates a social space within which a logic of pleasure will be permitted to operate and outside of which the older forms of coercion lie ready to hand.[38] (Mulcaster felt that the rod should always be kept in *sight* and that its visibility was if anything more important than its use.)[39] That force is available but not at first chosen provides the edifying spectacle of the pedagogue who restrains himself from violence. He is thus transformed from the bearer of a sovereign power into a *model* who can be emulated. He not only inculcates but visibly embodies the principles and techniques of self-regulation. In short, humanist pedagogy tries to establish an *imaginary* relationship (in the Lacanian sense) in which the teacher becomes an orthopedic mirror image for the student, whom Vives exhorts: "Listen to him intently—to his words, his forms of speech, note down his opinions, and make yourself as far as possible like him; take him for example, because when the teacher shall see this he will take pains that you shall not receive from him anything which would be unworthy of imitation."[40]

Imitation, therefore, is the principle that animates not only humanist stylistics but also humanist pedagogy. By *imitation* I mean a set of practices that places the subject in an imaginary relation with a governing model; it is the imaginary grasped *as* practice.[41] A mimetic education installs the subject in a play of mirrors, a dialectic of imaginary capture by a dominant form. It thus produces the ideological effect that Louis Althusser has dubbed "interpellation," or "hailing," wherein the subject comes both to recognize himself within and to depend upon a dominant specular image.[42] This mimetic or imaginary or imitative or "interpellating" mode of ideological domination is distinctive in that the subject comes to assimilate or internalize a set of practices and thus enacts his subjection "automatically," as if he himself had chosen it. It is a way of rerouting the subject's desires or energies for the purposes of ideological incorporation.

Humanism treats learning as *play* in order to tap the mimetic energies of the child; and conversely, it turns to the child because it finds in it the highest capacity for mimetic play, and hence for imaginary capture. "Nature," writes Erasmus, "has implanted in the youngest child an ape-like instinct of imitation and a delight in activity. From this quality springs his first capacity for learning."[43] The child is a quantum of energy that seeks of its own accord to be bound and shaped; it desires to invest itself in a governing model. Erasmus does not view children as passive recording surfaces that endure inscription; his model is not the classical one of the *tabula rasa*. Nor does he view them as sources of evil, insurrectional, or sinful desires that must be repressed. To be sure, the child's energies are morally and socially ambiguous; they will attach themselves to any model, and "perhaps it is easier at that age to copy evil than good."[44] Nevertheless, these energies are also a productive force that can be elicited and captured. Mimetic play directs them at a sanctioned model whose very form both disciplines and articulates them in an acceptable manner. Humanism no longer views the child's desires as a useless and dangerous force ranged against the violent counterforce of the instructor. It does not found itself on a wasteful neutralization of opposing charges but sets up an imaginary machine that feeds on the desires of the child, engaging them in a relation of constructive interference with those of the instructor. "Maisters," writes Brinsley, "may teach with much delight and comfort, and scholars learn with an ingenuous emulation, like as they recreate themselves in their ordinarie sports."[45] In theory, at least, humanism enables the schooled subject to desire his own ideological subordination.

In altering the monarchical model of political subordination, humanism sought at least occasionally to modify the patriarchal dynamic of the classroom as well. John Brinsley wrote that "masters must not be ashamed, nor weary, to do as the nurse with the child, as it were stammering and playing with them, to seeke by all meanes to breede in the little ones a love of their masters, with delight in their bookes, and a joy that they can understand; and also in the end to nourish in them that emulation mentioned, to strive who shall doe best."[46] There is a kind of Lacanian logic to all this: if the schoolmaster in his monarchical or paternal function dispenses the "law of the father," then the schoolmaster as focus of an imitative, mimetic, or imaginary logic begins to acquire the characteristics of a maternal body. Brinsley even suggests employing this maternal fascination to breed something like an oedipal rivalry or emulation among male students. Appropriating the maternal function is, of course, fully compatible with the actual exclusion of women from the Tudor classroom. Brinsley urges maternal simulation purely as an ideological lure, and to provoke the "playing" that underlies all mimetic assimilation of knowledge.

The Erasmian conception of imitation as a fundamental human practice deeply informs humanist theories of how language is acquired and hence of how literature is taught. Erasmus's views are particularly important given the breadth of his influence on Tudor education; as T. W. Baldwin puts it, his name "was written all over the sixteenth-century grammar school in England."[47] And Erasmus insists, "It is in speech that the imitative instinct is especially active."[48] With this concept Erasmus transforms the social relation between subject and language as taught in the schools.

"For it is not by learning rules that we acquire the power of speaking a language, but by daily intercourse with those accustomed to express themselves with exactness and refinement, and by the copious reading of the best authors."[49] By abandoning the memorization of rules for the imitation of linguistic practices Erasmus rejects a *juridical* conception of language which sees it as a collection of grammatical imperatives. Under the juridical model, language use is defined by obedience or disobedience to the laws of grammar; its governing criterion is correctness. In rejecting this for the notion of "daily intercourse," Erasmus in effect drops a model based on the legal apparatuses of the state for one based on the practices of civil society.[50] Thus the relation between language and its speakers no longer recalls that between the sovereign state and its subjects but rather that between familiar individuals. This is not, to be sure, a distinction between law and lawlessness but rather between the absolute, consistent, and above all explicit laws promulgated by the state and the informal, flexible, and above all implicit rules that govern everyday intercourse. An internalized and self-regulating code of behavior replaces the law and its enforcers; stylistic standards of "exactness and refinement" define a social mechanism that can afford to reduce its reliance on formalized rules.

In reality, of course, things weren't quite so simple. Although Erasmian humanism proposed a somewhat colloquial *method* for learning Latin, it ultimately aimed at producing a classical, literary style. John Stanbridge's *Vulgaria*, an early humanist grammar that for a time competed with Lily's, illustrated its grammatical rules with homely Latin and English phrases drawn from everyday life at school and home. Often crude in both content and vocabulary, Stanbridge's illustrative phrases were closer to "living speech" than what Erasmian humanism wished to teach, and they were ultimately rejected not because they were pedagogically ineffective but because they inculcated an inelegant and subliterary Latin. If Erasmus endorsed a pedagogical model of ordinary or everyday speech, he nevertheless didn't want a popular, vernacular milieu to infect the results of teaching. Indeed, the speaking of Latin in schools—presumably, the very epitome of the Erasmian method—soon came under criticism because it produced bad habits of expression.[51] The "barbarities" of medieval Latin against which humanists inveighed were not, after all, solely the product of scholastic philosophers; they were the result of ordinary (postclassical) usage and contamination by the linguistic properties of the vernaculars—the product, that is, of "daily intercourse." Erasmian humanism wished to teach classical literary Latin *as if* it were a colloquial tongue, and thus while it borrowed the methods of "natural" or spontaneous linguistic learning, it banished much of what had made Latin a practical or colloquial language. "Latin," in other words, was not an empirically given language but a *style*, and not all real Latin could meet its demands. If Erasmus tried in some respects to colloquialize the teaching of Latin, he also sought to *formalize the colloquial*, to subject it to stricter stylistic standards, and thus to purge it of genuinely popular or vernacular elements. Needless to say, many humanists regarded the vernacular itself—at least, in its early Tudor form—as inadequately refined for this kind of training.[52] Passage through the alienated medium of literary Latin provided a form of stylistic discipline which then enabled a reformed and more self-conscious use of English, the mother tongue.[53] The humanist flight from a juridical model of learning thus entailed, as its counterpart, an increasingly disciplinary approach to everyday or "civil" existence, including language.

It is no accident, then, that Erasmus, who reorganized the teaching of Latin around the concept of style, also wrote the first modern book of manners. *De civilitate morum puerilium* (1530) taught children the codes of civil behavior as a natural complement to the achievements of "lyberall science"; social manners and literary style thus cooperated to produce a subject "well fasshyoned in soule, in body, in gesture, and in apparayle."[54] The cultivation of a good Latin style now appears as part of a larger process of "fashioning" subjects—a process that submits not only language but also manners, dress, and comportment to ideals of "exactness and refinement."[55] If it is clear that stylistic pedagogy is a form of social discipline, it is equally certain that discipline is becoming stylized. For in defining civility as "outward honesty of the body" (externum ... corporis decorum), Erasmus transforms a set of social behaviors into a bodily *image*.[56] The "well-fashioned" or civil subject is an aesthetic ideal that expands the concept of "style" to cover the whole range of social bearing. To produce a civil subject *is* to produce a "style"—of manners, dress, and discourse. And social style, like the literary style that is now a part of it, is developed not through obedience to rules but through the mimetic assimilation of models. Thus *De civilitate* supplements a juridical approach to manners—the prescription and proscription of behaviors—with an imaginary logic. Norbert Elias distinguishes Erasmus's work from medieval books of manners by noting that "earlier, people were simply told" what to do, but in *De civilitate*, "such rules are embedded by Erasmus directly in his experience and observation of people. . . . Erasmus gives the same advice, but he sees people directly before him."[57] The presence of a mimetic register is clearly meant to establish an imaginary relation between text and reader. Imitation thus governs the mastery of prescribed social behaviors as well as the mastery of literary style. Conversely, humanist methods of teaching Latin style partake of a well-nigh global process for the ideological (imaginary) production of social subjects.

By abjuring or at least deferring an emphasis on grammar in favor of stylistic imitation, humanist pedagogy distinguished itself from both the late medieval traditions that preceded it and the classical methods of the late seventeenth and eighteenth centuries.[58] Erasmus introduced a relative destructuring of linguistic pedagogy in which "the primary impulse to write, and the act of writing itself, assert their domination over the mediation of technique."[59] The stylistic mimesis of literary texts thus replaced rote memorization; Vives urged students to "copy the same workmanship, but not the same words or conceptions" as the models they imitated.[60] Along with language, then, the concept of the text was transformed. From the incarnation of grammatical rules or governing concepts it came to be seen as an individualized voice or style. A model to be emulated rather than a law to be obeyed, the text thus served to bear those same imaginary effects that characterized the relation between student and teacher. Clearly, the juridical conception of the text befitted a situation in which the sovereign authority of the pedagogue stood in for the power of the state. The absolutism of grammatical rules made them all the more useful as the medium for a painful mnemotechnics. But like the humanist pedagogue, the humanist text provoked imitation rather than obedience, embodied the internal regulations of civil decorum rather than the violence of the state, and served as an orthopedic model rather than a threatening force. It offered an articulate receptacle for the subject's desires, instead of merely imposing restrictions on them.

The integration of stylistic and social training appears most clearly, perhaps, in Erasmus's *Colloquia familiaria*, widely used and reprinted as a Tudor school text. (Vives produced his own version of the same genre, *Linguae latinae exercitatio*, in 1538). Designed to produce "better Latinists and better characters," the colloquia teach a literate, conversational Latin through a series of dramatized discussions of everyday topics. Erasmus chooses the form of the colloquy "to allure the young," explaining that "to many people the rules of grammar are repulsive. Aristotle's *Ethics* is not suited to boys, the theology of Scotus still less."[61] Grammar, philosophy, and theology make up a trivium of juridical discourses in which the unassailable legitimacy of the medieval *auctor* and the irresistible violence of the pedagogue combine to impose a set of a priori principles or rules. In place of this Erasmus substitutes an *image* of speech—civil conversation among familiars—which also governs the relation between reader and text, for instead of memorizing rules, the reader is encouraged to imitate the stylistic gestures of the text's speakers and thus to mold himself into another "familiar" interlocutor. The colloquies thus make linguistic style a mode of social induction based on the imaginary (mimetic) mastery of decorums and gestural behaviors. Indeed, humanism treats style *as* a set of imitable linguistic behaviors or gestures, and so makes it assimilable to other kinds of social practice or discipline.[62] The colloquies can therefore build better "character" in the same way that they build better Latinists; though distributed along the axes of content and form, these two functions represent moments of a single mimetic process.

Mimetic assimilation was fundamental to all of humanist pedagogy. Histories and epic poetry were read for imitable *exempla*. The colloquies of Erasmus and dialogues of Vives were already protodramatic, and thus led naturally enough to the acting out of plays by Terence in the more prestigious academies such as St. Paul's School. Social roles, cultural *decora*, and literary style were all assimilable through imaginary identification and internalization.

The sovereign or juridical model of pedagogy, which operated on principles of punishment, inscription, and law, was thus transected by a "civil" model based on the assimilation of styles derived from everyday life. These two models seem to project very different cultural regimes, one based on the forcible imposition of order from above and the other based on hegemony and self-regulation. Yet they were not mutually exclusive in practice. Certainly, humanist interest in ideological persuasion did not signal a real or desired decay in the juridical apparatuses of the state; on the contrary, northern humanism took shape during the early consolidation of absolutist rule and was compatible with it.[63] Erasmian humanists emphasized the value of providing good counsel and education to princes but rarely questioned the legitimacy of royal power or its institutions. Thus Erasmian pedagogy adopted a "civil" rather than a "statist" model for itself not because it aimed at political liberty but because it abandoned it entirely. Humanist training delineated a civil realm in order to supplement and refine royal government, not in order to supplant it.

Within the confines of the school, as well, one model of pedagogy did not simply replace another. First of all, late medieval schooling did not rely solely on "juridical" discourses such as grammar, nor did humanism seek to eliminate these from its pedagogy. It simply put greater emphasis on mimetic practices and tried to theorize them in a more systematic way. Second, and more to the point, humanist theories of gentle schooling did not develop solely in reaction to long-standing traditions of cruelty; on the contrary, the sixteenth century simultaneously witnessed both an intensification of physical punishment in schools *and* the humanist alternative of persuasion. Unfortunately, the lack of anything but fragmentary and anecdotal evidence makes it difficult to say when and to what degree humanist pedagogical theory actually influenced the teaching practices of Tudor schools. Lawrence Stone vigorously contends that "Renaissance school practice . . . eventually came to bear little relation to Renaissance educational theory: the subject matter was more grammatical, the method of learning more by rote memory, the discipline more brutal."[64] But he too offers little more than anecdote. Recent evidence suggests that humanist methods and curricula may have established themselves more widely than Stone suggests.[65] Certainly, Erasmian texts such as *De copia* and *Colloquia familiarum* were widely popular, and not only do these texts encourage certain practices by their very form, but they probably would not have been adopted by schools that lacked all respect for the methods of Erasmian pedagogy.

In assessing the degree of violence in humanist schools Stone inadequately accounts for factors such as the influence of parents on teaching practices. Richard Mulcaster, who publicly defended corporal punishment in the classroom, complained bitterly of the restraining power that parents could exert over schoolmasters simply by threatening to remove their children to other schools.[66] Whereas medieval schoolteachers were generally clerics supported by the church, their Renaissance successors were frequently dependent on tuition and fees paid by parents and gifts given by them, and thus schoolmasters were accountable to them. Needless to say, wealthier parents had greater sway and greater choice, as Mulcaster also suggests, and their children were more likely to be treated with a lighter hand.[67] It is true that some of the most prestigious humanist pedagogues were notorious child-beaters, including Mulcaster himself, who taught at the Merchant Tailors' and St. Paul's schools, and Nicholas Udall, who taught at Eton.[68] Yet when Mulcaster defends beatings in his *Positions*, he sounds very much like a man who is bucking the general trend, and indeed, the very need to defend such practices suggests that they were far from universal.

In any case, despite some fundamental contradictions between them, the mimetic and juridical models of schooling were quite capable of coexisting and even served certain mutually complementary functions. Ciceronian humanism, in particular, tried to enforce stylistic norms that were perfectly assimilable to older methods of ideological control. Ascham, for instance, warned: "He that can neither like Aristotle in logic and philosphy, nor Tully in rhetoric and eloquence will from these steps likely enough presume by the like pride to mount higher, to the misliking of greater matters: that is either in religion to have a dissentious head, or in the commonwealth to have a factious heart."[69] In its more conservative manifestations, then, humanist pedagogy was perfectly conformable to juridical models of control. To theological and philosophical orthodoxies it simply appended a "law of style," whose normative embodiment was Cicero.

Not surprisingly, Erasmus was among the first to resist Ciceronianism as a stylistic-ideological norm. His *Ciceronianus* (1528) ridiculed the fashion for strict Ciceronianism, exposing both its historical contradictions and its cultural pathologies.[70] Erasmus depicted Ciceronian imitation as a kind of obsessional neurosis that transformed Cicero from a stylistic model into an idol or fetish. The goal of absolute imitation is not only degrading, Erasmus argued, but impossible; it will be thwarted by, among other things, the irreducible singularity of each writer, an innate "nature" that resists all attempts to overmaster it: "Every one of us has his own personal inborn characteristics, and these have such force that it is useless for a person fitted by nature for one style of speaking to strive to achieve a different one." Since the individuality of the subject impedes strict imitation of any one model, Erasmus endorses the study of multiple models, which, he insists, must then be "digested" and transformed by the reader's own personality.[71] A plurality of models prevents the reader from succumbing to the authority of any one of them and allows him to imprint his own mark on received materials.

Erasmian imitation theory thus seems to encourage not ideological subjection but the "self-fashioning" of autonomous subjects. Erasmus's ideal reader internalizes texts in the hope of mastering them, not of being mastered by them; instead of dutifully reproducing models, he emulates them in a competitive way. In so decisively challenging the authority of model texts, Erasmus seems to threaten the very mechanisms that make imitation a method of ideological control. When it abandons the ideal of a normative style, anti-Ciceronianism opens the way for a proliferation of styles, and with it the possible decay of certain kinds of traditional authority. Thomas Nashe revealed the anarchic potential within this movement by "proudly boast[ing]" that "the vaine which I have (be it a *median* vaine, or a madde vaine) is of my own begetting, and cals no man in England father but my selfe."[72] Gabriel Harvey, not at all amused by Nashe's posturings as a stylistic "masterless man," responded with sarcasm:

> It is for Cheeke or Ascham to stand levelling of Colons, or squaring of Periods, by measure and number: his [Nashe's] penne is like a spigot, and the wine presse a dullard to his Inke-presse. There is a certaine lively and frisking thing of a queint and capricious nature, as perelesse as namelesse, and as admirable as singular, that scorneth to be a bookworm, or to imitate the excellentest artificiality of the most renowned worke-masters that antiquity affourdeth.[73]

In the same vein, though in a very different context, Stephen Gosson decried the "abuses of . . . unthrifty scholars, that despise the good rules of their ancient masters, and run to the shop of their own devises, defacing old stampes, forging new printes, and coining strange precepts."[74] What unite Erasmus's liberal optimism, Gosson's conservative hysteria, and Nashe's self-vaunting iconoclasm are certain shared assumptions about the relation between imitation and sociocultural authority. All three writers view the revision of cultural models as a way of investing the individual subject with some degree of autonomous power. They differ only in their assessments of the value of cultural tradition and in the social effects that follow from weakening its hold. To be sure, both Nashe and Gosson seem to possess a more urgent sense of the political ramifications of innovation than does Erasmus, and not merely because Erasmus bore a more genial temperament. The charged religious and political atmosphere of Tudor and Stuart England, where polemical tracts flew daily from the presses, doubtless created a heightened sense of the social impact of rhetoric. From this perspective Erasmus's gentle attempts at stylistic reform appear as well-meaning and naïve as his efforts at religious reform came to seem when they were swallowed up in the storms of Protestant controversy. On the other hand, it may well be that Erasmus's more measured assessment is the correct one, and that the proliferation of styles was less liberating in its effects than Gosson feared or Nashe hoped—and not because style turns out to be socially irrelevant or nugatory but because the formation of individual styles merely restructures the social authority that it seems to reject.

That this is so becomes clearer if we interrogate Erasmus's conception of cultural authority and its relation to the individual subject. As we have seen, Erasmus's model for coercive authority is always juridical; hence he derides Ciceronianism as being "stricter than the Draconian code."[75] Power, for Erasmus, is always understood as the normalizing or regularizing force of law. Conversely, individual freedom is understood as the resistance to conformity, the creation of *difference*. Imitation, as he conceives it, engages the aggressivity that always inheres in a mimetic relation in order to produce a style that both follows and modifies its model.[76] The result is a style (or subject) that inhabits a collectively bounded field of imitation, yet clears out a differential space that defines its freedom.

What Gosson seems to fear are the entropic effects of this freedom, the possibility that multiplying differences will erode the model that constrains them. His images of stamping, printing, and coining figure imitation as exact reproduction. Like Erasmus's, therefore, his model of power is a juridical one, outside of which he sees only chaos howling. If we are to understand humanist style production as a mode of ideological control, we must try to fill the apparent void around the juridical model; we must theorize a social order that propagates itself not through the normalizing power of the law but through the regulated production of difference.

I believe that humanist stylistic pedagogy does produce such an order and that its mechanisms become visible if we attend to a metaphor that pervades humanist writings on style and rhetoric. When Erasmus writes in *De copia*, "[verbal] style is to thought as clothes are to the body,"[77] he expresses an analogy frequently encountered in the humanist rhetorical tradition and also something more than an analogy, since his conception of style production, as outlined in *De civilitate*, includes "apparayle" as well as "soule," "body," and "gesture." It is surprising, given the recent interest in Renaissance "fashionings" of subjects, that this process has not been more rigorously compared to the social dynamics of *fashion*.

Tudor society seems to have paid a good deal of attention to issues of fashion, to judge by the welter of sumptuary laws and the number of writers who moralized against contemporary "excesses" of apparel.[78] In *The Anatomy of Abuses* (1583), Philip Stubbes complained that "now there is such a confuse mingle mangle of apparell in [England], and such preposterous excesse therof, as every one is permitted to flaunt it out, in what apparell he lust himselfe, or can get by anie kind of meanes. So that it is verie hard to knowe, who is noble, who is worshipfull, who is a gentleman, who is not."[79] Stubbes's attack on "novell Inventions and new fangled fashions" in apparel recalls the railings of Stephen Gosson against dangerously innovative scholars, for in both cases the chaotic productiveness of style threatens to overturn customary authorities and distinctions. Fashion seemed a dangerously de-structuring phenomenon to a wide body of social observers. Not only did it blur traditional class lines, but it was subject to a bewildering mutability:

> The phantasticall follie of our nation, even from the courtier to the carter is such, that no forme of apparell liketh us longer than the first garment is in the wearing, if it continue so long and be not laid aside, to receive some other trinket newlie devised by the fickle headed tailors. . . . such is our mutabilitie, that to daie there is none to the Spanish guise, to morrow the French toies are most fine and delectable, yer long no such apparell as that which is after the high Alman fashion, by and by the Turkish maner is generallie best liked of.[80]

The notion of historical variation was by no means alien to humanism, which had, for instance, tried to historicize the study of law. But fashion changed with such velocity and capriciousness that it defied historical explanations of the kind generated by philological research. For Erasmus, historical and regional variations in clothing formed the basis of a skeptical anthropology that denied any positive grounding to social custom and revealed decorum to be a way of negotiating among cultural arbitraries.[81] Fashion seemed a perfectly aleatory movement that violated both customary social distinctions and the explanatory powers of human reason. Moreover, its arbitrariness was wedded to an almost coercive allure, so that it exhibited something like the force of law without its structure. Sumptuary laws were in part an attempt to recode the movement of fashion so as to give it the stability of a juridical form. Despite its seeming unpredictability, of course, fashion does have the coherence of a semiological system; it is, moreover, perfectly capable of both registering and reinforcing class distinctions, even in the absence of legal regulation.[82] What Tudor lawmakers and moralists saw as mere anarchy was in fact a nascent bourgeois form of social order. Tudor sumptuary legislation must therefore be seen in part as a misrecognition by a "traditional" society of a mode of domination which did not work on juridical models and in part as a defense of specifically feudal class distinctions that the fashion system did not protect.

For the purposes of my argument, fashion may be most usefully understood as a set of imitative practices. Thomas Dekker makes the connection explicit in *The Seven Deadly Sins of London* (1606), where he mocks fashion as a principal symptom of the sin of "apishness" and calls it "nothing but counterfetting or imitation."[83] As an imitative or mimetic practice, fashion partakes of all the ambiguities of the Lacanian imaginary, ambiguities exploited by Renaissance discourse on the topic. When Ophelia describes Hamlet as the "glass of fashion and the mold of form," she clearly invests him with the authority of a governing model or orthopedic image in which his subjects come to know themselves. In attacking English fashions, however, Thomas Dekker invokes the catastrophic counterpart of this imaginary ideal, namely the *corps morcelé*:

> For an English-mans suite is like a traitors bodie that hath beene hanged, drawne, and quartered, and is set up in severall places: his Cod-peece is in Denmarke, the coller of his Duble and the belly in France: the wing and narrow sleeve in Italy: the shorte waste hangs over a Dutch Botchers stall in Utrich: his huge sloppes speakes Spanish: Polonia gives him the Bootes: the blocke for his heade alters faster then the Feltmaker can fitte him, and thereupon we are called in scorne Blockheades. And thus we that mocke everie Nation, for keeping one fashion, yet steale patches from everie one of them, to peece out our pride, are now laughing stockes to them, because their cut so scurvily becomes us.[84]

Both the unifying and the disintegrative aspects of fashion, and consequently both its coercive allure and its threats, may thus be understood (in the first instance) as the dialectical poles of an imaginary relation. This relation, in turn, structures a *social* process that works by means of a mimetic rather than a juridical logic.

In this light it may be useful to pause for a moment over the wittiness of Dekker's invective, which figures the fashionably dressed Englishman as the hanged, drawn, and quartered body of a traitor. The comparison is surely apt, for the gentleman who borrows his dress from other nations is a kind of traitor, in Dekker's eyes at least, to his native land and its customs. There is, moreover, something amusing about describing ostentation as if it were a form of public punishment. In this case, as in others, the dismemberment of the fashionable body seems at least in part to project the aggressivity of the satirist; Dekker fantasizes about hitching his own resentment to the punishing machinery of the state. And yet invoking the state and its legal apparatus may point to a more basic conceptual difficulty. As a manifestation of "apishness," fashion represents a chaotic yet potent cultural phenomenon, a disquieting force that does not correspond to traditionally understood forms of social authority. In imagining its punishment, Dekker produces a slightly scrambled fantasy of what sumptuary legislation tried to effect. More fundamentally, however, he seems to summon up the image of the state in order to *conceptualize* the cultural force of fashion, to provide a kind of explanatory metaphor that would recode it according to an already-understood mode of power. Dekker's wit thus uncovers the deep conceptual aporia that arises when a juridical model of power confronts a mimetic or imaginary one.

It is as modes of imitation that sartorial and literary style converge, and Dekker suggests as much with his character Apishness, who not only wears the latest fashions but "feedes verie hungerlie on scraps of songs" and mouths "con'd speeches stolne from others, whose voices and actions he counterfeits."[85] Etienne Dolet attacked Erasmian imitation in terms that strongly resemble Dekker's attack on English fashion. Erasmus, he wrote, "has forged for himself a verbal persona . . . out of Horatian tags, filthy language from Apuleius, and the adages of Beroaldus; and after long and worthless labors his style has become impure like the face of a leper, repulsive and wretchedly disfigured with pallid rotten sores full of foul matter."[86] Both Dekker and Dolet focus on the perceived failure to synthesize disparate materials, so that the final product of imitation appears as mere bricolage, figured ultimately as a dismembered or diseased body. Terence Cave, whose translation of Dolet I am borrowing here, uses it to help deconstruct Erasmus's already shaky sense of a grounded self. Both literary and sartorial imitation, to be sure, reveal the constructed or "fashioned" quality of the Renaissance subject. What concerns me here, however, is less the failures of such practices, the moments in which their merely factitious character appears as a terrifying dissolution of the self, than those no less real moments in which an apparently unified and differentiated subject is produced.

My purpose in comparing literary style with fashion, in particular, is twofold. Historically, I simply wish to situate the practice of style production in a larger cultural field. But the strategy is also heuristic: the ideological character of the fashion system is more immediately apparent than that of the humanist style system that mirrors it. What I mean by this, and how it pertains to linguistic or literary style, may become clearer if we recall Erasmus's earlier-quoted dictum on how to learn languages:

> For it is not by learning rules that we acquire the power of speaking a language, but by daily intercourse with those accustomed to express themselves with exactness and refinement, and by the copious reading of the best authors.[87]

A few alterations and this passage serves as a surprisingly good guide to becoming fashionable:

> For it is not by learning rules that we aquire the power of dressing well, but by daily intercourse with those accustomed to dress themselves with exactness and refinement, and by the copious reading of the best fashion magazines.

The fashion system is not juridically structured and hence not mastered through the memorization of rules. Though my rewriting of Erasmus is flagrantly anachronistic, even in the sixtenth century one became fashionable not by methodically reproducing a given model in every detail (as Nosoponus might do) but through competitive emulation within the loose confines of a semiological field (the French style, the Spanish style, or an English admixture). Thus the general realm of the fashionable is always given a specific inflection by the subjects who enter into it. This differential character is not, however, a mode of resistance to the system but one of its principal lures, allowing the subject to claim a space within the larger framework of a collective representation. Fashionability propagates itself through the formation of nonidentical "individuals," who are nevertheless created within the confines of a governing system. Indeed, there is no original model that *can* be copied fully. Since the elements that define the semiological field of the fashionable are bound only by what Wittgenstein calls "family resemblances," they cannot all be present simultaneously in any one instance.[88] The fashion system is punctuated with virtualities and amorphisms; it exists only as its specific inflections; but it is no less a system for all that. Unlike the law, it does not demand a perfectly regularized conformity. Yet it by no means seeks to produce genuinely original or autonomous subjects. As critics such as Dekker contended, in fact, the proliferation of differences in fashion announced not a realm of freedom but the universal triumph of "apishness" as a form of cultural *domination.* Since fashion's power depends on the partial destructuring of codes allowed by a system of imitation, fashion could seem to Renaissance observers both incoherent and coercive—a paradox that was unattainable for juridical or state power. It is because humanist style production worked on identical principles that it could be variously construed as a mode of social control, a means of developing the expressiveness of the individual, or a sure road to cultural anarchy.

The Renaissance conception of subjectivity defines the individual in its relation to politico-juridical coercion of the kind that predominates in precapitalist formations. Freedom is conceived of as difference from or transgression of law. This mode of power by no means disappears under capitalism, but it is supplemented by other modes for which the differential subject is not an impediment but a conduit. The humanist "fashioning system," like the fashion system it both resembles and feeds into, extends its power through the production of *negligible* differences that bind the subject to it without challenging its boundaries. This is not to say that the system cannot produce genuinely revolutionary or aberrational styles, only that it tends not to. Even Thomas Nashe's rhetorical bark was worse than his ideological bite; his stylistic eccentricities, alarming as they may have been to a Gabriel Harvey, were not at all incompatible with a sometimes fawning social conformity.[89] His claim to being stylistically "fatherless" may remind us that the denial of paternal authority can be both a way of resisting *and* a way of propagating oedipal relations. The individualized styles generated by agonistic imitation allow the subject to "master" stylistic and textual authority as a way of internalizing it.

It has often been remarked that the practices of humanist imitation seem to betray the influence of an early capitalist milieu. As one recent formulation puts it, "The injunction to make the classical authors into one's own property—to create a style that belongs to oneself alone—has clear parallels in a culture of bourgeois acquisition."[90] This is exactly right, though, as I hope I have shown, humanist stylistics are "bourgeois" not only because they resemble the accumulation of capital but also because they deploy a normalizing social order based on the production of empty heterogeneity. By *bourgeois*, of course, I mean to designate the social formation in which these procedures will find their most efficient sphere of operation, not the class that invents them. Many of the imaginary practices I have outlined here originated in courtly society under the auspices of a late feudal nobility. Fashion, in particular, was almost exclusively a game for gentlemen, lending a fairly clear class character to the controversies surrounding it. Literary style, however—and this is its crucial difference from the fashion system it *formally* resembled—could circulate at other levels of the social edifice, largely for the simple reason that it was a more affordable (though by no means universally affordable) mode of display. Thus it was that a figure such as Erasmus could celebrate the cultivation of literary elegance while attacking "excesses" of costly dress. And thus it was, too, that humanist training could imbue the production of style with a more explicitly disciplinary character than that which appeared in the fashion system.

To the thesis that there is something fundamentally new about style as a mode of imaginary discipline it might be objected that imitational practices pervaded late medieval culture, most notably perhaps in the complex of religious ritual and doctrine that fell under the broad rubric of *imitatio christi*. Ciceronian imitation may even give a literary and secular inflection to some of these older religious practices, as the idolatry of Nosoponus, the hapless Ciceronian imitator in Erasmus's *Ciceronianus*, suggests. There are some crucial differences between medieval and Renaissance modes of imitation, however, one of which is that the *imitatio christi* always aimed—asymptotically, it is true—at the ideal of perfect imitation, so that the individual subject was ultimately absorbed and canceled by Christ as ideological model. Renaissance (or at least Erasmian) imitation, by contrast, posited and even encouraged an irreducible difference between model and copy, and thereby tended to redistribute some cultural authority to the latter. Medieval imitation may thus be visualized as a kind of planetary system in which imitations circled the model as mere satellites of a central sun, illuminated by it alone and ever spiraling toward it. Although Renaissance imitation could hardly be said to decenter this system, it granted a higher gravitational pull to its satellites and thus rendered the motion of the whole more eccentric. Here again the analogy of fashion may be helpful. When Ophelia describes Hamlet as "the glass of fashion and the mold of form," she installs him as the center of an "absolutist" system that revolves around its prince. But a very different description of the Renaissance fashion system occurs in *Pericles* when Cleon, recalling the lost glories of Tarsus, speaks of "men and dames so jetted and adorned" as to be "like *one another's glass* to trim them by" (1.4.27–28, my emphasis). Here the authority of the model has become dispersed and serialized; it is omnipresent and yet nowhere in particular. This centrifugal force, which is characteristic of the bourgeois style system, restructures without weakening the centripetal motion of the late-medieval, absolutist, or planetary system. In so doing it begins, ever so slightly, to confuse the distinction between imitation and model, copy and original, and thus to introduce the logic of simulation which Jean Baudrillard has traced from the Renaissance to postmodern culture.[91] The multiplication of stylistic-ideological mirrors in the Renaissance did not aim to democratize culture, however; rather, it began to recast cultural domination into forms that would suit a new kind of ruling class.

By imparting both juridical and mimetic forms of learning, Tudor schools were able at carry out two very different kinds of ideological work. The juridical model, as we have seen, helped to reproduce the dominant form of political authority. At the same time, the mimetic model helped to articulate a new class culture within the nascent bounds of "civil society." This it did by imparting behavioral discipline, encouraging the stylistic assimilation of cultural authority, and distributing individual differences within a regularized system. The transitional labor of the schools can thus be located at the sometimes tense intersection of these two systems, which both reproduced a more traditional model of cultural authority and helped to lay the basis for a new one.

Poetry and the Destruction of Content

Thus far I have portrayed the humanist style system as a complex but smoothly running ideological machine whose finer mo-tions may well have befuddled cultural conservatives. Their cries of anarchy, which merely complemented the humanists' own conception of their project as liberatory or enlightened, thereby mistook a metamorphosis of control for its collapse. Yet it is true that in enabling new ideological operations, humanism partly disabled some important older ones, specifically, those that relied on the inculcation of ideological *content* or representations. Moreover, there were apparently immanent boundaries to the reach and effectiveness of the humanist program, and these gave rise to symptomatic anxieties about literary training and about "poetic" language as such.

In some respects poetry occupied a perfectly innocuous position within the curricula of Tudor grammar schools. Practice in Latin versification was common in the upper forms, where students would read and imitate the works of Ovid, Virgil, Horace, and Juvenal just as they had been taught to imitate in prose.[92] Versification was just another technical skill to be mastered as part of a stylistic program, and poetry was simply another generic component of classical letters.

In other respects, however, poetry and drama posed special problems. Among these was the sense that the content or subject matter of Latin verse was often unwholesome for young boys. Ascham complained that Plautus and Terence were virtually the only surviving examples of the "perfect ripeness" of the Latin tongue and hence offered indispensable models for style. Yet, "the matter in both, is altogether within the meanest mens maners, . . . soch as in London commonlie cum to the hearing of the Masters of Bridewell. Here is base stuffe for that scholer that should becum hereafter, either a good minister in Religion, or a Civil Jentleman in service of his Prince and Countrie."[93] Ascham offers no clear or simple solution to this problem, though he unquestionably wishes the schoolmaster to focus on elocution or "utterance" and to denounce the baseness of dramatic "matter." Vives adopted the same strategy for teaching nondramatic verse. "The reading of poets," he cautions, "is more for the strengthening of the mind and raising it to the stars, *and for the cultivation of the ornaments of discourse* than for supplying subject-matter for conversation."[94] In other words, poetic texts were to be regarded as inventories of rhetorical styles and tropes, not as sources of instructive content. Robert Cawdrey expresses similar sentiments in *A Treasurie or Store-House of Similes* (1600): "As in slaughter, massacres or murther, painted in a Table, the cunning of the Painter is praysed, but the fact it selfe, is utterly deplored: So in Poetrie wee follow elocution, and the proper forme of wordes and sentences, but the ill matter wee do worthily despise."[95] Humanist pedagogy tried to solve the problem of poetic content by treating poetry as a source of *copia*, or elocutionary richness. Reading for copia tended to decode the poetic text by atomizing its larger structures of meaning and ideological content and by resolving it into generative strategies of style, on the one hand, and dissociated bits of elocutionary material, on the other.

Copia, then, was a means not only to the production of style but to the neutralization of foreign ideology. Late medieval culture had also tried to master the disturbing alterities of classical texts, but in a different, almost contrary manner. Allegorical constructions such as the *Ovide moralisée* overcoded the text with an officially sanctioned (Christian) narrative, whereas copia decoded the text into rhetorical and discursive components. The older method subsumed dangerous contents within a larger ideological unity; the newer method decomposed this same material into harmless, inert atoms. Allegorical readings continued to flourish during the Renaissance, but copia represented a decisive innovation in ideological control.

For Vives, the disintegrative effects of copia sometimes had to be supplemented by more direct, but not unrelated, forms of expurgation and censorship: "Obscene passages should be wholly cut out from the text, as though they were dead, and would infect whatever they touched. Does the human race, forsooth, suffer an irreparable loss, if a man cast the noxious part out of an unclean poet, and if he does to a book, what he would not hesitate to do to his own body, if necessary? The Emperor Justinian mutilated the writings of many lawyers."[96] Vives's easy endorsement of textual mutilation is especially striking if we think back to the first generations of Italian humanists, painstakingly reconstructing these same works from fragmentary manuscripts. "I saw the dismembered limbs of a beautiful body, and admiration mingled with grief seized me," wrote Petrarch upon viewing the old manuscripts of Quintilian.[97] The *Epistolae familiares* are light-years from Vives, their tender intimacy with the spirits of the classical dead contrasting sharply with the Spaniard's assertion that "reliance on the poets personally must be weakened."[98] It is worth recalling, in this context, that English humanism achieved few scholarly accomplishments to match those of its Italian counterpart. It produced no great editions and few works of deep learning; its strengths were in pedagogy, translation, and literature.[99] Strategies of reading and composition adopted by the early Tudor schools tended to convert the voices of the past into neutral sources of rhetorical ornament and expressive technique.

The problem of content was not the only one associated with poetry, as we shall see, but its political import is clear and its provisional solution suggestive. Althusser speaks of the school as carrying out processes of both technical and ideological reproduction, and here we can see a happy convergence of the two.[100] For the pedagogical transmission of poetry, which converts it into a technical resource for expression, *also* attempts to neutralize its ideological threat thereby. The ideological "work" performed here is merely negative—disturbing elements are purged without being replaced by any approved or official ones—but the two levels of social reproduction are nicely meshed. This is, in fact, a principal role of the school: to produce a unity of technical and ideological reproduction. To this end it not merely transmits a given curriculum but transforms it in specific ways.

There were limits to the ideological efficacy of the humanist program, however, and hence during Elizabeth's reign a concerted effort was made to substitute Protestant for humanist and classical materials.[101] Plays on sober, often religious topics replaced those of Terence in schools. Even the colloquies of Erasmus and Vives gave way in many places to those of the Genevans Castellion and Cordier.[102] This new insistence on religious conformity in school texts suggests, first, that humanism was not entirely successful in neutralizing the troubling contents of classical materials and, second, that mere censorship of such materials could not in the end substitute for the positive inculcation of religious dogma and outlook. Vives's worries about the content of classical poetry proved a harbinger for a more general anxiety about humanism itself which would eventually draw his own school texts into suspicion. This is, as we shall see, a recurrent phenomenon, for poetry served to focus and displace suspicions about humanist rhetoric.

In any case, the humanist destruction of content was never limited to poetry; it played a part in prose composition as well, though with less emphasis on direct cultural censorship. Nowhere, perhaps, is the way of handling prose content clearer than in the ideals of rhetorical abundance and fluency embraced by Erasmus's influential writings on copia. As Terence Cave has so brilliantly shown, copia tends to subordinate the idea of language as communicational medium or signifying grid to an emphasis on unbounded verbal productivity.[103] Evoking an inexhaustible source or treasure-house of speech, copia points to a primordial and demiurgic space of language which precedes any discursive content or contextual instantiation. This conception of language is, moreover, secured by an irreducibly figurative element in Erasmus's own writing which refuses to identify copia with technique and thereby distinguishes it from older forms of rhetorical amplification. Just as the figural productivity of copia can both exceed and cancel content, so the intuitive and extemporaneous elements of Erasmian composition can subvert both the intention or will to communicate and its technical means.[104]

Yet even the technical procedures for producing copia contributed to the destruction of content. Most influential among these was the so-called notebook method, which abstracted discursive raw materials from the text and collected them in what Bacon called a *"Promptuary* or Preparatory Store."[105] For Erasmus, the rhetorical disintegration of texts was no mere by-product of his method; he positively encouraged it as a way of reducing the authority of individual writers, thus freeing the formation of a personal style from the slavish imitation of a single prestigious model. Rhetorical decoding was not, however, a phenomenon limited to grammar students scribbling in their "copie" books. As Walter Ong has shown, printed books of commonplace materials—florilegia, emblem books, collections of apophthegms, similes, tropes and figures, moral dicta—proliferated wildly in the sixteenth and seventeenth centuries and even "formed the staple of the common man's reading."[106] Rhetorical culture found its most pervasive expression in the clouds of textual and discursive particles released by the printing press. Copia thus imposed its forms not only on pedagogy but on literate culture at large. To say that Tudor culture was rhetorical is in part to say that it was a culture of the excerpt, the ornament, and the fragment. Whole new literary forms such as the essay were made possible largely by the multiplication of commonplace materials.

Both within and outside the schools, the cultivation of eloquence had wide-ranging and complex effects. Vives and others encouraged the rhetorical decoding of texts as a way of defusing nonhegemonic materials, but this process was omnivorous: it did not always distinguish between "good" and "evil," licit and illicit texts but tended to neutralize all received ideological content. Tudor students were made to write Aphthonian themes *in utramque partem* on assigned topics, often drawing on materials stored under antithetical headings in commonplace books—a practice that tended to promote eloquence at the cost of dissolving conviction.[107] It has been suggested that the rise of skepticism in early modern Europe, with its attendant religious and intellectual crises, owed less to the revival of Greek Pyrrhonism than it did to the consequences of the humanist educational program.[108] The rhetoric fostered by the schools was of course ultimately meant to reinforce the ideological status quo. Ascham envisaged the production of student orators whose eloquence would buttress the order of the commonwealth; but more often the results may have been summed up by the character in a Marston play:

> I was a scholar: seven useful springs
> Did I deflower in quotation
> Of cross'd opinions 'bout the soul of man.
> The more I learnt the more I learnt to doubt:
> Knowledge and wit, faith's foe, turn faith about.[109]

Obviously, this skeptical "disposition" on the part of rhetoric was not new; it was more or less intrinsic to classical rhetorical practice, especially in its forensic applications. Renaissance humanism simply inherited, along with the rest of the classical tradition, a rhetoric that was, in Aristotle's words, "the faculty of observing in any case the available means of persuasion," or in Plato's less neutral description, "the universal art of enchanting the mind by arguments."[110] The enabling condition of rhetoric as a universal discursive instrument was an absolute disjunction between elocutionary force and any given content or ideological position, a disjunction that provoked not only philosophical controversy but pedagogical difficulties as well.

What appears within rhetorical discourse as a breach between "matter" and "utterance" or content and style manifests itself more globally as a contradiction between the discursive and ideological instrumentalities of rhetoric: its role in producing eloquent speech and its role in securing dominant values or ideologies (insofar as these are ideologies of content). This contradiction isn't necessarily uncontrollable, but it does complicate the school's double burden of technical and ideological reproduction, since these two functions are now not only autonomous but to some degree antagonistic. But this challenge actually defines the *role* of the school, which is to forge a (provisional, perhaps, and unstable) unity of these two forms of reproduction. In the case of humanist schooling, the concrete task was to recapture stylistic or rhetorical training for the dominant order, to provide a housing or total milieu for rhetoric in which its skeptical disposition might be contained. This task involved supplementary forms of ethical and religious training, a disciplinary regime, and (as I have argued) a displacement of much of the ideological burden onto style itself as a way of deploying and controlling subjectivities. But the success of this project was never a given, and it involved, in any case, a partial disabling of ideologies of content.

I began this section with the problem of poetic content, which humanist pedagogy attempted to solve by reducing content to *elocutio*, or style. Now, however, it is clear that a local solution created a global problem, for the autonomy of style, which served limited functions of censorship, posed the greater threat of the skeptical erosion of dominant values. Although this problem pertained to humanist rhetoric and pedagogy at large, however, these drew surprisingly little criticism to themselves. Even after the reforms demanded by Puritan educators, the humanist program remained largely intact.[111] Instead, *poetry* became the privileged sign of this ideological danger and in fact helped to deflect cultural anxiety away from rhetoric.

In the preface to his *Discourse of English Poetry* (1586), William Webbe comments on the very different cultural receptions given to poetry and rhetoric:

> Why should we think so basely of [poetry]? rather then of her sister, I mean Rhetoricall *Eloqution*? which as they were by birth Twyns, by kinde the same, by originall of one descent, so no doubt, as Eloquence hath found such favourers in the English tongue, as she frequenteth not any more gladly, so would Poetrye, if there were the like welcome and entertainment gyven her by our English Poets, without question aspyre to wonderful perfection, and appeare farre more gorgeous and delectable among us.

Webbe holds that poetry's disrepute results solely from its having been "pittifullie mangled and defaced by rude smatterers and barbarous imitators." The answer, he thinks, is to reform its prosody and style along classical lines, thus snatching poetry from "the rude multitude of rusticall Rhymers, who will be called Poets" and crowning it with the cultural respectability of humanism.[112] Whatever he says of poetry in the abstract, Webbe clearly views *English* poetry as a bastard that will stop playing Edmund to rhetoric's Edgar only when it renounces its plebeian and feudal ancestry and really does become the "twin" of humanist rhetoric. Webbe's aversion to popular verse is echoed in nearly all contemporary treatises on poetics, and it is certainly true that poetry suffered in some quarters through its associations with piping and playing and other popular diversions. Yet even classical poetry was viewed with concern by some humanist educators; so something more may be at stake here.

Webbe's own *Discourse* suggests as much when it traces poetry and rhetoric back to their origins. Webbe evokes the authority of Plato in asserting that poetry arose from the panegyrics sung at solemn festivals and thus began as a "vertuous and most devout" art. But when this religious performance provoked secular imitators, the original vatic "egg" began its split into poetry and rhetoric:

> So when other among them of the finest wits and aptest capacities beganne in imitation of these to frame ditties of lighter matters, and tuning them to the stroake of some of the pleasantest kind of Musicke, then began there to growe a distinction and great diversity betweene makers and makers. Whereby (I take it) beganne thys difference: that they which handled in the audience of the people grave and necessary matters were called wise men or eloquent men, which they meant by *Vates*; and the rest which sange of love matters, or other lighter devises alluring unto pleasure and delight, were called *Poetæ* or makers. Thus it appeareth both Eloquence and Poetrie to have had their beginning and originall from these exercises, beeing framed in such sweete measure of sentences and pleasant harmonie called 'Ρυθμός, which is an apt composition of wordes or clauses, drawing as it were by force the hearers eares even whether soever it lysteth, that *Plato* affirmeth therein to be contained γοητεία an inchauntment, as it were to perswade them anie thing whether they would or no.[113]

The distinction between poetry and rhetorical eloquence seems to reside only in their respective matters or contents. Rhetoric handles "grave and necessary matters," and poetry sings of "love matters, or other lighter devises alluring unto pleasure or delight." Here the erotic or amatory contents of poetry are subsumed within the larger category of the frivolous and are opposed to what is "grave and necessary." Poetry's subject matter is pleasure itself, or what conduces to pleasure, without reference to social utility or seriousness. But here content is an allegory of form; because poetic "matter" is merely pleasant, it signifies the possibility of detaching language's pleasurable or persuasive force from its ideological anchor in "grave and necessary matters." What poetry embodies—because it is fictional, and idle—is the discomfiting notion that elocution has no fundamental allegiance with what is serious or true but can "draw . . . as it were by force the hearers eares even whether soever it lysteth." Poetry thereby actualizes or manifests what is latently disturbing about rhetoric as well. Thus while Webbe begins his *Discourse* by contrasting the social prestige of rhetoric to that of poetry, he ends this passage with the Platonic insistence that both are forms of "inchauntment."

In discussing rhetoric earlier, I distinguished between its discursive and social instrumentalities: that is, between its capacity to persuade, and the possibility of subordinating this persuasive force to socially orthodox purposes. Not only are these two instrumentalities essentially unrelated, but the cultivation of the first has a tendency to impair the second; hence the function of the school and of scholastic rhetoric is to cobble together a unity of the two. Poetry foregrounds the breach between these two instrumentalities and also introduces a new breach, this time *within* the technical instrumentality that is persuasion. For rhetorical persuasion itself effects an (immanently unmotivated) unity of linguistic pleasure and discursive aim, thereby investing the pleasure with a certain "direction." But as Longinus (for instance) insists, poetic sublimity carries the listener not to persuasion but to ecstasy and it thus detaches linguistic pleasure from even a discursive instrumentality. Poetry does not *always* do this, of course, nor does it always divide discursive from social instrumentalities; it can be as "ideological" and as persuasive as any other form of discourse. Its specific gift is to reveal that the articulation of these discursive elements is immanently unmotivated and that they therefore have the potential, if not the tendency, to separate. Persuasion can free itself from "true" or dominant values, or it can devolve into linguistic pleasure without direction or purpose.

Poetry, therefore, is at once an innocent and a disquieting form of discourse: innocent because it tends to abandon "grave and necessary matters" and to pursue "lighter devises alluring unto pleasure and delight" (Webbe here anticipates George Puttenham's famous defense of the poet as a "pleader of pleasant and lovely causes, and nothing perilous"), disquieting because the very possibility of this detachment signals an instability within rhetorical discourse. That poetry can argue for anything, even unreal things, or for nothing at all suggests a similar disposition within its twin, rhetorical elocution. Nothing ties rhetoric to "grave and necessary matters" or to the correct position on them, but it falls to poetry at once to evoke this disconcerting disjunction and to draw its consequences onto itself because poetry is, in a sense, more rhetorical than rhetoric. Puttenham, for instance, wrote that poetry is "more eloquent and rethoricall then the ordinarie prose, which we use in our daily talke: because it is decked and set out with all maner of fresh colours and figures, which maketh that it sooner invegleth the judgement of man, and carieth his opinion this way and that, whither soever the heart by impression of the eare shalbe most affectionatly bent and directed."[114] When he writes that poetry "invegleth the judgement of man, and carieth his opinion this way and that," Puttenham echoes Webbe's language of errancy, which is quite widespread in contemporary descriptions of poetry. Puttenham, like Webbe again, grants poetry no powers different in kind from those of prose rhetoric; yet, as the slightly Platonic tilt of his language here suggests, poetry renders the power of elocution suspect.

Because it accented all the ways in which rhetoric might resist the aims of social reproduction, poetry also cast doubt on the assumptions of humanist pedagogy and so became for some humanists a kind of *bête noire*, not actually to be driven from the fold but certainly to be viewed with suspicion. For Ascham, poetry represented the threat of language cut free from ideological and rational restraint. "The quickest wittes," he writes, "commonlie may prove the best Poetes, but not the wisest Orators: readie of tonge to speak boldlie, not deepe of judgement, either for good counsell or wise writing."[115] He urged schoolmasters to distinguish the *vim demosthenis* from the *furorem poetæ* and to encourage only the former. Mulcaster, too, warned that "there must be heed taken, that we plant not any poeticall furie in the childes habit. For that rapt inclination is to ranging of its selfe, though it be not helpt forward, where it is, and would not in any case be forced where it is not."[116] In England, poetic theory never became an academic science or a significant part of the university curriculum as it did in Italy.[117] Rather, it tended to assume the form of the apology, written outside of the schools and attempting to redeem poetry by claiming for it a didactic or pedagogical function. Poetry's relatively minor role in humanist schooling bespoke anxiety more than neglect, for poetry revealed the degree to which the phrase "rhetorical education" might prove a contradiction in terms.

When he distinguishes between the *vim demosthenis* and the *furorem poetæ*, Ascham not only describes two different brands of textual force, or *energeia*, but also evokes, if only implicitly, a corresponding system of psychic faculties. Whereas Webbe, for instance, locates the differences between rhetoric and poetry in a mythicized history, Ascham treats them as arising from certain potentials or energies within the individual subject. Indeed, he seems to regard the poetic disposition as resulting from something like a humoral imbalance that produces, at best, an excessively quick "wit" and, at worst, something like madness. Ascham's brief remarks don't so much allude to as rely upon the historically complex traditions that contributed to the Renaissance theory of poetic imagination. This particular "take" on the problem of poetry seems to privatize or internalize what I have been treating as a social problem; yet, in tracing poetry's linguistic power or *energeia* back to certain psychosomatic energies within the individual subject, the discourse of imagination does little more than transcribe the linguistic properties of poetry onto the subject itself. Rather than lead us away from the social and institutional issues raised thus far, it allows us to read them in another key.

Among the better-known pronouncements on poetic imagination are Francis Bacon's. Poetry, he writes, "commonly exceeds the measure of nature, joining at pleasure things which in nature would never have come together, and introducing things which in nature would never have come to pass; just as Painting likewise does. This is the work of imagination," which "at pleasure makes unlawful matches and divorces of things."[118] Here poetry is once again described as an unusually—indeed, an unnaturally—free form of discourse. Only now its freedom seems more active, since, instead of simply detaching itself from the real, poetic imagination actually scrambles it. It does so, moreover, "at pleasure," but pleasure's pursuits are now described as "unlawful." Having thrown off the restraints of reason and nature, imaginative "pleasure" begins to resemble *furor*, or madness.

At the same time, however, the dissociational and recombinatory work of poetic imagination curiously resembles the kind of textual decoding that takes place in Erasmian composition. Indeed, the language used to describe poetic imagination often recalls the textual suturing that characterizes rhetorical copia. One author writes that poetic fancy not only "taketh what pleaseth it" but "addeth thereto or diminisheth, changeth and rechangeth, mingleth and commingleth, so that it cutteth asunder and seweth up again as it listeth."[119] In rhetorical composition, of course, this decoding serves a rational (that is, instrumental) purpose. But in the workings of imagination, humanist practices of textual decoding have become entirely automatic, following the drives of pleasure rather than the imperatives of technique.[120] Poetic imagination marks the point at which textual decoding breaks free from instrumental finalities and hence from social control.

Of course, the notion of autonomous or automatic decoding was by no means alien to Erasmus's theory of imitation. He too envisaged a "digestion" of texts which involved not only the keeping of commonplace books but also certain obscure and uncodifiable processes within the writing subject. Yet for Erasmus, this did not mean that writing could not ultimately be subordinated to rational or ideologically orthodox intents. Humanist pedagogy and writing theory both extended the realm of pleasure and granted it a certain autonomy, in the belief that it could be recuperated or "trained" in the end. This was in a sense humanism's great wager and the source of its distinctive optimism, which was by no means naïve. The sign of its success—when it succeeded—was the formation of a *style*, as we have seen. Style was the sign that textual decoding had ultimately been unified and reterritorialized and could now be inserted into a system of regular differences. When Puttenham defines style as "a constant & continual phrase or tenour of speaking and writing, extending to the whole tale or processe of the poeme or historie," it is clear the role of style is to reunify and homogenize the text, to recode its imaginative anarchy while guarding against sudden power surges of *energeia*.[121] By imposing a simulated ideological coherence on the text post facto, style also becomes the signature of a *subject*, in all senses of the word: one that has achieved a certain continuity and regularity, has learned to obey certain *decora*, is identifiable and individualized.

The concept of poetic imagination, however, implied a desire whose workings were more fully opaque and unpredictable, more resistant to attempts at rational or instrumental control. Bacon's remarks on imagination portray it as given to "unlawful" constructions, as prone to rebel against the sovereignty of reason. They thus project the image of a subject that is fundamentally less governable or trainable than the humanist one—if, indeed, the autonomy of the imagination allowed of a unified subjectivity at all. Poetic imagination was felt to be an outlaw faculty that, even if it did not coherently oppose the laws of moral or political reason, worked in blind indifference to them. Its dangers lay in its autonomy and automatism, which resisted instrumental control and thus threw a shadow on humanist optimism.

Above all, poetic imagination was felt to be dangerous owing to its decoding properties, its ability to scramble and recombine received materials. Once again, this was something that humanism had attempted to apply to instrumental purposes—of censorship in Vives's case, and of (fully socialized) individuation in Erasmus's. As we have seen, however, humanist textual decoding sometimes had the unintended effect of producing a generalized skepticism, and this was one of the contradictions in its ideological program. By presenting the specter of a decoding run rampant, poetic imagination highlighted the potential weaknesses in the system of rhetorical pedagogy while deflecting these away from rhetoric itself.

The relation between poetry and rhetorical culture, especially as practiced in the Tudor schools, was, in sum, thoroughly contradictory. On the one hand, even classical poetry was felt to pose a problem of illicit content, and this ideological problem was mastered through a process of rhetorical decoding. On the other hand, poetry also embodied the ideological instabilities of rhetoric by representing a textual decoding without limits, a persuasiveness without truth, and a discursive pleasure without aim. It thus signaled the immanent boundaries, and the potential crises, of rhetoric as a mode of ideological training.

Most of what I have said in this section is institutionally but not historically specific, for all the problems of Tudor rhetoric, poetics, and pedagogy pertain as well to their classical sources.[122] The next chapter attempts to make a more genuinely historical argument, which I anticipate here by returning to an issue I raised briefly before, that is, the widespread use of figures of errancy or wandering to describe the decoding effects of poetry.

One of the most striking examples of this figure occurs in a lovely but strongly equivocal passage in which Bacon writes: "But for poesy (whether we speak of stories or metre) it is (as I said before) like a luxuriant plant, that comes of the lust of the earth, without any formal seed. Wherefore it spreads everywhere and is scattered far and wide,—so that it would be vain to take thought about the defect of it."[123] The "formal seed" is what gives discourse its structural organization and thus its ideological and moral coherence. Without it, language becomes a decoded organism, a chaotic and luxuriant growth, a rhizomatic movement fed by "the lust of the earth"—itself a potent image of sexuality without a subject, pulsions of desire freely cathecting a terrestrial surface. What is noteworthy about this passage is the relatively direct way in which it connects the decoding properties of poetic discourse with figures of deterritorialization. As an autochthonous growth, poetry "spreads everywhere and is scattered far and wide," ignoring boundaries and fixed lines of transmission. In one sense this free ranging or errancy is simply the decoding of space and thus maps onto a territorial plain the poetic decoding of ideology (its opposite term is the staking out of a stable ideological "position"). It is not surprising, then, that figures of deterritorialization are, like Bacon's plant, "scattered far and wide" throughout sixteenth-century treatises as a way of figuring the decoding properties of poetic imagination. Sidney's *Apology for Poetry* portrays the ideal poet as both self-generating and nomadic. "Disdaining to be tied to any subjection," he is "lifted up with the vigor of his own invention, . . . freely ranging only within the zodiac of his own wit."[124] This self-vaunting moment, however, also seems designed to recall Phaeton's disastrous ride in the chariot of Helios, thus invoking the fear of imagination's power to usurp and destroy cultural authority.[125]

Since poetic creativity was felt to depend on the ideologically destructive effects of imagination, defenders such as Sidney were loath to deny its power. Instead, they tried to harness it to some restraining counterforce. Sometimes this was located within the poet's mind according to the taxonomies of faculty psychology— whence the frequent references to the controlling power of reason or to distinctions between eicastic and phantastic imagination. Just as frequently, however, this burden was shifted onto other levels of poetic discourse. Thus Bacon describes poetry as "a part of learning in measure of words for the most part restrained, but in all other points extremely free and licensed."[126] If the decoding effects of imagination cannot be inhibited, poetry seeks its principles of social and aesthetic order elsewhere, specifically in prosody and style. Thus Puttenham warns of the dangers of metrical excess:

> In every long verse the *Cesure* ought to be kept precisely, if it were but to serve as a law to correct the licentiousness of rymers, besides that it pleaseth the eare better, & sheweth more cunning in the maker by following the rule of his restraint. For a rymer that will be tyed to no rules at all, but range as he list, may easily utter what he will: but such maner of Poesie is called in our vulgar, ryme dogrell, with which rebuke we will in no case our maker should be touched.[127]

There is a distinctly Sidneyan flavor to the image of the poet "ranging as he list," but here Puttenham offers prosodic restraint as a way of taming and recoding the vagaries of poetic discourse. The composing or "civilizing" properties of poetic style and meter were frequently celebrated by invoking the myths of Orpheus and Amphion. William Webbe's version is standard:

> It was *Orpheus*, who by the sweete gyft of his heavenly Poetry withdrew men from raungyng uncertainly and wandring brutishly about, and made them gather together and keepe company, make houses, and keep fellowship together. . . . After him was *Amphion*, who was the first that caused Citties to be builded, and men therein to live decently and orderly according to lawe and right.[128]

The myth of Orpheus worked to legitimate poetry by portraying it as a purely pacifying force. Whereas Bacon, for instance, viewed poetic style as a way of reordering the chaos produced by poetic imagination—a chaos represented in images of wandering or vagrancy—the myth of Orpheus projected this decoding force outside of poetry altogether and pretended to encounter it in a primordial social mass, the "brutish wanderers" whom it seduces into civility. Bacon, in other words—and here he was joined by a host of other writers—would see Orpheus's song as creating the very nomadism that it attempts to master. But by suppressing or ignoring the faculty of imagination and assimilating poetry to music as a purely rhythmic or tonal force, the myth of Orpheus purged poetic discourse of its more threatening or disturbing properties.

This, too, was a concept inherited entirely from classical traditions. But the myth of Orpheus could take on more historically specific associations. Another Tudor version of the myth described the brutish wanderers tamed by Orpheus as "men, that in those dayes were in manner of brute beasts, wildely sparpled abrode in fieldes, forrestes and woody places, wandryng vagabondes, and peragrant peasants, living by rapine and raw flesh."[129] For at least one Tudor writer, the mythic landscape of the Orpheus story clearly evoked a displaced and fantasized version of the English countryside, with its deracinated peasants, wayward apprentices, highwaymen, and wandering beggars—in short, the whole welter of "masterless men" produced by the dissolution of the late feudal economy.

As we saw, even so innocuous a cultural practice as anti-Ciceronianism could evoke fears of masterless men in writers such as Gabriel Harvey. It should not be surprising, then, that as the discourse of poetic imagination focused even more anxiety on issues of ideological decontrol or decoding and as it employed figurations of vagrancy or errancy to depict this lawlessness, it should also call up the image of those deracinated poor who in the minds of the ruling groups most clearly represented a threat of cultural and social anarchy. In its successes the stylistic education offered by the Tudor schools helped produce a nascent form of bourgeois culture and thereby participated in the transition to capitalism, but in its real or perceived failures it evoked a very different part of that same transition, involving regions of society largely excluded from formal schooling. Tudor style production, though almost exclusively a game for the prosperous, could not quite banish from its unconscious the disturbing presence of a class which, barely subsisting at the margins of culture, neither perceived nor cared for its accomplishments. As we shall see, this class was more than a mere fantasy or symbolic presence in Tudor education and culture. To specify its role, however, will require a more global and rigorous description of the transition to capitalism.

# CHAPTER TWO

# Breeding Capital: Political Economy and the Renaissance

Humanist style production, as we have seen, engages a delicate interplay of ideological control and decontrol. As a transitional institution the Tudor grammar school oversaw the birth of a nascent bourgeois culture; yet at the same time it was troubled by the presence of other social classes, themselves products of the same transitional process. A curious blend of optimism and anxiety thus pervaded the discourse of humanist pedagogy. Understanding the relation between the two requires situating the local, institutional discourse of the schools within a more global transition. The next step, then, is to map out this transitional conjuncture, if only in a preliminary way, and I undertake this task by focusing on Marx's concept of primitive accumulation.

## Primitive Accumulation

I should begin, however, by admitting that this particular approach is bound to seem at least slightly quixotic. To anyone unfamiliar with Marx's *Capital* the term *primitive accumulation* is probably meaningless, and even among Marxist historians it seems to have fallen into a state of neglect tinged with disfavor. The only serious attempt to apply it to literary criticism (at least to my knowledge) is in Christopher Caudwell's *Illusion and Reality* (1937).[1] To make matters worse, Marx himself employed the term both as a mocking trope on Adam Smith's notion of "prior" accumulation *and* as a serious concept in its own right. This mongrel combination of theoretical and polemical concerns characterizes most of Marx's writings on precapitalist modes of production and has drawn cautionary warnings from some on the Althusserian flank of contemporary Marxism.[2] To unpack the meaning of primitive accumulation in Marx's own writings and to establish its relevance to contemporary Marxist accounts of the transition to capitalism is therefore no simple task. And to resuscitate a term that enjoys little currency outside of Marx's works is to risk the appearance of an outmoded orthodoxy. On the other hand, I believe that these are risks worth taking, for Marx's writings on the transition to capitalism are still immensely suggestive for any consideration of the historical transformations of the sixteenth and seventeenth centuries. Moreover, the theoretical method of his exposition has a subtlety and rigor that have not been sufficiently acknowledged by most historicist critics of the Renaissance. I intend, therefore, to "return to Marx" in an unabashed and somewhat systematic way in order to lay the basis of my own argument.

In the eighth and final section of the first volume of *Capital*, Marx sets out "the pre-history of capital, and of the mode of production corresponding to capital," and he recurs to this project again at various points in volume 3.[3] What precedes this is an essentially structural account of capitalist production, including its methods of surplus extraction and self-reproduction on an ever-expanding scale. A "pre-history" (*Vorgeschichte*) is necessary, Marx concludes, because the various elements of this mode of production—the separation of the direct producers from the means of production, the concentration of these means in the hands of the capitalist class, the production of surplus value, and so on—all dialectically presuppose one another. "The whole movement seems to turn around in a never-ending circle,"[4] with the result that a structural account of capitalism cannot explain its *origins* as a mode of production. Marx's prehistorical narrative thus arises in response to a theoretical necessity and raises interesting questions about the relation between historical (diachronic) and structural (synchronic) accounts of social life.

The specific task that Marx sets for himself is to account for the two main social elements of capitalist production: on the one hand, a propertyless class of wage laborers and, on the other, a class possessing capital for investment in labor and means of production. "The capital relation," he writes,

presupposes a complete separation between the workers and the ownership of the conditions for the realization of their labor. As soon as
capitalist production stands on its own two feet, it not only maintains this relation but reproduces it on a constantly expanding scale.
The process, therefore, which creates the capital-relation can be nothing other than the process which divorces the worker from the ownership of the conditions of labor; it is a process which operates two
transformations, whereby the social means of subsistence and production are turned into capital, and the immediate producers are turned
into wage-laborerers. So-called primitive accumulation, therefore, is
nothing else than the historical process of divorcing the producer
from the means of production. It appears as "primitive" because it
forms the pre-history of capital, and of the mode of production corresponding to capital.

The economic structure of capitalist society has grown out of the
economic structure of feudal society. The dissolution of the latter set
free the elements of the former.[5]

Marx takes England as the earliest and fullest example of capitalist development, and his historical exposition, which ranges
from the sixteenth to the eighteenth centuries, focuses mainly on
the ways in which a class of propertyless workers was produced.
His principal themes are the expropriation of agricultural land
through enclosure and engrossment and the resulting dispossess-
sion of the small peasant class; the dissolution of monastic holdings; the discharge of feudal retainers; repressive Tudor and Stuart
legislation directed against the dispossessed classes; state-imposed
limits on wages; the genesis of agricultural and industrial capitalism; and the effects of early colonialism on the accumulation of
capital.[6] Marx's emphasis is on the forcible and violent methods,
often state supported, used to dispossess certain fractions of the
feudal producing class and to amass large sums of monetary
wealth: "The spoliation of the Church's property, the fraudulent
alienation of the state domains, the theft of the common lands,
the usurpation of feudal and clan property under conditions of
ruthless terrorism, all these things were just so many idyllic methods of primitive accumulation."[7]

Etienne Balibar has given a theoretically precise meaning to
Marx's claim that this exposition is a prehistory: "The analysis
of primitive accumulation," he writes, "is ... strictly speaking,
merely *the genealogy of the elements which constitute the structure of the capitalist mode of production.*"[8] In other words, Marx's
purpose in constructing this history was to trace the genesis of

those elements that would *later* combine in capitalist production.[9] This strategy does not make his analysis teleological, but it does rescue it from blind empiricism by employing a principle of selection which is strongly *retrospective*.[10] (Facts, as Walter Benjamin points out, become historical only "posthumously." The historian's task is to "grasp the constellation which his own era has formed with a definite earlier one.")[11] Marx's prehistory narrates the class struggles of the early modern period to show how they produced the elements of capitalist production, but it does not give a coherent account of how these struggles were informed by the structures of the feudal mode of production within which they arose. Hence, writes Balibar, "we are not dealing with a true history in the theoretical sense (since, as we know, such a history can only be produced by thinking the dependence of the elements with respect to a structure)."[12] Marx thus writes a prehistory of capitalism in two different senses: it is a genealogy of that which is *not yet* capitalism and this genealogy itself is *not yet* a history. This is not to say that Marx's account is faulty; it is only to guard against taking it for something it is not by remembering the theoretical project that informs it. As Barry Hindess and Paul Q. Hirst maintain, "The object of *Capital* is to construct a theory of the capitalist mode of production, where pre-capitalist modes of production are discussed in the discourse of *Capital* it is to illustrate features of capitalism and not in order to construct a general theory of modes of production."[13]

Marx's decision to write a prehistory of capital is determined by the theoretical project of *Capital*, not only because it "illustrates features of capitalism" but because it contributes to Marx's critique of the classical political economists. In particular, Marx wishes to explode Adam Smith's view that the "accumulation of stock necessary for capitalist production" results exclusively from the industry and thrift of the capitalist class. Smith's contention that "capitals are increased by parsimony, and diminished by prodigality and misconduct" both explained and justified the division of society into competing classes by substituting a myth of primary ethical differences for a real historical process.[14] "This primitive accumulation [of Smith's]," writes Marx,

> plays approximately the same role in political economy as original
> sin does in theology. Adam bit the apple, and thereupon sin fell on
> the human race. Its origin is supposed to be explained when it is told
> as an anecdote about the past. Long, long ago there were two sorts of

people: one, the diligent, intelligent and above all frugal elite; the other, lazy rascals, spending their substance, and more, in riotous living. The legend of theological original sin tells us certainly how man came to be condemned to eat his bread in the sweat of his brow; but the history of economic original sin reveals to us that there are people to whom this is by no means essential. Never mind! Thus it came to pass that the former sort accumulated wealth, and the latter sort finally had nothing to sell except their own skins. And from this original sin dates the poverty of the great majority who, despite all their labour, have up to now nothing to sell but themselves, and the wealth of the few that increases constantly, although they have long ceased to work.[15]

It is in the battle with Smith and the political economists that the tactical and theoretical significance of Marx's prehistory appears most clearly. (Smith's actual views, as we shall see, differ significantly from Marx's rendition of them, but for the moment I shall treat Marx's version as accurate). The reference to the myth of Eden is no mere rhetorical flourish but a stab at two interdependent elements in Smith's account: ethics and teleology. In place of Smith's assumption of some mysterious and originary distribution of ethical merits (of industry, thrift, frugality)—a tale that betrays a residual Calvinist theology—Marx substitutes an account of the violent expropriation of one class by another. Adam's prelapsarian innocence, Marx suggests, finds its avatar in a later "Adam" whose idyllic vision of primitive accumulation obscures the material processes of class formation. Marx's emphasis on forcible expropriation uncovers violence where Smith saw only thrift, and the collective logic of class struggle where Smith saw only individual acts. The point is not so much to reverse Smith's attribution of virtue as it is to reject an ethical problematic entirely. The petty producing class, Marx implies, was not booted from its fields and gardens because of the sin of sloth; the hand of the enclosing landlord, and not the hand of God, shut the gates of this "Eden" (such as it was).

In substituting historically specific acts of expropriation for the timeless realm of ethics, Marx also rejects the teleological view that capitalism originates in the same acts of thrift that are thought to sustain it, and thus in effect calls itself into being. Emphasizing that the *original* separation of the producing class from its means of production relied on the use of politico-juridical force, Marx contrasts this method with capitalism's ability to reproduce the separation primarily through economic means. Primitive accumulation thus "belongs among the antediluvian conditions of capital, belongs to its *historic presuppositions,* which, precisely as such *historic presuppositions,* are past and gone, and hence belong to the *history of its formation,* but in no way to its *contemporary* history, i.e., not to the real system of the mode of production ruled by it."[16] Marx's "retrospective" view, far from being teleological, is actually a critique of teleology; the prehistory of capital tells a tale not of embryonic development but of a fundamental *break* between modes of production. Thus Marx emphasizes that the dominance of merchant's capital, which prepares the way for capitalist production by encouraging the spread of markets and commodity production, is nevertheless structurally incompatible with the capitalist mode of production itself.[17]

The somewhat "disarticulated" character of Marx's prehistory serves a theoretical purpose by illustrating that the elements of capitalism, in their genesis, lack any direct structural relation to one another or to the mode of production they will help to compose. The very notion of primitive accumulation thus arises as part of a negative hermeneutics whose purpose is to banish the illusions of political economy. Since these illusions are still with us, along with the mode of production they help to support, the narrative of primitive accumulation still has a critical value. The question remains, however, whether it has any positive or independent conceptual value outside of this critical project.

In one sense, the answer is no. As a prehistory of capital, a constellation of events with no internal articulation, Marx's narrative seems merely to identify a space where a history ought to be. The prehistory would then be erased and subsumed by such a history in the same way that the outline of a half-solved jigsaw puzzle would disappear when the puzzle was completed. And yet, since all histories are *also* prehistories—that is, since they always contain a retrospective element as a founding condition of existence— the concept of primitive accumulation cannot simply disappear into a "full" narrative of the transition from feudalism to capitalism. At the very least it is a set of ineradicable (because constitutive) emphases within such a narrative. While it is not quite a structural concept on the order of a mode of production it is not quite nothing, either. Its value is in isolating and focusing certain crucial aspects of the transition.

At the same time, the presence of a genealogical discourse within *Capital* does not merely indicate a lack waiting to be filled by theory. Or if it does, this particular lack has been asked to show unusual patience, for Marxism has not yet provided either a definitive general theory of the transition between modes of production or a conclusive historical account of the transition from feudalism to capitalism. On the contrary, such issues have been the occasion for exceptionally vigorous and long-standing debates.[18] Our understanding of the transitional process today is rich and detailed, and we have indeed "filled in" many of the theoretical and historical spaces left empty by Marx. Yet at the same time, certain problems posed by the transition have proven intractable and have therefore placed limits on the very possibility of theoretical closure. Even Hindess and Hirst, who attack the problem with extraordinary rigor, define a "transitional conjuncture" as "one in which the transformation of the dominant relations of production is a *possible* outcome of class struggle conducted under the conditions of that conjuncture."[19] Even a "full" history of the transitional process would not, therefore, be fully determined in a theoretical sense; it would contain elements that if not exactly aleatory would be at least contingent. As a genealogical discourse, then, primitive accumulation signifies both a history to be written and the limits such a history must observe. Its vocation is to provide not a conclusive narrative but a useful one.

One of its uses, in fact, is to refine our sense of what we mean by the transition to capitalism and how it pertains to the sixteenth century. The very notion of a "transitional" era has, of course, become a notorious commonplace, and must be delimited somehow if it is to have any interesting or useful meaning. One of the virtues of a Marxist theory of transition is that it involves modes of production which can be defined with considerable rigor. (This is not to ignore debates over the concept of the feudal mode of production and of the mechanisms of the transition to capitalism; the point is that all sides in this debate operate with a carefully defined, though contested, set of concepts.) Even so, the transition to capitalism is a process so complex, lengthy, and overdetermined that it has been dated by one economist as extending "from the end of the fourteenth to the end of the eighteenth century."[20] At one point in *Capital*, Marx boldly states that "the capitalist era dates from the sixteenth century," but then he revises this a few pages later to the more prudent claim that "the *prelude* to the revolution that *laid the foundation* of the capitalist mode of production was played out in the last third of the fifteenth century and the first few decades of the sixteenth."[21] These issues of periodization are in themselves only symptoms of the need for a more fully elaborated set of distinctions.

More precisely, a *theoretical periodization*, which is not directly convertible into historical periods but which would form one of their bases, will help to refine our sense of the transition. Here again the work of Etienne Balibar is extremely suggestive. In examining Marx's analysis of the capitalist labor process, Balibar has pointed out that capitalism's separation of the producer from the means of production is a complex concept combining two elements. The first of these is the *formal* subsumption of labor by capital, which involves a mere transfer of economic and legal property. "At first," writes Marx, "capital subordinates labor on the basis of the technical conditions given by historical development. It does not change immediately the mode of production."[22] But once this formal separation has been effected, and under the incentive of relative surplus value, capital revolutionizes the means of production themselves, replacing handicraft tools that can be set in motion by individual laborers with industrial machines that require a complex division and cooperation of labor. This is the *real subsumption* of labor by capital, wherein not only the relations of production but the productive process itself prevent the individual worker from setting the means of production into operation on his own.

The distinction between the real and formal subsumptions of labor, along with the "chronological dislocation" this entails,[23] enables Balibar to identify *manufacture* as a transitional creature in which the formal relations of production are capitalist but the forces of production (technical apparatus, division and cooperation of labor) are derived from feudal crafts. It is clear, however, that the formal subsumption of labor itself involves two stages: one in which the direct producers are separated from the means of production (that is, primitives accumulation) and one in which they are "recombined" with them as wage laborers under conditions of capitalist production.[24] Here again a chronological dislocation separates these two stages: the dispossession of the feudal petty producing class was in no sense a planned preparation for capitalist manufacture. On the contrary, the lack of employment for the dispossessed classes in the sixteenth and early seventeenth centuries was one of the factors that made primitive accumulation an explicit social crisis.

This theoretical periodization, it should be clear, derives not from an empirical survey of historical development but from a structural analysis of the capitalist labor process. That is to say, the various "stages" are not temporal or chronological but structural, in that each is a necessary precondition for the next. Structural necessity certainly implies a temporal order, but it allows a considerable field for historical variation.[25] It should be equally clear that this sequence does not provide causal mechanisms for the movement from one structural stage to the next. Such mechanisms—economic, social, legal, and political—interact strongly with the productive relations but are in no sense reducible to them. Finally, just as this theoretical periodization is not derived from a historical chronology, so it cannot be directly converted into a set of historical "periods." For one thing, the component stages can overlap; in England, primitive accumulation continued well into the eighteenth century as parliamentary enclosure uprooted the remnants of precapitalist agriculture. For another, these stages cannot be inserted into a linear continuum because, as Althusser and Balibar have shown, historical time is not a uniform and pregiven "container" of different modes of production and their components but rather the product of a set of heterogeneous socioeconomic mechanisms, each with its own differential temporality, interacting in a complex and overdetermined fashion.[26]

One of the reasons primitive accumulation has fallen into disfavor as a concept may be Maurice Dobb's ill-advised attempt to convert it directly from a theoretical to historical "stage" based on windfall profits in the land market.[27] While avoiding this kind of reductivist historicism we may nevertheless look to the sixteenth and early seventeenth centuries as the historical period in which primitive accumulation played its first important role. The concept therefore has a preliminary value in defining the meaning of the transition to capitalism as it applies to the Tudor and Stuart periods. (I offer a convenient historical terminus of 1660, when economic expansion and employment in manufacture began significantly to mitigate the vagrancy problem.)[28] In particular, it allows us to say that the really decisive transformation—that is, the institution of capitalist productive relations—occurs only in nascent and nondominant forms. What does characterize this period is the development of various preconditions for capitalist production—the spread of markets, the development of merchant's capital, the creation of a dispossessed class—within a complex conjuncture that combines both the late mutation and the partial dissolution of the feudal economy.

By the late fifteenth and sixteenth centuries, what I shall call a "primary decoding" of feudal production was under way. In the countryside, the peasant struggles of the fifteenth century led to the virtual abolition of villeinage and the establishment of small holdings, generally of insecure tenure.[29] The towns witnessed the spread of petty production as the older craft guilds were replaced by amalgamated trading companies in which merchants employed small masters, while the so-called "domestic" system spread to the suburbs and countryside.[30] This decoding was not in any sense a dissolution of feudal production but rather its reorganization in a way that was both more atomized and more centralized. If the hold of feudalism was not abrogated, however, it is true that the predominance of small holdings and petty production tended to dissolve the cellular unity of manor and guild. Customary land tenure gave way to forms that approximated "absolute" property—either freehold or varieties of copyhold that granted virtually total control to landlord or to tenant. These new forms of tenure, combined with the spread of market relations, led to a decoding of feudal production on the local level or, in other words, to the stripping of economic relations from their direct encoding (embeddedness) in legal and political forms, and their reorganization at a more abstract regional or national level (the absolutist state, mercantilism).

This process of decoding was limited, however, by the nature of merchant's capital, which, as a system of "profit upon alienation," extracted its profits primarily from the sphere of circulation, "continually speculating with the maintained territories, so as to buy where prices are low and sell where they are high."[31] Thus while it connected local markets and expanded commerce, it also employed monopoly powers to reinforce traditional territorial privileges and thereby safeguard its means of profit. Within the sphere of circulation, then, merchant's capital was restricted to a primary decoding or deterritorialization. And within the sphere of production it could accomplish nothing more. Even the so-called domestic system, which helped to subvert the old craft guilds, still left workers in possession of their means of production while it extracted a profit through monopoly control over the supply of raw materials and finished products. "Without revolutionizing the mode of production," merchant's capital "simply worsens the conditions of the direct producers, appropriating their surplus labor on the basis of the old mode of production."[32] Relying on political and legal monopoly for its surplus extraction, merchant's capital was still feudal in form.

While the spread of commodity production helped effect a late mutation of feudalism, however, primitive accumulation laid the basis for its replacement. If commodity production brought a primary decoding of feudal productive relations, primitive accumulation represented an *absolute* decoding through the total separation of the direct producer and the means of production:

> The immediate producer, the worker, could dispose of his own person only after he had ceased to be bound to the soil, and ceased to be the slave or serf of another person. To become a free seller of labour-power, who carries his commodity wherever he can find a market for it, he must further have escaped from the regime of the guilds, their rules for apprentices and journeymen, and their restrictive labour regulations. Hence the historical movement which changes the producers into wage-labourers appears, on the one hand, as their emancipation from serfdom and from the fetters of the guilds, and it is this aspect of the movement alone which exists for our bourgeois historians. But, on the other hand, these newly freed men became sellers of themselves only after they had been robbed of all their own means of production, and all the guarantees of existence afforded by the old feudal arrangements. And this history, the history of their expropriation, is written in the annals of mankind in blood and fire.[33]

Primitive accumulation thus laid the basis for an abstract recoding on the basis of the capitalist wage contract, while it thrust the decoding process beyond the structural limits imposed by the feudal mode of production. I do not mean that feudalism underwent a full-scale "dissolution" prior to the advent of capitalism; rather, a fraction of the petty producing class was extruded from its economic and social system in order to become what Marx called a *vogelfrei Proletariat.*

This expulsion resulted primarily from changes in agrarian relations. Land was profitable to feudal landowners mainly because of the tenants who occupied and worked it. With the rise of markets for land and wool and with the development of improved methods of agriculture, however, land became transferable and in some cases more profitable when stripped of its customary inhabitants. This is where the various elements of primitive accumulation described by Marx come into play, though it should be pointed out that the landlords' successful efforts at expropriation were conditioned by two developments of the fifteenth century: the failure of the small peasants to achieve a secure form of freehold tenure and the economic differentiation of the peasantry itself, which acted to destroy class solidarity and thus the basis for collective resistance to expropriation.[34]

One of the most controversial elements in Marx's account of the transition has proven to be his insistence that the enclosure movement played a leading role in the transformation of sixteenth-century agrarian relations.[35] But even if the chronology of enclosure does not support the emphasis Marx gives to it in his account of the sixteenth century, a good fourth to a third of the rural population was composed of cottagers, squatters, and wage laborers whose land tenure and economic status were so insecure that they could easily be dispossessed by a variety of other means, such as entry fines and legal challenges, if landlords chose to do so.[36] And there were a number of enclosing landlords who did depopulate whole villages, including that notable patron of letters the earl of Leicester, who wrote in a moment of remorse, "I am like the ogre in the old tale, and have eaten up all my neighbors."[37]

Marx's focus on enclosure is in any case meant to illustrate the more general role of *force* in the transition. Politically, this argument is directed against the historical idealism of Adam Smith and his followers. "In the tender annals of political economy," notes Marx, "the idyllic reigns from time immemorial," while "in actual history it is a notorious fact that conquest, enslavery, robbery, murder, in short, force, play the greatest part" in the birth of capitalism.[38] At the same time, this political argument avoids a teleological view of the transition by contrasting the forcible initial separation of the producer from the means of production with capitalism's ability to reproduce this separation primarily through economic means.

"Force," writes Marx, "is the midwife of every society which is pregnant with a new one. It is itself an economic power."[39] Force does play a privileged role in the transition to capitalism, but since it is also integral to the reproduction of the feudal economy, Marx's formula requires some commentary. What is at stake is a reversal of the direction of force with respect to the existing economic relations. The feudal landowning class generally exerted its politico-juridical coercion "inward" so as to secure both the existing forces of production (that is, the unity of the peasant and land) and the existing relations of production (that is, enforced rents or labor services), expressed in the cellular unity of the manor as a productive unit. The proto-capitalist landowners who effected so-called primitive accumulation, however, began to direct force "outward" so as to dissolve these relations and methods of production. Force became expulsive rather than binding, centrifugal rather than centripetal, and on the other side the small peasantry now tried to secure its place on the land, whereas before it had struggled to free itself from villeinage. It was this redirection of force, its novel deployment as an expulsive mechanism, that carried out the absolute decoding of feudal production.

The result was a sizable mass of impoverished and vagrant persons who lost their domestic, social, and cultural habitations along with their means of subsistence. There are some excellent recent studies of vagrancy in the sixteenth and seventeenth centuries, and even though these tend to treat it as a social problem rather than as a structural symptom, they nevertheless reveal a crisis of major proportions.[40] The Tudor and Stuart eras saw an explosion in the size of the vagrant population that overwhelmed traditional institutions for poor relief.[41] The problem was compounded by a number of factors, including trade crises, the dissolution of many monasteries and hospitals that had done charitable work, and increasing restrictiveness by craft guilds that might have provided employment. And the magnitude of the problem, great as it was, appeared even greater because the vagrant poor frequented towns and markets to beg, find shelter, or otherwise seek subsistence.[42] Vagrants attended holiday gatherings of all sorts: plays, bearbaitings, horse races, sermons and Sunday services, aristocrats' funerals, even official functions such as quarter sessions, assizes, and elections.[43] And since they were continually on the move, the local rogues' gallery was always changing, magnifying the apparent numbers still more. The beggars, it seemed, were *always* coming to town.

The dramatic rise in the real and seeming numbers of the vagrant poor, the collapse of traditional institutions for relieving and controlling them, and the actual and imagined dangers they posed to the sedentary population resulted in a major change of social attitudes, what A. L. Beier has termed the "desanctification of the poor." Traditions of holy poverty in the Middle Ages had made the poor seem worthy of charity, and because their numbers were relatively small and they tended to remain in their village or parish, they were regarded and treated as members of a local community. In the early sixteenth century, however, this attitude changed radically. The poor were increasingly viewed with indifference, suspicion, or fear, and instead of being given charity they were frequently persecuted or punished. They became, in a sense, the quintessential "other" of English society. If primitive accumulation was marked by a reversal of the direction of juridico-political force, then, it also witnessed a strikingly similar reversal of ideological "force." For whereas late feudal ideology tended to bind the poor to a corporative social or religious body, early modern ideology worked to expel them as alien and threatening.

This position as "other" within the dominant ideology resulted in part from the vagrancy of the poor, which kept them beyond the reach of ideological apparatuses that were designed to control a mainly sedentary population. "Children of the needy," wrote Vives, "receive a deplorable upbringing. Together with their brood, the poor are cast out of the churches and wander over the land; they do not receive the sacraments and they hear no services. We do not know by what law they live, nor what their practices or beliefs."[44] What primitive accumulation produced was a class of men and women unlike any other in late feudal society. While popular and official images of the poor should not be confused with reality, it is nevertheless clear that the new class of "masterless" men came to represent as well as to embody a force that was decoded with respect to the economic, social, and ideological structures of late feudalism.[45] In some sense they could be said to mimic the qualities of capital itself, whose ceaseless movements tended to ignore or to dissolve traditional social bonds and beliefs. Yet—and this is the point—they represented a decoding more thorough than capital, in its late feudal forms, was able to effect. If merchant's capital helped achieve a primary deterritorialization of the late feudal polity, connecting and expanding traditional markets while maintaining a web of monopoly restrictions among them, the vagrant poor obeyed an absolute deterritorialization that sent them sprawling over the countryside and prompted an urgent—and brutal—reterritorializing effort on the part of the state. If merchant's capital brought about a primary decoding of late feudal production in order to recode it in the sphere of exchange, the vagrant poor represented an absolute decoding, the decisive separation of the producer from the means of production. The dispossessed classes thus had a strongly anticipatory force; by "mirroring" the decoding effects of capital in a way that overstepped the structural limitations of late feudal production they became a precocious and nightmarishly exaggerated image of *modernity.* They were a kind of volatile fluid, coursing irregularly through the social body and visible everywhere in it, representing the possibility of a total and anarchic breakdown of the existing social mechanisms of order and control.

Paradoxically, the vagrant poor were able to "mimic" capital precisely because, by a chronological dislocation, industrial capital (including its agricultural forms) was not yet in existence. Capitalism as a mode of production would bring about an abstract recoding of the dispossessed classes through the system of wage labor, thus reabsorbing them into the productive regime (though under radically different conditions) and to a large degree resettling them. Industrial capital would also produce unemployment, but in the form of a "reserve army of labor" which played a functional role in depressing wages. Likewise, it would impose a disastrous but strictly functional mobility on portions of the labor force. Under capitalism, in other words, vagrancy and unemployment are largely useful to the system of production, even though they fall outside of the actual process of production. Thus in *The Wealth of Nations*, Adam Smith would attack the so-called "settlement laws" for impeding "the free circulation of labour and stock both from employment to employment and from place to place." In England, he fumes, "it is often more difficult for a poor man to cross the artificial boundary of a parish, than an arm of the sea or a ridge of high mountains."[46] Movement is no longer seen as a catastrophe inflicted on the working classes by means of their expropriation; instead it is considered an inherent liberty or "right," which can be guaranteed only by the free market. For Smith, vagrants are simply potential laborers in search of capital; they are therefore part of the nation's economic and social life. It was only during the heyday of primitive accumulation that the vagrant classes played the role of a fully decoded body with respect to the dominant social order.

Vagrancy and the Schools

The primitive accumulation of church lands under Henry VIII and Edward VI necessarily entailed something like a primitive accumulation of *schools* as well, for the dissolution of ecclesiastical property led to a wholesale refounding of medieval chantry schools, collegiate churches, monastic schools, religious guilds, song and grammar schools under the secular jurisdiction of the Tudor state.[47] Through their assimilation to the state apparatus, Tudor schools were also constituted for the first time as relatively autonomous social institutions with their own techniques and subject matter, and in this conversion the advent of humanism played an opportune part.

In detaching themselves from the corporative body of the church, moreover, Tudor schools also distanced themselves from older institutions of secular education, which were almost entirely associated with vocational apprenticeship in the guild system.[48] Craft and trade guilds were primarily economic organizations, of course, but they were also social, cultural, and religious ones; they thus embodied as clearly as any other feudal institution the direct imbrication of economic production with the political and ideological levels of society. Education within the guild system was at once vocational and cultural in a way that suggested an organic bond between the two. "Obviously," as John Lawson and Harold Silver note, "more than technical training was involved, for in the master's family and in the corporate life of the guild, its worship, moots, feasts, plays and pageants, adolescent apprentices must have gained much of their moral and social education."[49] In both its secular and religious branches, then, medieval schooling was conducted under the vocational and cultural auspices of a guild structure, and its knowledge was always in some sense vocational. Even Latin was "learnt as a written and spoken language in daily use for most official and professional purposes and therefore more as a vocational skill than as part of a liberal education."[50] A humanist curriculum, however, tended to spurn such direct vocational ties. By converting Latin from a directly practical to an expressive or stylistic medium and from a vocational to a literary one, humanism helped to divorce the teaching of grammar from its old affiliations with apprenticeship and the guild structure. Thus, while a humanist education by means of its disciplinary functions was felt to be compatible with apprenticeship, it frequently did all it could to distance itself from vocational training.[51] Unlike those they replaced, then, Tudor schools aimed to fashion not corporative-productive subjects but political and "civil" ones. The relative autonomy of the schools, enabled in part by the state's role in primitive accumulation, was a precondition for the kinds of transitional effects described in my first chapter.

Schools were not only implicated in the material process of primitive accumulation, however; they also represented part of a strategic response to it by the governing authorities. The social dislocation, vagrancy, and unemployment that attended changes in agrarian production were thought to pose a major threat to the stability of the nation, and in attempting to control them the Tudor state took on the difficult double imperative of the capitalist state: to serve as a class state, upholding the interests of the ruling groups, while acting relatively autonomously to safeguard the global stability of the social order. The state's response to vagrancy in the sixteenth century included attempts to pass and enforce anti-enclosure laws, generally opposed by the gentry in Commons; more successful efforts to pass antivagrancy laws which harassed, punished, and controlled the victims of enclosure; and forms of poor relief which sought to succor the new vagrant poor, keep track of them, and if possible employ them.

Schools formed part of the state's proposed effort at poor relief, as institutions intended to control English youth and prepare them for gainful employment. Children and adolescents made up a disproportionately large part of the vagrant population during the early modern era, and were "singled out in numerous statutes," writes A. L. Beier. "By the end of Elizabeth's reign, London was experiencing large-scale 'juvenile delinquency,' and officials feared these vagrant youths as potential rioters."[52] It should not be surprising, then, that schooling came to be seen as an important instrument for controlling and relieving the poor. In a royal injunction issued following the Pilgrimage of Grace, a northern uprising in 1535, Thomas Cromwell ordered that parents, masters, and governors should

> forsee that the said youth be in no manner wise kept or brought up in idleness, lest at any time afterwards they be driven for lack of some mystery or profession to live by, to fall to begging, stealing, or some other unthriftiness; forasmuch as we may daily see, through sloth and idleness divers valiant men fall, some to be begging and some to theft and murder, which after brought to calamity and misery impute a great part thereof to their friends and governors, which suffered them to be brought up so idly in their youth; where if they had been well educated and brought up in some good literature, occupation or mystery, they should, being rulers of their own family, have profited as well themselves as divers other persons, to the great commodity and ornament of the commonwealth.[53]

Hugh Latimer ominously warned England's magistrates that "if ye will not maintain schools and universities ye shall have a brutality."[54] The state's burden was, of course, increased by its dissolution of the monasteries, hospitals, schools, and other agencies of poor relief that had traditionally belonged to the Catholic church. Tudor legislation tended to lump schools together with other charitable institutions in its attempts to control the effects of primitive accumulation.

Humanists were only too happy to encourage the idea that schooling offered a solution to the problem of vagrancy and crime. In *A Remedy for Sedition* (1536), another response to the Pilgrimage of Grace, Richard Morison denied that theft, vagabondage, and rebellion were caused by poverty and insisted that "The root is lower. . . . Education, evil education, is a great cause of these and all other mischiefs that grow in a commonwealth."[55] Vives, as well, declared that abandoned children should "enter a publicly supported school where they would be educated in letters and morals, and be maintained," and he argued that "no greater danger for the sons of the poor exists than a cheap, inferior and demoralizing education."[56]

In fact, however, Tudor schools did not generally serve as institutions for controlling vagrant youth. This was the job of poor laws and, beginning with Elizabeth's reign, the failed experiment with "bridewells" or work-prisons in which masterless children were to be supplied with raw materials and subjected to the wholesome discipline of enforced labor.[57] Free schools and scholarships were available for some children of the poor; yet economic factors often prevented them from taking advantage of such opportunities.[58] Both tradition and the interests of the Tudor state nevertheless caused schools to be regarded as institutions of poor relief; and if various factors tended to thwart this purpose, it is still true that the problem of vagrancy informed pedagogical intentions and anxieties.

The figurative language used by Tudor pedagogues frequently depicted children as innately or potentially vagrant; against this disposition the disciplinary and sedentarizing regime of the school was felt to exert a prophylactic effect. Mulcaster wrote that "being in the schoole, [a child] may do somewhat very well, though not very much, wheras roming about, he might hap to do ill, and that very much."[59] It is not that children were necessarily seen as morally evil, but they were felt to have, on the one hand, an alarming capacity for idleness and, on the other, a kind of directionless energy that, if not properly harnessed, might develop into criminal behavior. John Brinsley suggested combining play and pleasure with a measured severity so that the school would be "*ludus a non ludendo*, a place voyd of al fruitless play & loytering,"[60] using phrases that evoke both the excesses of popular festivity and the aimlessness of the vagrant. If this connection seems tenuous, it is useful to consider the history of the word *truant*, which originally denoted a vagabond or sturdy beggar but in the sixteenth century began to be applied to lazy or absent schoolboys.

The class character of the schools' disciplinary mechanism thus sometimes assumed the mediated form of an opposition between sedentary and nomadic regimes. Actual vagrants, or likely candidates for vagrancy, were excluded from formal schooling, but since vagrancy was often regarded not as a class condition but as a moral or disciplinary failing, Tudor pedagogues still felt the need to ward it off. It may now be clearer how humanist conceptions of poetic imagination as vagrant or errant might produce anxiety within an educational apparatus intended to control just such things, and how the decoding properties of humanist style production might provoke an ambivalent response from a culture in which the recoding of vagrant elements was a constant concern. Humanist schooling provided an essentially sedentarizing regime into which certain "nomadic" elements were nevertheless absorbed.

A particularly suggestive instance of this phenomenon was the teaching of penmanship, in which ideological, literary, and pedagogical matters could clearly intersect.[61] One of the more intriguing discussions of penmanship occurs in John Brinsley's *Ludus literarius* (1612), a book that collects most of the reigning humanist wisdom about pedagogy and frames it within a candid discussion of the problems and shortcomings faced by teachers in the "common" petty and grammar schools. One of the complaints made by parents, he notes, is that their children don't learn penmanship in school. As a result their writing is unfit for any trade, and they must be sent to a scrivener to learn to write. Brinsley admits that these complaints are often justified and that many schoolteachers themselves set a bad example, "For many of the best Schollars, have beene wont to write very ill; in so much, as it hath beene a received opinion, as you know, amongst very many, That a good Schollar can hardly be a good pen-man."[62] For their part, scriveners were often equally uninterested in scholarship. Many fifteenth-century scriveners knew no grammar at all, and to protect their trade the Company of Scriveners of London passed regulations demanding that they attend grammar school.[63] Writing, therefore, was subject to a division between manual and mental labor; scriveners were artisanal masters of its technology, and scholars treated it as a disembodied medium of thought and expression. Erasmus attributed this division to the advent of printing, arguing that whereas scholars of old had to copy almost everything they read, some of their descendants in the age of print wrote nothing at all.[64] In any case the scrivener was not only a counterpart to but in some cases an economic rival of the schoolmaster. Brinsley thus urged teachers to master the art of writing themselves and to produce *penmen* who possessed the whole art of writing: "For these properties should be joyned together in every pen-man, who would have any approbation; to be able as well to write a good stile (I mean to indite, and to expresse his mind in some good forme of wordes, and true Orthographie) as to write fair."[65]

Penmanship itself, as taught in the Renaissance, can be divided into two phases or regimes, each with its own goals, practices, techniques, and even social relations: these are copying, or letter production, and drawing, or line production. The first of these is the one still practiced today as a part of elementary education and has come to represent the whole of what we now mean by "penmanship": the copying of the forms of letters. Like style production, the copying of letters is a mimetic or imitative practice; Renaissance students were provided with "copybooks" containing model letters, and they practiced reproducing them. Like all mimetic practices, penmanship could assimilate certain elements of play. Erasmus, not surprisingly, urged that writing should be taught so that it feels like playing, not studying.[66] And in its more advanced forms, handwriting was every bit as expressive or stylistic as literary style. Students were urged to practice writing "still viewing your Coppie, and observing everie grace and comelines thereof."[67] Fads and fashions arose in handwriting as in clothing, and like fashion, handwriting engaged a dialectic between a general style or model (known as a "script") and its individual inflections (known as a "hand").[68] Handwriting thus complemented the stylistic practices associated with literary training to produce a unified aesthetic of rhetorical and graphic elements known as penmanship.

At the same time, and particularly in its elementary phases, the teaching of handwriting had a noticeably disciplinary character, with an emphasis on exactness and uniformity (of shape, size, and spacing) in the production of letters.[69] Penmanship demanded not only patience, concentration, and coordination of hand and eye but also a rudimentary sort of bodily orthopedics involving the control of hand, elbow, and sitting posture. Cross-hatching on the page was also recommended as an aid for beginning students

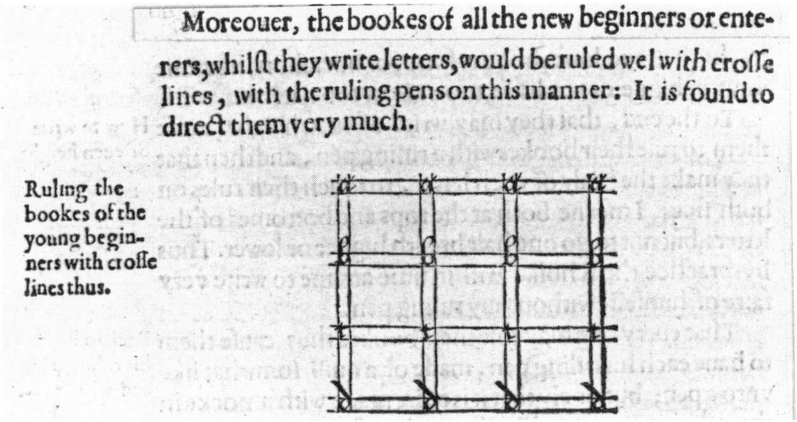

> Moreouer, the bookes of all the new beginners or ente-
> rers, whilſt they write letters, would be ruled wel *with* croſſe
> lines, with the ruling pens on this manner: It is found to
> direct them very much.

Ruling the
bookes of the
young begin-
ners with croſſe
lines thus.

*Figure 1.* John Brinsley, *Ludius Literarius* (1612), sigs. E3v and F1r.
Courtesy The Beinecke Rare Book and Manuscript Library, Yale University

(see figure 1). Penmanship as copying thus emerged from a striated or "ruled" space (in every sense of the word).

The disciplinary and stylistic practice of letter production was, however, erected on a foundation of a very different nature. Line production, which derived from the technology of ink and the quill pen, was an art whose difficulty may be hard to appreciate today. The trick was to produce a controlled and even flow of ink without runs, blotting, or skipping, and it involved careful cutting of the pen, adjusting the viscosity of the ink, attending to the roughness and absorbency of paper—in short, a kind of minor hydraulics. Before writing could be a means of copying or reproduction, then, it was a production of regulated *flows*. It is worth pondering, perhaps, the way in which a concept of writing as inscription derives from the classical technology of stylus and wax tablet, a technology that bore little relation to the material practice of writing in the Middle Ages and Renaissance. Advances in writing technology since that time have aimed at controlling (and as far as possible eliminating) precisely the physical fluidity of writing, the release of a volatile liquid onto a smooth surface.

Line production involved a technique as well as a technology: the hand had to move quickly and lightly over the page in order to avoid blotting or an excessively thick line. Brinsley recommended that the student "learne to carry his pen as lightly as he can, to glide or swim upon the paper." If letter production required a slow, exact motion, line production required speed and fluidity of the

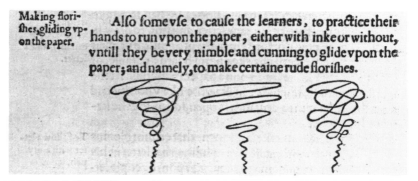

**Making flori-ſhes,gliding vp-on the paper.** Alſo ſome vſe to cauſe the learners, to practice their hands to run vpon the paper, either with inke or without, vntill they be very nimble and cunning to glide vpon the paper; and namely, to make certaine rude floriſhes.

*Figure 2.* John Brinsley, *Ludus Literarius* (1612), sig. F2v. Courtesy The Beinecke Rare Book and Manuscript Library, Yale University

hand: the child must learn to draw "as the Painter doth." While letter production required a disciplinary orthopedics, line production required the free flow of bodily humors: writing lessons were to be scheduled "about one of the clock: for then commonly their hands are warmest and nimblest."[70] Finally, if letter production took shape in the striated or ruled space of cross-hatching, line production occupied a free or smooth space and aimed not at forming accurate letters but at creating "rude flourishes" (see figure 2). A comparison of the crosshatch and the flourish illustrates quite graphically the difference between letter production, as a disciplinary and sedentarizing regime, and line production, as a fluid and nomadic one.[71] Ultimately, of course, the two were conjoined in an unstable union, under the dominance, one might say, of letter production, though some of the great handwriting masters of the Renaissance also elaborated a grotesque art of the flourish.

This opposition between letter and line production was embodied socially in the competition between schoolmaster and scrivener. It was the scrivener who possessed an artisinal mastery of writing as a species of hydraulics, and it was he who therefore competed with the schoolmaster for control over the teaching of writing. Scriveners were seen as threatening not only because they were the purveyors of a nomadic art, however, but because they were themselves often nomadic or itinerant.[72] Brinsley urges schoolmasters to teach penmanship in order to "avoyde the evils by wandering Scriveners," who "draw away the mindes of many of the Schollars from their bookes; even of such as cannot endure to take paines, nor have any great love of learning, and cause many, of good hope to leave the school utterly."[73] The scrivener, like an uncanny pied piper, was especially alluring to those students who "cannot endure to take pains"—that is, who were given to idleness and resistant to discipline and were thus prone to the contagion of vagrancy. His deterritorializing motion threatened to sweep away the sedentarizing regime of the school. But who exactly was he?

The "wandering scrivener" or itinerant writing master was a legacy of the late Middle Ages; he not only taught the art of writing but also copied documents and performed other secretarial tasks. Moreover, he often taught subjects other than calligraphy and might operate as a "schoolmaster at large," which is why Brinsley would find him especially worrisome.[74] As a wandering artisan or peddler, the writing master tended to be lumped together with the larger vagrant population both in Tudor legislation and in the popular mind. Many, in fact, supplemented their incomes by forging passports and begging licences for vagabonds, making the connection between the two seem even stronger. In *The Fraternitye of Vacabondes* (1575), John Awdelay identified a species of rogue called the Jarkeman, who "can read and write, and sometimes speake Latin. He useth to make couterfaite licenses which they call Gybes, and sets to seales, in their language called Jarkes."[75] In the person of the wandering scrivener the schoolmaster might see his own demonic double, for scholars themselves had a strong heritage of wandering in the Middle Ages, and the sixteenth-century crisis of vagabondage had led to a crackdown on begging and wandering scholars and clerics.[76] Moreover, some country schoolmasters themselves were not immune to the temptation of forging licenses, doubtless encouraged by their marginal economic status.[77] An antivagrancy act of 1572 significantly juxtaposes "all counterfeytures of Lycenses Passeportes and all users of the same" with "all Scollars of the Universityes of Oxford and Cambridge that goe about begginge, not beinge aucthorized under the seale of the said Universities."[78] Teaching in a common grammar school was a notoriously low-paying profession that often attracted scholars in desperate straits. With a bad turn of fortune a poor schoolmaster might easily find himself cast out on the road.

Not only in their ideological programs but in their material situations, then, many Tudor grammar schools had to ward off vagrancy, whose threat can no longer be seen as merely external but was at least potentially immanent as well. Brinsley's reaction to the wandering scriveners is interesting in this regard. After ranting against the whole species, he draws back a bit and insists that his warning is directed "not at all" against honest scriveners; rather, "it only helpeth to redresse the great abuse by som shifters, who go under the name of Scriveners" (though the term *shifter* may only compound the confusion between movement and roguery). Furthermore, scriveners are not to be banished from the school-house entirely but may be admitted at appointed times and for certain limited functions, as allowed and supervised by the schoolmaster.[79] The itinerant scrivener was therefore assimilated into the sedentarizing regime of the school in a compromise dictated in part by the material nature of writing itself.

I have chosen to focus on the case of writing both for its intrinsic interest and for its exemplary value in illustrating the ideological effects of teaching. As a formal and technological practice, Renaissance writing included a set of virtual regimes—principally nomadic and sedentarizing—each of which encoded a potential set of social relations. These virtual regimes are transhistorical in that they are more or less intrinsic to the practice of writing, or at least to technologies that enjoyed a secular endurance; they exist as a set of social valences within a cultural practice, valences that may form a variety of bonds with different institutions. Here the schoolmaster and the scrivener serve as "mediating" figures who actualize or energize these virtual regimes by inserting them into a larger sociocultural process. They thus allow the different regimes within writing to resonate, as it were, in response to another conflict of nomadic and sedentarizing forces within the school, which is in turn informed by global transformations in the social order. These different "levels" may be regarded as merely homologous in that the mediations among them are not fully genetic (that is, they do not clearly "cause" or "determine" one another, though mutual influences are apparent). It is the lack of a genetic or causal line that may raise doubt as to whether this is a historical analysis at all or only a clever set of adjacencies. I respond that my procedure is inspired by Marx's conception of prehistory; that is, I have constructed a genealogy of elements that enter into a specific conjuncture and whose structural relations are neither determined nor explained by their genesis. The ideological force of writing is the specific pressure that is virtual regimes can exert within this conjuncture, either to reinforce or to oppose the reproduction of the social order. In this case the pressure is neither especially great nor particularly focused, since handwriting is both a rarefied and a relatively innocuous social practice and since the "double" nature of writing renders its allegiances ambiguous. Its interest is therefore primarily that of a symptom (taken in its strictest sense—as a "falling together" rather than as an "effect") of the complex and somewhat contradictory role of the schools and their literary culture within the transition. At the very least it helps to situate the more wide-ranging problem of stylistic or rhetorical education, of which it formed a part, and to suggest why poetry posed a problem for humanist educators. For like handwriting, poetry was a nomadic discipline[80] that was only provisionally and unstably assimilated to the program of Tudor schooling, and like handwriting, its virtual regimes were activated by a specific historical and institutional conjuncture. It is this conjuncture that renders humanist training "ideological" in the specifically Marxist sense by engaging a more global transformation in the dominant relations of production and of social class. Another aspect of this process involved the school's labor in generating a discourse of literary and social capacities.

## Social Mobility and the Discourse of Capacities

Marx's critique of Adam Smith can be seen as, among other things, an exercise in practical narratology. For attacking the myth of primitive accumulation requires more than revealing its lack of basis in historical fact; it involves uncovering the hidden metaphysics of its narrative and developing a critical resistance to the lure of storytelling. The fall into poverty, like the fall into original sin, "is supposed to be explained when it is told as an anecdote about the past"; Marx's project is thus in part to dispel the ideological power of a tale that shimmers with the romance of the long ago. Yet Adam Smith's tale of the "two sorts of people" is not only a story about the past; it is a story from the past, whose roots can be traced to the sixteenth century and earlier. Smith, in fact, can hardly be said to have fathered the myth that Marx credits him with; at most he simply borrows it for the purpose of political economy. The myth of primitive accumulation was authored collectively by the cultural voices of one of the "two sorts of people"; it was already a piece of middle-class folklore centuries before Marx showed that it was, in Shakespeare's words, "so like an old tale that the verity of it is in strong suspicion."

At the least, then, Marx treats Smith with perverse generosity, depicting him as a kind of intellectual manufacturer, whereas he is really only an importer of goods made elsewhere. But a more troubling issue of authorial attribution is at stake here. The problem, to put it succinctly, is that Smith's actual views are almost entirely contrary to those of which Marx accuses him. In *The Wealth of Nations*, Smith does not base the division of labor and classes on the existence of "two sorts of people"; rather, he explains the existence of the "two sorts of people" by means of the social division of labor. Thus, individual differences in ethics or talent are not used to explain or justify the class structure of capitalism. Smith, like Marx, seeks a structural and not an ethical understanding of economic behavior.[81] He is innocent of the etiological mythmaking with which Marx charges him.[82] Smith has, in fact, almost nothing to say about the origins of the system of wage-labor, nor is he a defender of its grosser inequities.[83] Marx was not unknown to engage in polemical exaggeration from time to time, but he was certainly not given to systematic misrepresentations of this sort. He was, furthermore, an (ambivalent) admirer of Smith's work and—as anyone who has read *Capital* knows—one of his most precise and attentive readers. Neither malice nor carelessness can plausibly explain the discrepencies I have pointed out. Besides, the views that Marx attacks were widely enough held to make them worth demolishing in any case. What could be gained by misattributing them to Smith, especially when this error would be obvious to anyone who had also read *The Wealth of Nations* (including many, if not most, of the early readers of *Capital*)?

Without pretending to pluck out the heart of this mystery I may nevertheless observe that Marx's misattribution produces an interesting result: a collective social discourse anterior to Smith and which he positively rejects is nevertheless foisted onto him. The historical product of a social class is thereby rewritten as the fault of an individual's shortcomings or dishonesties. The rhetoric of *Capital* thus reenacts or performs the myth of primitive accumulation itself, in that Adam Smith, like the poor, comes to bear a moral burden that is not rightfully his. Marx's play on the name of "Adam" Smith is then rich indeed: just as theological myth makes Adam the author of all human sinfulness, so Marx's myth makes Adam Smith the author of all the sins of political economy. Smith becomes an eponymous villain, bringer of the poisonous "knowledge of good and evil"—that is to say, of the *ethical* discourse that clouds the minds of men.

The scapegoating of Adam Smith—for this is what it is—has a serious theoretical consequence. For the critique of primitive accumulation surpasses a single historical myth to embrace the whole "ethical" conception of history. At stake here is the status of the subject as economic agent, and with it, the method of *Capital*, which attempts to give a structural and hence impersonal account of the dynamics of capital without grounding it in any particular view (psychological, moral, utilitarian, humanist, or other) of the economic subject. Marx warns early on, "As we proceed to develop our investigation, we shall find, in general, that the characters who appear on the economic stage are merely personifications of economic relations; it is as the bearers [*Träger*] of these economic relations that they come into contact with each other."[84] For Marx, the subject as economic agent is merely the *bearer*, meaning the personification or instantiation, of an economic relation and therefore cannot form the starting point of an economic analysis. This approach makes capitalism as a system, rather than the capitalist as an individual, the object of attack; it defines revolution as an effort to transform social relations and thus distinguishes it from a witch hunt or the actions of a lynch mob. Among other things, then, it attempts to ward off scapegoating as a mode of political action. In this context the lexical richness of the term *Träger*, or bearer, comes into play, signaling that the concept of a structural support has come to displace the older ethical conception of the "bearer" of (economic) sins.

Primitive accumulation brings this problem to the fore again because it is an "originary" myth in two senses: it purports to describe the origins of capitalism, and it defines the problematic (that is, ethics) which will form the starting point of economic analysis. Indeed, it builds or fabricates its history *from* this problematic. Marx's scapegoating of Smith is thus pertinent to his theoretical task, "performing" in an ironic fashion the errors of an ethical ideology. In a sense he sets up "two sorts" of political economists—his kind and Smith's—so that this false polarity can give way once more to a materialist analysis. In so doing he activates an "ethical" disposition or tendency within rhetoric itself and its modes of address.

By *ethical* I mean to identify a mode of thought which takes a free and volitional subject as its basis and starting point. Yet the term fits rather loosely with its use here. In one sense it is too broad, since qualities such as diligence and frugality, while they do occupy a place among the traditional virtues, pertain only to economic productivity—of labor in the case of diligence, of capital in the case of frugality. In another sense it is too narrow, since intelligence—the third term in Marx's unholy trinity—does not pertain to ethics at all. What we really have here is a discourse of *capacities* which ranges from concepts such as intelligence, talent, creativity, or cleverness to the abilities to impose and endure various kinds of self-discipline such as industry, parsimony, and persistence. The discourse of capacities is individualizing, but it further conceives of the individual as a set of given potentialities that manifest themselves in economic activity. In particular they reveal themselves in economic "movement," also known as social mobility—the diachronic myth whose synchronic basis is the discourse of capacities. What this discourse does is to reduce the narrative of mobility, with its uncertainties, its chances made and lost, its sudden peripeties, to the workings of an immanent providence. Success or failure is the narrative outcome of a process that always turns out to be the manifestation of an essence, and the result reveals one to have been, from the very start, one of the "two sorts of people." The myth of primitive accumulation is nothing other than this collusion between a narrative of social mobility and a discourse of capacities.

Yet to speak of the "myth" of social mobility is not to deny it all empirical basis. As Lawrence Stone has demonstrated, the period from 1500 to 1650 was one of extraordinary and unprecedented economic movement, both "vertical" (up and down the ranks of the social hierarchy) and "horizontal" (from one profession, trade, or location to another within a social rank).[85] Economic conditions certainly benefited some who practiced industry and thrift, and new opportunities opened for individuals with drive, talent, or persistence. The myth of primitive accumulation was not made up of whole cloth, nor was it Marx's purpose to suggest that it was. The ideological narrative of social mobility derived from reality but selectively filtered it through the experience and prejudices of the rising classes. Elizabethan middle-class culture was already providing numerous "lessons in diligence and thrift" in the form of sermons, pamphlets, plays such as Thomas Heywood's *Four Prentices of London,* and novels such as Thomas Deloney's *Jack of Newberry,*—all of which promised success for the hardworking and parsimonious and ruin for the lazy and extravagant.[86] The ideological work carried out by the myth or narrative of social mobility was to reduce a complex social phenomenon to a discourse of capacities which explained vertical movement exclusively by means of quasi-ethical powers within the individual. It is not especially surprising that the rising classes would want to attribute their success to their own virtues while ignoring factors such as inheritance, economic monopoly, political patronage, exploitation, plunder, criminal activity, or even the luck of inhabiting a particularly fertile or well-placed piece of land. Nor is it surprising that they would want to attribute the ruin of others to shortcomings such as laziness or extravagance. These undoubtedly could contribute to economic ruin. For the working classes, however, a more pertinent factor was a decline in real wages of as much as 50 percent during the sixteenth century, the result of an excess supply of labor caused in part by the effects of primitive accumulation. This fall of wages, writes Stone,

> was undoubtedly of a magnitude for which there is no parallel in English history since the thirteenth century. The living standards of the labouring classes went down sharply in the sixteenth century, and stayed down throughout the seventeenth. On the other hand, throughout the whole of the sixteenth century and much of the seventeenth, there was a striking rise in the material comforts of all classes from the yeomen upwards, groups who benefitted from rising agricultural prices, increased commercial activity, and increased demand for professional services.[87]

This economic pressure on the lower classes was further intensified when traditional channels of upward social mobility, including the recruitment of apprentices, began closing in the first half of the seventeenth century.[88] The myth of social mobility not only worked to legitimate a widening class gulf in the early modern period but helped to explain economic changes whose causes lay beyond the reach of contemporary thought. A discourse of individual capacities productively obscured the roles of class power and structural determination and assured that in the minds of the rising classes "the idyllic reigns from time immemorial."

This discourse of capacities becomes especially clear in contemporary attitudes toward the vagrant poor, who were classified according to whether they were able or unable to work. So-called sturdy beggars were persecuted for what was felt to be a wilful witholding of labor power or productive capacity, despite the fact that most had worked or were still employed.[89] In *The Description of England* (1577), William Harrison described vagabonds as the "thriftless sort" who "lick the sweat from the true labourers' brows" and "do what they can to continue their misery . . . to stray and wander about, as creatures abhorring all labour and every honest exercise."[90] "Captivated as they are by a certain sweetness of inertia and idleness," opined Vives, the poor "think activity, labor, industry, and frugality more painful than death."[91] Although such sentiments draw heavily on traditional notions of the sin of sloth, this had by no means always been associated with poverty, which had formerly been regarded as a kind of vocation involving hardship and effort rather than ease. The new attitude toward the poor is generally associated with the rise of the "Protestant ethic" but the conditions for it were already present in the petty producing culture of the late Middle Ages. J. Thomas Kelly argues convincingly that the overwhelming of traditional means of poor relief, rather than changes in theological outlook, played the leading role here.[92]

The discourse of capacities was by no means new to the sixteenth century. The rising classes had long employed meritocratic arguments about what constitutes true nobility (Chaucer's "Franklin's Tale" comes readily to mind). Conversely, this discourse had also played a role in legitimating the positions of the three feudal estates. The great innovation of the sixteenth century was to employ it in a major way to explain *downward* mobility and to cope ideologically with the swelling tides of the new poor.

The schools, of course, contributed significantly both to the historical fact of social mobility and to the ideological discourse of capacities. Lawrence Stone contends that the expansion of secondary and university education between 1570 and 1650 resulted in a "free-for-all competitive struggle uncontrolled by the existing elite."[93] While the schools' ability to promote upward mobility was probably more limited than contemporaries thought, and was certainly greater for the middle and upper classes than it was for unskilled workers, still its effects were not inconsiderable. The humanists who encouraged educational reform had no interest in overturning the traditional social hierarchy, but they did see the schools as a way of introducing merit into it. In the course of attempting to provide for poor scholars at a school in Canterbury, Thomas Cranmer gave what has been called a "radical" oration on the rights of the lower classes to receive an education. "Poor men's children," he said, "are many times endued with more singular gifts of nature, which are also the gifts of God, as with eloquence, memory, apt pronunciation, sobriety, with suchlike, and also commonly more given to apply their study, than is the gentleman's son delicately educated."[94] While the names of Colet, Cheke, Ascham, and Elyot are associated with elite schooling, educators such as Edmund Coote and John Brinsley wrote "for the weakest, & for the common countrey schools," in the hopes that they "may be either equall, or at least come neare to those of greater name." Brinsley addressed his work to "the meaner sort, that even their children may the more easily attaine to learning, that so some of them being advanced thereby, may become a stay to their parents, a comfort to their kinsfolkes, a credit to their country which brought them up."[95] Clearly, the discourse of capacities did not carry only one ideological charge; it could be employed for progressive as well as conservative purposes.

If the schools attempted to inject merit into the larger social order, they themselves aspired to offer a model meritocracy in which diligence, talent, and obedience were duly rewarded. Schoolmasters were urged to set students in competition with one another so that "emulation, and feare of discredite, will make them envie who shall excell."[96] Brinsley wrote that students "should be placed as adversaries, that they may contend in all things, whether of them shall doe the better, and beare the bell away."[97] This method clearly had other, unstated advantages, including the important one that competition among students discouraged collective resistance to the authority of the teacher. But it clearly also converted the classroom into a midget "market society," in which the paternal guidance of the schoolmaster kept things from degenerating into a Hobbesian free-for-all.

The practices of a literary education also contained lessons in diligence and thrift. Copia, for instance, had always had metaphorical associations with wealth, and Renaissance humanists were quick to point out that the habits learned in gathering literary materials were like those needed to achieve material prosperity: "A good thriftie man will gather his goodes together in time of plentie, and lay them out againe in time of need: and shal not an Oratour have in store good matter, in the chest of his memorie, to use and bestow in time of necessitie?"[98] At the beginning of book 2 of *De copia*, which treats of "abundance of subject matter" (*copia rerum*), Erasmus offers two significantly antithetical phrases for rhetorical amplification: "He wasted all his substance in riotous living" and "He completed a thoroughly comprehensive education."[99] Copia clearly offered an analogy to material wealth, and the collection of commonplaces an analogy to "Smith's" primitive accumulation. More concretely, though, the habits of thrift, diligence, and application gained through a literary education were felt to be transferable to the economic world.

Nevertheless, the success of this training was held to depend ultimately on the presence of certain native capacities—Mulcaster calls them "ingenerate abilities"—in the student.[100] Brinsley declared that only the "most ingenious" were to be encouraged to continue in school while the others were to be fitted for trades or some other calling.[101] "Neither is it possible," he writes, "by all the means and paines in the world, to make such to be scholars, to whom God in their naturall constitution seemeth to have denied it."[102]

The discourse of capacities has a complex relationship with the humanist interest in the power of education or training. In Erasmian composition theory, training relies on a mimetic capacity that, Erasmus seems to suggest, is universally distributed. Innate differences in temperament and constitution tend to "color" or inflect literary style, and may even render some individuals incapable of certain kinds of style (Ciceronianism, for example), but they render no one incapable of writing. The notion of capacity, however, could also be used to explain the limits of training and account for the failures of the humanist educational project. Elsewhere Erasmus maintains that if a student fails to respond to gentle persuasion, the teacher should not punish him but "turn him out to the plough or the packsaddle . . . [for] there are boys good only for the farm and manual toil."[103] The contradictions in Erasmus's statements point to a deeper conflict between a disciplinary and what I shall call a "demonstrative" function. As a disciplinary mechanism, the school employs training to develop some capacities (for scholarship, literary expression, diligence, and thrift) and to master or eradicate others (for idleness, vagrancy, and criminality). As a demonstrative mechanism, however, schooling is meant to "uncover" relatively immutable capacities and thereby to separate out the incorrigible and unfit from the gifted and industrious. The disciplinary function will tend to adopt a relatively ecumenical attitude that regards training as desirable and possible for all while the demonstrative function will attempt to establish distinctions among individuals or social groups.

It is important to recognize that in Renaissance schooling, the "failure" of students was not an occasional, accidental, or even undesirable phenomenon. A number of writers worried in print that too much education would leave the realm bereft of farmers, artisans, and common laborers. It was therefore the duty of the schoolmaster to police the boundaries of upward mobility. Mulcaster wrote that the schoolmaster must observe his students closely, and "then as his delite wilbe to have the towarde continue, so must his desire be, how to procure the diverting and removing of the duller and lesse toward, to some other course, more agreeing with their natural, then learning is."[104] Moreover, he advises, in order to prevent discontent and possible social upheaval, the schoolmaster must weed out these less-gifted students at an early age, before they come to understand what rejection signifies.[105] The demonstrative function was therefore not an adventitious effect of Renaissance schooling but a coherent strategy.

In the case of upward social mobility the disciplinary and demonstrative functions cooperated to the degree that unusually talented youths from the lower classes could be trained for and advanced to one of the professions or skilled trades. In the case of downward mobility, however, they came into conflict. It was the incorrigible, unapt, or lazy youths who were felt to be most liable to come to a bad end and were thus most in need of disciplinary training, but it was also these who, Erasmus suggests, should not be punished or disciplined but simply turned out of the school. Brinsley also argued that incorrigible students should be expelled because they provided a bad example for the others.[106] Of course, punishment was always readily available in Tudor schools and especially in the poorer ones. The gentleness of the Erasmian method, if not explicitly designed for middle- and upper-class students, seems to have been applied to them more often. Where discipline failed, however, the demonstrative function was always waiting. If recalcitrant students could not be forced to learn or obey, they could at least be ejected—not without having had an ideological labor performed on them, however, for they were now shown to lack the capacities necessary for advancement or to possess those that led to beggary or crime and, in either case, to be unfit for training or advancement.

To whatever degree it was actually applied, then, the Erasmian preference for persuasion over punishment had the effect of transferring the burden of educability largely onto the individual student. Failure indicated a lack of both the intellectual gifts and the ethical predisposition necessary for training. If the discourse of capacities was individualizing, however, Erasmus's reference to the "plough or the packsaddle" suggests that a lack of capacity was felt to be characteristic of the lower classes, whose position was now justified as the result of a mass incapacity. Such views were not alien to medieval thinking about the three estates; Erasmus's pastoral language, which suggests that the failed student would return to the harsh but stable existence of the medieval peasant, seems to draw on that tradition. Only this mode of life was becoming increasingly precarious in the sixteenth century, when many small peasants and petty artisans experienced something closer to an economic free fall than to the durable servility of a feudal estate.

The ideological effect of schooling and its discourse of capacities was to understand economic movement—both upward and downward—as an effect of individual talents and drives, and thus to posit "two sorts of people." If the schools helped some people to advance economically, they also tended to legitimate the widening class gulf of the sixteenth century. This intervention could have very specific and concrete effects: the Elizabethan bridewells, for instance, were designed for youths who proved "unapt to learning."[107] If humanist theory divided the cultural "space" of the school into areas of play and persuasion for the cooperative and firmer sorts of discipline for the more resistant, the school itself was a site of relatively gentle discipline compared to some of the social institutions waiting for those who were "unapt." More generally, the schools helped to produce the ideological category of the *willful* poor, those who were "captivated by a certain sweetness of inertia and idleness," as Vives so delicately put it, and were therefore subject to the brutalities of Tudor and Stuart poor laws. The demonstrative function of the schools, which operated quite clearly here, was not limited to persons who actually attended them. Rather, the schools helped create an ideological climate in which economic success and failure were understood through the categories of diligence and laziness, self-discipline and excess, talent and the lack of it. They thus provided a material and institutional support for the tendency to read structural upheavals and class struggles in terms of individualized, ethical differences.

They did so, moreover, by means of a curriculum that was essentially literary. Literature was humanism's way of attempting to pry education free from vocational training, from this or that productive skill. A literary education was not a preparation for any single profession but a sign of admissibility to them all. For humanism, the literary capacity was felt not only to provide the base of all learning but almost to constitute the human as such, or at least what it meant to be fully human. In this context the Erasmian conception of literary style, which places so much weight on individual capacities and differences, can be seen to be fully if unconsciously complicit with the school's larger discourse of capacities.

The individuating tendencies of the style system take on their
ideological significance (in the strictest sense) when inserted into a
more inclusive cultural tendency to construe economic transformations through individual differences and abilities. The humanist discourse of capacities was often self-consciously progressive
and meritocratic and, when harnessed to the institutional force of
the schools, provided some talented or industrious individuals
with a means of social advancement. But this same institutional
discourse simultaneously helped to legitimate the economic decline and state-enforced punishment inflicted on growing numbers
of the new poor.

My argument has now, it seems, come full circle. I began by situating Tudor education within the transition described by Marx
(that is, "real" primitive accumulation) and I now end by suggest-
ing how humanist theory and scholastic practices contributed to
the ideological narrative of that transition, elaborated (according to
Marx) by Smith and his brethren. Approaching humanism through
the lens of one version of political economy, we now find it influ-
encing another. Moreover, this influence is not limited to the
general social myths and cultural climate I have just described,
for humanism was one of the genetic threads that fed into the
discourse of political economy. Despite some obvious shifts in polemical and theoretical direction, it is simple enough to trace a
genealogical line from Renaissance humanism to Hobbes, Locke,
and Mandeville, and thence to figures such as Joseph Priestley,
Adam Ferguson, and Adam Smith. If one were searching for the
origins of Marx's "two sorts of people," for instance, one could do
worse than follow a lead suggested by Mandeville, who, in the
course of rebutting the "flatteries" of humanist philosophy, writes:

To introduce, moreover, an Emulation amongst Men, they [the human-
ists] divided the Species into two Classes, vastly differing from one
another: The one consisted of abject, low-minded People, that always
hunting after immediate Enjoyment, were wholly incapable of self-
denial, and without regard to the good of others, had no higher aim
than their private Advantage; such as being enslaved by Voluptuous-
ness, yielded without Resistance to every gross desire, and made
no use of their Rational Faculties, but to heighten their Sensual
Pleasure. These vile grov'ling Wretches, they said, were the Dross
of their Kind, and having only the Shape of Men, differ'd from Brutes
in nothing but their outward Figure. But the other Class was made
up of lofty high-spirited Creatures, that free from sordid Selfishness,
esteem'd the Improvements of the Mind to be their fairest Posses-

sions; . . . and making a continual War with themselves to promote
the Peace of others, aim'd at no less than the Publick Welfare and the
Conquest of their own Passion.[108]

Whatever its intuitive appeal, however, this apparent line of influence is ultimately misleading, and tracing its failures will lead us
to the historical unraveling of humanism as a literary and educational program.

What cuts the discursive line running from humanism to political economy is in large part a historical rupture, that between
primitive accumulation and early capitalist manufacture. To be
sure, the Tudor-humanist discourse of capacities survives this rupture and extends well into the discourse of political economy. The
progressive line, which holds that human capacities are roughly
equal and that social inequality is therefore to be explained by educational and environmental factors, can be found in Hobbes and
Locke,[109] in a number of Restoration economists and pamphleteers, including Sir Matthew Hale, Sir William Petty, Sir Joshua
Child, Sir Thomas Culpepper, and Sir Francis Brewster,[110] and in
the liberal tradition of political economy represented by Adam
Smith. The more conservative line, which explains wealth and
poverty by means of innate differences of industry, frugality, or intelligence (or which simply rails against the laziness and shiftless-
ness of the poor without trying to explain them), can *also* be found
in Locke and his disciples, in conservative Restoration economists, and in Adam Ferguson and others.[111] But while both strands
of argument survive in the discourse of political economy, they do
so largely as residual elements of an older cultural formation, for
the advent of capitalist manufacture begins decisively to transform
thinking about the poor.

In the Tudor and Stuart periods, the poor and vagrant were
economically unassimilable and so viewed primarily as potential
sources of crime and social unrest. Attempts to employ them were
largely intended as punishment, and were in any case rendered
impractical by the limitations of guild production and traditional
agriculture. Hence the vagrant poor were more often imprisoned,
punished, licensed, given charity, or shipped abroad. These views
and practices also continued after the Restoration, but the rise of
capitalist manufacture then gave birth to a new way of thinking in
which the poor were seriously viewed as a productive—or potentially productive—source of labor power.[112] One pamphleteer promised a day when "those that whilst unhived were a Swarm of Droans

and Pest to the Society, become (oh a Miracle) Industrious Bees, each contributing something to the Support of the General."[113]

This new emphasis on productivity does not so much resolve as displace the older questions about poverty. The essential issue for post-Restoration economists is not whether people are poor because they are lazy and thriftless or lazy and thriftless because they are poor. Though both positions are advanced, these ethical and etiological matters increasingly cede their place to the practical question of how an undisciplined mass of unemployed can be made into a productive labor force. Instead of raising moral or political questions about social class, the discourse of capacities is increasingly invoked to justify a more complex and efficient division of labor: "Men are endowed with various talents and propensities, which naturally dispose and fit them for different occupations."[114]

Once a system of manufacture is in place, and the poor *as* poor become a potential economic resource, talk about upward mobility begins to wane. Mandeville is, as usual, brutally direct:

> If here and there one of the lowest Class by uncommon Industry, and pinching his Belly, lifts himself above the condition he was brought up in, no body ought to hinder him; Nay it is undeniably the wisest course for every Person in the Society, and for every private Family to be frugal; but it is the Interest of all rich Nations, that the greatest part of the Poor should almost never be idle, and yet continually spend what they get.[115]

In this new climate, formal education for the poor is increasingly attacked as irrelevant to their economic role, and labor itself is viewed as the only appropriate form of discipline:

> The children of the poor should be brought up and inured, as early as may be, to some useful labour; and be taught with due care, the great principles of religion and morality. But all are not agreed that reading and writing, are qualifications necessary for the obtaining of those ends; some think, that these accomplishments are useful only in higher stations; and that to instruct at a public expense the youth of the lower class in reading, writing, &c. is a kind of intrusion upon the class next above them; that these qualifications, instead of being advantageous to the poor who possess them, serve only to render their state more irksome, and to inspire them with notions subversive of society. There must be labourers; and that most useful class of men should be duly cherished and taken care of: But books and pens

will not alleviate the weight of the spade, or at all contribute to dry the sweat off the labourer's brow.[116]

This shift in social attitude is predicated on a change in the labor process itself. Artisanal or guild production involved skilled labor, long apprenticeships, and technical training that often required the ability to read; manufacture increasingly involved unskilled and repetitive work for which education was irrelevant.

Despite the attempts of Renaissance humanists to distance education from apprenticeship, it is clear enough that Renaissance education relied on a general congruity of the two. The discipline of the classroom was roughly comparable to that of apprenticeship, and indeed, the Erasmian emphasis on the imitation of literary models involved a kind of mimetic labor not entirely different in kind from the apprentice's imitation of his master's skills. But the advent of manufacture brought about an intensification and simplification of labor for which neither the level nor the formal model of scholastic discipline was adequate preparation. In his attack on charity schools, Mandeville writes that "going to School in comparison to Working is Idleness, and the longer Boys continue in this easy sort of life, the more unfit they'll be when grown up for downright Labour, both as to Strength and Inclination."[117] Adam Smith, who opposed both public and private endowment of education, also attacked long apprenticeships and the guild system, arguing that the abstract pressures of the marketplace provided better and stricter discipline than did the personal authority of a master.[118] The decay of crafts and the decay of Renaissance education went hand in hand.

It is worth noting that in its considerations of schooling and social mobility, classical political economy rarely argued that the poor were inherently incapable of social advancement. The issue was simply how to fit them productively, efficiently, and (if possible) happily to their new role as a source of capitalist labor power. In fact, arguments about the "two sorts of people," while still an ambient ideology, played their least important role precisely in the discourse of political economy. Most often they occupied, more or less implicitly, the silence left by political economy's disinclination to consider the real origins of capitalism.

In any case, if schooling of the humanist type was now often considered irrelevant for one of the "two sorts of people," gentlemen were still receiving an old-style education in classical letters. Here too a hardening of class lines was visible in attacks on the social diversity of free schools. In "General Directions for the Better Education of a Child of Great Quality," the Oxford tutor Stephen Penton warned of "the inconvenient mixture of Persons of Quality in the *same School* with Tinkers and Coblers Children, which perhaps may teach them base, dirty Qualities (they were never born to) of Lying, Filching, Pailing, Swearing, &c."[119] Though he expressed himself with greater delicacy, Locke held the same views and, moreover, urged that gentlemen's children should be kept as much as possible away from the bad influence of servants—advice rarely given before the Restoration.[120]

Locke's attacks on classical education are also of interest, for although largely at odds with contemporary practice, they point to the decay of humanist pedagogy. And this is so not because Locke sounds so little like a humanist but because, in his educational writings, he often sounds so much like one. In *Some Thoughts concerning Education* (1693), Locke insists that learning springs from the imitation of examples and the acquiring of habits, not from the memorizing of rules and facts, and that its purpose is to impart civility and breeding along with knowledge.[121] He repeats humanist assaults on physical punishment and grammatical drill and insists that the tutor or schoolmaster should offer a model for the student to imitate. In fact, he resumes and clarifies almost everything of importance that humanism had to say about mimetic education, but—and this is the point—he simultaneously rejects the current emphasis on classical letters and style. Locke's intention is to make education more practical and productive, given the increasing involvement of gentlemen in the world of business. Hence he insists on "how much more use it is to judge right of Men, and manage their affairs wisely with them, than to speak Greek and Latin, or argue in Mood and Figure," and he fits his ideal education to "a Gentleman's Calling; which is to have the Knowledge of a Man of Business, a Carriage suitable to his Rank, and to be Eminent and Useful in his Country according to his Station."[122] In order to train gentlemen for their new economic roles Locke rejects an education in the classics, just as other writers rejected it in order to fit the laboring poor for *their* new roles. More important, perhaps, Locke also unravels the union of behavioral and literary imitation that formed the core of humanist theory. The genius of Erasmian pedagogy was its attempt to incorporate literary stylistics into a total system of moral and ideological training, and to incorporate it not just as subject matter or content but as ideological *form*. Yet Latinity, while perfectly conformable to mimetic training, was not an indispensable part of it, and Locke was able to retain the behavioral and ideological program of humanism while shunting aside its classical curriculum. Imitation survives in his educational program, but detached from its humanist context of classical language and literature.

With this proposed separation of schooling and the literary my treatment of Renaissance education also comes to an end. Its purpose is to offer a general institutional context for literature as an ideological form during the sixteenth and early seventeenth centuries, but I do not mean to propose this context as a determining or constraining one. If schooling could disengage itself from the literary, it is also true that literary production led a life apart from the schools, encoding its own virtual regimes, which had other and multiple points of contact with social life. The second part of this book, which looks at four writers of the Renaissance, situates them not primarily with respect to the culture of the schools but within other areas of a broader transitional conjuncture. My focus is on how literary texts are informed by this conjuncture and how, in their turn, they help to illuminate and articulate it.

# PART TWO

# CHAPTER THREE

# The Twittering Machine: John Skelton's Ornithology of the Early Tudor State

If he was nothing else, John Skelton was certainly one of the most obstreperous English poets; his literary gifts were inseparable from a bottomless and apparently free-floating aggression. Henry VIII employed him briefly as a writer of vituperative verses against the French and Scots and then to entertain the court in a display of "flytyng," a crude form of poetical name-calling. Yet the self-styled *orator regius* remained a marginal figure at court, and in his resentment he composed a series of vicious and ill-considered satires against the powerful Cardinal Wolsey, even taking a few swipes at Henry himself. Just as abruptly he then changed face and put himself in Wolsey's employ to write attacks on Protestant heretics and a rebellious Scots duke. Yet Wolsey witheld the promised reward of an ecclesiastical living, and the poet never succeeded in making nastiness anything more than an intermittently profitable vocation. Even after his death Skelton was regarded largely as a bundle of quirky and unassimilable energies. Despite his priestly calling, his name soon became attached to a collection of "merry tales," according to which he kept a woman in his church at Diss, fathered a bastard, defecated on a sleeping friar, and otherwise distinguished himself for piety and devotion.[1] Wordsworth complimented him as "a demon in point of genius,"[2] but Pope simply dismissed him as "beastly Skelton."

In matters of poetic influence he was no less difficult. Skelton portrayed his own genius as both autogenerated and prodigious; he describes himself as England's incomparable "phoenix" in *Ware the Hawk,* and he seems largely to have arrogated to himself the titles of poet laureate and king's orator. Indeed, as C. S. Lewis correctly observed, he had "no real predecessors and no important disciples."[3] His turbulent verse owed little to the polish of Chaucer and even less to the dullness of fifteenth-century predecessors such as Hoccleve or Lydgate.[4] His influence on English verse was just as small as its influence on him. It is true that he enjoyed brief fame as a prophet of the Reformation and that Spenser borrowed the name of Skelton's Colin Clout for his Protestant pastorals. Yet no important successors took up Skelton's distinctive verse form, doubtless finding it too colloquial, too jarring, and too deeply imprinted with his personality. Skelton also developed a bitter hatred for the Erasmian humanism that began to take hold in the early sixteenth century. He was a vigorous participant in the so-called Grammarians' War of 1519, during which he and his fellow "Trojans" defended the old scholastic method of learning Latin against the humanist innovations of the "Greeks."[5] Skelton deemed it absurd that

> Platus with his comedies a chyld shall now reherse,
> And medyll with Quintylyan in his *Declemacyons,*
> That *Pety Caton* can scantly construe a verse,
> With, *"Aveto"* in *Greco,* and such solempne salutacyons,
> Can skantly the tensis of his conjugacyons;
> Settyng theyr myndys so moch of eloquens,
> That of theyr scole maters lost is the hole sentens.
>
> (*Speke Parott,* 176–82)[6]

Skelton even exchanged insulting Latin verses with the humanist grammarian William Lily. Here, as elsewhere, his conservative instincts put him on the losing side, and in rejecting humanism he cut himself off from the future of Renaissance verse. Skelton's relative uninterest in "eloquens" also probably impeded his career as a court poet.[7] It sometimes seems as if Skelton tried to write himself out of literary history by sheer force of will. His career testifies to the fact that a poet can indeed be too original.

Skelton's idiosyncracies have caused problems for critics trying to fit him into the scheme of cultural periodization which characterizes traditional literary history. Ian Gordon delineated the problem in 1943 when he wrote that "Skelton fell between two periods, the receding Middle Ages and the advancing Renaissance, without being a part of either." Reverting, Pope-like, to the vocabulary of the monstrous, Gordon calls Skelton "a Mr. Facing-Both-Ways" and adds, "Seldom has a poet borne the marks of a transition age so clearly as Skelton."[8] In *John Skelton's Poetry* (1965), Stanley Fish nuances Gordon's formulation but does not fundamentally alter it. "Skelton's poetry," he writes, "gives us neither the old made new nor the new made old, but a statement of the potentiality for disturbance of the unassimilated. It is a poetry which could only have been written between 1498 and 1530, when the intrusive could no longer be ignored as Lydgate had ignored it and before it would become part of a new and difficult stability as it would after 1536."[9] Fish's formulation suggests that Skelton's poetry is historically determined, or at least bounded; yet the agent of this determination is, paradoxically, a gap or hiatus between periods. It is as if Skelton sailed his lyrical boat by the force of a vacuum. A. C. Spearing conveys a similar sense of paradox, arguing that "Skelton's attitude is more, not less medieval than Chaucer's," yet finding that the difficulty and poetic manner of *Speke Parott* strongly anticipate *The Waste Land.*[10] The problem here is Skelton's seemingly perverse refusal to act like a "transitional" figure. He was the only poet of really considerable talents writing at the beginning of the sixteenth century and was therefore in a perfect position to bridge the gap between medieval and Renaissance poetics. Yet he seems somehow to have sensed his literary-historical mission and then mischievously to have dodged it. Or perhaps his mission *was* to dodge it, to occupy the transitional space in such a way as to reveal a dramatic gap or break between periods, and even to scramble the linear model that underlies this history.

One way around this problem is to look for influences outside of the literary canon and thus to situate Skelton's poetics in a larger cultural field. Some scholarly work has elucidated Skelton's poetry by demonstrating both the formal and thematic influence of church liturgy and by considering Skelton's vocation as poet-priest.[11] A very different approach has traced Skelton's career as failed or frustrated courtier and read his work in relation to the political events of the 1520s. These two paths intersect, of course, especially when Skelton begins his series of satires against Cardinal Wolsey. Yet they have not so much resolved the problems of Skelton's difficult transitional status as they have displaced and enlarged them. For the Christian interpreters have produced a conservative and strongly "medieval" Skelton, the orthodox and devoted priest who fights for traditional church and aristocratic privileges and against the encroachments of the early Tudor state. But the courtly Skelton is a more recognizably modern figure— self-promoting, dissatisfied with his duties in a rural parish, lacking strong convictions or social allegiances, willing to use his literary talents in any way that will serve his own ambitions.[12] Skelton's alleged social role thus splits as well into irreconcilably "medieval" and "Renaissance" components.

This is, clearly, the moment to wheel a Marxist theoretical apparatus onstage and triumphantly announce its ability to sublate these contradictions within a larger totalizing movement. I will not do so, however, because Skelton's poetical career signifies in its most interesting way when it remains fissured. It is these Skeltonic gaps and discontinuities that I want to articulate more precisely, by posing them in relation to the rise of the absolutist state and its role in reorganizing the late feudal polity.

## Cultural Territoriality in *Ware the Hawk*

It has long been recognized that the absolutist state played a decisive part in the transition to capitalism, though precisely what this part was has been the subject of extended debate. Marx and Engels held that absolutism represented a balance of political power between the feudal ruling class and the emergent bourgeoisie and that it prepared the way for capitalist production by carrying out many of the functions of primitive accumulation.[13] Nicos Poulantzas rejects the first half of this thesis and develops the second in order to argue for the relative autonomy of the absolutist state, as I discuss in the Introduction. Perry Anderson takes a somewhat different (though not irreconcilable) approach, contending that absolutism reorganized the rule of the nobility in response to certain mutations in the late feudal economy:

Feudalism as a mode of production was originally defined by an organic *unity* of economy and polity, paradoxically distributed in a chain of parcellized sovereignties throughout the social formation. The institution of serfdom as a mechanism of surplus extraction fused economic exploitation and politico-legal coercion at the molecular level of the village. The lord in his turn typically owed liege–loyalty and knight–service to the seigneurial overlord, who claimed the land as his ultimate domain. With the generalized commutation of dues into money rents, the cellular unity of political and economic oppression of the peasantry was gravely weakened, and threatened to become dissociated (the end of this road was "free labor" and the "wage contract"). The class power of the feudal lords was thus directly at stake with the gradual disappearance of serfdom. The result was a *displacement* of politico-legal coercion upwards towards a centralized, militarized summit—the Absolutist State. Diluted at village level, it became concentrated at "national" level.[14]

Yet while Anderson argues that the absolutist state reorganized the conditions of feudal class rule, he does not hold that it was in any simple sense the instrument of the landowning classes. For one thing, the whole process was overdetermined by the interests of the mercantile bourgeoisie.[15] For another, political centralization was achieved at the expense of baronial power, beginning with Henry VII's "primitive accumulation" of state power after the Wars of the Roses.[16] The emergence of absolutism thus dislocated the structural conditions of feudal rule; insofar as it protected the economic interests of the landlord class, it did so by drastically reducing their independent political authority. By de- and reterritorializing the parcelized sovereignty of feudalism, the absolutist state dissolved its own concrete implication in a structure of pyramidized dependency in order to *represent* the ruling groups. "The sovereign commanded authority not as the person residing at the apex of the hierarchy," John E. Martin notes, "but as the detached symbolic representative of the unity of the landlord class."[17] The state thereby achieved a relative autonomy with respect to the class it represented and could claim to act in the interests of the nation as a whole.

The relations between state and church in the early Tudor period—of central importance to Skelton's career—were largely determined by absolutism's rearticulation of class rule, for the church represented a significant fraction of the landlord class. It owned about one-third of the land in England, enjoyed a jurisdiction at least partially independent of the king's law, and exercised an especially rigorous, conservative, and tenacious form of feudal land-ownership.[18] The crown viewed the church as at once a desired source of wealth, an impediment to political centralization, and even a potential source of sedition (aristocratic families often furnished monastic leaders). The Dissolution was therefore prompted by political as well as economic considerations.[19] Even before the Dissolution, however, the Tudors made significant efforts to restrict the independent jurisdiction of the church, for the most part by attacking sanctuary rights. The privilege of sanctuary was "purely secular and jurisdictional," according to Isabel Thornley, that is to say, purely an effect of the church's political authority as feudal landowner, "but long before the Tudor period had opened, circumstances had given it a false ecclesiastical cover," and this enabled the church to retain its protective jurisdiction after similar rights had already been taken from lay persons.[20] Sanctuary was both a symbolic and a real affront to royal jurisdiction, and one that could be exploited for seditious purposes.

Significantly, Henry VII's first major assault on the sanctuary privilege was designed to suppress a threat of political revolt. In 1486 when the Yorkist Thomas Stafford was dragged from sanctuary and taken to the Tower, the King's Bench ruled that "sanctuary was a common-law matter in which the Pope could not interfere . . . and that the privilege did not cover treasonable offenses."[21] As Henry VIII's lord chancellor, Cardinal Wolsey continued this assault on church privilege by dissolving some monasteries and further restricting rights of sanctuary.

> For all privileged places
> He brekes and defaces,
> All placis of relygion
> He hathe them in derisyon.
> (1089–92)

So wrote Skelton in *Why Come Ye Nat to Courte?* (1522).

If the jurisdictional privilege represented by sanctuary was, in one sense, indistinguishable from secular forms of parcelized sovereignty, its "false ecclesiastical covering" nevertheless imparted a significant ideological difference, for sanctuary was not perceived as just another expression of feudal landownership. It was, rather, invested with a sacred character, and its inviolability was thus hedged about with the massive ideological resources of the medieval church. It is largely for this reason that sanctuary outlived secular forms of independent jurisdiction. Indeed, I think it is fair to view sanctuary as the ideological *paradigm* for such jurisdiction, and thus to say that the distinction between "sacred" and "profane" ground provided an ideological undergirding for the entire feudal system of parcelized sovereignties. This is why attacks on sanctuary were of political as well as cultural or religious significance, and why the early Tudor state directed such considerable energies toward incorporating the church in its jurisdiction.

The traditional account of Skelton's life and career places him in a simple and unitary relation to this process: as a vigorous, life-long opponent. According to this account, Skelton was for most of his career a client of the Howard family. They in turn belonged to a group of conservative lords opposed to Wolsey, whom they blamed for the execution in 1521 of Edward Stafford, third duke of Buckingham and a relative by marriage of the Howards.[22] The anti-Wolsey satires, in this view, grew in part from the patronage of a group of powerful northern lords frustrated by the loss of influence over the king and angered by the death of an ally on possibly trumped-up charges of treason. If this version is correct, Skelton would be in the employ of powerful victims of Tudor centralization. At the same time, he was a priest, whose work was deeply influenced by Christian liturgy and belief, and he therefore felt a more purely personal and religious objection to Wolsey's attacks on church privilege.[23] The anti-Wolsey satires were all prompted in part by Wolsey's dissolution of some monasteries in 1521. They were, moreover, written from the confines of the Abbey at Westminster, where Skelton had lived since 1518 and where he enjoyed the relative protection of sanctuary.[24] By combining political loyalty to a group of aggrieved feudal lords with personal dependence on and fervent religious belief in the church's rights of sanctuary, Skelton allied himself in every conceivable fashion with the conservative forces fighting the consolidation of absolutist rule.

Recently, however, this portrait of Skelton has been subjected to a devastating revisionist critique by Greg Walker. He finds no evidence for a Howard-Wolsey feud in the 1520s; on the contrary, the Howards seem to have been loyal and happy supporters of Wolsey's handling of crown policy. Further, the theory that they were patrons of Skelton is based on spurious suppositions and misdatings of poems.[25] There is reason to doubt the sincerity of Skelton's religious convictions as well, for he clearly viewed his move to a rectory at Diss in Norfolk as a calamitous falling off from his earlier position at court, where he had served as a Latin tutor to the young Prince Henry. When Henry ascended the throne, Skelton sent his former pupil a desperate letter describing himself as "a man utterly doomed to oblivion and, so to say, dead in his heart" and then compared his exile to Ovid's.[26] In any case, he abandoned Diss forever at his earliest opportunity and never resumed his priestly duties.[27] The notion that the anti-Wolsey satires were prompted by sincere outrage is challenged by the reversal in 1523, when Skelton turned around and wrote not only on behalf of Wolsey but in apparent collaboration with him.[28] "He seems to have swiftly considered the advantages to be gained from aligning himself with his erstwhile target," writes Walker, "compared them with the less certain gains to be won by continuing his wooing of patronage from the city [of London], and promptly thrown in his lot with Wolsey."[29]

In place of the conservative and somewhat romantic image of Skelton as defender of church and nobility Walker offers a rather less flattering image of the poet as a self-serving mercenary whose rise was inhibited by misjudgments and ineptitude. He makes a largely compelling case for viewing the satires not as expressions of prophetic wrath but as a search for patronage and advancement, first from the king and then, failing that, from among the prosperous and disaffected citizens of London. This Skelton is neither a sworn enemy of absolutism nor a reliable defender of it but someone who is ready to profit from it if given the chance.

Walker successfully destroys many of the historical assumptions that underlie the traditional view of Skelton, but his own version isn't quite coherent either. He argues, for instance, that *Speke Parott* attempts to profit from apparent tensions between Henry and Wolsey in order to secure royal patronage.[30] Yet if this is the case, how does one explain lines such as "Bo-ho [Henry] doth bark wel, Hough-ho [Wolsey] he rulyth the ring" (130)? Even someone as eccentric as Skelton couldn't possibly expect to please the king with language like this. It also seems likely that Skelton's ultimate reconciliation (or cooperation) with Wolsey was at least partly determined by ideological commitments as well as by considerations of personal gain, for his poetic assignments on Wolsey's behalf involved writing satires against foreign invasion (Skelton was, if nothing else, a sincere xenophobe) and religious heresy. A residue of the "old" Skelton thus persists despite attempts to banish him. The fact is that no fully coherent or unified account of his career is possible. Skelton is neither the conservative prophet nor the self-serving courtier, neither the consistent opponent nor the consistent parasite of the Tudor court, but someone who oscillates erratically between these positions, and whose career is therefore full of strange folds and detours. His poetry is obsessed with the changes in the late feudal polity wrought by absolutism, but his reactions to them are shifting and contradictory. Skelton's historical significance can be read primarily through his internal divisions and fissures if he is understood as a kind of relay or switching station through which conflicting social energies are routed.

*Ware the Hawk* was composed while Skelton was rector at Diss, presumably around the time he wrote *Phyllyp Sparowe* (1505?). This period witnessed Skelton's peculiar and somewhat inexplicable "break" with the conventional formulas of late medieval lyric. The poem, which exemplifies the beginnings of Skelton's distinctive poetics, describes and denounces the actions of a neighboring priest who becomes so involved in his hawking that he pursues his prey right into Skelton's church. There the hawks tear a pigeon apart on the holy altar and defecate on the communion cloth, while the priest himself overturns the offering box, cross, and lectern. The poem vents its rage at the desecration of holy places, flinging both crude and pedantic insults at the offending priest.

*Ware the Hawk* directs its anger at an act of profanation which it understands primarily as the violation of a boundary or territory; it condemns those who

> playe the daw
> To hawke, or els to hunt
> From the auter to the funt,
> Wyth cry unreverent,
> Before the sacrament,
> Wythin the holy church bowndis,
> That of our fayth the grownd is.
>
> (8–14)

Skelton's church is, of course, the literal as well as the metaphorical "ground" of faith; the hawking priest offends not only because he has intruded on divine territory but because he has intruded on Skelton's territory. "For sure he wrought amys / To hawke in *my* church of Dys" (41–42, my emphasis). I do not wish to suggest that the concept of the holy place merely expresses property rights, either for Skelton or in general. But the sanctity of the medieval church, which was articulated within the feudal structure of parceled sovereignty, represents Skelton's primary experience of this structure. Certainly the violation of the church's boundaries in *Ware the Hawk* seems to threaten its sovereignty:

> Or els is thys Goddis law,
>
> . . . . .
> Thus within the wals
> Of holy church to deale,

Thus to ryng a peale
Wyth his hawkys bels?
Dowtles such losels
Make the churche to be
In smale auctoryte.
(130, 134–40)

For Skelton, the whole hierarchical taxonomy of late medieval culture is interwritten with the church's territorial sanctity. When this is broken, all other structures collapse like a house of cards.[31]

These objections are not particularly novel in themselves. The interest of Skelton's poem arises from its formal reaction to the trespass, for *Ware the Hawk* responds to the violation of a politico-religious territory by subjecting itself to a strict rhetorical territoriality. The poem is meticulously constructed according to what Stanley Fish aptly calls the "machinery of the artes praedicandi." After a formal exordium (*prologus*), "the text is punctuated by eight hortatory exclamations (*Observate, Deliberate, Vigilate, Deplorate, Divinitate*—probably for *Divinate*—*Reformate,* and *Pensitate*) which correspond to the development of the *thema* as taught in the manuals."[32] The conspicuous rhetorical formalism of the poem clearly represents a kind of reaction formation to the disturbance of the church's boundaries; the anarchic trajectory of the hawk finds its answering principle in an exaggerated reterritorialization by the poet, thus producing a striking—and, for Skelton, characteristic—cohesion between political and rhetorical topographies. This coincidence of spaces produces brilliant formal effects in *Phyllyp Sparowe* and offers the privileged means by which Skelton transcodes history into literature.

But an additional element transforms the nature of the poem's process. Stanley Fish describes *Ware the Hawk* as "a burlesque in the Chaucerian tradition." Both the incident itself and Skelton's indignation, Fish argues, are ironized; despite its obsessive formalism, the poem's rhetoric constantly undercuts itself, thereby dissolving the seriousness of the priest's offense.[33] *Ware the Hawk* may not be as thoroughly ironic as that, but a festive excess of rhetoric certainly renders the poem and its defensive reterritorialization highly ambivalent. A gay destructiveness delights in the violation of boundaries and in the consequent evaporation of the authority constituted by them. At least part of Skelton's imagination both enjoys and extends the profanities committed by the neighboring priest, who, the poet claims,

wysshed withall
That the dowves donge downe myght fall
Into my chalys at mas,
When consecratyd was
The blessyd sacrament.

(182–86)

The pleasurable onomatopoeia of "dowves donge downe" exemplifies the festive counterlogic of *Ware the Hawk*, which can enjoy polluting even that final cultural territory, the space of the blessed sacrament. The poem's very title, which seems at first to mean "beware the hawk" and thus to make a defensive or warning gesture, was actually "a proverbial cry used to encourage the hawk to obtain its prey."[34] It is as if Skelton had marshaled the forces of rhetorical territoriality in a mock-defensive gesture, the better to overthrow *all* boundaries in one totalizing motion.

## *Phyllyp Sparowe* and the Decoding of the Body Politic

Like *Ware the Hawk*, *Phyllyp Sparowe* is set in a chapel and concerns a bird whose presence disrupts the sanctity of the church. The first part of the poem takes place at Carrow Abbey, where Jane Scrope, a young woman, composes a fanciful elegy for her pet sparrow. Against the backdrop of the Vespers of the Office for the Dead, Jane produces a rambling discourse, sometimes reminiscing about Phyllyp—their physical intimacies, his endearing habits, his death at the hands (or paws) of Gib the cat—sometimes engaging in reveries that arise from the thought of his death (she imagines Phyllyp's journey to the classical underworld, organizes a fanciful bird mass for him, tries to write a Latin epitaph). Parallels in theme and content suffice to suggest that the poem continues the project of *Ware the Hawk*, particularly with regard to the question of rhetorical territoriality. C. S. Lewis's evaluation of the poem is pertinent:

It is indeed the lightest—the most like a bubble—of all the poems I know. It would break at a touch: but hold your breath, watch it, and it is almost perfect. The Skeltonics are essential to its perfection. Their prattling and hopping and their inconsequence, so birdlike and so childlike, are the best possible embodiment of the theme. We should not, I think, refuse to call the poem great.[35]

The fragility of the poem, its tendency to break apart when handled, constitutes an important element of its form; Lewis shrewdly connects this to the birdlike wandering of its discourse, the "inconsequential" arrangement of its topics.

A sense of the poem's method can be gotten from an opening passage in which Jane enumerates her fears for Phyllyp's soul:

> Of God nothynge els crave I
> But Phyllypes soule to kepe
> From the marees depe
> Of Acherontes well,
> That is a flode of hell;
> And from the great Pluto,
> The prynce of endles wo;
> And from foule Alecto,
> With vysage blacke and blo;
> And from Medusa, that mare,
> That lyke a fende doth stare;
> And from Megeras edders,
> For rufflynge of Phillips fethers,
> And from her fyry sparklynges,
> For burnynge of his wynges;
> And from the smokes sowre
> Of Proserpinas bowre;
> And from the dennes darke
> Wher Cerberus doth barke,
> Whom Theseus dyd afraye,
> Whom Hercules dyd outraye,
> As famous poetes say;
> From that hell-hounde
> That lyeth in cheynes bounde,
> With gastly hedes thre;
> To Jupyter pray we
> That Phyllyp preserved may be!
> Amen, say ye with me!
>
> (67–94)

This lengthy quotation conveys the peculiarly agglomerative style of the poem, in which literary references, authors, myths, or, elsewhere, body parts or kinds of birds are collected into unstructured catalogs.[36] *Phyllyp Sparowe*'s encyclopedic prolixity plays on medieval traditions of amplification rather than on Erasmian copia,[37] for its discursive raw materials are not digested by the homogenizing flow of style or hemmed in by the restraints of rhetorical decorum. Although they lack the prodigious mass of Rabelaisian catalogs, Skelton's are similarly unwieldy hoards of inert and ornamental elements. The allusions, though they sometimes evoke epic, do not contribute to a unified or allegorical whole.

If both the internal ordering of these lists or strings of references and their succession in the poem follow a loosely associative flow and on a dramatic or characterological level produce something like a "stream of consciousness," individual lists do exhibit a strong topical coherence. In the passage just quoted, mythological figures collected from the classical underworld obey no evident pattern of disposition, but they do draw fairly clear boundaries between catalogical sections of the poem. The resultant parceling of *Phyllyp Sparowe* recalls the rhetorical divisions that characterize *Ware the Hawk* and forms one of the many correspondences between the two poems. Yet the formal partitioning of *Phyllyp Sparowe* is of a much more complete and radical kind. In *Ware the Hawk*, the headings of each section announce the divisions of the *thema*. Thus, at the same time as they partition the poem, they organize its parts into a global rhetorical scheme. The rhetorical headings form a kind of sectional exoskeleton for a unified discourse. Indeed, they imbue the sections with the appearance of a necessary *order* since the development of the *thema* follows an established sequence.

In the first part of *Phyllyp Sparowe*, however, the topical parcels are genuinely autonomous and do not unite the poem into a rhetorical whole. Although some of the *topoi* draw on established literary practices and subgenres—such as the heroic katabasis and the medieval bird mass—yet these derive from different and often incommensurable traditions (an explicit concern of Jane's when she thinks of composing an epitaph for Phyllyp) and are, furthermore, interspersed with such heterogeneous materials as Phyllyp's erotic wanderings, his reactions to various bugs, and Jane's fantasies about torturing the cat. Although the poem is punctuated by overheard scraps of the Office for the Dead, these do not organize Jane's discourse; rather, the poem fragments and absorbs the mass.

This parceled form complements a neutralization of cultural authority in which it also plays a role. When Phyllyp Sparowe is substituted for the hero of the classical katabasis in the passage quoted, the comic disproportionality of the bird tends to dissipate the grandeur of the epic machinery. Thus C. S. Lewis describes the poem as "mock-heroic, though the term must here be stretched to cover the mock-religious as well," and he goes on to compare it with *The Rape of the Lock.*[38] Yet *Phyllyp Sparowe*'s innocent destruction of authority must be clearly distinguished from parody or satire. Mock epic depicts the inversion of epic authority precisely in order to reassert it as the measure of a contemporary decadence. It thus depends on maintaining hierarchical differences, whereas Skelton's poem collapses and neutralizes them. Like Jane herself, *Phyllyp Sparowe* does not mock cultural authority; it is ultimately indifferent to it. Thus the poem must also be distinguished from those forms of inversion through degradation which characterize the popular culture of the time and which Mikhail Bakhtin has so brilliantly described. Skelton does employ methods of festive degradation elsewhere, most notably in *Eleanor Rumming*, but also in *Ware the Hawk*, where the church's spirituality is degraded and materialized when the hawk defecates on the altar and where sacred icons and implements are literally inverted in an emblematic representation of "the world turned upside down."

Unlike *Ware the Hawk*, which displays an ambivalence between orthodox and heterodox, hierarchizing and degrading tendencies, *Phyllyp Sparowe* simply neutralizes both. The poem's resistance to parody or blasphemy is all the more surprising given the opportunities offered by its impromptu mass for a dead bird. But while the poem draws on traditions associated with goliardic parodies of the mass, it never engages in such parodies itself.[39] For to imitate or to parody the mass it is necessary to take it as a formal and ethical paradigm that the text then necessarily reflects, either in direct or inverted form. In either case, the liturgy would impose the same kind of order on *Phyllyp Sparowe* that Skelton's rhetorical schema imposes on *Ware the Hawk*. Its failure to do so typifies the nature of the poem: any number of *potential* master codes may operate in localized parcels of the text, but none succeeds in establishing either a temporary or a global dominance.[40] No religious text overcodes the poem, nor is any form of dominance distributed among an "oligarchy" of master codes or texts.

We have seen how the absolutist state partly deterritorializes the parceled sovereignty of feudalism, recoding local structures so as to produce the centralized and ultimate form of the feudal polity. Skelton engages this process by establishing a correspondence between political and literary territoriality—in effect, by reviving in its fullness the concept of the literary *topos.* Having done so, however, he does not produce in *Phyllyp Sparowe* a representational *inversion* of the polity, a "world turned upside down" or, if you will, a pyramid standing on its head. Rather, he throws the deterritorializing machine into reverse; responding to centralized sovereignty, the poem radically relocalizes its own structure and neutralizes cultural authorities. The result can only be described as parceled anarchy in a poem whose autonomous localities resist hierarchical organization both in respect to one another and in respect to their own internal forms. This is obviously not mere reflection of a historical process but a utopian strategy within its field.

It is worth recalling here that there was a real Jane Scrope, with whom Skelton was apparently infatuated. She, her sisters, and her mother took up residence at Carrow Abbey in 1502, after her stepfather, Sir John Wyndham, was beheaded by order of the king for his (rather distant) association with a Yorkist conspiracy. While the widow's move to Carrow was made for reasons of economy rather than security, the whole affair casts a political shadow over the poem's formal and ideological project and suggests one motivation behind its deterritorialization.[41]

A complementary though in some sense contradictory logic pervades the libidinal register of the poem, where parceling gives way to decoding. A territorial field is still at stake, though here it is not directly the form of the poem but rather the human body with its sociosexually inscribed regions. The first publication of *Phyllyp Sparowe* caused something of a scandal, owing in part to its boldness in depicting what is clearly an erotic relationship between Jane Scrope and her sparrow. To some degree this was simply an instance of reviving and extending a Catullan tradition in inappropriate circumstances, but the "beastly" transgressions on both Skelton's and Jane's parts contribute to a larger program of erotic decoding which bears a visible relationship to the politics of the poem's form.

While *Phyllyp Sparowe* returns intermittently to the topic of Jane's and Phyllyp's physical intimacy, the most extended passage on this matter is the first:[42]

For it wold come and go,
And fly so to and fro;
And on me it wolde lepe
When I was aslepe,
And his fethers shake,
Wherewith he wolde make
Me often for to wake
And for to take him in

> Upon my naked skyn.
> God wot, we thought no syn—
> What though he crept so lowe?
> It was no hurt, I trowe.
> He dyd nothynge, perde,
> By syt upon my kne.
> Phyllyp, though he were nyse,
> In him it was no vyse;
> Phyllyp had leve to go
> To pyke my lytell too,
> Phillip myght be bolde
> And do what he wolde;
> Phillip would seke and take
> All the flees blake
> That he coulde there espye
> With his wanton eye.
> (159–82)

Fish's reading of this and the other erotic passages is instructive, based as it is on the presumed contrast between a sophisticated male reader and the charming but naïve figure of Jane:

> We are aware, as [Jane] is not, of the sexual implications of her demonstratio's. . . . It is perhaps difficult to read these lines without questioning her innocence, but we make the necessary effort and accept her demurral. . . . It is, however, a conscious effort, and Skelton insists that we make it. If his poem is to succeed, we must be continually aware of the distance between what Jane in her innocence would intend and what we would interpolate.[43]

Fish thus arrives at a choice partially justified by the text itself: either Phyllyp's wanderings are innocent, or they arouse Jane sexually. Or again (if I am reading Fish correctly), there is a sexual component that Jane is not aware of, though "we" know it is there. But what exactly do we know that Jane does not? That the relationship is erotic *and therefore transgressive.* But if we take Jane at her word, she does not deny that Phyllyp's actions may be erotically pleasurable, only that there is anything wrong with this. Nothing has been transgressed ("It was no hurt, I trowe," "In him it was no vyse"). Recourse to Freudian negation ignores that Jane's denials are secondary and formal compared with the pleasurability of the erotic narrative. Fish's analysis is not explicitly psychoanalytic, but it does rely on a supposed latency, the pressure of a not-said.

A "transgressive" reading would garner its strongest support from thematic parallels to *Ware the Hawk:* just as the hawk's errant flight leads it to violate the sacred territory of the church, so Phyllyp's wanderings violate the sacred territory of the virgin's body. Phyllyp's search for fleas provides a delicate, comic, and titillating parallel to the passage in which the priest's hawk murders pigeons on the sacred altar. In both cases, animal instinct proves sublimely indifferent to the boundaries of cultural taboo. But whereas *Ware the Hawk* summons up at least a mock horror at this outrage, *Phyllyp Sparowe* regards only its pleasures (emblematically, the poem's opening word is "placebo," its closing phrase "rien que playsere").[44] Phyllyp's libidinal nomadism does not transgress the sociosexual inscriptions of the body, therefore; rather, it erases them and thus decodes the body's territoriality.

*Phyllyp Sparowe* can thus be understood best in terms of the anoedipal, schizophrenic sexuality described by Gilles Deleuze and Félix Guattari in the *Anti-Oedipus:* a regime in which desire flows (or rather, break-flows) between machinic part-objects, unchanneled by oedipal law and the rule of the phallus. It is thus inappropriate to view Phyllyp as a "phallic symbol," a substitute for a genital satisfaction that is lacking.[45] To do so is to fall into the teleology of the Oedipus, to interpret the desiring production of part-objects as the secondary effects of a dominant, "mature," and genital sexuality, governed by the unitary structures of the phallus. Jane's body is composed of desiring machines—the toe, the knee, the tongue, the breast—all of which produce pleasure and all of which are connected *not* by the globalizing stroke of the Oedipus (which would organize the parts into a whole inscribed with taboos) but only by Phyllyp's random and nomadic wandering, which is the movement of desire itself.[46] This process has no *telos*—reproduction or even genital orgasm—nor does it hide or repress anything or substitute for something lacking; it is simply a decoded and polymorphous flow of desire.

Here it is well to recall Deleuze and Guattari's observation that "global persons do not exist prior to the prohibitions that found them," prior, that is, to their establishment as structural points on the oedipal triangle, which is in turn constituted by subjugating the diverse break-flows of desire to the law of the phallus or castration.[47] In her libidinal functioning, then, Jane should not be regarded as a unified subject but as the site of polyvocal and decoded flows.[48] Her desiring-production resists subordination to the Oedipus in much the same way that the parceled anarchy of the poem resists subordination to the unitary rule of a master text. The utopian and schizophrenic alternative to overcoding thus proceeds simultaneously on political, sexual, and formal levels. Yet while mutually implicated, these levels do not bear an expressive relation to one another; the "same thing" does not happen on each. Formally, the poem reterritorializes itself into autonomous parcels, while its libidinal register is characterized by a deterritorialized nomadism, not autonomy but an unchanneled flow between part-objects. This deterritorialization does not, however, correspond to that carried out by the state; it does not unify the body in order to subject it to the rule of the despot.

I have thus far separated the issues of poetic form and Jane's desiring-production, but in fact, these two converge, for Jane desires to be a poet, and a good third of her discourse concerns her attempt to write an epitaph for Phyllyp. Here Jane fulfills her eminently *practical* critique of the metaphysics of lack as all her supposed deficiencies conclusively evaporate. In particular, this section of the poem turns on a witty and, for Jane, quite conscious contradiction between an abundance of poetic material and the "lack" of a disposing style. On the one hand, Jane falls most completely into the alibi of insufficiency, and on the other she refutes it in the practice of her discourse:

> Yet one thynge is behynde,
> That now commeth to mynde:
> An epytaphe I wold have
> For Phyllyppes grave.
> But for I am a mayde,
> Tymerous, halfe afrayde,
> That never yet asayde
> Of Elyconys well,
> Where the muses dwell:
> Though I can rede and spell,
> Recounte, reporte, and tell
> Of the *Tales of Caunterbury*
> Some sad storyes, some mery,
> As Palamon and Arcet,
> Duke Theseus, and Partelet;
> And of the Wyfe of Bath,
> That worketh moch scath
> Whan her tale is tolde
> Amonge huswyves bolde,
> How she controlde
> Her husbandes as she wolde,

. . . . .
And though that rede have I
Of Gawen, and Syr Guy,
And can tell a great pece
Of the Golden Flece,
How Jason it wan,
Lyke a valyaunt man;
Or Arturs rounde table,
With his knightes commendable.
(603–23, 628–35)

And so on. In the succeeding list of "though" clauses her productivity reaches its zenith as she reels off a miniature encyclopedia of classical and medieval fables. But then the "though" clauses reach their conclusion, at which point there appears the "lack":

Though I have enrold
A thousand new and old
Of these historious tales,
To fyll bougets and males
With bokes that I have red,
Yet I am nothyng sped,
And can but lytell skyll
Of Ovyd or Virgyll,
Or of Plutharke,
Or Frauncys Petrarke,

. . . . .
For as I tofore have sayd,
I am but a yong mayd,
And can not in effect
My style as yet direct
With Englysh wordes elect.
(749–58, 769–73)

What Jane has, then, is matter—enough to "fyll bougets and males"—but she cannot "direct" her "style." Here, for purely tactical reasons, the poem does succumb to a phallic symbolization. A *bouget* is a pouch, bag, or wallet; the word, related to *bulge*, comes from the Latin *bulga*, a leather bag or a womb. A *male* is also a leather bag or wallet, but the word lends itself to witty associations with the testicles.[49] Jane thus bulges with the necessary matter for a poem but cannot "direct" her "style"; that is, she cannot subject her materials to a unitary disposition or mode of expression. But also, she cannot direct her stylus, or writing stick, with its all-too-obvious symbolization: she cannot wield the phallus, she is a maid, she lacks that with which she could subject her materials to a unifying stroke. Jane thus comes to "know" herself in the void of castration.

Yet Jane's lack is ironized, not because she eventually manages to scribble a few Latin verses but because she has been speaking prodigious poetry all along. Her lack is assigned to her only retroactively, as a kind of phallic *ressentiment*, by the ideal of a unified style that her own productivity continuously exceeds and overflows. The strength of her practice defeats the weakness of her alibi; thus the momentary but intensely phallic symbolization of the passage is not only provisional but in some deeper sense derisory. Like the defensive reterritorialization of *Ware the Hawk* it is invoked only in order to accomplish a more thorough decoding.

And yet *Phyllyp Sparowe* is, in some sense, founded on the void, specifically that left by the disappearance of its namesake. Elegy is supremely the genre of lack; Jane's creativity may seem intended to refill a universe that has been hollowed out by her sparrow's disappearance. But Jane lacks Phyllyp only in the sense that she lacks a style. As the extraordinary digressiveness of the poem shows, Jane's verbal cosmos is not "sparrow-centric." Which is only to say once again that Phyllyp is not the phallus; his disappearance does not overcode the text.

In fact, it does the opposite. The death of a sparrow recalls not only Catullus's poem but—especially in this liturgical context—Jesus's words to his disciples: "Are not two sparrows sold for a farthing? and one of them shall not fall to the ground without your Father" (Matthew 10:29). The providential fall of the sparrow symbolizes the total saturation of the cosmos by God's law, its complete structuration down to the smallest portion; in short, the totalizing efficacy of the *logos*. Yet the poem neutralizes this, like so many other signs, for Jane's grandiose execrations on Gib the cat and her comic hope that

> Phyllyp may fly
> Above the starry sky,
> To treade the prety wren
> That is our Ladyes hen.
> (598–601)

only reinforce our sense of the triviality and meaninglessness of the event. The desymbolization of Phyllyp's death thus destructures the poem's universe instead of reordering it. What has disappeared is not a phallus but a linchpin, and the removal of this "weak link" allows an entire structure to collapse.

This destructuration, at least, applies to the poem's first part. But Jane's discourse makes up only half of the original poem; the second part, consisting of Skelton's "commendations" of Jane, follows far different rules.[50] Drawing on materials from the cult of the Virgin and on the formulas of courtly love poetry, Skelton constructs an intense but sometimes routinized praise of his beloved. The first and second parts of the poem exhibit clear stylistic contrasts, as Jane's digressiveness is replaced by Skelton's fidelity to his subject.[51] In general, a more restrained and frugal economy of style pervades the second part.

Setting sophistication against naïveté, difficulty against simplicity, and male against female, the second part of the poem quite clearly tries to master the first, beginning with the rather disquieting entrance of Skelton's authorial persona. At the end of Jane's section, when she finally manages to write an epitaph for Phyllyp in "Latyne playne and lyght," Skelton suddenly manifests himself in the midst of her composition:

> Per me laurigerum
> Britanum Skeltonida vatem
> Hec cecinisse licet
> Ficta sub imagine texta.
> (834–37)

It was permitted that this should be sung by me, Skelton the laureate poet, in the guise of a fictive image.

By this epiphanic entrance, Skelton disperses the imaginary voice of Jane and appropriates the whole of the poem for himself. Not only the second part but also Jane's discourse was an effect of Skelton's rhetorical mastery, which henceforth becomes the poem's ultimate referent.[52] The Skelton persona thus reorganizes the poem's territoriality so that it is entirely expressive of his rule.

Not surprisingly, "Skelton's" poetry emphasizes symmetry and stasis and reduces Jane to the commonplaces of the medieval blazon: her face is as white as orient pearl, her cheeks are like rose buds, her lips are like cherries, her mouth is "sugred" (1031–40). Her otherwise formalized appearance does include a blemish, though, which draws the poet's most sustained attention:

> Her beautye to augment
> Dame Nature hath her lent
> A warte upon her cheke,
> Who so lyst to seke
> In her vysage a skar
> That semyth from afar
> Lyke to a radyant star,
> All with favour fret,
> So properly is it set.
> (1041–49)

The wart is a random excrescence, a surd element that resists the poet's efforts to cleanse and spiritualize his beloved. Hence it must be subjected to the most strenuous kind of poetic sublimation and, more important, *fixed* within a structure. The wart is

> set so womanly,
> And nothynge wantonly,
> But ryght convenyently,
> And full congruently,
> As Nature cold devyse,
> In most goodly wyse.
> (1067–72)

As if the wart were threatening to wander or had already reached its position by an aleatory movement, Skelton makes it into a fixed locus of chaste fascination and thus into an antitype of Phyllyp the libidinal nomad. The wart transgresses no boundaries on a body that has been precisely and definitively inscribed.

This thematic project of overcoding Jane has its formal counterpart in the structural and stylistic unity of the second part. Although the commendations are formally divided by the periodic repetition of a refrain, yet the regions produced thereby are essentially homogeneous, as they were in *Ware the Hawk*. The second part of *Phyllyp Sparowe* thus truly forms a whole, into which it tries to incorporate, retroactively, the first part as well.

Yet despite his initially absolutist claims, the Skelton persona's powers are not unlimited, for his rhetorical mastery of Jane balances an equally powerful erotic submissiveness. Each repetition of the refrain incorporates different paraphrases of the Psalms, such as "Quomodo dilexi legem tuam, domina! [How I have loved your laws, o mistress"!] and "Legem pone michi, domina, in viam justificationem tuarum! [Set laws down for me, mistress, in your just ways!]." Skelton addresses Jane as if she were a sixteenth-century leather lady and asks her to bind him down. Unlike Phyllyp, the poet will walk only in "just ways"; the second part of the poem is a virtual web of obligations, decorums, entreaties, restrictions, and taboos.

It is clear, then, that the Skelton persona does not emerge merely to master Jane. She also ironizes his neurotic obsessiveness, his sadistic instrumentality, his stiff formalism, his emptiness of invention. "Skelton" unwittingly illustrates his shortcomings in his very first English phrase, when he promises to devote his "hole imagination" to praising his mistress. If this persona organizes things into wholes, he also reduces them to holes. This is a motivated pun, for "Skelton" unifies by draining the copiousness of localized difference. The phallic organizer who pretends to totalize and complete the poem proves to be precisely the space of its "hole," or lack.

But if the second part of *Phyllyp Sparowe* does not entirely succeed in subsuming the first, neither is its attempt to do so completely neutralized. At best the poem achieves a balance of forces; "Skelton" reveals the fragility of Jane's poetics, the susceptibility of its anarchic logic to a subsequent structuration and mastery. The project of the poem's first part is thus shown to be utopian in a bad sense as well. Radical as they are, the poem's localizing and destructuring movements depend on a localized freedom, the private imaginings of a young woman whose daydreams flow unimpeded only because they confront nothing outside of themselves. Here is the truth of Lewis's remark that *Phyllyp Sparowe* is "indeed the lightest—the most like a bubble—of all the poems I know." Not just the structural soundness but the utopian logic of the poem proves evanescent.

It is no accidental irony that the opening word of the poem—placebo—also designates a flatterer or sycophant. Thus the very sign that announces the poem's flight from absolutism also suggests its possible capitulation to it. In later and more dangerous days, Skelton would chastise those who

> occupy them so
> With syngynge *Placebo*,
> They wyll no farder go.
> They had lever to please
> And take theyr worldly ease
> Than to take on hande

> Worshypfully to withstande
> Suche temporall warre and bate
> As now is made of late
> Agaynst holy churche estate,
> Or to maynteyne good quarelles.
> *(Collyn Clout, 906–16)*

These lines may be taken as a retrospective critique of *Phyllyp Sparowe* as well, which did "no farder go" than to outline a regime of pleasure.

## Speke Parott and the Delegation of Speech

*Speke Parott*, the first of Skelton's anti-Wolsey satires, does go considerably farther than *Phyllyp Sparowe* in maintaining a quarrel with state authority. Written in 1521, when Skelton was already residing in sanctuary at Westminster, *Speke Parott* both develops and dramatically revises the poetics of *Phyllyp Sparowe*. A bird is once again the center of attention, but this bird is very much alive—immortal, in fact—and is no longer merely the subject but the speaker of the poem:

> My name ys Parott, a byrde of Paradyse,
> By Nature devysed of a wonderowus kynde,
> Deyntely dyetyd with dyvers delycate spyce,
> Tyll Eufrates, that flodde, dryvythe me into Ynde,
> Where men of that contre by fortune me fynde,
> And send me to greate ladyes of estate;
> Then Parot moste have an almon or a date.
>
> A cage curyowsly carven, with sylver pynne,
> Properly payntyd to be my coverture;
> A myrrour of glasse, that I may tote therin;
> These maydens full meryly with many a dyvers flowur
> Fresshely they dresse and make swete my bowur,
> With "Speke, Parott, I pray yow," full curteslye they sey,
> "Parott ys a goodlye byrde and a pratye popagay."
>
> Wythe my beke bente, and my lytell wanton iye,
> My fethyrs fresshe as ys the emerawde grene,
> Abowte my necke a cerculett lyke the ryche rubye,
> My lytell legges, my fete both fete and clene,

I am a mynyon to wayte apon a quene;
"My propyr Parott, my lytell pratye fole."
With ladyes I lerne and goe with them to scole.

(1–21)

With his "lytell wanton iye," Parott is clearly a ladies' bird, just as
Phyllyp Sparowe was.[53] One of the literary models for *Speke Parott*
is the *Epistres de l 'amant verd* by Jean Lemaire de Belges, a series
of despairingly erotic letters from a pet parrot to his departing
mistress. Yet even from these opening lines it is clear that Skelton's Parott, unlike Lemaire's, is primarily autoerotic. He lovingly
enumerates his *own* body parts, "totes" in his mirror, and seems to
value the ladies of the court mostly because they make much of
him. Parott thus appropriates not only speech but sexuality as well;
in his disturbing autonomy he is like a strange hybrid of Phyllyp
and Jane.[54] Parott's sexuality is not entirely innocent, however,
and his is given to knowing, phallic innuendo.[55]

Not only sexually but more generally, *Speke Parott* may be said
to rewrite *Phyllyp Sparowe* into a song of experience. Parott has
fallen from Paradise, "that place of pleasure perdurable" (186),
which may in part be identified with *Phyllyp Sparowe*'s realm of
"rien que playsere." Parott is a polyglot who both embodies and
masters the curse of Babel. "Yn Latyn, in Ebrue, and in Caldee, /In
Greke tong Parott can bothe speke and sey" (25–26)—as well as in
French, Spanish, Dutch, and several English dialects. And he employs this multilingualism together with dense layers of figure to
protect himself in the dangerous world of court:

But of that supposicyon that callyd is arte,
*Confuse distrybutyve,* as Parrot hath devysed,
Let every man after his merit take his parte;
For in this processe, Parrot nothing hath surmysed,
No matter pretendyd, nor nothyng enterprysed,
But that *metaphora, alegoria* withall,
Shall be his protectyon, his pavys [shield] and his wall.

(197–203)

But allegory is not the only means of defense on which the poem
relies. A. C. Spearing has suggested that Parott's cage may represent the confinement and relative safety of the sanctuary of Westminster.[56] I say "relative safety" because one of the poem's satirical targets is Wolsey's assaults on sanctuary rights: "So myche

sayntuary brekyng, and prevylegidde barryd— / Syns Dewcalyons flodde was nevyr sene nor lyerd" (503–4).[57] In every way, the world of *Speke Parott* is therefore more dangerous, covert, and sinister than that of *Phyllyp Sparowe*, and accordingly, Parott is a cannier type of bird.

In its rambling course, *Speke Parott* criticizes numerous evils in the early Tudor polity, for almost all of which it blames Thomas Cardinal Wolsey. As Greg Walker has observed, Skelton's satires almost entirely abjure social analysis in favor of ad hominem attacks[58] against a man who seemed to embody in his person the entire machinery of the Tudor state. Nor was Skelton alone in this perception. The Venetian ambassador Sebastian Giustiani described Wolsey as a man "of vast ability and indefatigable. He alone transacts the same business as that which occupies all the magistracies, offices and councils of Venice, both civil and criminal, and all state affairs are likewise handled by him let their nature be what it may."[59] Even more than Henry VIII, Wolsey represented the concentration of administrative and jurisdictional power carried out by early absolutism. Not only did he run most of the governmental apparatus as lord chancellor, but in 1518 he was granted vast ecclesiastical powers when he was named papal legate *a latere*. Wolsey used his new authority to reorganize and interfere with the government of every diocese, "appointing his own protégés, regardless of the rights of patrons, and set[ting] up legatine courts to which he summoned men from all over England,"[60] in addition to dissolving monasteries and attempting to curtail rights of sanctuary. By centralizing diocesan government and subjecting it to the interests of the crown, Wolsey helped prepare the way for the Tudor state's more formal rule of the church. It is Wolsey, far more than Henry, who embodies for Skelton the centralizing force of early Tudor absolutism.

Superficially, *Speke Parott* seems to react to Wolsey as *Phyllyp Sparowe* reacted to its own despotic signifiers: by de- and reterritorializing into autonomous parcels. Parott even devises a name for this poetic mode—*"confuse distrybutyve"* (198)—and describes the recombinatory method that produces it:

> Suche shredis of sentence, strowed in the shop
> Of auncyent Aristippus and such other mo,
> I gader togyther and close in my crop,
> Of my wanton conseyt, *unde depromo*
> *Dilemata docta in pedagogio*

*Sacro vatum*,[61] whereof to you I breke;
I pray you, let Parot have lyberte to speke.

(92–98)

Parott's "wanton conseyt" works according to the mechanisms of poetic imagination I described in Chapter 1, atomizing and scrambling received texts so as to decode them ideologically. The poem thus registers a tension between Parott's role as a conscious and unified speaker who is an apparent source of speech and his position as mere relay or switching station in an uncontrolled and seemingly random field of language-flows. The figure of the parrot, a bird who memorizes "scraps of sentence" and repeats them unexpectedly, offers a striking image for the decontextualizing labor of poetic imagination. The more speech that is fed into Parott, the more uncanny and disconcerting he becomes: "Thus dyvers of language by lernyng I grow" (103). Unlike those of *Phyllyp Sparowe*, the textual fragments shuttled through *Speke Parott* are not even subjected to the constraints of a consistent poetic voice or persona; Parott shifts abruptly between languages and dialects, like a tape recorder gone mad:

*Ulula*, Esebon, for Jeromy doth wepe!
Sion is in sadness, Rachell ruly doth loke;
Midionita Jetro, our Moyses kepyth his shepe;
Gedeon is gon, that Zalmane undertoke,
Oreb *et* Zeb, of *Judicum* rede the boke.
Now Geball, Amon and Amaloch—"Harke, harke,
Parrot pretendith to be a bybyll clarke!"

(113–19)

Yet the slippery, obscure, and seemingly aleatory surface of the poem conceals a dense allegorical coherence. While "some folys say ye arre furnysshyd with knakkes, / That hang togedyr as fethyrs in the wynde" (292–93), they lack the learning to construe the poem's message—so says the first of the envoys that Skelton attached to *Speke Parott* in an attempt to explain it to an uncomprehending audience.[62] Recent commentators have unveiled most of the poem's linguistic, scriptural, and allegorical mysteries and found a coherent, detailed attack on Cardinal Wolsey. Once interpreted, the poem reveals not incoherence but, if anything, a hypercoherence verging on paranoia that traces almost all of England's social, political, and religious disorders back to this one source. It is around the cardinal as fetishized signifier that all the poem's allegorical codes crystallize and congeal, thus establishing a stark dialectic between de- and reterritorialization. What *Phyllyp Sparowe* distributed between two parts of the poem *Speke Parott* enacts simultaneously, at once flying apart to avoid capture and recomposing itself to direct all its obsessive force at a single target.

The formal and lingusitic strategies of *Speke Parott*, though they owe more than a little to some of Skelton's earlier works, are both honed and transformed by the poet's engagement with real political authority. Wolsey, in fact, confronts Skelton with a very specific model for the relation between language and power: that of *delegation*, the transfer of juridical or administrative authority by means of speech or language. Wolsey had recently become the recipient of two different forms of delegated power. Having already been appointed papal legate in 1518, he was then sent by King Henry to Calais for a series of diplomatic negotiations in the fall of 1521. Wolsey's ostensible purpose was to mediate between French and imperial forces in order to avoid a war into which England would be drawn by treaty, but his real purpose was to arrange a secret agreement with the imperial delegates for a combined assault on France. In any case, Wolsey brought the Great Seal of England with him to Calais as a sign of his plenipotentiary powers—an event of some symbolic importance.[63]

Delegation is itself a complex symbolic act in that the delegate becomes an actual bearer of authority but only by representing or standing in for the delegating power. Paradoxically, the act of delegation can grant a certain autonomy if delegates are asked to exercise their own judgment; yet ultimately their decisions must all serve the interests of another, so that they are at once both actant and symbol. Delegation as speech act, the sending forth of the delegate to act on behalf of another, is a real linguistic transfer or exchange of power but one that is bounded by the relation of representing or signifying. It serves as a linguistic conduit for centralized power, allowing it to extend its operations and jurisdiction over a wide territorial field. Delegation is therefore a characteristic mode of propagating authority within despotic, absolutist, or bureaucratic states.

That Wolsey tended to drive the tensions or complexities of delegation into open contradiction was, I think, part of his fascination for Skelton. Wolsey accumulated enormous jurisdictional and administrative authority in the course of his various duties, and if this allowed him to carry out the will of his superiors more fully, it also threatened to destabilize or overturn the relations of power that bound him to them. England's papal legate was well known to covet the papacy himself and had already engaged in unsuccessful machinations to attain it. "Hyt ys to fere leste he wolde were the garland on hys pate," warns Parott (435). As to secular power, the Venetian ambassador observed that "the Cardinal, for authority, may in point of fact be styled *ipse rex*,"[64] and *Speke Parott* likewise warns Henry that his indulgence allows Wolsey to "rule the ring." Skelton apparently took advantage of some tensions that developed between king and lord chancellor during the course of the Calais negotiations to launch his satire, though in the end he misread both these and the true nature of Wolsey's mission.[65] *Speke Parott* thus finds an opening for satire in the assumption that Wolsey has arrogated so much power that he betrays his diplomatic tasks.

It is in relation to Wolsey's position as unreliable or usurping delegate, I believe, that the persona of Parott takes on his full satirical force. Parrots, of course, are known for repeating only what their masters teach them. Incapable of independent thought, they can only mimic the words of others, and they thus represent a simple and absolute relation between language and authority. The parrot is pure linguistic instrument, subject to another, without understanding, unable to argue back. "Speke Parott," the phrase that titles Skelton's poem, suggests an absolutist brand of linguistic delegation which determines both the moment and the content of speech. Accordingly, Parott can be a shameless flatterer of authority:

> In Englysshe to God Parott can supple:
> "Cryste save Kyng Herry the viiith, owur royall kyng,
> The red rose in honour to flowrysshe and sprynge!"
>
> "With Kateryne incomporabyll, owur royall quene also,
> That pereles pomegarnat, Cryste save her nobyll grace!"
> (33–37)

In one sense, then, Parott's role is to debase or degrade Wolsey's position as delegate. Skelton's satire relies on an implicit parallel between Parott's position as poetic persona, speaking only the words that his creator supplies, and the lord chancellor's role as mere instrument or tool of royal policy: "A narrow unfethered and without an hed, / A bagpype without blowynge standeth in no sted" (74–75). In one sense the arrow is Wolsey, whose flight has taken him from England to Calais, and Skelton reminds him that without his "head" (Henry) and "feathers" (presumably, diplomatic finery and status), the lord chancellor is useless and impotent.[66] But this image also figures Skelton's poem as satirical arrow, with its feathered persona and guiding poetical author or "head." However much he may plume himself on his borrowed authority, Skelton suggests, Wolsey is just a trained bird, provided with a few phrases to utter on behalf of another. Like Parott, Wolsey is only a vain and lascivious "popagay."

The notion of parroting, incidentally, connects the satire of Wolsey with another, apparently unrelated part of the poem: Skelton's attack on humanist methods of language instruction. Wolsey was known to have sponsored the "Greeks" at Oxford, and this in itself was sufficient provocation for Skelton's attack.[67] But what *Speke Parott* objects to more specifically is humanism's divorce of speech from content or "matter" and hence from understanding. The child who can say " '*Aveto*' in *Greco*, and such solempne salutacyons," yet "Can skantly the tensis of his conjugacyons" (179–80) seems uncomfortably like a parrot who can repeat phrases without knowing what they mean or how to use them. Skelton regarded humanist education as a degrading form of linguistic delegation producing servile and ignorant speakers, a reflection of its hated patron.

If the parrot symbolized a flattering and obedient form of imitation, however, another and somewhat contradictory tradition viewed it as a wanton, mischievous, or satirical speaker, "roughly comparable to the court jester who offers garbled scraps of wisdom in snatches of foreign tongues, an outspoken revealer of confidences, indulged because he is not responsible for his sometimes telling juxtaposition of random phrases."[68] The seemingly mechanical repetition of speech which makes parrots seem so subservient from one perspective can also make them appear uncanny or disturbing from another. Maybe they really are independent intellects whose phrases aren't random. In mimicking us, do they mock us? Skelton's articulate Parott raises just this doubt; he derives more than a little of his satirical energy from his ability to twist and garble various kinds of speech, thus rendering them either strange or risible. Parott embodies repetition as alienation, where it gives birth to the illusion of a weirdly autonomous mind. Parott is "wanton"; he demands "lyberty to speke" and thus appropriates a power that was seemingly only lent to him. In this, of course, he also represents Wolsey, another mouthpiece or verbal instrument who (Skelton thinks) has gotten out of hand. Like Parott, Wolsey is a delegated speaker who mysteriously becomes a *source* of speech and authority.

Through its feathered persona, *Speke Parott* adopts a complex and contradictory stance toward linguistic delegation. In some respects the poem enacts a kind of latent pun on the word: it "delegalizes" speech, not only by investing it with unofficial or seditious meanings but, more fundamentally, by collapsing the law of speech, by disarticulating or decoding those linguistic structures that make language a reliable conduit for the transmission of authority. Here Parott plays his crucial role as a language machine run amok, switching suddenly from shrewdness to frenzy, from wisdom to foolery, shuttling textual fragments and lingusitic flows in unpredictable directions, oscillating unexpectedly between communication and mechanical sound production. Parott dislocates the speaking subject, referring to himself by name and in the third person, as if he were elsewhere, not in this voice that emerges from his body. Parott, in fact, does for language what Jane Scrope does for sexuality, snatching it from the stroke of a despotic signifier.

But *Speke Parott* is not *Phyllyp Sparowe*, and thus while it traces lines of flight from power it also tries to mount a counterattack by harnessing the force of delegation for its own purposes. If Greg Walker's reading of the poem is accepted—and I think it should be, at least in part—then *Speke Parott* is Skelton's attempt to regain royal favor by exploiting what he thought to be Henry's serious dissatisfactions with Wolsey's diplomatic efforts. The poem is thus an unsolicited barb loosed on Henry's "behalf" and a proleptic resumption of Skelton's post as *orator regius*, the title by which he identifies himself at the poem's end. The second envoy, dated three days after Henry sent a letter recalling Wolsey from Calais, rejoices over the apparent failure of the lord chancellor's mission, and contrasts what it takes to be Skelton's new poetic delegation with Wolsey's failed diplomatic one:

> Passe forthe, Parotte, towardes some passengere;
> Require hym to convey yow ovyr the salte fome;
> Addressyng your selfe, lyke a sadde messengere,
> To owur soleyne Seigneour Sadoke, desire hym to cum home,
> Makyng hys pylgrimage by *Nostre Dame de Crome:*
> For Jerico and Jerssey shall mete togethyr as sone
> As he to exployte the man owte of the mone.
>
> (301–7)

Skelton's poetic missive steps in for Henry's letter recalling the failed and wayward ambassador; just as Parott is sent to speak for his author, so Skelton believes himself now to be speaking for the king. The only problem with this royal delegation is that it was entirely fictive, an autodelegation. Relying on gossip and rumor, Skelton was uninformed of Wolsey's real mission at Calais and was apparently taken by surprise when the king welcomed and thanked the returning lord chancellor.[69] Ironically, then, it was Skelton, not Wolsey, who abused the power of delegation by appropriating royal powers of speech while only posing as the representative of authority. If he thought Wolsey capable of almost magical powers of usurpation, mightn't this be in part because his own career was based on the usurpation of titles, those of poet laureate and king's orator?

At the same time that Skelton puts his pretended authority as *orator regius* up against the secular power of the lord chancellor, however, he also invokes a second, prophetic delegation with which to berate the worldly cardinal. The poem's prophetic voice and vocation emerge most clearly in the final envoy, where a complaint against contemporary abuses is joined to an implicit threat of divine retribution:

> So many thevys hangyd, and thevys neverthelesse;
> So myche presonment, for matyrs not worth a hawe;
> So myche papers werying for ryghte a smalle exesse;
> So myche pelory pajauntes undyr colowur of good lawe;
> So myche towrnyng on the cooke-stole for every guy-gaw;
> So myche mokkyshe makyng of statutes of array—
> Syns Dewcalyons flodde was nevyr, I dar sey.
>
> .  .  .  .  .
>
> So many trusys takyn, and so lytyll perfyte trowthe;
> So myche bely-joye, and so wastefull banketyng;
> So pynchyng and sparyng, and so lytell profyte growth;
> So many howgye howsys byldyng, and so small howse-holdyng;
> Such statutes apon diettes, suche pyllyng and pollyng—
>
> .  .  .  .  .
>
> So many vacabondes, so many beggers bolde,
> So myche decay of monesteries and relygious places;
> So hote hatered agaynste the Chyrche, and cheryte so colde;
> So myche of my lordes grace, and in hym no grace ys;
> So many holow hartes, and so dowbyll faces;
> So myche sayntuary brekyng, and prevylegidde barryd—
> Syns Dewcalyons flodde was nevyr sene nor lyerd.
>
> (477–83, 491–95, 498–504)

Skelton's jeremiad nicely balances a sense of social dissolution with an awareness of the increasing centralization and severity of royal power, so that his depicted polity is at once anarchic and totalitarian. If only empirically, he manages to grasp the dynamic of primitive accumulation. But this contradictory state is also that of his poem and its two delegations. For as *orator regius*, Skelton attempts to recall the aberrant and excessive Wolsey in the name of the king, and thus to restore the political order of the kingdom. From this perspective Henry is viewed as a "mercyfull" ruler (60), the embodiment of a feudal or limited monarchy, and emergent absolutism is mistakenly regarded as the product of a renegade lord chancellor. As prophet, however, Skelton stands apart from all political authority. Now he seems to promise not the restoration of a lost order but the loss of all order, for "Dewcalyons flodde" suggests a divine punishment that would both complete and literalize the dissolution of the late feudal polity.

The de- and recoding operations of Skelton's later poetics are thus tied to two incompatible concepts of poetic delegation, explaining, I think, the sometimes contradictory stance of *Speke Parott*, which seems on the whole to criticize Wolsey on behalf of the king, yet sometimes inexplicably attacks Henry as well. As papal legate and lord chancellor Wolsey was able to effect a preliminary subordination of church to state, and this double role was reflected in an unacceptably "worldly" manner. Skelton, by contrast, endures an unstable alternation between his delegated roles, and this constitutes his divided experience of early absolutism. Ironically, however, his most fully elaborated statement on the prophetic nature of poetry occurs in his final work, *A Replycacion* (1528), written on behalf of the formerly reviled Wolsey, whom it fulsomely praises. This final turn of Skelton's career has proven to be a puzzling one, at least to those who thought that Skelton had fought a principled and even dangerous battle against the lord chancellor. It certainly suggests a mercenary or at least an opportunistic side to his character. This development is foreshadowed, however, by Skelton's own poetical birds, all of whom have undergone some degree of taming. Even the irascible Parott "must have an almon or a date" and probably isn't too choosy about where he gets it. Yet it is also unfair to privilege *A Replycacion* just because it was Skelton's last poem. Had he lived, the poet might well have turned wild once more and bitten the hand that fed him.

# Rational Kernel, Mystical Shell: Reification and Desire in Thomas More's *Utopia*

Frederick Engels sums up in a small space the ambivalence with which classical Marxism viewed the tradition of utopian socialism:

> We can leave it to the literary small fry to solemnly quibble over these [utopian] phantasies, which today only make us smile, and to crow over the superiority of their own bald reasoning, as compared with such "insanity." For ourselves, we delight in the stupendously grand thoughts and germs of thought that everywhere break out through their phantastic covering, and to which these philistines are blind.[1]

At once respectful and condescending, Engels assigns utopia an indeterminate position between scientific socialism and ideology. For him, Saint-Simon, Fourier, and Robert Owen were visionary heroes; if they failed to construct a viable socialism from reason alone, this was because they wrote when capitalism had not achieved its full historical development, had not yet revealed its essential contradictions and hence the way beyond them. Even so, utopian fantasy had a prophetic insight that put it miles ahead of its bourgeois detractors, whose dismissive "bald reasoning" was the thinnest cover for their own class interests.[2]

Engels values utopias because they generate "stupendously grand thoughts and germs of thought"—because, that is, they pave the way for theory. Yet Engels's assessment is as much affective as intellectual. At their best, utopias "delight"; otherwise, they elicit a knowing smile. It is unclear whether the "phantasy" and "insanity" of the utopia play a passive or an active role, whether they inhibit or promote its intellectual greatness. The final sentence, at least, seems to relegate fantasy to a position of pure exteriority in relation to utopian thoughts, which "everywhere break through their phantastic covering." Engels's figure clearly harks back to the well-known passage in Marx's *Capital:* "With [Hegel, the dialectic] is standing on its head. It must be turned right side up again, if you would discover the rational kernel within the mystical shell."[3] What "matters" in utopias, then, is the rational kernel; the fantasy is a husk to be peeled and discarded. But as Althusser has pointed out, the figure of kernel and shell "poses a *pre-dialectical question*" and is therefore inadequate to Marx's actual theoretical practice.[4] In Engels's work, this inadequacy infects the figure itself, for the "rational kernel" of the utopia does not sit quietly in its fantastic covering, waiting to be shelled; rather, it "breaks through" everywhere. The image of utopia as an exploding or erupting text is one we will encounter repeatedly. But we may note from the start that it is a peculiar way of picturing rationality. What kind of reason *erupts*? The figure of rupture and release seems better suited to questions of pleasure or desire, to the liberation of the repressed, or to the production of copia. What kind of reason gives "delight" but not knowledge? For Engels, the specifically literary elements of the utopia, its articulations of fantasy and desire, occupy the troubling position of the supplement, at once interior and exterior to utopian rationality. Since he is not fishing for "literary small fry," he does not take time to pause over these questions. A fully dialectical approach to the genre of the utopia, however, requires us to read its pleasures as well as its knowledge politically.

The legacy of Engels appears in what is indisputably the greatest and one of the few truly *critical* works on More's *Utopia* and utopias, Louis Marin's book *Utopiques: Jeux d'espaces.* I don't intend to discuss Marin's arguments or his brilliant readings here, but it will be clear to anyone familiar with his book that they provide a critical basis for my own analysis, and a few remarks on his theoretical approach are pertinent.[5] Clearly taking his cue from Althusser and Pierre Macherey, Marin defines the utopia as an

ideological critique of ideology. Utopia is a critique of dominant ideology to the degree to which it reconstructs present or contemporary society by displacing and projecting the latter's structures into a fictive discourse. It differs thereby from the philosophical discourse of ideology which is the totalizing expression of existing reality as well as the latter's ideal discourse.[6]

As opposed to ideological thinking, which effaces or smooths over social contradictions, utopias conserve and represent them in the form of literary figures. Yet "the utopian critique is [itself] ideological insofar as utopia, as discourse, does not contain the method which allows it to take place, nor the methodology which would legitimate it: does not, in other words, contain the theory of its own production." Because it lacks methodological self-awareness, including an awareness of its own production in history, utopia cannot offer a scientific theory of society; rather, "utopian discourse accompanies ideological discourse as its obverse and *designates the as yet empty place of a scientific theory of society* (Marxism)."[7] Like Engels, Marin inserts utopia in a historical narrative of development whose final term is the appearance of theory.[8] At first glance this approach might seem crudely teleological; in fact, it is not so. Marin knows fully what it means to read utopias backward from the perspective of theory. Nor by placing utopian discourse in the "as yet empty place" of theory does he designate it as an embryonic *form* of theory, one whose later development will manifest and fulfill a (latent) essence. Marin situates the figural squarely in the *literary* realm, and this is not a realm that will ever become theory. On the contrary, the irreducible distance between the literary and the theoretical enables the constitutive and defining practice of utopian discourse, which Marin calls neutralization, to occur. Precisely because it does not attain conceptual clarity, the utopian figure can maintain contradictions in a kind of half-life, neither erased nor resolved nor even, strictly speaking, contradictory, since contradiction pertains to conceptual rather than figurative discourse. Thus, the utopian figure "neutralizes" social contradictions.

While Marin retains the literary quality of the utopian figure he nevertheless defines it in its relation to theoretical discourse. Simply, the figure is to utopia what the concept is to theory; thus, through a series of analogies, the utopia is converted into an object of (scientific) scrutiny. But like Engels, Marin introduces an entirely different element into his analysis. The utopian figure is not to be read as a crystallized structure but as the trace of a process of literary production. "For the immobilizing effect [*le blocage*] of the system of ideological representation, utopia substitutes the mobility of a figure."[9] If the final "image" of utopia seems coherent and lucidly described, nevertheless the text itself arises from a mobile and heterogeneous set of productive forces that emerge to disrupt the representational surface. In his reading of More's *Utopia*, Marin shows how the apparently maplike precision of Hythlodaeus's description outlines a social space that could not possibly exist, whose various elements are mutually exclusive and dislocating. Such an approach shifts our attention, Fredric Jameson notes, from utopia as product to utopia as process: "To understand Utopian discourse in terms of neutralization is indeed precisely to propose to grasp it as a process, as *energeia*, enunciation, productivity, and implicitly or explicitly to repudiate that more traditional and conventional view of Utopia as sheer representation, as the 'realized' vision of this or that society or social ideal."[10] What matters for Marin, then, are the "plays of spaces" which disrupt the descriptive surface of the final product. "In this discourse, closed by the synopsis of a totalizing (or totalitarian) gaze, that multifarious production is signified by the noncongruence of the spaces produced: plays of spaces at once imaginary . . . and non-superimposable (multiple spaces) within the strictest coherence of a totalizing discourse." Like Engels, Marin posits utopia as an exploding text: "Utopia always appears as a rupture in a discursive continuity," a continuity established only by repressing the productive forces of the text.[11] Two points are noteworthy here. The first is that Marin's own critical figuration comes largely from the domain of psychoanalysis: the demiurgic play of utopian spaces, with their various condensations and displacements, recalls the primary processes of the Freudian dream work. And utopian figuration, which allows contradictions to emerge in a neutralized but still readable form, produces a text rather like the manifest content of a dream—not least because the "synopsis" of More's totalizing gaze, which imposes a rational structure on the primary material, performs a function like that of the Freudian secondary revision, reworking dream images into a more or less coherent narrative[12] Hence Marin's exploding text inverts Engels's: instead of thoughts bursting through fantasy, here figural plays of space erupt through a "rational shell"—the orderly and descriptive map of Utopia. At the core of the utopia there now lies play, *energeia*, productivity.

The second point, intimately connected with the first, concerns the political values Marin assigns to these primary and secondary processes. The utopian product or image, that is, the secondary revision of the utopian process, is immobilized and "totalitarian," caught in the toils of a relentlessly instrumental rationality. The primary process, by contrast, is productive and anarchic; its rupture of the totalizing shell seems somehow liberating. As Marin admits, his own politics and approach are decisively influenced by the events of May 1968, itself a utopian breach of late capitalist society.[13] "Plays of space" within the utopia are not, therefore, exclusively the register of impersonal, historical forces; there is something festive, pleasurable, *playful* about them. This side of Marin's argument remains relatively undeveloped, however, partly out of strategic considerations dictated by the tradition of *Utopia* criticism. The question of the pleasurability of utopia did not play a great (or at least a clear) role in Marxist criticism, but it did influence critics who were more methodologically and politically conservative. C. S. Lewis, for example, explicitly tried to depoliticize *Utopia* by declaring it a simple *jeu d'esprit*, which "becomes intelligible and delightful as soon as we take it for what it is—a holiday work, a spontaneous overflow [eruption?] of intellectual high spirits, a revel of debate, paradox, comedy and (above all) of invention, which starts many hares and kills none."[14] There is some truth in what Lewis says here, but he says it in order to trivialize the work and stifle debate. Interestingly, he seems in silent agreement with Engels on one point: that only a "rational kernel" could give *Utopia* political interest. But Lewis insists that there isn't one. At the same time that he characterizes the utopian text as purely pleasurable, moreover, Lewis damns the imagined Utopia as a totalitarian dungeon: "There is no freedom of speech in Utopia. There is nothing liberal in Utopia. From it, as from all other imaginary states, liberty is more successfully banished than the real world, even at its worst, allows.[15] (Lewis's ideological disciple in this regard is J. H. Hexter, who likens Utopia to Maoist China.)[16]

Before going on, we would do well to pause over Lewis's thoughts for a moment. "There is no freedom of speech in Utopia." In fact, only one restriction on speech appears in Hythlodaeus's entire description of the island: none may express their religious views so violently as to prevent others from pursuing their own beliefs in peace.[17] Far from forbidding free speech, Utopia allows more of it than any commonwealth existing in More's time or in Lewis's. And is there "nothing liberal" about an imaginary polity based on representative democracy and religious toleration at a time when no European state was? If Lewis really believed that Utopia banishes liberty more completely "than the world, even at its worst, allows," one can only conclude that he never saw the world at its worst. I enumerate these points because, while I too intend to explore the "unpleasantness" of Utopia, I believe that this unpleasantness has been exaggerated by a conservative tradition of *Utopia* criticism which thrives on ideological delusion, cold-war hysteria, and sheer intellectual dishonesty.

Nevertheless, Lewis is not alone in his assessment of *Utopia*. Marin too finds the utopian image totalitarian and thus shifts attention to the figural or rhetorical "play" of the text. Yet, if only by omission, Marin and the entire progressive tradition of *Utopia* criticism have ceded questions of pleasure and nonpleasure to the right, along with any sustained consideration of how the utopian image works to produce nonpleasure. It is as if the whole issue were an embarrassment; yet surely it is to its more or less coherent and more or less pleasing image of a socialist society that *Utopia* owes its continuing cultural life.[18]

A reading of *Utopia* along these lines may raise issues relevant to cultural Marxism as well. Fredric Jameson has done much to reopen the question of the utopian, principally (though not exclusively) as it applies to mass culture. For Jameson, the utopian is the necessary partner and other of ideology, the "bait" of fantasy or desire which the mass cultural text must dangle in front of its consumer before any ideological defusing, repression, or management can occur.[19] Jameson and Marin both regard the utopian fantasy or play as occupying a position that is somehow *primary;* this fantasy is only subsequently defused by an ideological process of "secondary revision," through whose constraining form it nevertheless continues to escape, thus granting the cultural artifact its fundamental ambivalence. As I shall argue, however, More's *Utopia* takes this model of (utopian) kernel and (ideological) shell and, in Marx's suggestively mixed metaphor, turns it on its head. For whereas *Utopia*'s finished form depicts a utopian-socialist society, this surface conceals an "interior" realm whose primal fantasy and pleasurable substance turn out to be—the logic of capital itself.

## The Monkey in the Middle

From the beginning, *Utopia* announces its independence from the tradition of philosophical discourse. Included in the parerga, or prefatory materials, is what claims to be a "quatrain in the Utopian vernacular," in which the island itself seems to speak. It begins: "Utopus, my ruler, converted me, formerly not an island, into an island. Alone of all lands, without the aid of abstract philosophy, I have represented to mortals the philosophical city [absque philosophia / Civitatem philosophicam expressi mortalibus]" (18–19). "Without philosophy." That is to say, Utopia results from practice rather than from dialectical argument; it is the product of labor, not cognition. Yet this island expresses itself in ways other than merely being: it speaks, and does so in a pleasanter discourse than that of philosophical reasoning. The poem as a mode of discourse embodies the island's antiphilosophical bias.

In *Utopia* proper, the island "speaks" by means of its visitor and advocate, Raphael Hythlodaeus, whose surname the Yale edition translates as "expert in trifles" or "well-learned in nonsense" (p. 301). Now both translations are misleading, especially the latter, whose elegant paradox seems to place Hythlodaeus in the position of a bearer of false knowledge. The point is an important one, since Hythlodaeus's name has been used to ironize his entire discourse, both his criticism of contemporary European society and his description of Utopia. The Penguin edition of *Utopia* substitutes "Nonsenso" for Hythlodaeus, with predictable results.[20] More almost certainly encountered the word *hythlos* in Plato, where to be sure it is used pejoratively to mean "idle talk" or "nonsense." In the *Theaetetus*, the word appears in the phrase *graon hythlos*, or "old wives' chatter" (176b). In the *Lysis*, Socrates asks, "[Was] our earlier statement about friends . . . all mere drivel [*hythlos*], like a poem strung out for mere length?"(221d).[21] In neither case does *hythlos* designate that which is false within the sphere of philosophical discourse. Rather, it designates nonphilosophical speech, the gossip of old women or poetry spun out for its own sake. The word seems to describe speech that aims at pleasure rather than knowledge. Plato uses it consistently to denote the *evasion* of dialectic (for example, *Republic* 336d). Similarly, *daios*, the second half of Hythlodaeus, does not mean "learned," in a philosophical or a scholarly sense, but "experienced," "cunning," "skilled" as an artisan might be skilled at his craft. A better translation of "Hythlodaeus" might be "skilled in pleasant speech."[22]

Hythlodaeus thus represents a mode of discourse which finds no place—not even the place of the false—within philosophical dialectic, just as Utopia finds no place within a society that produces such a dialectic. As the humanist Guillaume Budé writes in a prefatory letter, "Utopia lies outside the limits of the known world" (12–13), where *mundi cogniti* might also be taken to mean the world proper to or produced by cognition. Marin designates this extraterritorial realm, this utopia of philosophy, as the space of the figure. I shall call it that of the *hythlos*, of pleasurable speech. In book 1 of *Utopia*, Peter Giles introduces Hythlodaeus to More as "one whose conversation he hoped would give me pleasure" (51); later, when Hythlodaeus has recounted the events at Cardinal Morton's table, More responds: "To be sure, my dear Raphael, [with your narrative] you have given me great pleasure [*voluptate*]" (85). In book 2 Hythlodaeus describes the island, which is also known as "eutopia," or "the happy place."

Utopia, then, represents itself by means of discourse that privileges pleasure over knowledge and employs knowledge primarily to produce pleasure. And yet the image of Utopia is not always pleasurable; in many respects life there seems regimented and spiritually impoverished. Stephen Greenblatt notes a "pattern [that] is repeated again and again in Hythlodaeus's account: freedoms are heralded, only to shrink in the course of the description."[23] Greenblatt catches not only the existence but also the rhythm of the dystopian countertheme, the way in which an initial sense of liberation or well-being progressively and almost imperceptibly degenerates into a feeling of entrapment. This rhythm is familiar from certain kinds of anxiety dreams, a resource on which antiutopian literature continually battens.

As an example of withering freedom Greenblatt offers the case of travel.[24] Utopians who desire to visit cities other than their own may do so, but (we soon learn) only after receiving a certificate of permission from the local governor. Persons caught traveling without this certificate are subject to punishment of enslavement (145–47). The image of bureaucratic intrusiveness and penal excess is disturbing enough, but something else, even stranger, is going on here. Long before the section on travel, Hythlodaeus informs us that the island's fifty-four cities are "identical in language, traditions, customs, and laws. They are similar also in layout and everywhere, so far as the nature of the ground permits, similar even in appearance" (113). Indeed, "the person who knows one of the cities will know them all, since they are exactly alike insofar as the terrain admits" (117). One cannot help wondering, then, what could incite Utopians to visit other cities in the first place. It seems to make as little sense as exchanging their identical garments would. Restrictions on travel are not only confining, then; they are apparently unmotivated. The prohibition prompts us to infer an underlying wish, but here that wish is impossible to

locate; Utopia simply provides no place for it. Utopians, one sup-
poses, would no more understand the desire to visit new places
than they understand the desire of the Anemolian ambassadors to
deck themselves with gold. Europeans, on the other hand, would
understand it perfectly. And here we come to one of the characteristic features of Utopia. It prohibits desires that, strictly speaking,
can only arise elsewhere—specifically, in that dystopian "other" of
Europe, whose failings motivated the production of the utopian
image in the first place.

This repressed mode of reference works oddly in conjunction
with the clear topical allusions Utopia makes to England. As Jameson points out, "such play of topical allusion is structurally indispensable in the constitution of the Utopian text as such and
provides one of the distinctive traits necessary if we are to mark
the Utopia off from its generic neighbors in the realm of fantasy or
idyll."[25] These allusions signal that Utopia is a determinate reworking or transformation of an ideological image of England. Several paradigms have been offered to describe this transformational
practice. Utopia may be seen as the Platonic form of England or as
its anagogical redemption. For Marin, the Utopian figure is the
"neutral" of English social contradictions. In the repressed reference, however, an entirely different relationship obtains. England
does not appear as historical or geographical or social referent. It is
simply the imputed site of a desire whose existence is marked only
by a prohibition against it. England becomes that *andere Schau-
platz* (to use Freud's term) on which Utopian desire is staged. In
short, England occupies the position of the unconscious with respect to Utopia. It arises as a wish rather than a contradiction, although it gives birth to both contradiction and repression in the
Utopian narrative. And the emergent wish does not cause a dislocation of the Utopian topography; it does not assume the form of a
"space" that breaks up the Utopian "map" (Marin). Instead, it disrupts the *logic* of the text and, moreover, converts Utopia into the
repression of a wish that it cannot possibly contain (in any
sense).[26]

A telling example of this phenomenon occurs in the famous passage that describes how the Utopians store their gold. In their socialized economy gold has no use as a means of exchange;
nevertheless the island hoards it in case of war. But the storage of
the metal presents difficulties.

> If in Utopia these metals were kept locked up in a tower, it might
> be suspected that the governor and the senate—for such is the fool-

ish imagination of the common folk—were deceiving the people by the scheme and they themselves were deriving some benefit therefrom. Moreover, if they made them into drinking vessels and other such skilled handiwork, then if occasion arose for them all to be melted down again and applied to the pay of soldiers, they realize that people would be unwilling to be deprived of what they had once begun to treasure.

To avoid these dangers, they have devised a means which, as it is consonant with the rest of their institutions, so it is extremely unlike our own—seeing that we value gold so much and are so careful in safeguarding it—and therefore incredible except to those who have experience of it. While they eat and drink from earthenware and glassware of fine workmanship but of little value, from gold and silver they make chamber pots and all the humblest vessels for use everywhere, not only in the common halls but in private homes also. Moreover, they employ the same metals to make the chains and solid fetters which they put on their slaves. Finally, as for those who bear the stigma of disgrace on account of some crime, they have gold ornaments hanging from their ears, gold rings encircling their fingers, and, as a last touch a gold crown encircling their temples. Thus by every means in their power they make gold and silver a mark of illfame. (151–53)

This ritual debasement of gold is in some ways *the* quintessentially Utopian act. Economically, it signals the ascendancy of use value over exchange value and demonstrates that the production of goods in Utopia aims at satisfying needs rather than extracting profit. More generally, it manifests the cultural origin of all values and thus underwrites the Utopian project as a whole. The desire to accumulate gold is not part of human nature but the product of an institutional system of private property. It can thus be overcome; society can create itself anew.

The logic of this Utopian practice is contradictory, however, as C. S. Lewis points out: "The suggestion that the acquisitive impulse should be mortified by using gold to purposes of dishonor is infantile if we take it as a practical proposal. If gold in Utopia were plentiful enough to be so used, gold in Utopia would not be a precious metal."[27] To debase gold in Utopia in order to discourage private hoarding would be like debasing iron for similar purposes in Europe. Gold is superabundant in Utopia; moreover, the whole sphere of exchange value does not exist there. Thus a Utopian indifference to gold would make sense; a ritual debasement of it, on the other hand, suggests a desire that must be repressed.[28] The situation recalls that of travel, which arises as a question only because of a prohibition against it. Thus the passage on gold turns against itself. Far from devaluing gold, the Utopian practice invests it with an innate desirability that transcends all social contexts. What the text has done is to transform social value (gold as the congealed product of social labor: exploration, mining, refining, and so on) into a quality of the thing itself. This is the very process Marx immortalized as the fetishism of the commodity.

> The mysterious character of the commodity-form consists therefore simply in the fact that the commodity reflects the social characteristics of men's own labor as objective characteristics of the products of labor themselves, as the socio-natural properties of these things. . . . [But] the commodity-form, and the value-relation of the products of labor within which it appears, have absolutely no connection with the physical nature of the commodity and the natural [*dinglich*] relations arising out of this. It is nothing but the definite social relation between men themselves which assumes here, for them, the fantastic form of a relation between things. . . . I call this the fetishism that attaches itself to the products of labor as soon as they are produced as commodities, and is therefore inseparable from the production of commodities.[29]

Commodity fetishism causes the social origin of value to disappear from consciousness. What replaces it is, on the one hand, an innately valuable "thing" and, on the other hand, an equally mysterious valuation of it on the part of the subject. Value, Marx notes, "does not have its description branded on its forehead; it rather transforms every product of labor into a social hieroglyphic."[30] A hieroglyphic: on the surface, a figure or discourse of valuable objects and their relations and, beneath, an occulted figure or discourse of social relations, which becomes the unconscious of the system of commodity production, revealing itself only through the "symptom" of mysterious value relations among objects. It is this fetishism that causes values to become naturalized or reified in Utopia. And it is this same fetishism that puts English social relations in the position of the "unconscious" of Utopia, to emerge as inexplicable and imperishable desires. Ironically, then, the famous passage on the debasement of gold is shot through with the logic of the commodity. *Utopia* thus takes its place as a transitional work by testifying both to the birth of a capitalist economy and to its foreclosure from discourse. For these two developments are necessarily intertwined. The fetishism of the commodity is nothing but the repression of the social content of productive labor, a repression that results from the social decoding of commodity exchange through the use of abstract labor power as a universal equivalent. Historically, the economy could become an autonomous social instance, and hence the object of its own "science," only at the same moment that its real workings were repressed from the field of vision. The same contradictions that would soon afflict economics as a scientific discourse are here anticipated by *Utopia*'s literary discourse.

We have not yet exhausted the peculiarities of this passage, however. Its more general motivation—to demonstrate the social origin of value—is disrupted by the phenomenon of reification, as we have seen, but so is its more specific motivation—to exalt use value or utility over exchange value. Utopia devalues gold by working it into objects of low prestige, which the Utopians presumably wouldn't mind relinquishing in times of war. But here again the logic of the scheme is flawed. Chamber pots may be unglamorous, but they are hardly useless; their sudden confiscation would prove inconvenient. And this is as nothing compared to the idea of liquidating the chains of slaves and criminals at the very moment that the country is going to war. The image of Utopia during wartime—toiletless and ranged by newly freed malcontents—is not an appealing one. It is use value, then, that is finally debased here. In their storage of gold, the Utopians operate a system of pure social prestige to which utility must be sacrificed. The items used to debase gold aren't at all useless; they simply occupy a low rung on a scale of invidious differences and thus are expendable in the end.

That the Utopians have only redistributed the elements in a system of social difference becomes clear in the episode of the Anemolian ambassadors. Not only do the ambassadors fail to impress the Utopians by decking themselves in gold and jewels, but they find themselves subjected to scorn and laughter. Nor is the Utopians' laughter of a popular festive variety designed to bring the haughty Anemolians down to their level. Rather, the Utopians "looked with contempt on silk and regarded gold as a badge of disgrace. . . . They therefore bowed to the lowest of the party as to the masters but took the ambassadors themselves to be slaves because they were wearing gold chains, and passed them over without any deference whatever" (155). The Utopians observe a punctilious social decorum, scraping before the powerful and ignoring what they take to be servants. They thus act like Europeans, only they misread the elements that constitute social prestige.

While the problem of reification assumes a particularly direct and striking form in the treatment of gold, it informs a wide range of Utopian social strategies. Utopia frequently tries to reform social desire by manipulating the *things* that serve as the apparent objects of desire. Such is the case with clothing: "As for clothes, these are of one and the same style throughout the island and down the centuries, though there is a distinction between the sexes and between the single and married. The garments are comely to the eye [literally, "nec ad oculam indecora (not displeasing to the eye)"], convenient for bodily movement, and fit for wear in heat and cold" (127). Stephen Greenblatt comments: "The Utopians . . . take pains to reduce sharply the number of points of reference by which men mark themselves off from each other. The uniformity of dress strikes out not only against vanity but against the elaborate distinctions of rank and occupation that were reflected (and legally regulated) in Tudor dress."[31] Recognizing that the English aristocracy uses fashion as a form of social domination, More helps to destroy the class system by destroying the fashion code. Only in this case he does so by substituting a numbing uniformity for invidious distinction. Not only do Utopians dress like monks, but their very plainness assumes a strange prestige when they confront foreigners. What Utopia (and More) is finally unable to imagine is an aesthetics of dress which would be sumptuous without being invidious—something the island's community of property could supply. Nothing prevents the Utopians from using part of their seemingly endless surplus to dress everyone on the island attractively, but More cannot finally disengage clothing—or the aesthetic in general—from its articulation within class society. In a sense, More is not always adequate to his social conception in *Utopia*. He falls back on reified strategies of ascetic manipulation, and the result of his excessive utilitarianism is that paradoxical state, a "starvation" of luxury. The Utopian dress code must look like a proscription, even if it is not framed as one. As usual, it evokes desire by means of repression or privation.

Stylistically, this phenomenon expresses itself in the figure of litotes, which Elizabeth McCutcheon has shown to be the dominant rhetorical figure in *Utopia*.[32] McCutcheon brilliantly connects More's use of the double negative both to the fictional structure of *Utopia* and to the problems of humanist irony and rhetorical undecidability. I suggest another symbolic use of litotes: it expresses how Utopian pleasure arises as the opposite of that which is forbidden, unavailable, or withheld, that is to say, as the negation of a negation. In the passage on clothing, for example, "comeliness" is expressed in the phrase "nec ad oculum indecora [not displeasing to the eye]." Not only does this expression tend to minimize the beauty of Utopian clothing, but more paradigmatically it posits pleasurableness as the negation of displeasure. On a microlevel, this expression performs similarly to the island's travel restrictions.

Utopia, then, is locked in a tension of opposites. The island itself is constructed as the repression of desires it cannot locate and of which it cannot take account. This is why the deconstruction of its surface is experienced as a liberation. It is not enough to say, with Macherey, that the literary text fails to cohere, or with Marin, that the Utopian space is "noncongruent" with itself. Utopia is not merely incoherent; it *explodes*, and this explosion is felt as a pleasurable release. Utopian negation is not, therefore, always neutralizing. It can also function as a barrier or dam.

In one of the more important prefatory letters to Utopia, Peter Giles (the real one writing as the character) explains why the directions to Utopia were lost. Hythlodaeus, it turns out, did give the island's latitude and longitude.

> But, somehow or other, an unlucky accident caused us both to fail to catch what he said. While Raphael was speaking on the topic, one of More's servants had come up to him to whisper something or other in his ear. I was therefore listening all the more intently when one of our company who had, I suppose, caught cold on shipboard, coughed so loudly that I lost some phrases of what Raphael said. (23)

That a cough obscures the way to Utopia is not accidental. If not a positive pleasure, coughing is at least an explosive release of bodily tension or an irritating pressure. It is therefore the body's revolt against Utopia. Of course, the materiality of the body does define the structure of pleasure; it imposes, if you will, a certain figuration on it. But in *Utopia*, this figuration is also made to bear all that the work's social vision cannot account for. It becomes the repository for the social desire that the Utopian image reifies and thus works to naturalize the antiutopian elements of the work. The ideological lesson is clear enough: "Human nature," even the body itself, essentially resists all forms of socialization. Utopia is impossible because it denies our "deepest urges." What this formulation misses, however, is how the book *installs* these "deepest urges" by its reification of social desire. What escapes a problematic can return as myth, often as the myth of nature. In *Utopia* this problem is emblematized in the episode of the ape and the Greek books, which Hythlodaeus recounts in the course of explaining how readily the Utopians assimilate Western culture, especially Greek culture.

> When about to go on the fourth voyage, I put on board, in place of wares to sell, a fairly large package of books, having made up my mind never to return rather than to come back soon. They received from me most of Plato's works, several of Aristotle's, as well as Theophrastus on plants, which I regret to say was mutilated in parts. During the voyage an ape found the book, left lying carelessly about, and in wanton sport tore out and destroyed several pages in various sections. (181)

Marin interprets the ape as the symbol of a nonrational, mutilating, and consummative form of reading.[33] The ape materializes the text, converting it from spiritual to bodily nourishment (wittily, the text is a study of plants, the ape's natural food). The ape thus represents a festive alternative to the Utopian assimilation of Western culture. In a way, the image complements the themes of the Utopian "quatrain" in the parerga to the work. To "eat" the text is to engage in an antiphilosophical mode of reading that elevates pleasure over knowledge. By its mode of consumption, the ape converts philosophy/science into *hythlos*. Of course, the pleasure produced here is more destructive and feral than that which emerged from the quatrain. Furthermore, the figure of the ape and the Greek books does not apply only to Utopia's external relations; it also emblematizes the internal structure of Utopia itself by producing a dystopian counterimage of it. The ape clearly represents those "baser urges" that underlie human rationality (embodied in the books) and anarchically consume all structures of order. As the representative of an animalistic pleasure principle, the ape ruptures the "rational shell" of Utopia in the same way that the cough obscures the position of the island. As an ideological figure the ape is a proto-Hobbesian "natural man" who blindly tears all intellectual and social fabrics. He happens to eat a work of Theophrastus, but he might as well have eaten *Utopia* itself. By embodying "nature," the ape grounds the dystopian countertheme of the work in the most ideologically powerful of myths. But it must be recalled that this bundle of irrational impulses is the ideological precipitate of the text itself. If Utopia has a monkey in the middle, one which "everywhere tears through its . . . [rational] covering," this is because the reified impulse is the necessary and dialectical mirror image of the reified commodity.

## Capital in Sheep's Clothing

Recent criticism of *Utopia*—and again I am thinking especially of Marin and Jameson—has suggested how reification informs the very generic constitution of utopian discourse. As a mode of writing that relies primarily on description, the utopia tends invariably to replace the dynamics of social or historical process with the stasis of the image, the representation, the map. In More's *Utopia*, certainly, the abstraction and stasis of the descriptions contribute to the sense of moribund rigidity that pervades Utopian society. More reinforces this effect by downplaying Hythlodaeus's role as narrator, thus producing a "white" discourse: an objective, autonomous, and seemingly self-generating description that lacks human origin or agency.

Any reading of book 2 thus has as its prerequisite the disruption of Utopia's discursive self-sufficiency, the resolution of its apparently lucid descriptions into textual and social processes. And here the first book of *Utopia* plays a critical role. Hythlodaeus's discussions of the contemporary social crisis, which provide a rationale for the utopian project itself, also expose the historical processes that later congeal into the reified descriptions of book 2. And this is so even if More's depiction of historical conditions is itself ideological, as we must assume if book 1 is not also to take on a false transparency.

But book 1 carries out its dereifying work on the level of form as well. The dialogical structure of the book foregrounds the human and social agency that frames the production of discourse, while the disruptive temporality of narrative undoes the illusory stasis that settles over book 2's descriptions. For Marin, narrative is the supreme figural embodiment of history, hence the privileged decoder of descriptive reification.[34] Of course Utopian narrative can itself be resolved into the temporal (diachronic) displacements of contemporary (synchronic) contradictions. It may be that neither description nor narration enjoys a privileged figural relation to history. In More's work, at least, each tends to collapse into the other. I myself explore book 1 not because its figural or representational elements can "interpret" the rest of the work but simply because it expands the range of such figures and interpretations.

In defending his decision not to become an adviser to kings, Raphael Hythlodaeus constructs a wide-ranging critique of the political and economic institutions of his day. If his discourse is ultimately incoherent, if it, like the rest of More's text, is structured by contradictions it cannot fully grasp, it nevertheless displays an astonishing and recurrent clarity regarding the fundamental historical processes at work in sixteenth-century England.[35] For our purposes the most directly relevant part of Hythlodaeus's discourse is his narrated conversation at the table of Cardinal Morton, especially his debate with the lawyer about the causes of thievery in England.

> It happened one day that I was at [Morton's] table when a layman, learned in the laws of your country, was present. Availing himself of some opportunity or other, he began to speak punctiliously of the strict justice which was then dealt out to thieves. They were everywhere executed, he reported, as many as twenty at a time being hanged on one gallows, and he added that he wondered all the more, though so few escaped execution, by what bad luck the whole country was still infested with them. (60)

The lawyer's evident satisfaction at the strictness of English justice is clouded by the inexplicable proliferation of the very crime it is meant to eliminate. His bafflement thus reproduces a characteristically Utopian structure: a proscription becomes the site of a mysterious surplus, which in turn proves to be a mysterious desire or impulse. Thieves "voluntarily prefer to be rascals [sponte mali esse mallent]" (61), though this preference obeys no evident logic. An ethical discourse, which posits an innate will to transgress, here comes to the aid of a legal system whose social logic is evidently foundering.

Hythlodaeus dereifies this magical "will to steal" by revealing that thievery is actually the result of class domination.[36] Theft proliferates in England, he argues, not because men are evil but because large portions of the population have been thrown out of work and have turned to stealing as the only way to support themselves. This vagrant population is composed of dismissed feudal retainers and manorial servants, on the one hand, and agricultural populations deracinated by sheep enclosure, on the other. Hythlodaeus's eloquent response thus completes the homology between the lawyer's discourse and the structure of Utopia. Not only does a proscription signal a magical excess of desire, but this desire is shown to originate "elsewhere," only in this case that elsewhere is discursive rather than geographical. The displacement is not from Utopia to England but from ethical to sociohistorical discourse. History now emerges as the repressed "political unconscious" of the ethical; to reveal the structuring effects of history is to dereify and dissolve the mysterious impulses of ethical thought.

The lawyer's reified logic doesn't so much displace social relations onto things as produce a fictive subjectivity for its own purposes. When economic necessity forces a certain class to steal, their prosecution is justified, ideologically sealed, by falsely taking the prohibition against theft to oppose a *wish*, on the assumption that all prohibitions arise in response to desires that predate them.[37] Not desire but its simulacrum intervenes to shore up the coherence of an ideological discourse. Moreover, Hythlodaeus's explanation, which reveals the fictive quality of this purported will or impulse to steal, also replaces this "thing" with a nothing, a lack (of productive work, of subsistence). I shall return to this point later.

In the meantime I call attention to the rhetorical as well as the conceptual brilliance of Hythlodaeus's discourse. His discussion of sheep enclosures deserves quoting at length:

> "Yet this [the presence of discharged retainers and standing armies] is not the only situation that makes thieving necessary. There is another which, as I believe, is more special to you Englishmen."
>
> "What is that?" asked the Cardinal
>
> "Your sheep," I answered, "which are usually so tame and so cheaply fed, begin now, according to report, to be so greedy and wild that they devour human beings themselves and devastate and depopulate fields, houses, and towns. In all those parts of the realm where the finest and therefore the costliest wool is produced, there are noblemen, gentlemen, and even some abbots, though otherwise holy men, who are not satisfied with the annual revenues and profits which their predecessors used to derive from the estates. They are not content, by leading an idle and sumptuous life, to do no good to their country; they must also do it positive harm. They leave no ground to be tilled; they enclose every bit of land for pasture; they pull down houses and destroy towns, leaving only the church to pen the sheep in. . . .
>
> Consequently, in order that one insatiable glutton and accursed plague of his native land may join field to field and surround many thousand acres with his fence, tenants are evicted. Some of them either circumvented by fraud or overwhelmed by violence, are stripped

> even of their own property, or else, wearied by unjust acts, are driven
> to sell. . . . All their household goods which would not fetch a great
> price if they could wait for a purchaser, since they must be thrust
> out, they sell for a trifle.
>
> After they have soon spent that trifle in wandering from place to
> place, what remains for them but to steal and be hanged—justly, you
> may say!—or to wander and beg." (66–67)

Hythlodaeus's attack on enclosure begins with a witty metonymy:
not the landowners but the sheep themselves depopulate the countryside. By blaming the animal victims of this process Hythlodaeus parodies the corresponding metonymy that allows the
lawyer to blame its human victims. Moreover, he invests the sheep
with a malignant *will*. Like the deracinated farmers they used to
be "tame and cheaply fed" but now have become "greedy and
wild." By reproducing the lawyer's logic on these dummy subjects,
Hythlodaeus reveals the purely simulacral nature of the "voluntary preference" for stealing and thus dereifies the lawyer's ethical
discourse. The sheep may be taken as answering figures to the ape
in book 2, revealing how natural and human drives can be constructed ideologically.[38]

In a number of respects Hythlodaeus's battle with the lawyer anticipates, and even influences, Marx's later critique of "so-called
primitive accumulation."[39] Like those conservative political economists who revert to ethical thinking in order to explain poverty—
inventing a class of "lazy rascals, spending all their substance, and
more, in riotous living"—More's lawyer claims that impoverished
thieves "voluntarily prefer to be rascals." And in response Hythlodaeus employs a series of dereifying strategies strikingly similar to
Marx's, replacing ethical categories with a historical narrative focusing on enclosure and other violent acts of class expropriation.
Like Marx, too, Hythlodaeus sees the abolition of private property
as the only real solution to class violence. But this option he saves
for his discussion with More; at Morton's table his proposals are
much less radical. Antienclosure legislation, the abolition of monopolies, the encouragement of crafts, the employment of the poor
(69–71): while passionately stated, Hythlodaeus's proposals are not
very different from some of the legislative measures halfheartedly
adopted by the Tudor state. In fact, the lawyer and Hythlodaeus
divide Tudor antivagrancy strategies between them: one sort demands punishment and repression and the other hopes to *recode*
the vagrant poor within the traditional productive regime. But

Hythlodaeus's response is no more practical than the lawyer's. Indeed, although his analysis is keener and more progressive, Hythlodaeus also shares the lawyer's fear of the vagrant poor, particularly of discharged retainers and former soldiers trained in violence. His proposed reforms, while humane, are already tainted with the failure of Tudor attempts at recoding and thus point to the need for a more radical utopian solution.

Yet Utopia's obsession with surveillance and control seems also to be a recoding operation conducted with the vagrant masses silently in mind. In this respect its project is largely consonant with that of the Tudor state, despite its apparent opposition to it. Utopia's fully productive citizens are the direct antitypes of English vagrants, as is suggested by their very names. If the residents of book 2 are "Utopians" because they live in a place called "Nowhere," the vagrants of book 1 are also "utopian" in the very different sense that they have nowhere to live.[40] Their territorial nomadism, the lack of an inhabitable *topos,* merely expresses the fact that they occupy no place within the productive regime, or indeed within the polity at large. Yet if English vagrants in one sense embody the dysfunctional or "dystopian" aspects of the English polity, if they represent a problem Utopia will attempt to recode, yet from another perspective they are already latently utopian. Precisely because they have been expelled from society, the decoded masses are perfect subjects for imaginative recombination. Stripped of all prior social bonds, they have been suitably prepared for entrance into the utopian polity.[41] Since More cannot imagine a transition from the structures of English society to those of its Utopian counterpart, he proceeds by means of the destructured excrescences of that society. Thus if Utopia represents an attempt to "recode" late feudalism, in another sense it requires the complete decoding of this formation in order to realize itself. While it strains against social dissolution, it must also push it to its limits. The Utopian polity will thus rework, in a displaced form, the English contradiction between economic decoding and attempted juridical recoding by the Tudor state.

One example of such decoding/recoding is the Utopian management of residence. All Utopian citizens spend at least two years doing agricultural labor, resulting in a regulated exchange of urban and rural populations: "Twenty from each household [in the country] return every year to the city, namely, those having completed two years in the country. As substitutes in their place, the same number are sent from the city" (115). Like English vagrants,

Utopians have no permanent residence. But in this case deracination is part of a social logic, indeed the very basis of a productive regime, rather than its discarded precipitate. Within the cities, too, the doors of all houses are unlocked and "every ten years they actually exchange their very houses by lot" (121). In the practice of a purely aleatory exchange, the principle of absolute decoding appears as such. Yet that which in England produces a mass outside the polity (that is, renders it u-topian with respect to the polity) here produces an interiorized and regulated flow. Traveling without permission, on the other hand, brings a penalty from the Utopian state just as it would from Tudor. But note: in Utopia such vagrancy *really is* voluntary, though inexplicably so, since Utopian vagrants really do have someplace to live, unlike the deracinated masses of England. In a sense, then, Utopia fulfills the rationale of Tudor vagrancy laws better than England ever could. Hythlodaeus shows English vagrants to be social victims and coerced lawbreakers. But by eliminating the alibi of need, Utopia produces exactly what the law craves: a voluntary transgressor, the perfect juridical subject.

Not that the Utopian polity achieves any ideological closure thereby. In fact, restrictions on travel prove to be a prime example of utopian incoherence. What emerges as striking is rather a structural affinity between English and Utopian disruptions. The debate over theft began with the concept of a prohibition, hence with the categories of the licit and the illicit. But this dipole or antithesis was almost immediately disrupted by the problem of excess: for the lawyer, an excess of thieves and, for Hythlodaeus, an excess of punishment. "This manner of punishing thieves goes beyond justice and is not for the public good," he says. "It is too harsh a penalty for theft and yet is not a sufficient deterrent" (61). Hythlodaeus then introduces the complementary concept of lack: theft arises from a lack of subsistence, employment, a place to live. The ideological structure of the debate may be represented by a pair of perpendicular (and hence incommensurable) axes: one of the licit and the illicit, the other of excess and lack. Utopian legality, as embodied in travel restrictions, is similarly transected. The desire to travel appears as a mysterious excess, mysterious (and excessive) because nothing could prompt it, because when we search for its motivation we find nothing, an absence. Not a positive lack, as in England, the lack that drives vagrants to steal, a need that cries out for fulfillment. Rather, a neutral lack, the blank absence of any motivation (Utopian monotony). In one case a lack that causes motion; in the other a lack that renders motion incomprehensible. In one case a lack that founds a social explanation and thus solves a mystery; in the other a lack that signals a reification and is itself a mystery.

Classical Greek knew two forms of the negative. The negative of will or thought, *me*, signaled an impediment or prohibition. The negative of fact or statement, *ou*, signaled nonfact, nonbeing, emptiness. It is the latter that attaches itself to Utopia, marking it as the absence rather than the denial of place. We originally approached Utopia through the problem of prohibition, but (as in the debate on theft) the categories of the licit or illicit were at least partially displaced by the problems of excess and lack. In a prefatory poem to *Utopia*, Cornelius de Schrijver invites the reader to "experience the great emptiness lying at the heart of things [quantum rebus inane latet]" (30–31). In fact, Utopia does have an emptiness at its heart; the island itself is moon-shaped, curving around a placid body of water at its center: "The bay is like a huge lake, smooth rather than rough, and thus converts almost the whole center [alvum] of the country into a harbor" (111). The Latin *alvum*, translated as "center," literally means stomach or womb. Ironically, this island of abundance has an empty stomach, subtly recalling the hungry English vagrants for whom it might serve as haven. England is filled with the empty stomachs of need, a positive lack; the Utopian stomach is a neutral lack, the calm lake of nondesire.

In the debate on theft the concept of lack helps to dereify an ethicolegal discourse by revealing the social causes of criminal behavior. More generally stated, the ideologeme excess/lack disrupts or destabilizes the ideologeme licit/illicit.[42] I would go so far as to suggest that this volatile noncongruence between ideologemes dominates the workings of *Utopia* as a whole and that it conceptually figures (for and through More) some important elements in the transition to capitalism. In book 1 Hythlodaeus's analysis of the contemporary social crisis centers on two of these elements: the depredations of absolutist monarchy and the displacement of the agricultural populations. Both may be discussed in terms of "power," but it is crucial to distinguish between political and economic power if we are not to homogenize a complex historical process. The Tudor state operated mainly through its politico-juridical apparatuses, issuing laws and decrees, granting monopolies, levying taxes, and so forth. State power assumes the forms of injunctions and prohibitions, and thus aligns itself with the axis of the licit and the illicit. In book 1 the reformer is always encountering a web of decorums and prohibitions, some explicitly stated, others implicitly. The "practical philosophy" of More the persona, which employs an "indirect method" (99) of political counsel, tries not to overstep the bounds of licit discourse, but it cannot erase these bounds. Likewise, the author More's whole method of political critique, with its masking personae (Hythlodaeus) and displacing substitutions (of, say, Henry VII's England for that of Henry VIII), enacts an elaborate dance around the borders of allowable speech. Like so many Renaissance texts, *Utopia* renders visible the prohibitions under which it labors.

The concept of lack, however, cannot be contained by either the licit or the illicit; it is decoded with respect to this axis and hence with respect to the politico-juridical discourse of the state. Hythlodaeus introduces this concept in reference to an economic process (enclosures prompted by a new market in wool) and uses it primarily to describe economic realities (lack of means of subsistence or of a place in the productive regime). I suggest that the axis of lack/excess serves in More's text as the ideologeme of the economic and that its disruption of the axis licit/illicit figures a crucial aspect of the transitional period: the preliminary emergence of the economic as an autonomous instance, its initial disengagement from the politico-juridical, with which it had been implicated in feudal production. I speak here of an ideologeme of the economic because the axis of excess and lack cannot fully represent a real economic process; rather, it works negatively by pointing out the incompleteness of a politico-juridical discourse, by revealing its decoded other. (It is, significantly, the failure of the *lawyer's* arguments that first allows an economic discourse to emerge.) Under generalized commodity production all exchanges occur within a code of equivalence, that of abstract value, and this includes the purchase of labor power which is the basis of capitalist exploitation. The extraction of surplus value within capitalist production can occur without any coercion by the state; exploitation of this sort eludes any politico-juridical discourse of "power" because it is decoded with respect to it. The coded homogeneity of commodity exchange in turn produces a class structure that is both decoded and heterogeneous; that is, whose heterogeneity is not defined by a law or coded boundary. No prohibition separates classes under advanced Western capitalism; no sumptuary laws, for instance, legislate modes of dress. It is simply that the extraction of surplus value survives within, and often thrives on, the politico-juridical equality of all classes.[43]

In book 1 of *Utopia* the deracinated classes play the role of this decoded other with respect to a penal system whose victims they become but whose logic they defy. The penal practices of Utopia itself seem designed primarily to recontain or recode the system of punishment and thus to render the juridico-political discourse of the state "full" again. In response to the threat of a decoded mass, Utopia revives the institution of slavery as final form of recoding, producing a caste or a signed social division. In a sense, the Utopian penal system tries to please both Hythlodaeus and the lawyer. By eliminating need, the island can punish its citizens in good conscience: "Their own countrymen are dealt with more harshly [than prisoners of war], since their conduct is regarded as all the more regrettable and deserving a more severe punishment as an object lesson because, having had an excellent rearing to a virtuous life, they still could not be restrained from crime" (185). Since Utopia has eliminated private property, the crime of theft is impossible there. But the persistence of other crimes might seem to contradict Hythlodaeus's need theory. Apparently, Utopian criminals "voluntarily prefer to be rascals," to quote the lawyer at Morton's table. In fact, however, neither Hythlodaeus's arguments in book 1 nor the Utopian project of book 2 were ever designed to eliminate the ethical concept of the will. By introducing the topic of need, Hythlodaeus hopes to correct but not abandon traditional concepts of legality; his reformist project aims to save not only a population but a kind of discourse as well. By banishing need, Utopia similarly produces a perfected ethical and juridical subject whose moral workings are "unclouded" by economic factors.

Marin sees the survival of criminal behavior in Utopia and among the Polylerites are marking a textual contradiction: the persistence of the "ethicotheological" despite the fulfillment of Hythlodaeus's "sociohistorical" thesis. But this apparent contradiction arises because Marin attends to only half of this thesis. Lack's corresponding term is excess, which also comes into play when Hythlodaeus describes enclosers as "insatiable glutton[s]" (67) and declares that "the unscrupulous greed of a few [paucorum improba cupiditas] is ruining the very thing by virtue of which your island was once counted fortunate in the extreme" (69). Hythlodaeus's attempt to rewrite the ethical as the social now appears to be only partly successful, asymmetrically so. The criminality of the poor is shown to be prompted by need, which in turn results from the depredations of the wealthy. But this only pushes the mystery one step back; in place of men who "voluntarily prefer to be rascals," we now find "insatiable gluttons" driven by "unscrupulous greed." Another desire now founds the social process, this time the *auri sacra fames.* Nor is this hunger the property of a particular social class: "Not only the servants of noblemen but the craftsmen and almost the clodhoppers themselves, in fact all classes alike, are given to much ostentatious sumptuousness of dress and to excessive indulgence at table" (69). The concept of need can serve Hythlodaeus as a rational principle for social discourse, both because it offers a causal explanation of other phenomena and because it is self-limiting: hunger ends with a certain degree of nourishment, need ends at a certain zero level of satisfaction. Greed, on the other hand, takes off inexplicably from that purported zero degree and knows no limit: "When every man aims at *absolute ownership of all the property he can get*, it is all shared by a handful who leave all the rest in poverty" (105, my emphasis).[44] Excess erases the supposed zero degree of need; since the desire to accumulate is infinite, eliminating abject poverty will not eliminate theft. Expropriation is now the normal state of society. The persistence of theft among the Polylerites is no mystery (pace Marin), for they still use money, hence recognize private ownership, hence allow of infinite accumulation, hence occasionally steal to get things. The land of the Polylerites is only a partial utopia, the imaginary projection of a reformist policy. For Hythlodaeus, the problem of excess knows of only one solution, and that is systemic: elimination of private ownership. Thus yet another asymmetry straddles the axis of lack and excess. Not only is lack rational and self-limiting while excess is irrational and infinite, but in addition (and as a consequence) lack admits of reformist solutions while excess demands a radical, utopian one. If hunger and vagrancy were the only problems, then Hythlodaeus's reformist scheme of manorial production might suffice—if not "really," at least as set down by the text. But the problem of excess, which Hythlodaeus calls "greed," "pride," "the madness of kings," destabilizes any reformist solution by removing the internal limits of need. Lack and excess are not really discrete, antithetical terms standing at equal distances from a purported center of rational satisfaction. Rather, excess engulfs lack, sends it surging off the scale. Utopia will solve the problem of need easily enough; its challenge is to manage the crisis of surplus.

Going Native

Granted that *Utopia* cannot be comprehended by any one concept or reduced to a single theme, still it is possible to isolate that
element which makes it historically *new* and which distinguishes
it from the array of imaginary polities that predate it. Simply put,
Utopia is organized primarily around the satisfaction of needs; its
governing rationale is the production and consumption of use
values.[45] Book 1 has paved the road, first, by way of its defense of
the deracinated masses who lack the most basic means of subsistence and, second, by way of its attack on the kings and nobles
whose unjust appropriation and wasteful expenditure of goods lead
to the impoverishment of society. In answer to the double bind of
excess and lack, Utopia installs a rational and equitable distribution of goods, which supplies basic needs and yet avoids invidious
accumulation or waste. Utopia exists primarily to house, feed, and
clothe its inhabitants; its governing logic is that of utility.

This conceptual basis is furthermore related to the text's formal
and generic features, as may be illustrated through comparison
with two other paradigmatic texts. The first of these, Plato's *Republic*, is perhaps the most obvious precursor of More's work.
Nevertheless, *The Republic* is primarily the elaboration of a *political* idea; its economic and cultural aspects—say, its abolition of
private property—are subordinated to what is essentially a scheme
of political organization. Accordingly, the text openly proclaims
that its imagined polity is just that—the projection of a philosophical reasoning—and consequently devotes little energy to *embodying* it in any imaginative or figural way. *The Republic* is more
sparing than *Utopia* in its use of descriptive or anecdotal detail,
more rigorous in its use of analytical schemata. *Utopia*, by contrast, is politically "underdeveloped" in relation to *The Republic*.
The description of Utopia's state apparatus, while daring in its
democratic orientation, is bland and perfunctory. Despite the web
of often obscure prohibitions that span it, the Utopian polity is
relatively apolitical; most of the text's descriptive energies are directed toward what might better be called "civil society."[46]

If Plato's *Republic* is born of reason, then *The Land of Cockayne*, our other paradigm, is born of the sleep of reason. Part
dream-vision, part paradise, this medieval poem describes not a
utopian polity but a landscape of wish fulfillment: "In Cockaygne
is mete and drink, / Withoute care, how and swink" (17–18).[47] Day
shines eternally in this land; rivers run with milk, honey, and

wine; insects, wild animals, and beasts of burden are nonexistent; everyone is happy. If *The Republic* articulates a strict system of political reason, *The Land of Cockayne* depicts the pleasant excesses of desire. Its mode is purely descriptive; the poem is thick with imagery unfettered by any rational grid. Individual images are densely, often grotesquely overdetermined: buildings have walls made of meat pies, and hot roasted geese fly through the air and offer themselves for consumption. The poem reels in the grip of an intoxicating yet whimsical descriptive excess. Naturally, such a concretely imagined place claims to exist: "Fer in see by west Spaygne / Is a land y-hote Cokaygne" (1–2).

These two precursor texts map out a set of antitheses which Utopia may be said to meditate. More's imagined polity is neither the ascetic operation of a *logos* nor a delirium of pleasure; rather, it tries to imagine a rational consumption embodied in the practicality of the use value. Its descriptive method is correspondingly measured as well; avoiding both the colorlessness of Plato's dialectical city and the oneiric density of *The Land of Cockayne*, it achieves a spare but believable mimesis. While it may be rhetorically undercut, the ontological solidity of the island is neither sapped by a *stated* fictiveness nor muddied by fantastic pigments. It must *be there*, in response to its claim to fulfill the needs of the body; but by restraining need before it spills over into excess, it reins itself back—for the most part—from the overtly imaginary. In short, the rationality of the Utopian description accords with the rationality of use value; both answer the call of utility. Like the island's clothing or houses, Utopian mimesis is functional but not extravagant or beautiful. It mostly operates at a bare sufficiency, within the limits set down by the moral economy of the use value.

But if *Utopia*'s descriptive characteristics can be squared with its conceptual reliance on utility, this would seem to contradict my earlier point that description is a *reifying* mode, since reification signals the global dominance of exchange value over use value. For Marx, use value and exchange value embody the incommensurable spheres of the qualitative and the quantitative, the concrete and the abstract, consumption and exchange. We have therefore fallen into a disturbing conceptual loop, but not a random one; it is the loop that founds political economy.

Engels found utopias interesting because they dimly anticipated the idea of a communist society. But *Utopia*'s historical "pre-science" consists not only in its ability to imagine a particular social organization but also in its premature capture by the ideology of political economy, resulting in a conception of Utopia as a society that effects the "liberation" of use value. This liberation is promised by Marxism as well, which sees communism as a system of production for use rather than profit. The split between communist and capitalist societies can be viewed as a macroversion of a split within the commodity form itself, that which divides it into use value and exchange value. More cannot conceive of the split in this way; for the most part, exchange value lies outside the practical and figural vocabularies of *Utopia*, though as we shall see, it plays a key structural role all the same. More is less a proto-Marxist than a proto-Veblenite, contrasting the rational utility of the use value with the conspicuous consumption of the feudal aristocracy. In book 1 use value forms the absent, rational center of a society divided between ostentatious gluttons, on the one hand, and impoverished wretches, on the other. Utopia hopes to rescue use values from the ab-usive effects of a system of aristocratic expenditure which engages in wasteful sumptuary excess. The project is truly one of "liberating" use values, with all that that entails—namely, the belief that conspicuous consumption distorts the natural and proper use of things. In this view, use value is the irreducible and primary essence of social goods, their innate rationality—clothing for warmth, food for nourishment, housing for shelter. To return to a prior metaphor, use value is the essential kernel obscured by the husk of aristocratic waste. Peel off that loathsome husk, which one can do by abolishing private property, and the original, nutritious kernel will be revealed. This metaphor of outer and inner is literally reproduced in the case of utopian clothing. Since clothing is meant for warmth, Utopian clothing of undyed leather embodies its immanent essence as use value. Dyes or ornamentation, which other societies might add on later, represent the artificial exteriority of conspicuous consumption. by eschewing them, Utopia returns both to the "inner" and to the "natural" (and Utopia conceives of itself generally as promoting a more natural state of life). Utopian clothing enshrines a whole strategy against feudal ostentation in which wretched excess is pared down to rational use.

This strategy silently relies on what Jean Baudrillard has called "the myth of primary needs," of "an irreducible zone where the individual chooses himself, since he knows what he wants: to eat, to drink, to sleep, to make love, to find shelter, etc. At this level he cannot, it is supposed, be alienated in his need as such: only deprived of the means to satisfy it."[48] From the perspective of this myth, "excess" or surplus is defined as what remains once primary needs are satisfied. Things actually work quite differently, however:

> In fact, the "vital anthropological minimum" doesn't exist: in all societies, it is determined residually by the fundamental urgency of an excess: the divine or sacrificial share, sumptuous discharge, economic profit. It is this pre-dedication of luxury that negatively determines the level of survival, and not the reverse (which is an idealist fiction). Advantages, profit, sacrifice (in the sense of social wealth) and "useless" expenditure are all deducted in advance. And the priority of this claim works everywhere at the expense of the functional side of the balance sheet—at the expense, when necessary, of minimal subsistence.[49]

The asymmetry of the ideologeme excess/lack finds its logic in a social process wherein excess is always the primary term, both defining and deconstructing the mythical rationality of need. On the level of practice this takes the form of what Georges Bataille has called "destructive expenditure," in which the subject sacrifices itself by effecting the pure loss of values. Destructive expenditure, he notes, can assume many forms: "luxury, mourning, cults, the construction of sumptuary monuments, games, spectacles, arts, perverse sexual activity (i.e., deflected from genital finality)—all these represent activities which, at least in primitive circumstances, have no end beyond themselves."[50] Aristocratic consumption, which More opposes, is a functional and reactionary version of such expenditure, recouping apparent sacrifice for a surplus of prestige and political power.[51] More's practical exaltation of use value thus reacts to a historical moment in which destructive expenditure appears primarily as a form of social domination.

*Utopia* constructs its two realms, Utopia and "England," by totalizing the logics of utility and aristocratic consumption. But this schematic opposition comes from separating out the competing and overdetermined elements in a real social formation, that of early sixteenth-century England. In Hythlodaeus's "England," productive labor (embodied primarily as agricultural labor) is being squeezed out by an excessive demand for profit and ostentation. By squandering even the nation's productive resources, aristocratic consumption initiates a disintegrating downward spiral, a disequilibrium of expenditure over production that can only end in general impoverishment. Utopia, by contrast, offers a perfected and idealized arena for communalized petty production and thus for the production of useful values.[52] However, Utopia does not balance output and production. A strong work ethic combined with a rather ascetic devotion to utility assures a constant surplus of production over consumption—that is to say, a disequilibrium that reverses England's. This surplus symbolizes the dominance of productive values as such.

The opposition between Utopia and England, or between utility and waste, derives from the class division of English society into petty producers and aristocracy. Or rather, it results from the reduction of these classes to schematized social functions and dysfunctions. Petty producers embody production and utility; they are "well-behaved, simple, and by their daily industry more beneficial to the commonwealth than to themselves." The aristocracy are "greedy, unscrupulous, and useless" (105), engaged only in the wasteful destruction of useful values. In Hythlodaeus's England, however, the reign of wasteful expenditure has not only deprived the petty classes of their land and means of production; it has "infected" them with the ostentatious manners of the aristocracy, as Hythlodaeus claims. In Utopia, the petty producer's paradise, this class can be reduced to its pure idea: useful production and rational consumption.

The schematic resolution of English society is mapped onto the longitudinal axis leading from England to Utopia, which is "as far removed from our [world] by the equator as their life and character are different from ours" (197). But how can this distance be traveled? In general, it cannot; the inaccessibility of Utopia expresses (among other things) the incommensurability of usefulness and expenditure. Yet Hythlodaeus's unrepeatable journey there is carefully mapped out, as Marin has shown.[53] Leaving from his homeland of Portugal, Hythlodaeus travels first to South America, then to the utopian southern hemisphere, then to Ceylon and Calcutta and home again, thus establishing two pairs of "toponyms" or answering places. South America and Ceylon/Calcutta, the new world and the ancient, define an equatorial axis that bisects the (impossible) latitude leading from Portugal/England to Utopia. Hythlodaeus, furthermore, describes an elaborate and symmetrical series of climatic and cultural bands that parallel the equatorial axis, thus making the utopian southern hemisphere into a figural mirror image of the northern.

Hythlodaeus begins his Utopian travels by joining Vespucci on the final three of his four voyages to the New World. On the last of

these he and twenty-three companions are left behind in a fort
somewhere near what is now Ponta de Baleia, on the eastern coast
of Brazil. What happens then is sketchy but significant.

> He recounted how, after the departure of Vespucci, he and his
> friends who had stayed behind in the fort began by degrees through
> continued meetings and civilities to ingratiate themselves with the
> natives until they not only stood in no danger from them but were
> actually on friendly terms and, moreover, were in good repute and
> favor with a ruler (whose name and country I have forgotten).
> Through the ruler's generosity, he and his five companions were sup-
> plied with ample provision and travel resources and, moreover, with a
> trusty guide on their journey ... to take them to other rulers with
> careful recommendations to their favor.

Others repeat the generosity of this ruler: "Then they had opportunity of visiting many countries in all directions, for every ship
which was got ready for any voyage made him and his companions
welcome as passengers [ille, comitesque eius libentissime admitte-
bantur]" (52–53). The liberality of these peoples, which was clearly
suggested to More by Vespucci's own description of his voyages,[54]
clearly derives from the Italian's encounter with the unexpected
workings of a gift economy in which expenditure dominates both
accumulation and use. Vespucci's letter chronicles his repeated as-
tonishment at, and exploitation of, the practice of gift exchange.
He writes of one tribe: "They are so liberal in giving that it is the
exception that they deny you anything; and on the other hand,
they are free in begging when they show themselves to be your
friends." At their very first landing Vespucci and his men experience this excessive reciprocity:

> And we anchored a half league from shore, where we saw an im-
> mense number of people. And we leaped ashore, full well equipped
> men, and the people ashore still showed themselves shy of associat-
> ing with us. And we could not so reassure them that they would
> come to talk with us. And this day we so persistently endeavored in
> giving them of our wares, such as bells, mirrors, glass beads and
> other trash that some of them were rendered confident and came to
> converse with us. And when we had established friendly relations
> with them, inasmuch as night was falling, we took leave of them and
> returned to the ships. And the next day, when dawn broke, we saw
> that infinite hordes were on the beach; and they had with them their
> wives and children. We put ashore and found that all came laden
> with their possessions, which are such as will be told in its place.

Later Vespucci turns generosity to his own profit: "At [another] spot we traded for 150 pearls, which they gave us for a bell, and for some little gold which they gave us gratis." Other tribes, however, exhibit equally incomprehensible hostility; one engages in a mock ritual of gift exchange only in order to capture, dismember, and cook one of Vespucci's men.[55] Vespucci cannot even begin to explain such behavior; he can only recount it. His experiences with the indigenous people violate all economies of "rational" expectation.

The practice of destructive expenditure is exemplified in More's work by the well-known episode of the compass:

> [The] mariners [of the southern hemisphere] were skilled in adapting themselves to sea and weather. But he reported that he won their extraordinary favor by showing them the use of the magnetic needle of which they had hitherto been quite ignorant so that they had hesitated to trust themselves to the sea and had boldly done so in the summer only. Now, trusting to the magnet, they do not fear wintry weather, being dangerously confident. Thus, there is a risk that what was thought to be a great benefit to them may, through their imprudence, cause them great mischief. (53)

This episode has been read—reasonably, I think—as a cautionary tale about the proper "use" of *Utopia*.[56] But it can also be read as a broader fable about the concept of use, since the compass represents in a privileged way the Western practice of utility. The compass is not only marked by a specific function, like all use values; it is also explicitly *about* measurement, scientific rationality, technical functionalism. In itself the compass presents a microallegory about the scientific and moral consciousness of the West, about the "measured" quality of its scientific and moral prudence.

The "imprudent" natives waste and abuse the compass, of course, not, however, as English aristocrats waste things to produce invidious difference. This is rather a case of abuse through overuse, the spilling over of need into desire, of practical navigation into a wager of life itself.[57] The abuse of the compass explodes the supposedly immanent and self-limiting rationality of use value, sacrificing it to an antieconomy of destructive expenditure. The mariners of the southern hemisphere invest their gift perversely, with excessive and dangerous desires, and thus succeed in unsettling the concept of utility as it is enshrined in the more "temperate" clime of Utopia. Their zone is the zone of expenditure itself, which must be traversed and abandoned on the way to Utopia's productive regime.

Only it cannot really be left behind. For the exigencies of surplus, waste, excess are primary; they form the arena in which the provisional boundaries of need take form. The logic of expenditure always returns to energize and embarrass Utopia—for example, in the golden chamber pots, emblems of the Utopian commitment to utility, which are simultaneously an immense indulgence in luxury. This waste of gold is moreover tied directly to defecation, thus engaging the bodily pleasures of expenditure or discharge. The chamber pots offer a two-sided emblem, a card whose one face reads chaste utility and whose other reads filthy excess.

The Utopian marketplace is a point at which these competing logics are both condensed and globalized:

> Every city is divided into four equal districts. In the middle of each quarter is a market of all kinds of commodities. To designated market buildings the products of each family are conveyed. Each kind of goods is arranged separately in storehouses. From the latter any head of a household seeks what he and his require and, without money or any kind of compensation, carries off what he seeks. Why should anything be refused? First, there is a plentiful supply of all things and, secondly, there is no underlying fear that anyone will demand more than he needs. Why should there be any suspicion that someone may demand an excessive amount when he is certain of never being in want? No doubt about it, avarice and greed are aroused in every kind of living creature by the fear of want, but only in man are they motivated by pride alone—pride which counts it a personal glory to excel others by superfluous display of possessions. The latter vice can have no place at all in the Utopian scheme of things. (137–39)

The marketplace is the most volatile site in all of Utopia, the crucial point at which the island must prove "equal" to itself. Demand must not exceed supply, desire must not exceed need. Otherwise, Utopia could degenerate into a mass of competing and hostile hoarders of goods. Hythlodaeus's exposition, of course, draws attention to precisely this danger, and his arguments are transparently flawed. Men only take more than they need, he says, when faced with the danger of want, and Utopia has eliminated this danger. But the absence of want in Utopia is equally predicated on the fact that no one takes more than he needs; so the argument is circular. Further, Hythlodaeus introduces the exclusively human problem of excess of pride, the desire to "excel others by superfluous display of possessions," and then insists that such desires "can have no place at all [nullum omnino locum habet] in the Utopian scheme of things," using a form of expression that should be familiar by now. Nonproductive expenditure is the utopia of Utopia, the practice that has "no place" there—though Hythlodaeus has just described a possible place for it.

The description of the Utopian marketplace pretends to represent an institution founded on the reduction of desire to need. The marketplace *works*, which means that it balances its accounts, by means of that deadening of desire effected by the global dominance of utility. Utopian goods themselves resist wasteful or destructive expenditure; they are emblems of their own imperturbable practicality. But by invoking a set of possible fragilities, Hythlodaeus turns the "sure thing" of the marketplace into a gamble after all. A defensive rhetoric undercuts the purported logic of the market, which now appears to expose itself at every moment to at least the possibility of a catastrophic depletion. Thus the Utopian marketplace stakes a wage after all: you are free to exhaust me anytime; I offer myself fully to you. As a textual construction, the market really works by the logic of destructive expenditure, not utility. We may in fact describe it as the socialization of such expenditure. By constantly offering itself up for limitless waste, the Utopian market dwarfs any petty or individual gestures of ostentation or accumulation. Utopian society as a whole thus becomes the source of an intimidating and unrequitable largess. But this largess is hidden by the modesty of Utopian goods, which lends the appearance of an orderly and practical flow of use values. The repressed logic of destructive expenditure emerges only in the form of an aristocratic gesture, now performed by a collective institution rather than an individual.[58]

The conflict between need and desire, utility and expenditure emerges with the greatest clarity in the Utopian philosophy of pleasure, which forms the topic of Hythlodaeus's longest theoretical digression.[59] The concept of pleasure, we learn, occupies a central place in the religious and ethical thought of the Utopians—so much so that this is the one thing Hythlodaeus finds possibly excessive or blameworthy: "In this matter they seem to lean more than they should to the school that espouses pleasure as the object by which to define either the whole or the chief part of human happiness" (161). Even "vital commodities" are nothing but "the matter of pleasure" (165). For all that, the Utopian theory of pleasure is "excessive" only at first blush, for "they hold that happiness rests not in every kind of pleasure but only in good and decent pleasure" (163), which turns out to exclude not only dicing, gambling, hunting, and the keeping of superfluous wealth, as well as delight in clothes, honors, and jewels, but also eating, drinking, defecating, and sex. "True" pleasure finally means a state of bodily health, the avoidance of excessive labor or self-mortification, and the contemplation of truth.

The most interesting part of all this is the Utopian doctrine of bodily pleasure:

> Bodily pleasure they divide into two kinds. The first is that which fills the sense with clearly perceptible sweetness. Sometimes it comes from the renewal of those organs which have been weakened by our natural heat. These organs are then restored by food and drink. Sometimes it comes from the elimination of things which overload the body. This agreeable sensation occurs when we discharge feces from our bowels or perform the activity generative of children or relieve the itching of some part by rubbing or scratching. Now and then, however, pleasure arises, not in process of restoring anything that our members lack, nor in process of eliminating anything that causes distress, but from something that tickles and affects our sense with a secret but remarkable moving force and so draws them to itself. Such is that pleasure that is engendered by music.
>
> The second kind of bodily pleasure they claim to be that which consists in a calm and harmonious state of the body. This is nothing other than each man's health undisturbed by any disorder. Health, if assailed by no pain, gives delight of itself, though there be no motion arising from pleasure applied from without. Even though it is less obvious and less perceptible by the sense than that overblown craving for eating and drinking, yet none the less they hold it to be the greatest of pleasures. Almost all Utopians regard it as great and as practically the foundation and basis of all pleasures. Even by itself it can make the state of life peaceful and desirable, whereas without it no place is left for any pleasure. (173–75)

The first kind of bodily pleasure, involving repletion or discharge, is clearly homologous to those forbidden social pleasures that involve the consumption or destruction of a surplus. This is specifically a pleasure of imbalances, arising from the perception of differential pressures among bodily organs. The brief description refers repeatedly to "organs" or "parts" in general as well as to the specific organic processes of ingestion, defecation, and sexual orgasm. The "perceptible sweetness" of this kind of pleasure involves not only a noticeable affect but one that is located within a body conceived as an articulated system of organs. Yet even this formulation does not do justice to what is at stake here. Strictly speaking, the word *organ* suggests a functional part within a total-ized whole—an organism. But More's hesitation about organic pleasures arises from the fact that the organs do not serve any pro-ductive finality that would constitute the body as system. It is bet-ter to think of the organs as desiring machines that *themselves* produce pleasure, than to say that a global subject feels pleasure "in" this or that organ. The organs of pleasure are not "parts" of anything; they really form a disarticulated nonsystem.

The second kind of pleasure, that of health, "consists in a calm and harmonious state of the body," which is "unperturbed by any disorder." The healthy body is a body without surpluses or lacks, a body whose internal parts have been decoded, resulting in a har-monious but undifferentiated plenum—in short, a body without organs.[60] One does not feel health in a specific part of the body; indeed, Hythlodaeus devotes much energy to the question of whether one feels its pleasure at all. The Utopians "give the palm to health" (177) as the superior pleasure, and their image of the healthy body clearly offers a microcosm of the "calm and harmo-nious state" of Utopia itself. The regulated flows (of goods, of pop-ulations) which characterize Utopian society are meant to keep it in a healthy state, without surpluses or depletions. Conversely, the other kind of pleasure is dystopian because it always relieves a prior irritation, on which it thus depends: "If a person thinks that his felicity consists in this kind of pleasure, he must admit that he will be in the greatest happiness if his lot happens to be a life which is spent in perpetual hunger, thirst, itching, eating, drink-ing, scratching, and rubbing. Who does not see that such a life is not only disgusting but wretched?" (177). Wretched indeed, and precisely the condition of the English body politic, divided as it is between those whose lives are spent in perpetual hunger and thirst and others whose lives are spent in perpetual eating and drinking. England is a "sick body" and Utopia a "healthy condition" (105), according to Hythlodaeus.

The Utopians endorse repletive or excretive pleasures only inso-far as they lead back to the zero level of imperceptible satisfaction: "The delight of eating and drinking, and anything that gives the same sort of enjoyment, they think desirable, but only for the state of health" (177). Despite Hythlodaeus's weak insistence that health is a conscious state, and his proviso that "the absence of pain without the presence of health they regard as insensibility rather than pleasure" (175), nevertheless Utopian pleasure is mostly defined negatively, as the avoidance of sensation and the search for a state "undisturbed by any disorder." One is reminded of Freud's definition of pleasure in *Beyond the Pleasure Principle* as the reduction of excitations and its connection with the death drive as tending toward an ideal state of complete rest. In More's punning title, Eu-topia, or the happy place, is also U-topia, the place of nonbeing.[61] Utopian happiness is the Nirvana principle of reduced excitation, the zero state of the decoded body.

In the *Philebus* Socrates endorses the view that "pleasure is something that comes to be but in no case ever is . . . Hence it is an alternation of passing away and becoming that will be chosen by those that choose a life like that in preference to . . . the life which included neither pleasure nor pain, but the purest possible activity of thought" (54d, 55a).[62] The kind of pleasure Socrates rejects is clearly the organic, dystopian variety. For him, pleasure lacks ontological stability because it is a pure process of becoming, a passing from a state of irritation to one of satisfaction. Symbolic of the whole world of becoming, it must therefore be neutralized before the comtemplation of being can begin. Put differently, pleasure and pain are to the body what history is to the world: its motor activity, the conflict of its differences, the pressure of its imbalances. The Utopian rejection of such pleasures is thus of a piece with Utopia's transcendence of history. Utopia is not a becoming but a being, "the best *state* of a commonwealth" (the Latin title: *De optimo reipublicae statu*), just a bodily health is a "calm and harmonious *state* of the body [quieto, atque aequabili corporis statu]."

Death, being, health, Utopia—all participate in the general economy of the zero degree. According to taste, one can rewrite the whole series in terms of Platonic ontology or Freudian metapsychology. The latter is more compelling nowadays, but both are versions of essentialism (all becoming tends toward being, all life tends toward death). In either case, Utopia ends up being moralized identically: life to them would be death to us. My purpose is not to oppose such moralizations but to examine their common origin. Whence the economy of the zero degree? In particular, what is the origin of the healthy or neutralized body, happy in the absence of lack or surplus?

For Hythlodaeus, the pleasure of health originates in nature. To "good and decent pleasure . . . our nature is drawn by virtue itself, [and] . . . the Utopians define virtue as living according to nature"

(163). Conversely, "whatever things mortals imagine by a futile consensus to be sweet to them in spite of being against nature (as though they had the power to change the nature of things as they do their names) are all so far from making for happiness that they are even a great hindrance to it" (167). The pleasures of excess or of expenditure for its own sake (as opposed to expenditure aimed at restoring the zero degree) are all products of a false social agreement. They are *artificial* pleasures, added on to the core of rational pleasures provided by nature.[63] Like the dyes or ornaments excluded from "natural" Utopian clothing, perverse or artificial pleasures merely obscure and supplement the stable and irreducible zone of nature whose ideal of rational consumption always tends toward the zero degree.

The belief in a natural tendency toward equilibrium is what makes More's mythology so congenial to Freud's. The only problem is that it is frequently refuted by social practice. So-called primitive societies, for example, may decide to squander their resources in feasts and spend the intervals in famine rather than engage in rational or measured consumption.[64] Even Hythlodaeus complains that *all* European social classes engage in destructive and ostentatious expenditure. He interprets this behavior as an indication that society has gotten the best of nature, but the truth is that the myth of rational or measured consumption is the most artificial of all—first elaborated by Hellenic philosophy but realized as a social practice only by bourgeois society under the influence of political economy.[65] "Natural" consumption is nothing but productive consumption, which could become a norm only in a society governed by the logic of utility. It is thus difficult to speak of Utopia as expressing a "petty wish" insofar as it reforms the feudal petty producing class into the rational consumers of political economy. The myth of the neutral or healthy subject, containing its own self-limiting needs, is the dialectical counterimage of the use value, an ideological construct needed to effect the tautological calibration of needs and goods under capitalism. The decoded body without organs, the body that "uses" goods so as to fulfill its needs and return to the zero state, that consumes social products only so as to discharge all contracts with society and resume an isolated plenitude, underlies More's ideology and Freud's. But this subject of the death drive is only the bourgeois subject who wishes to pay his debts and be left alone or, alternatively, the proletarian subject who is paid just enough to restore his labor power in undiminished quantities. Both are provided with use values whose consumption stokes the fires of a productive regime. The notion of perverse or heterogeneous investments of objects (of compasses, for instance) or of expenditure outside of a productive logic knows no place here.

On all levels productive consumption is governed by an ideology of self-equivalence. The body at the zero state has returned *to itself*, having discharged the distortions of excess or lack. Rational consumption always leads back to equilibrium or self-balance. The use value too is always equivalent to its function, while need simply equates or calibrates the unitary subject and its objects. But the secret of this system lies elsewhere, in the practice of commodity exchange. As Guy Debord observes, *"The commodity-form is through and through equal to itself*, the category of the quantitative. The quantitative is what the commodity-form develops, and it can develop only within the quantitative."[66] Only by means of its quantitative self-equivalence as exchange value does the commodity first learn of its "qualitative" self-equivalence as use value. The homogenizing effects of commodity exchange produce the unitary and rational objects of utility; hence use-value is really the product and satellite of exchange value. The notion of the use value as an object that prescribes the modes and limits of its own consumption is the crowning illusion of reification; hence there is no contradiction in posing Utopian description in relation to both use *and* exchange value. Both can sustain the reified logic of political economy, which Utopia's form and content continually express.

By saying this I do not mean to belittle *Utopia*'s political significance. Useful or rational consumption strikes directly at an aristocratic mode of expenditure which aims primarily at class domination, and More's devotion to the moral economy of use value represents an important bourgeois strategy for wresting economic and cultural power from the aristocracy. What *Utopia* cannot imagine in any coherent way, however, is the socialization, rather than the elimination, of destructive expenditure, and therefore, Utopia is always rooting out sources of potential excess: "Now you can see how nowhere is there any license to waste time, nowhere any pretext to evade work—no wine shop, no brothel anywhere, no opportunity for corruption, no lurking hole, no secret meeting place" (147). "Nowhere . . . nowhere": the utopias of Utopia are the spaces of excess or destruction, folds or "lurking places" in the otherwise seamless skin of a productive regime. Alehouse and brothel, fulfillers of the "bad" sorts of pleasure, would be to the body of Utopia what organs are to the human body—sites of accumulation and discharge, producers of imbalance and heterogeneity. Their excision attempts to produce the homogeneous body of the zero state. The repressed logic of expenditure, however, bursts forth in grotesque or symptomatic ways: those unforgettable chamber pots or the perilous Utopian marketplace. These are the new organs of Utopian discharge, covertly effecting either democratized or communalized operations of waste in the midst of a generalized utility.

I am not arguing here that expenditure constitutes a more "basic" social logic than that of production, or that is status as the repressed confers on it a special privilege to effect a transvaluation of values. A social order based solely on expenditure would be as absurd as one based solely on utility. Rather, expenditure operates as the supplement of utility, its uncontainable yet contaminating other. It is perhaps appropriate, then, that this supplemental logic emerges primarily in moments of textual "excess"—the digression, the whimsical detail, the anecdote—when the rationality of Utopian description loosens its grip a bit. In other words, it is as a work of fantasy that *Utopia* both embodies and expresses a practice of unproductive expenditure. And here, I think, we come to the heart of *Utopia*'s mysterious duplicity as a work that is at once serious social critique and *jeu d'esprit,* blueprint for a new society and whimsical dream. The work's rationality constitutes a political "use value" in the battle against aristocratic excess, but its supplemental and fantastic expenditures save it from its own utilitarian practice. In short, *Utopia* is and is not equal to itself, it does and does not approach the homogeneity of the body without organs. As use value and as literary "waste," it is both ambitious and trifling; thus does it achieve its full and ambivalent radicalism. To speak of the "proper use" of *Utopia* is thus falsely to reduce it to a function. *Utopia* is neither more nor less useful than the compass that both measures a position and stakes the wager of a dangerous, frivolous journey.

# Margins and Modernity: The Shepheardes Calender and the Politics of Interpretation

In *The Shepheardes Calender* Spenser clearly fashioned a cultural manifesto that introduced both a new poet and a new poetics. The self-importance of the work is registered above all by the inclusion of a critical commentary on the poems whose style and format was meant to recall humanist editions of Virgil.[1] "No English poet," remarks William Nelson, "had ever been announced so pretentiously."[2] As manifestos go, however, Spenser's is remarkably unclear: no one is quite sure what it means to say. Through its highly self-conscious imitation of Virgilian and continental pastoral, it seems to declare its allegiance to humanist poetics and culture. Yet its language and form also invoke medieval poets such as Chaucer and Langland, and its title and woodcuts allude to the old *Kalender and Compost of Shepherdes*.[3] It is possible, of course, that Spenser envisioned a simple fusion of classical and native literary traditions; yet the success and even the possibility of such a fusion was not clear to many of Spenser's first readers, in large part because humanists looked upon medieval works such as *The Kalender of Shepherdes* as barbarous and contemptible. Sidney complained that the "framing of his style to an old rustic language I dare not allow, sith neither Theocritus in Greek, Virgil in Latin, nor Sanazarro in Italian, did affect it."[4] Even "E. K.," who provides the critical commentary and introduction to Spenser's pastorals, is unable to decide whether the poet employs archaic diction "by . . . casualtye and custome, or of set purpose and choyse, as thinking them fittest for such rusticall rudenesse of shepheards."[5] E. K., that is, doesn't know whether this diction is the result of unintended influence and hence possibly naïve or the sign of an artistically self-conscious (indeed, humanist) attention to rhetorical decorum.

Further ambiguities surround the poems' religious meaning. It is clear that the so-called "moral" pastorals draw on native traditions of ecclesiastical satire and that they allude allegorically to a number of contemporary figures and events. Yet critical arguments continue about the nature of Spenser's theological and ecclesiastical loyalties and so about the objects of his satire—if indeed the moral eclogues are satirical at all.[6] Even David Norbrook, who makes a strong case for reading the moral eclogues in the context of popular Protestant satire, admits that *The Shepheardes Calender* "is a much less clear-cut case than the more explicit religious satires. . . . the volume does generate an atmosphere of skepticism and uncertainty."[7]

These interpretive problems are explicitly thematized, moreover, by the presence of a critical apparatus within the work. E. K.'s commentary claims to elucidate some of the poems' aesthetic, religious, and political significance by employing the techniques of humanist philological criticism. Yet the function of the commentary seems inconsistent. Sometimes E. K. dutifully supplies a literary allusion or elucidates an allegory. At other times he clearly mangles the meaning of the verse, drifts off on tangents, piles on useless pedantry, or engages in hysterical and irrelevant polemics. The sheer weight of his prefaces and commentaries borders on parodic excess, and so looks forward to such works as *A Tale of a Tub* or *The Dunciad*.[8] The whole scholarly apparatus is poised unstably between the serious and the ludic, with the result that it has proven difficult to say whether E. K. is a parodic creation of Spenser's or a real though anonymous glossator.

What this troubling apparatus puts into play, then, is the space and function of commentary itself. "It is part of the fiction of *The Shepheardes Calender*," writes Michael McCanles, "that E. K.'s glosses and commentary are not part of the fiction."[9] Yet it may be more exact to say that they raise the question of what is or isn't fiction. In a way that is typical of Renaissance texts they both suggest a set of stable or normalizing oppositions—commentary/work, fact/fiction, margin/center—and upset or subvert them. Instead of merely removing obscurities and pinning down meanings, they actually extend the reach of textual uncertainty, and they do so, moreover, in ways that thematize the relation between interpretation and cultural power. Such an observation is hardly critical news, of course; in fact it merely rehearses the thematics of what is by now an all-too-familiar form of deconstructive reading. I nevertheless wish briefly to pursue such a reading and through it to trace some of the formal and epistemological paradoxes of E. K.'s commentary, in order to prepare the way for a more historical approach to the problem of interpretation.

In the Dedicatory Epistle to Gabriel Harvey, E. K. introduces a significant figure while defending Spenser's use of obsolete language:

> But all as in most exquisite pictures they use to blaze and portraict not onely the daintie lineaments of beautye, but also rounde about it to shadow the rude thickets and craggy clifts, that by the basenesse of such parts, more excellency may accrew to the principall; for oftimes we fynde ourselves, I knowe not how, singularly delighted with the shewe of such naturall rudenesse, and take great pleasure in that disorderly order. Even so doe those rough and harsh termes enlumine and make more clearly to appeare the brightnesse of brave and glorious words. (p. 8)

By alluding to the use of landscape in contemporary portraiture, E. K. invokes a whole set of aesthetic and political hierarchies. In the late sixteenth century, landscape "was regarded chiefly, if not altogether, as a kind of painting suitable for backgrounds."[10] The foreground was to be reserved "from the rest of the landskip for the standing of such as are principall to the history."[11] In *The Art of Drawing with the Pen* (1606), Henry Peacham writes:

> Landtskip is a Dutch word, & it is as much as wee shoulde say in English landship, or expressing of the land by hills, woods, Castles, seas, valleys, ruines, hanging rocks, Citties, Townes, &c. as farre as may be shewed within our Horizon. Seldome is it drawne by it selfe, but in respect & for the sake of something else: wherefore it falleth out among those things which we call *Parerga*, which are additions or adjuncts rather of ornament, than otherwise necessary.[12]

As a parergon, landscape stands in a relation of subordinate exteriority to the *ergon*, or work proper, embellishing by contrast the "principal" figure that it frames. But this spatial or formal relation expresses a certain articulation of power, as the political connotations of the word *principal* suggest. The aesthetic subordination of landscape to figure is modeled on the political subordination of countryside to prince or monarch—a subordination that is dramat-

ically enacted in the "Aprill" eclogue when the natural and mythical elements of the pastoral landscape arrange themselves around
the figure of Eliza:

> And whither rennes this bevie of Ladies bright,
> raunged in a row?
> They bene all Ladyes of the lake behight,
> that unto her goe.
> *Chloris*, that is the chiefest Nymph of al,
> Of Olive braunches beares a Coronall:
> Olives bene for peace,
> When wars doe surcease,
> Such for a Princesse bene principall.
>
> (118–26)

Eliza becomes the "principall" figure in a pastoral landscape
whose formal subordination represents political obedience by
"framing" the queen in a flattering and stable way. Like Wallace
Stevens's jar, she "takes dominion everywhere." In a less literal
fashion, the whole technique of pastoral allegory serves the same
political aesthetic. For just as painters "blaze and portraict the
daintie lineaments of beautye" by surrounding them with "rude
thickets and craggy clifts," so the pastoral allegorist employs
"rude" and "craggy" characters in order that "more excellency
may accrew" to the "principall" figures whom they represent. Like
landscape, the allegorical herdsmen of courtly pastoral maintain a
strictly subordinate exteriority to their noble referents. E. K.'s invocation of landscape therefore pertains to more than Spenser's diction; it adumbrates the political aesthetic of *The Shepheardes
Calender* as a whole.

In addition, the figure of landscape and portrait may be read as a
metaphor for the relation between commentary and text, for E. K.'s
glosses are meant to "enlumine and make more clearly to appeare
the brightnesse of [Spenser's] brave and glorious words." The commentator maintains the same subordinate exteriority to the literary ergon that landscape maintains to the painterly ergon: his
purpose is to magnify the poetic "principal." This spatial metaphor emerges in the General Argument, where E. K. discusses the
etymology of the work *aeglogue.*

> They were first of the Greekes the inventours of them called Æglogai
> as it were *aigon* or *aigonomon. logoi.* that is Goteheards tales. . . .

> This being, who seeth not the grossenesse of such as by colour of learning would make us beleeve that they are more rightly termed Eclogai, as they would say, extraordinary discourses of unnecessarie matter, which difinition albe in substaunce and meaning it agree with the nature of the thing, yet nowhit answereth with the *analysis* and interpretation of the word. (p. 12)

E. K. backs the wrong etymological horse, but his translation of *eklogoi*, the correct etymon of "eclogue," is canny. Eclogues are "extraordinary discourses" in the sense of being choice or selected works. But they are also "extraordinary" in the sense of standing outside or beyond a certain order; *ek-logoi* are words on the outside. The term might well be used to denote not the pastoral verses themselves but the commentary that frames their perimeter—not the ergon but the parergon. "Extraordinary discourses of unnecessarie matter" nicely describes E. K.'s often pompous and irrelevant commentary. (Another rendering of *EK-logoi* might be "E. K.'s words.") The "false" etymon itself is offered as a piece of "unnecessarie matter," an example of how the mere "colour of learning" can turn commentary's functional exteriority dysfunctional. The figure of the painterly parergon therefore creates ambiguities when applied to the relation between commentary and text. In painting, a rude and natural landscape frames an elegant "principal." But here the natural rudeness of pastoral occupies the typographical center, framed by the refined learning of the commentary. Which is "principal," the ergon or the parergon?[13] The impossibility of a formal or conceptual subordination, if it is not already the mere effect of power, is at the very least a conduit for it. Instabilities produced by framing signal the potential for a revolt at the margins: the outside may always decide to mount an assault on the center.

E. K.'s "excessive" commentaries are such a bid for power, a simultaneous effort to colonize the existing center and to shift that center to the outside. While the *ressentiment* of the commentator is familiar enough, there is something telling in the way E. K. establishes his critical authority by appealing to principles of philological accuracy. In his remarks on the meaning of *aeglogue*, he insists that the "false" etymon (*eclogai*) does well enough in a practical way, by expressing "the nature of the thing," but it falls short of the standards of scientific philology established by humanist scholarship. Commentary's proper role is therefore defined not by the pragmatics of reading but by the standards of a scientific method. That E. K. turns out to be wrong may or may not be intentional, but it foreshadows an argument I will make at greater length later: that rhetorical uncertainty of this sort is the dialectical *product* of "scientific" philology and thus a counterproduct of the procedures and protocols of humanist knowledge. The immediate point is that whereas E. K.'s claims to certainty may temporarily stave off the threat of critical irrelevance, they simultaneously create new possibilities for critical insubordination. E. K. gets a bit uppity when he endorses the descriptive relevance of *eclogai* as "extraordinary discourses of unnecessarie matter." Although "unnecessarie matter" primarily means "matter of whatever sort," it may also designate matter that is unnecessary or trifling and thus pass an unfavorable judgment on the pastoral form. (Earlier, E. K. describes eclogues as being "base for the matter, and homely for the manner" [10].) At the same time, however, these attempts to master the pastoral text are motivated in part by an equally evident sense of alienated longing. The pastoral myth of an organically unified world seems to exert a nostalgic attraction on a commentary doomed to rest outside of it. The warm simplicity of pastoral fiction contrasts with the exteriorized and alienated technics of "scientific" philology.

This formulation, however, rests on a by now untenable dichotomy of outside and inside. For *The Shepheardes Calender* contains a number of "cold pastorals," whose melancholy alienation internally redoubles the relation of commentary to text. "Januarye," the first of these, engages the painterly problem of landscape and figure rather directly as Colin Clout's bitter longings for the lost Rosalind disrupt the normal relation between self and nature:

> Thou barrein ground, whome winters wrath hath wasted,
> Art made a myrrhour, to behold my plight:
> Whilome thy fresh spring flowrd, and after hasted
> Thy sommer prowde with Daffadillies dight.
> And now is come thy wynters stormy state,
> Thy mantle mard, wherein thou maskedst late.
>
> · · · ·
>
> All so my lustfull leafe is drye and sere,
> My timely buds with wayling all are wasted:
> The blossome, which my braunch of youth did beare,
> With breathed sighes is blowne away, and blasted,
> And from mine eyes the drizling teares descend,
> As on your boughes the ysicles depend.
>
> (19–24, 37–42)

Instead of merely framing the principal figure of Colin, rough nature rejects its position of subordinate exteriority and penetrates into the ergon itself. Mirroring replaces contrast, thus confusing the relation between outside and inside, frame and portrait. When Colin claims that the "ground" has become a mirror, we should take this word in its formal, aesthetic, and even ontological senses. The landscape that should "ground" the principal has mastered it instead; the basis of certainty now produces uncertainty. The pastoral itself is caught in a pastoral nostalgia for happier, earlier times. This mirroring does not take place only inside the eclogue, though. E. K.'s preface, which both offers and withdraws a normative version of the relation between figure and landscape, anticipates the uncertainties within the eclogue itself and thus helps to *produce* them. It is not for nothing that E. K.'s annotations are called a "glosse," with its connotations of shining, glazing, deception. Despite its claims to be grounded in a scientific practice, the critical commentary on these pastorals seems able to project its uncertainties into the poems themselves.

E. K.'s glosses anticipate the critical difficulties faced by some of Spenser's more recent readers. They also lock Spenserian pastoral into a tightly dialectical relation with humanist scholarship. *The Shepheardes Calender* is almost obsessed with questions of knowledge, method, and interpretation, which it also poses as questions of social and political power. I hope to show that for Spenser, the aesthetics of pastoral are inseparable from the social production of knowledge, both in broadly paradigmatic and in more local and directly political ways. Questions about the protocols and legitimation of knowledge lie at the very heart of *The Shepheardes Calender* and help to define its transitional status.

### Scientific and Narrative Knowledge

The interplay of certainty and uncertainty which marks E. K.'s commentaries was at least latent in humanism from its very beginnings. Quattrocento humanists adopted a deliberative rhetoric that was strongly informed by skepticism. Yet by elevating practical reason, or *phronesis*, over theoretical reason and by rejecting scientific certainty in favor of moral prudence, these early humanists achieved a kind of happy and untroubled pragmatism. Relying on principles of decorum rather than universal truth, humanism was "defined by its resistance to the epistemological implications of its own rhetoric."[14] This pragmatic and rhetorical posture served early humanism in its cultural and academic battles with scholastic philosophy. Yet it generated a complex relation with the attempts of Valla, Poliziano, Patrizi, and others to formulate a scientific historiography based on the principles of philological scholarship. Barbara J. Shapiro remarks: "As history moved away from the rhetorical tradition . . . and emphasized impartial accuracy, it was forced to relate its claims of truth to those of logic and 'science,' and thus to confront disciplines it had earlier rejected and epistemological issues it had previously ignored.[15]

As an empirical rather than a demonstrative or syllogistic science, humanist philology was largely compatible with the practical or prudential truth claims of humanist rhetoric. Lorenzo Valla's *scientia sermocinans* drew its principles "not from reason but from example, not from a law of speech but from observation."[16] Hence the attempts of Valla and Poliziano to determine the unequivocal and historically concrete meanings of the words in a text were bounded by the understanding that their results could attain nothing more than practical certainty.[17] On the other hand, humanist historiography strongly insisted on the need for objectivity and accuracy, for determining the validity of sources, and for distinguishing between fact and legend. And the practice of placing their work at the service of political or religious interests encouraged humanists to insist on the scientific validity of results. Valla's famous *Declamation on the Donation of Constantine*, for example, was written to support the king of Naples in a territorial dispute with the pope; thus while Valla employs arguments based on probability of motivation and result, he also has to make his philological critique seem as convincing and "scientific" as possible.[18] Humanist historiography thus combined a strong theoretical distinction between fact and fiction with the skeptical recognition that this could not be fully achieved in practice.

Yet this apparent contradiction was not always experienced as crisis. Barbara Shapiro points out that for seventeenth-century England, "the skeptical critique tended to emphasize the fallibility of human knowledge and to inspire reluctance to make claims of certitude rather than to repudiate all claims to knowledge."[19] In fact, the humanist rhetoric of prudential knowledge seems to have set an optimistic style for both history and the natural sciences in England, which confidently expected a constant but never complete refinement of human knowledge through continuing experimentation and empirical research.[20]

Other areas of culture, however, were less amenable to philological scrutiny or to skeptical forms of knowledge, principally religion. Valla's researches cast doubt on the authenticity not only of the Donation of Constantine but also of the Apostle's Creed, and Erasmus's editorial work on the New Testament eroded the authority of the Vulgate. In his debates with Luther, Erasmus repeatedly employed the term *opinion* to describe religious doctrine and was denounced by Luther for treating Christian truth "as nothing better than the opinions of philosophers or men."[21] Erasmus's skeptical style of religious thought found a few answering voices in England, in William Chillingworth and the Great Society of Tew, and in the latitudinarian movement after the Restoration. But religious controversy led generally in the direction of greater insistence on conformity and certitude.[22]

A more suggestive and more extreme version of Erasmian skepticism is *The Praise of Folly*, whose rhetorical excesses, logical conundrums, and textual uncertainties are the most direct counterproducts of Erasmus's classical scholarship, particularly of his editorial work on the *Adages*[23] and the New Testament. *The Praise of Folly* is largely "about" the impossibility of legitimating humanist discourse. Not only does the form of the paradoxical encomium liberate the destructive forces of a sophistical rhetoric, but the formal proximity of the encomium to prayer helps to destabilize prayer as a traditional form of religious worship. *The Praise of Folly* is perhaps the finest example of how humanist techniques of scientific knowledge *could* be harnessed to create an unlimited skepticism and a vertiginous literary undecidability. It thus showed that the humanist dialectic of certainty and uncertainty had the potential to be driven into open contradiction. Montaigne's skepticism, which set a pessimistic tone for French thought in the early seventeenth century, followed a similar road.

English reception of humanist history and philology came by paths that would bring them in proximity to Spenser. *The true order and Methode of wryting and reading Hystories* (1574), Thomas Blundeville's translation of excerpts from Patrizi and Acontius, was dedicated to the earl of Leicester, who was also Spenser's patron. Acontius, an exiled Protestant, was a follower of Leicester, to whom he dedicated an unpublished work on history.[24] Even closer to home was Spenser's friend Gabriel Harvey, who championed the new humanist historiography, attacked old-style chroniclers such as Holinshed, and repeatedly expressed his admiration for Valla.[25] (E. K.'s dedication to *The Shepheardes Calender* asks Harvey to be a patron for Spenser and plays to his prejudices by citing Valla's criticisms of Livy. [p. 8].) Spenser himself, in the letter to Raleigh which accompanied the first edition of *The Faerie Queene*, distinguished between "historiographers," who are bound to tell only what is true, and "poets historical," who are allowed to employ myth and fable.[26] And in *A View of the Present State of Ireland*, he insisted on the danger of relying on the "remembraunces of bardes which use to forge and falsefye everie thinge as they liste." Emulating the methods of antiquarians, Spenser argued that from

> comparison of times likenes of manners and Customes Affinytie of wordes and names properties of natures and uses resemblaunces of rightes and Ceremonies monimentes of Churches and Tombes and manie other like circumstances I doe gather a likelyhode of truethe, not certainlye affirminge anye thinge but by Conferringe of times nacions languages monimentes and suche like I doe hunte out a probabilitye of thinges.[27]

*A View* is obviously riddled with inaccuracies and colonialist assumptions, which its "scientific" and probabilistic approach merely serves to legitimate. But it is a sign of how thoroughly Spenser had absorbed the principles of the new humanist historiography.

In *The Shepheardes Calender*, the dialectic of humanist knowledge is embedded in the very form of the work. By framing the eclogues, and thereby creating what Michael McCanles calls "a historical and typographical gulf between the text of the poems and the text of the commentaries,"[28] E. K.'s glosses reflect the sharp fact/fiction distinction insisted on by humanist historians and textual critics. But by folding this commentary back into the fiction of the work, *The Shepheardes Calender* turns this impassable gulf into a space of unstable reversals and oscillations. Whereas *A View of the State of Ireland* resolves the contradictions of humanist knowledge into a "responsible" probabilistic method, *The Shepheardes Calender* more playfully separates its two component parts into pedantic and often absolute claims of knowledge, on the one hand, and complete undecidability and a skeptical rejection of knowledge, on the other. The work both produces and contains a crisis of legitimation by rehearsing it in a playful and literary form.

A social framework for this crisis might be suggested by drawing on what Jean-François Lyotard has called the "pragmatics" of narrative and of scientific knowledge.[29] As embodied, for instance, in storytelling, epic, or myth, narrative knowledge is marked by certain procedures of transmission (oral recitation, rhythmic and verbal formulas, particular relations of authority between sender and receiver) which lend it a relatively fixed and self-validating quality.[30] "Narration is the quintessential form of *customary* knowledge," says Lyotard. Moreover, it is both directly constituted by and directly constitutive of a social bond. What it produces is not knowledge in the scientific sense but a set of social relations and practices, chiefly of a customary sort. As a result, "narrative knowledge does not give priority to the question of its own legitimation. . . . it certifies itself in the pragmatics of its own transmission without having recourse to argumentation and 'proof.'"[31]

Scientific knowledge operates under protocols entirely different from these. It "requires that one language game, denotation, be retained and all others excluded. . . . [It] is in this way set apart from the language games that combine to form the social bond. Unlike narrative knowledge, it is no longer a direct and shared component of the social bond. . . . The relation between knowledge and society . . . becomes one of mutual exteriority."[32] What distinguishes scientific from narrative knowledge is not only a difference in content but a shift in the protocols of transmission and legitimation.[33] Scientific knowledge no longer directly reproduces customary social relations; it issues denotative statements that attempt to validate themselves by means of formal criteria. But it is precisely in so doing that it opens a broad new field for the delegitimation of knowledge and the production of *uncertainty*. It is because a scientific pragmatics ultimately cannot ground its own procedures in a satisfying way that it must frequently have recourse to a legitimating narrative of some sort: a narrative of Enlightenment, of scientific progress, or in the case of humanism, of the recovery or "renaissance" of classical culture and the rejection of medieval darkness or "barbarism."

Lyotard's categories are especially suggestive, I think, for understanding the relation between humanist commentary and pastoral poetry in *The Shepheardes Calender*. For what Spenser's eclogues manage to evoke, fitfully and belatedly, is the image of a precritical, customary, or "narrative" form of knowledge transmitted by piping and poetry and articulated within an idealized rural collectivity: precisely the kind of bardic knowledge that Spenser would judge untrustworthy in *A View of the State of Ireland*. E. K.'s glosses, separated from this pastoral world by the "impassable gulf" between commentary and text, quite graphically represent the "mutual exteriority" of knowledge and society which characterizes a scientific pragmatics. The Shepheardes Calender thus invokes two very different and incompatible regimes of knowledge as part of the work's generic and cultural heterogeneity.

The simultaneous presence of these two regimes enables The Shepheardes Calender to be construed as a "transitional" work. For while the difference between scientific and narrative knowledge cannot be directly reduced to that between capitalist and precapitalist discourse, Lyotard's language at least partly encourages assimilation to these categories.[34] The transformation of knowledge from customary social bond to socially autonomous discourse clearly involves a social decoding of intellectual production very like that described in the first part of this book. Yet Lyotard's categories require considerable expansion and retooling if they are to be assimilated to a Marxist account of the transition to capitalism: in particular, the nature and procedures of "narrative" knowledge as they apply to medieval culture need to be explained, and questions of the legitimation of knowledge need to be tied more rigorously to issues of *ideological* legitimation and social reproduction.

An appropriate point of entry for this question is medieval textual criticism and commentary, which differs significantly from the philological criticism of the Renaissance humanists.[35] Medieval biblical commentary was actually a complex hybrid of scientific and narrative practices. Although it achieved a high degree of formal sophistication, branching out into logical, semiotic, and grammatical studies,[36] these forms were effectively subordinated to a narrativizing project. Medieval commentary and figural interpretation aimed, despite their formal complexities, to reduce the heterogeneous texts that composed the Bible to a coherent and simplified narrative order, to transform the Bible into the expression of a salvational myth that could ultimately be condensed to the incantatory formulas of a credo.[37] This "narrative reduction" actually suppressed biblical textuality by integrating all biblical stories into a master narrative and by identifying history with the "literal sense" of scripture.[38] Its ultimate purpose was not to expound or elucidate the text of the Bible in a critical sense but to overcode it with a narrative that, though largely derived from Scripture, came to occupy a more powerful ideological position. The Thomist fourfold allegory, adopted by Dante for his allegory of the poets, reorganized individual, secular, cosmic, and divine histories into an overarching narrative totality.[39]

To describe this mode of interpretation as "totalizing" is not, however, to suggest that it banishes all alternative cultural or interpretive modes. Scholastic logic, for example, was an alien body within the church's field of narrative knowledge but coexisted peacefully with it, largely by being granted a local or parcelized authority. For although scholasticism made important advances over Aristotle in the "scientific" field of formal logic, these were bounded and in effect ideologically neutralized by the guild structure of the universities.[40] Logic fell under the jurisdiction of arts faculties, which were forbidden to discuss theological issues; it thus developed its procedures in splendid isolation from the narrative apparatuses of the church. This material-institutional isolation was reflected, moreover, in the internal contours of the discipline itself. Medieval logic shed all Aristotelian interest in rhetorical, enthymemic, or probabilistic arguments—precisely those that would open it up to epistemological or metaphysical questions.[41] (Aristotle himself fell into relative disregard compared to formal logicians such as Peter of Spain, who considered an enthymeme only a syllogism with one term suppressed). Whereas this bounding of logic allowed significant advances in areas such as predication theory, it reflected a situation in which the lines of an intellectual field were drawn not as a consequence of its internal protocols but rather to establish domains of privilege. As a result, logic was effectively prevented from posing critical questions to theology (though it influenced the discursive language of theology) or to the narrative apparatuses of the church. It created intellectual conflict only when it overstepped its domain and tried to pass judgment on theological matters, as the crisis of Averroism and the career of Reginald Pecock both suggest.[42]

This parceling out of autonomous discursive areas under the dominance of a narrative apparatus is widespread in medieval Christianity. While it reflects a characteristic mode of articulating power within the feudal polity (as discussed in the chapter on Skelton), it also answers to the pragmatics of narrative knowledge, which, as Lyotard points out, are more "tolerant" than scientific ones.[43] The narrative apparatuses of the church tended to exercise a form of flexible domination which is especially evident in the handling of non-Christian culture. A good example is Ralph Higden's *Polychronicon*, a world history from the creation to 1360, "divided into seven books according to the several ages of human history in order to display the providential plan."[44] Employing what has been called the usual "scissors and paste" method of the medieval chronicler, Higden attempted to "reconcile the bibilical account of the beginning of history with pagan sources."[45] Here the materials of classical culture are not expelled but simply absorbed into an authorized narrative unity. Yet they need not directly support the Christian narrative of history; they need only not contradict it. A similar approach characterized late medieval criticism of classical and secular literature, which simply applied the allegorical techniques of biblical interpretation to a wider and more heterogeneous body of texts. In a study of the literary criticism practiced by classicizing friars, Judson Boyce Allen shrewdly observes that "the spiritual sense of fiction probably results from a colonizing triumph of exegesis, rather than a coup d'etat by fiction."[46] The function of medieval literary commentary was to assimilate heterogeneous materials to the dominant cultural narrative, to "colonize" sources of potential dissonance or uncertainty. This is a totalizing gesture, to be sure, but an extremely loose one. In fact, the metaphor of colonization ought to be taken quite seriously here. Successful colonization does not involve an attempt to reform every aspect of the colony's political, cultural, and economic life according to the example of the colonizer. On the contrary, it often entails a minimalist project allowing the greatest possible autonomy consistent with the demands of continued domination. Likewise, medieval exegesis of classical texts did not characteristically seek a scrupulous or thorough assimilation to the dominant narrative but only a working correspondence that would neutralize areas of possible ideological friction. In general, the margins of officially sanctioned culture tended to be rather loosely policed, allowing a sometimes surprising interpenetration of Christian and non-Christian cultures: "The figures of romance invaded the churches themselves, creeping into the carvings of the portals, along the choirstalls, and into the historiated margins of the service books."[47] The narrative apparatuses of the church thus exerted something analogous to Althusser's "determination in the last instance" within the cultural field—establishing structures in dominance, parceling out areas of relative autonomy, all the while being overdetermined by the elements it controlled. It constructed a "loose" totality whose elements were not reduced to mere epiphenomena of the structure that organizes it or even required to play an ideologically functional role.

The characteristic workings and structures of narrative knowledge are perfectly exemplified in *The Kalendar of Shepherdes*, from which Spenser drew both the title and some of the formal characteristics of his volume of eclogues. That the *Kalendar* is in fact concerned with knowledge is suggested by the full title of one of its English editions: "The arte / scyence / and practyke of the great Kalendar of Shepeherdes . . . "[48] Primarily a work of religious instruction intended for a rural, semiliterate audience, the *Kalendar* defines its readership and ideological slant in describing its own fictional author,

> a shepherde kepynge his shepe in the feldes which was no clerke ne understode no manere of scrypture nor wretynge but only by his naturall wyt. He sayeth that lyvynge and dyenge is all at the wyll and pleasure of almyghty god. . . . And he sayeth . he that offerith himselfe here to live vertuesly in this worlde . after this lyfe . he shall receyve the swete lyfe that is sure and lastyth ever with out end. . . . Therefore saythe this shepharde . I will lyve soberly with these smale temporall goodes that Ihesu hath lente me and ever to exyle the desyre of wordely [*sic*] ryches and wordely worshype.[49]

The *Kalendar* largely consists of religious and moral information delivered in mnemonic formulas or narrative or graphic forms: the Pater Noster, the Salutation of Our Lady, the Apostle's Creed, the Ten Commandments of the Lord, the five commandments of the church, the ten commandments of the devil (rhymed), the visions of Lazarus depicting the torments of the damned, the "trees" of vice and virtue, and so on. Encompassing and loosely organizing all of this is the liturgical calendar with its saints' and feast days; the *Kalendar* is ultimately grounded in the narrative of the church year, which subsumes within its rhythms both the agricultural seasons and the metaphorical "seasons" of individual human lives.[50] The *Kalendar* thus effects an overcoding of experience rather like that carried out by medieval allegory: it structures a wide range of cultural materials under the loose governance of the church's narrative apparatus. Typically, the kinds of knowledge it distributes are not subject to questions of legitimation; they verify themselves in the social processes of their transmission, which subject the hearer or reader to the corporative body and sacramental practices of the church.

The *Kalendar* is thus a massively and almost naïvely ideological document; but for all that, it is also a diverse one, which does not require formal or ideological unity to do its work. It is, in fact, a cultural grab bag. Its religious materials coexist happily with all kinds of "practical" information and superstitious lore: zodiacs

and astrological tables, calendars of solar and lunar eclipses, die-
tetic advice, anatomical diagrams, poems, a handy guide to phle-
botomy, and so forth. New editions added material with no sense
of violating boundaries. To be sure, there are sometimes explicit
and sometimes implicit principles of unity that connect the
work's various parts: notions of spiritual and bodily health, of different modes of heavenly determination, and so forth. But there is
very little effort to "frame" its component parts, to separate orthodox religious beliefs from superstitious ones, to distinguish between true and false information, to establish any particular order
or sequence of knowledge, or even to impose linguistic unity (the
*Kalendar* includes both English and Latin).

In its very form, the *Kalendar* reflects the loose articulation of
religious and customary practices whereby the church tried to impose its hegemony in rural areas. Keith Thomas has shown how
the sacramental rites of the medieval church were given a "magical" turn and interpretation by rural communities.[51] Blessing of
the fields, for example, reformed traditional religious practices in
accordance with the needs and understanding of rural peasants,
even as it broadened the range of ideological practices through
which the church could extend its influence.[52] If this blend of religion and magic was determined in part by the struggle among
competing class cultures, and thus represented a kind of forced
compromise exacted from the ruling ideology, it is also true that
the church's brand of hegemony allowed cultural interpenetration
and compromises even when it was not under similar kinds of
stress. The relative tolerance of narrative knowledge, with its
loose or "colonial" totalities, is reflected both in the real practices
of the rural church and in the literary compilation of those practices within the *Kalendar of Shepherdes*.

The *Kalendar* thus represents more than just another generic
component or allusion in Spenser's eclogues; it encodes a pragmatics of knowledge which is different from, and largely incompatible
with, the poems' humanist commentary. As a variant of a scientific pragmatics, humanist philology is intolerant of nonscientific
discourses. It insists on a strict theoretical distinction between the
true and the false, or between fact and fiction, which it embodies
in the "framing" of poem by commentary and by the imposition of
an impassable gulf between them. The humanist insistence on certainty and scientific knowledge is, however, attended by problems
of legitimation, which can manifest themselves either in a probabilistic, empirical, and "prudential" concept of truth or in a more

radical brand of skepticism and uncertainty. As an example of narrative knowledge, however, the *Kalendar of Shepherdes* encodes a much more tolerant (though no less effective) regime. Instead of excluding or framing other knowledge forms, it subsumes them within a colonial totality. Instead of policing a strict boundary between true and false, or orthodox and unorthodox, it allows and even encourages indeterminacy and vagueness. If the humanist insistence on certainty generates a corresponding and sometimes anxious form of uncertainty, narrative tolerance encourages a relative indifference to matters of fact and fiction.[53]

A suggestive and amusing collision between these two regimes of knowledge occurs in the General Argument to the *Shepheardes Calender.* Here, E. K. tries to justify Spenser's decision to begin his calendar with the month of January, thus violating classical precedent, which would begin the year with March. After a lengthy and pedantic excursus on the Greek, Roman, Egyptian, Jewish, and Christian calendars, all of which results in a complex knot of irreconcilable precedents, E. K. concludes: "But our Authour respecting nether the subtiltie of thone parte, nor the antiquitie of thother, thinketh it fittest according to the simplicitie of commen understanding, to begin with Januarie, wening it perhaps no decorum, that Shepheard should be seene in matter of so deepe insight, or canvase a case of so doubtful judgment. So therefore beginneth he, and so continueth he throughout" (p.14). Without reading all that precedes this conclusion it is hard to appreciate its comic bathos. It isn't really a conclusion at all but an abandonment of a scholarly tangle. Yet if this ending noticeably falls off from the high erudition that precedes it, it also renders that erudition superfluous. The final position may well suffice, without any further why. It is as if E. K. is suddenly struck with the Wittgensteinian insight that the chain of reasons has an end. By abandoning the humanist search for a determinate historical cause, he indulges in a bit of pastoralism himself, abjuring the criteria of scientific knowledge and falling back on the shepherd's logic of custom ("commen understanding"). He thus abandons his earlier insistence on scientific certainty, as, for instance, in his attempt to define the word *eclogue,* when a merely pragmatic solution was deemed insufficient because it did not answer to "the *analysis* and interpretation of the word."

Earlier I spoke of the form of *The Shepheardes Calender*—the pastoral eclogues framed by a humanist commentary—as graphically representing the "mutual exteriority" of knowledge and society which marks a scientific pragmatics. I also suggested that the pastoral world of the poems might represent an imaginary version of a society governed by narrative pragmatics. If so, it might be concluded that *The Shepheardes Calendar* is marked by a nostalgia of the outside for the inside, of margin or frame for center. But in fact *all* aspects of framing—both its stabilities and its uncertainties—pertain to a scientific pragmatics. If there is an ambivalent "nostalgia" in *The Shepheardes Calender* or, more precisely, in E. K.'s commentary it is not for another position within a framed world but for something anterior to all framing. In other words, the contradiction in the poem is not between outside and inside or between certainty and uncertainty but between a scientific pragmatics that encompasses all of these and a narrative pragmatics that produces undifferentiation, indetermination, and a precritical knowledge that involves neither certainty nor uncertainty in a scientific sense.

If E. K.'s commentary offers a relatively "pure" instance of scientific knowledge, the woodcuts that illustrate each eclogue offer a relatively pure instance of narrative pragmatics—or of its aesthetic equivalent. With the exception of the title, the woodcuts represent the clearest allusion to the old *Kalendar of Shepherdes* in Spenser's volume. Not only was the use of woodcuts self-consciously archaic, but the sight of depictive rather than emblematic illustrations would have struck a sophisticated reader of 1579 as being "so out-of-date as to be, if not scorned, certainly looked down on."[54] In their internal organization as well as their style the woodcuts are markedly old-fashioned, as the illustration to "Februarie" shows (figure 3). The eclogue itself is a carefully framed debate between two shepherds, Cuddie and Thenot, on the traditional theme of youth versus age. Forming the centerpiece of the poem is the tale of the oak and the briar, told by Thenot, the aged shepherd, to illustrate the dangers arising from youth's efforts to supplant the old. Now, within the eclogue the fable is clearly set off from the "real" world of Cuddie and Thenot, and the meaning of the eclogue depends in large part on certain ironic discrepancies between the fable and its effects (or noneffects) on the debate between Thenot and Cuddie.[55] In the woodcut, however, this sharp framing disappears. The characters in the fable occupy the same representational space as Cuddie and Thenot—one of Cuddie's cattle even munches on the briar!—and all these "depictive" characters share their locale with a sign of the zodiac. Within this "tapestry-like space,"[56] humanist distinctions between fact and

Figure 3. Edmund Spenser, *The Shepheardes Calender* (1591 ed.), sig. A3r. Courtesy The Beinecke Rare Book and Manuscript Library, Yale University

fiction evaporate, along with a "painterly" sense of perspective or of differences between figure and landscape, ergon and parergon. The "tolerant" aesthetic of the woodcut thus complements the narrative pragmatics of knowledge represented by the old *Kalendar of Shepherdes*, and in its absence of differentiating frames it forms a counterpoint to E. K.'s humanist commentary.

In general, the strict or scientific rigor of humanist philology was accompanied by a corresponding strictness in the realm of aesthetics. Just as humanist historians scorned the medieval chronicler's apparently naïve mix of fact and fiction, so humanist writers scorned the barbarousness of scholastic Latin, the naïve fictions of medieval romance, even, in some cases, the vernacular practices of rhyming or accentual verse. *The Kalendar of Shepherdes* was precisely the kind of crudely "native," popular, and unshapely work that humanists viewed with contempt, in large part for tolerating a degree of internal heterogeneity that a more classical poetics proscribed. This is why it is not enough to say that *The Shepheardes Calender* aims to "fuse" or "amalgamate" humanist and native medieval poetics. For the fact is that the structure and even the possibility of such an amalgamation differ radically under the conditions of humanist and prehumanist culture. The tensions generated by the coexistence of two incompatible aesthetics within *The Shepheardes Calender* are registered most clearly on the level of linguistic style, particularly by Spenser's use of archaisms. E. K. writes in the Dedicatory Epistle that

> it is one special prayse, of many whych are dew to this Poete, that he hath laboured to restore, as to theyr rightfull heritage such good and naturall English words, as have ben long time out of use and almost cleane disherited. Which is the onely cause, that our Mother tonge, which truely of it self is both ful enough for prose and stately enough for verse, hath long time ben counted most bare and barrein of both. (pp. 8–9)

Yet Dr. Johnson famously deplored the "studied barbarity" of Spenser's eclogues, claiming that it produced "a mingled dialect, which no human being could ever have spoken."[57] Much of the dedicatory epistle is an apology for Spenser's language, as if E. K. anticipated the work's critical reception. Characteristically, he defends Spenser's practice partly on the basis of *decorum*, speculating that the poet may use archaic words "of set purpose and choyse, as thinking them fittest for such rusticall rudenesse of shepheards, eyther for that theyr rough sounde would make his rymes more ragged and rustical, or els because such olde and obsolete wordes are most used of country folke." Archaisms are thus allowable if they reflect a scientifically based knowledge of historical usage: that is to say, if they are framed by a flawless sense of artistic and historical decorum and not merely floating free or contaminating the text. Humanist stylistics is not fully separable from humanist science, for linguistic decorum depends on the ability to distinguish between usages in different historical and cultural contexts. Conversely, humanist historiography was based in large part on philological studies of language and style; Valla had proved the Donation of Constantine a forgery by revealing its anachronisms of vocabulary and phrasing. A strict concept of linguistic decorum thus arises together with a scientific study of language and style. As a result, language is no longer an unreflexive set of customary usages but an object of scientific knowledge and, as such, subject to questions of legitimation.

The problem is not, therefore, that *The Shepheardes Calender* is a stylistic and cultural amalgam. The problem is that this is seen

as a problem, that it generates a set of decisions and discrimina-
tions based on a sense of cultural decorum. As a humanist text,
*The Shepheardes Calender* is obliged to account for and enframe
its moments of stylistic heterogeneity and especially its archaisms
and medievalisms, whereas a precritical or narrative text such as
*The Kalendar of Shepherdes* could tolerate a mixed or heterogeneous mode without anxiety. Thus Spenser is faced with two very
different models for cultural amalgamation. And of course the notion of strict or scientific decorum generates its own uncertainties
and paradoxes as well. For if Spenser is accurately "imitating" the
*Kalendar*, his sense of historical decorum should, logically, cause
him to suspend his sense of history and decorum, since the *Kalendar* recognizes neither of these. (The paradoxes of decorum similarly led Erasmus to conclude that imitating Cicero forbids writing
like Cicero. Because Cicero wrote like a man of his time, modern-
day Ciceronians should write like men of *their* time.) *The Shepheardes Calender* may thus be a humanist text that employs
medievalisms within its strict frame of decorum, a prehumanist
text that employs medievalisms uncritically (E. K. considers both
possibilities), or even a humanist *simulation* of a prehumanist text
which wittily abandons its sense of decorum out of a sense of decorum. Or it may be a mixture of the three. The point is that *The
Kalendar of Shepherdes* not only offers a set of stylistic and cultural materials for assimilation, it offers a different paradigm or
pragmatics to govern the conditions of that assimilation, and both
the materials and the paradigm are unacceptable to humanism.

The incompatibility of these two pragmatics—and of their accompanying aesthetics—is one of the subjects of Spenser's "Februarie" eclogue. Thenot's and Cuddie's debate, including the fable of
the oak and the briar, has been read as an allegorical discourse
about the conflict between traditional authority and social aspira-
tion, and even more specifically as a battle among some of Elizabeth's courtiers.[58] But the eclogue is also clearly about competing
modes of cultural and literary authority, and thus to some degree
about the contradictory status of *The Shepheardes Calender* itself.
In "Februarie," Thenot tries to settle the debate between youth
and age by telling an Aesopian fable about an aged oak and a
"bragging brere." Thenot describes his fable as

> a tale of truth,
> Which I cond of *Tityrus* in my youth,
> Keeping his sheepe on the hils of Kent.
> (91–93)

E. K. informs us that *"Tityrus"* is Chaucer, and thereby alerts us to Spenser's—and Thenot's—indebtedness to medieval poetics. But this imagined scene of pastoral instruction embeds Thenot's Chaucerian apologue within an immemorial process of narrative transmission and thus invokes a whole cultural pragmatics as well.

The narrative "rooting" of fable and apologue finds its emblem in the aged oak, which represents the decaying remnants of traditional culture and authority to which Thenot himself clings:

> A goodly Oake sometime had it bene,
> With armes full strong and largely displayd,
> But of their leaves they were disarayde:
> The bodie bigge, and mightely pight,
> Throughly rooted, and of wonderous hight;
> Whilome had bene the King of the field,
>
> . . . . . .
>
> But now the gray mosse marred his rine,
> His bared boughes were beaten with stormes,
> His toppe was bald, and wasted with wormes,
> His honor decayed, his braunches sere.
>
> (103–8, 111–14)

Later Thenot describes it as

> an auncient tree,
> Sacred with many a mysteree,
> And often crost with the priestes crewe,
> And often halowed with holy water dewe.
> But sike fancies weren foolerie,
> And broughten this Oake to this miserye.
>
> (207–12)

Associated with priestly sacraments and the blessing of fields, the oak thus defines a larger field connecting a Chaucerian and native medieval poetics with the narrative apparatuses of the church. In an indirect way, it might even be said to describe the *Kalendar of Shepherdes*, a venerable but somewhat mossy remnant of late medieval culture, and one that was viewed with suspicion because of its associations with Roman Catholicism and the old liturgical calendar.

Alongside the oak grows a "bragging brere," who taunts him for his age and then complains to a passing husbandman that the oak mars his beautiful flowers. Enraged, the husbandman chops down the oak, leaving the briar lord of the field: that is, until the winter comes, and the briar, now deprived of the oak's protection, is killed by harsh weather. This literal deracination or "uprooting" of narrative tradition is then replicated in the framing tale when Cuddie interrupts Thenot and prevents him from finishing his fable. Noting that Thenot is "conningly cutte of by Cuddye," E. K. punningly ties the rejection of Thenot's Chaucerian apologue to the chopping down of the oak.

The character of the "bragging brere" who provokes this uprooting resembles that of an ambitious courtier, but more generally he seems to represent rhetoricity itself, and particularly a guileful or sophistical rhetoric; he uses "painted words . . . / His colowred crime with craft to cloke" (160–62). Though hollow, however, the briar is beautiful:

> Yt was embellisht with blossomes fayre,
> And thereto aye wonned to repayre
> The shepheards daughters, to gather flowres,
> To peinct their girlonds with his colowres.
> And in his small bushes used to shrowde
> The sweete Nightingale singing so lowde.
>
> (118–23)

The nightingale and the coded words "flowres" and "girlonds" evoke the notion of poetry, particularly the "new poetry" of the court. The briar's lament to the husbandman recalls the styles of Wyatt and Surrey, and his complaint to the oak, "The mouldie mosse, which thee accloieth, / My Sinamon smell too much annoieth" (135–36), may allude to the tendency of both courtly and humanist poets to eschew their homely and native traditions in favor of more refined foreign models. In sum, the upstart briar offers a highly ambivalent image of the new poetry: cunning, delicate, proud of its sophistical rhetoricity, artfully plaining, obsessed with foreign elegance, and contemptuous of native sturdiness—all flower and no stalk.

In the oak and the briar, then, Spenser has embodied two of the cultural and literary strains that constitute *The Shepheardes Calender*. Thus whatever their external referents may be, they also represent the unstable amalgamation of elements that founds his own poetics, and they reveal the *Calender* to be not an organic "fusion" but an unwieldy and tense juxtaposition of two cultural traditions. Moreover, the tension between the two is asymmetrical: the oak is perfectly willing to tolerate the parasitical briar, but the briar insists on uprooting and eliminating its host. The "Feb-ruarie" eclogue thus meditates on cultural and ideological ten-sions that set *The Shepheardes Calender* irreparably at odds with itself. Dr. Johnson's phrase "studied barbarity" sums up these con-tradictions and signals the desire of later literary husbandmen to prune away or deracinate the work's prehumanist elements. "Feb-ruarie" is thus also, perhaps, a baleful prognostic of Spenser's own literary reception.

In fact, the early reception of *The Shepheardes Calender* in-volved not only criticism of the work's archaic elements but radi-cal and sometimes bizarre attempts to eliminate them. Some humanists who approved of the work's classical aesthetics but dis-liked its use of medieval and regional diction found a simple but total solution: translate it into Latin. *The Shepheardes Calender* was twice so translated—first in an unpublished version by John Dove of Christ Church, Oxford (c. 1585–1589)[59] and then by The-odore Bathurst of Pembroke College, Cambridge (Spenser's col-lege), whose version was published posthumously in 1653. In a dedicatory epistle, William Dillingham praised Bathurst's edition of Spenser, "dressed in a Roman toga,"[60] because it saved the work from the oblivion that would result from changes in the English language—a fairly direct reference to the work's archaic diction. The Latin rendering, claimed Dillingham, would "bring light to those parts which are obscure, fluency to those which are rough, and splendor and elegance to the whole."[61] This is clearly more than a translation. It is a reformation of the original, meant to re-duce its messy heterogeneity to Virgilian purity.

A far stranger and, for my purposes, more telling appropriation of Spenser's eclogues was carried out by the English Ramist Abra-ham Fraunce. In *The Lawiers Logike* (1588), Fraunce employed Ramist dialectic in an attempt to reduce the practice of English common law to a logical and scientifically self-conscious disci-pline. What bothered Fraunce most about the common law as it was then practiced was its reliance on custom. This rendered it both unmethodical (and hence difficult to learn) and also bereft of scientifically grounded principles. Significantly, Fraunce compared lawyers who naïvely relied on legal precedent to "good Catholics and modest-minded men, [who] beleeved as the Church beleeved, but why the Church beleeved so, it never came within the com-passe of their cogitation."[62] From the perspective of a scientific pragmatics, the self-validating character of narrative or customary knowledge seems mere tautology.

The common law could nevertheless be saved, Fraunce believed, because even custom is constructed according to the principles of "natural reason" and is therefore susceptible to analysis by the "artificial reason" of Ramist dialectic. Indeed, Fraunce believed that all cultural practices, even poetry, were informed by an immanent rationality that needed only to be revealed and organized: "Reade *Homer*, reade *Demosthenes*, read *Virgill*, read *Cicero*, reade *Bartas*, reade *Torquato Tasso*, reade that most worthie ornament of our English tongue, the *Countesse of Penbrookes Arcadia*, and therein see the true effectes of natural Logicke which is the ground of artificiall."[63] *The Lawiers Logike* is based on an earlier, unpublished work by Fraunce titled "The Sheapheardes Logike" (c. 1585?), which illustrated the principles of "natural reason" solely by means of copious examples taken from *The Shepheardes Calender*. *The Lawiers Logike* retains these examples, and thus astonishingly jumps back and forth between the *Calender* and common law to fetch examples for Ramist analysis. For instance, Fraunce quotes the following lines from Spenser's "Julye":

> But nothing such thilk shephearde was,
>   whom *Ida* hyll dyd beare,
> That left hys flocke, to fetch a lasse,
>   whose love he bought to deare.
>
> (145–48)

and resolves them into this syllogism: "Hee that leaveth his flocke to fetch a lasse, is no good sheepherd: But *Paris* did leave his flocke to fetch a lasse, Therefore, *Paris* is no good sheepherd."[64] Like E. K., Fraunce has complete confidence in the scientific certainty of his method, despite the absurd readings and conclusions to which it often leads. But his articulation of science and poetry is very different from E. K.'s, and deserves some scrutiny. Within *The Shepheardes Calender*, poem and commentary are defined by the relation of framing: E. K.'s glosses remain exterior to a pastoral world that sometimes images a naïve and idyllic narrative culture. The practices of the commentary clearly bear no resemblance to what occurs within the fiction of the poem, and this disjunction generates conflicting feelings of superiority and nostalgic longing on the part of the commentator. For Fraunce, however, logic and poetry are both informed by the same reason; hence the poet is an unmethodical philosopher. Indeed, all persons, regardless of social status or profession, reason alike. What Fraunce finds especially appealing about Spenser's eclogues is that they represent shep herds, the simplest and most naïve of men, engaged in reasonable discussion and debate. Thus the pastoral world is not disjoined from the scientific one; it contains an immanent and "natural" form of philosophical reason. Accordingly, Fraunce does not observe the rules of framing. Since he does not regard the poems or their fictional world as representing an organic totality, he happily breaks them up into fragments for analysis. For him, unlike E. K., there is nothing about pastoral that is essentially foreign to science, and hence there is no need merely to circle around the poems with a commentary on their alien world. He does not even regard his procedures as an "uprooting" of pastoral, because he does not recognize an opposing or anterior cultural logic at work there.

Fraunce's work is not, however, antipastoral; it merely construes pastoral differently. In *The Shepheardes Calender* pastoral is often the site of a narrativized knowledge certified by the procedures of its own social transmission, a knowledge that is derived from and reproduces a customary social relation and is hence inseparable from it. Fraunce's scientific knowledge is, by contrast, exterior to all concrete social collectivities: "Men reason in schooles as Philosophers, in Westminster as Lawyers, in Court as Lords, in Country as worldly husbands."[65] But logic underlies each of these instances as a metadiscourse that belongs to none of them. If this formulation reduces knowledge and society to a state of "mutual exteriority," however, it founds a different kind of social bond based on universal participation in reason. Indeed, it effects a potentially radical leveling and reunification of discursive subjects: "Coblers bee men, why therefore not logicians? and Carters have reason, why therefore not Logicke?"[66] Scientific discourse imagines a new social collectivity founded on the pact of reason rather than the bonds of narrative culture or material production. Knowledge is no longer derived from or legitimated by existing social relations; rather, it signifies a virtual and utopian community of radically equal interpreters. This is the pastoral of science, a social order of transparent simplicity and universal equality—the shepherd's (il)logic: all shepherds have reason; all men have reason; therefore all men are shepherds.


Unsettling the Elizabethan Settlement

Like many other Ramists in England, Abraham Fraunce seems also to have been a Puritan.[67] It is, at least, easy to see how his leveling conception of human reason might support antiprelatical views of church government. What seems a merely utopian or virtual equality within Ramist theory could take on more serious consequences in the religious sphere, where it engages not only theoretical but practical attempts to reorganize traditional institutions of interpretive authority. In *The Shepheardes Calender* too, the humanist "game" of interpretation suddenly turns solemn when transposed to religious and political contexts. E. K.'s claims and foibles as interpreter are easily assimilated to the fictional play of the work; and generic and stylistic contradictions raise, at most, purely aesthetic complaints from readers. But the act of interpretation becomes much graver in the "moral" eclogues, where it bears upon contested issues of religious belief and political authority. "Maye," "Julye," and "September" all deal with politically sensitive questions of church discipline and ceremony, the financial and moral conduct of the episcopate, and the role of state authority in ecclesiastical conduct—matters that formed the basis of serious sectarian disputes. In these eclogues, the pastoral world turns allegorical and dangerous; wolves and foxes, the representatives of theological fraud and deception, are on the prowl for unwary shepherds and their flocks. Interpretation thus becomes fraught with anxiety, sometimes literally a matter of life and death. In "Maye," an innocent kid captured by a wily fox learns too late that "deceitfull meaning is double eyed" (254)—a warning to the unwary about the dangers posed by High Anglicans who are really papists at heart.[68]

Theological disputes always have an ideological gravity of their own, but since religious conformity was an important goal of Elizabethan policy the political stakes were especially high. A national church supplied an important prop for absolutist rule by helping to secure the ideological unity and internal solidity of the nation-state. Religious policy also guarded the borders of absolutism's national arena by forging external policies and alliances. Conversely, it was feared that religious controversy would open the way for factionalism at court, class conflict in the polity, and foreign intrigue or invasion.

This intersection of Protestant, nationalist, and absolutist politics was brought home to Spenser around the time of *The Shepheardes Calender* by the queen's marital negotiations with the French and Catholic duke of Alençon. The proposed match horrified a number of nationalist Protestants, including those of Leicester's circle. It has been argued that some of Spenser's eclogues covertly criticize these negotiations and that the evident dangers awaiting critics of the queen may have prompted Spenser to publish his work anonymously, thereby starting a potentially risky game of interpretation and concealment.[69] The more paradigmatic questions of knowledge and interpretation raised by E. K.'s commentary thus provide a general context for more specific and sensitive interventions into the political and religious spheres.

Sometimes, politics threaten to invade E. K.'s commentary itself. His pedantic discourse on the history of the calendar stages the apparently innocuous and even playful paradoxes of humanist knowledge. But things become more pointed in historical context. In 1577 Pope Gregory announced his proposals for the reform of the secular calendar; yet despite its manifest superiority, English scholars and church officials felt that to accept the Gregorian calendar would be to acknowledge Rome's jurisdiction over England. Hence just before or after 1580 John Dee proposed an alternative "Protestant" calendar. In this atmosphere the very topic of scholarship on the calendar became politically charged.[70] E. K. steadfastly refuses even to allude to this polemical context, which nevertheless hovers ominously in the background and attests to the position of religious controversy as a particularly dense field for the intersection of knowledge and political power.

In *The Shepheardes Calender* the interplay between a narrative and scientific pragmatics, or between humanist and prehumanist knowledge, is overdetermined throughout by issues of religious controversy, nationalist ideology, and Protestant interpretation. More precisely, Spenser's work raises questions of interpretation in order to probe the strains that were beginning to show in the Elizabethan settlement by 1579. One of the theoretical foundations of this settlement was the doctrine of adiaphorism, or the distinction between those religious matters that were eternal, unchanging, and divinely instituted and those that were of human origin and so historically conditioned.[71] Adiaphorism was primarily a theological instrument for defining the role of the state in church government. It set aside a core of religious doctrine as divinely sanctioned and hence beyond secular control, while regarding most other matters, including ceremonies and church discipline and government, as human inventions, subject to the political authority of the crown. It thus placed the visible church under the jurisdiction of the state while holding that the invisible church was a *corpus mysticum*, the body of the elect, which existed outside of historical time.[72]

While the doctrine of adiaphorism negotiated the lines between state and church authority, it also defined the boundaries of scientific thought. Because they were of human and historical origin, adiaphora were also susceptible to humanist methods of historical analysis; the core beliefs, however, were regarded as eternal, divinely enjoined, and immune to such analysis. Adiaphorism thus effected a parceling of narrative and scientific practices not unlike that practiced by the medieval church and resulted in a theology "that could be defended with some mixture of reason, history, tradition, and scripture."[73] By defining adiaphora as things not essential to salvation, the church was able to adopt, in some instances, a relatively tolerant attitude toward heterodox beliefs or practices. On the other hand, adiaphorism granted the state enormous powers to define and enforce its version of church discipline. In fact, although adiaphorism was intended to draw lines of jurisdiction, it did so primarily to express the dominance of the state over religious practice, interpretation, and doctrine. It granted the state both the power and the flexibility to impose a national church on a body of citizens with often diverse religious beliefs.

However much the church visible might be distinguished from the church invisible in theory, in practice the Elizabethan settlement drew much of its strength from identifying the nation-state as a cultural and political entity with the body of the elect. Anglicanism left many of the traditional forms of church government and discipline intact but reorganized the narrative apparatuses of the medieval church so that the social organism that legitimated religious knowledge and practice was now the state. In *The Shepheardes Calender* this unity of national and religious ideology comes closest to realization in "Aprill, " and specifically in Colin Clout's ode to "fayre *Elisa*, Queene of shepheardes all" (34). Throughout, Colin's ode celebrates Elizabeth's double role as queen of England and head of the English church.[74] Formally, the ode attempts to forge a unity of courtly and Protestant allegory while the pastoral fiction treats England itself as a harmonious garden in which state and ecclesiastical authority are perfectly fused. Glossing lines that describe Elisa as the daughter of Pan and Syrinx, E. K. writes that "by Pan is here meant the most famous and victorious King, her highnesse Father, late of worthy memorye, K. Henry the eyght. And by that name, oftymes (as hereafter appeareth) be noted kings and mighty Potentates: And in some place Christ himself, who is the verye Pan and god of Shepheardes" (50). King and Christ can substitute as allegorical referents, just as Elizabeth, who is indirectly compared to Solomon throughout the ode, represents both political and divine wisdom.[75]

The panegyric ode of "Aprill" is the closest *The Shepheardes Calender* comes to expressing a complete and idyllic unity of nation and church in which class and religious differences have disappeared into a naïve organicism. It is the most directly "ideological" of the pastorals in that it implies (to borrow William Empson's famous phrase) a beautiful relation between rich and poor. But Spenser makes it clear that this beauty is merely imagined. Even within "Aprill" Colin's ode is reported at second hand to a framing world of danger and sorrow; its harmonies are already presented as irrevocably lost. And much of the rest of the *Shepheardes Calender* is devoted to registering the forces that disrupt this imaginary idyll. Spenser does not, I think, rise to direct criticism of the Elizabethan settlement; rather, he allows just enough dissonance within the work to create *doubt* or uncertainty about the precritical innocence of Colin's ode. He thus accomplishes in the political realm something very much like what E. K. accomplishes in the philological.

*The Shepheardes Calender* directs the force of critical doubt at both of the imaginary communities that together under write England's ideological coherence or unity: the nation-state and the church. It is true that nationalist mythology, the first of these ideological forms, plays a less important role in *The Shepheardes Calender* than it does in *The Faerie Queene* (the ode in "Aprill" again being an exception), but nationalism does enter the work at the level of language. E. K., at least, describes Spenser as aiming at a verbal Reformation that will purify English of its foreign elements and restore it to a native simplicity. He writes in the dedicatory epistle:

> It is one special prayse, of many whych are dew to this Poete, that he hath laboured to restore, as to theyr rightfull heritage such good and naturall English words, as have ben long time out of use and almost cleane disherited. Which is the onely cause, that our Mother tonge, which truely of it self is both ful enough for prose and stately enough for verse, hath long time ben counted most bare and barrein of both. (pp. 8–9)

E. K.'s language is steeped in the rhetoric of pastoral melancholy: his nostalgia for the "good and naturall English words" that flourished in a cultural golden age before language grew "bare and barrein" anticipates Colin Clout's lament for the "barrein ground" of pastoral in "Januarye." This pastoralism of language is subtended, moreover, by E. K.'s praise of the "mother tongue" and his attack on those who neglect "their owne country and natural speach, which together with their Nources milk they sucked" (p. 9). The concept of the mother tongue indulges both the psychological satisfaction of the maternal presence and the metaphysical satisfactions of voice. A language as familiar as the nursing breast evokes an imaginary fullness of meaning. Yet it is not language as such but the native tongue that is mythicized here; "natural" speech is really only "country" speech. What the nurse's breast figures is a primary *localization* of culture; it anticipates the pastoral space while the relation between nurse and child foreshadows the idealized and nourishing bonds of a pastoral collectivity. The act of nursing thus offers a metonymic blueprint for a language whose exchange is entirely and directly a social relation. The milk of the native word is the medium of a narrative knowledge—precritical, intuitively familiar, passed among members of a localized collective. Conversely, the neglect of this language is construed as antisocial. E. K. attacks those who "are not ashamed, in their own mother tonge straungers to be counted and alienes" (p. 9). Not to adorn the mother tongue is both an act of filial impiety and a self-imposed exile from the community of native speakers. Here the alienation of meaning betokens a social alienation from narrative culture; the pastoral of language is inseparable from pastoral as a social myth. To restore the native tongue is to restore the cultural medium ("milk") of pastoral.

Of course, this linguistic project is directly nationalist as well, for the attempt to forge a native language for poetry imagines the cultural reformation of England into a pastoral collectivity, the reduction of the nation to an oversized village. Both terms of this equation are contained in the phrase "their owne country . . . speach," which conflates rural and national culture. E. K. contrasts the simple pastoral tongue to one adulterated with foreign substitutions, reviling those who "patched up the holes [in English] with peces and rags of other languages, borrowing here of the french, there of the Italian, every where of the Latine, not weighing how il those tongues accorde with themselves, but much worse with ours: So now they have made our Englishe tongue, a gallimaufray or hodgepodge of al other speches" (p. 9). This cultural xenophobia was probably reinforced by the queen's ongoing marital negotiations with the duke of Alençon. E. K.'s desire to seal off the cultural and linguistic borders stems the threat of religious, political, and sexual "contamination" posed by the queen's possible marriage to a French Catholic.[76]

This desire for a linguistic pastoral is, however, riddled with contradictions. For one thing, E. K.'s literary nationalism is often betrayed by Spenser's eclogues, which borrow freely from Marot, Ronsard, Du Bellay, Sanazzaro, and Mantuan.[77] Moreover, the *Kalendar of Shepherdes*, which provides an important cultural and generic model for Spenser's volume, was translated from a French original and harks back to a time when the narrative apparatuses of the church were not organized around the nation-state. More important, archaisms and regionalisms do not produce the kind of prereflective national unity that E. K. desires. Their most pertinent advantage for this purpose was their supposed familiarity, that they had been imbibed from youth like milk from the nurse's breast. Yet as E. K. admits, it is precisely these "good and naturall English words" that strike the reader as barbarous and obscure, making him "crye out streight way, that we speak no English, but gibbrish" (p. 9). In fact, the incorporation of such native words does not project a pastoral collectivity; it rather attests to the irreducible contradictions within the nation-state. In *The Arte of Rhetoricke* (1560), Thomas Wilson warned: "Either we must make a difference of English, and say some is learned English and other some is rude English, or the one is court talke, the other is countrey speech, or els we must . . . use altogether one maner of language."[78]

The differences of which Wilson complains were of course insoluble at the level of speech alone, and even the relative flattening effected by political and economic unification could not eliminate the multiplicity of regional, class, and professional dialects. The "internal" polyglossia of English represents both the historical sedimentations and the social contradictions that resist sublimation into a cultural unity. Stubborn fissures of language trace those material and ideological struggles that cannot be resolved by the nation-state. If Spenser's language does not offer anything so coherent as a critique or rejection of nationalist mythology, it at least problematizes and unsettles the courtly fiction of the nation-state as a hierarchically unified pastoral landscape. Alexander Pope complained that "the old English and country phrases of Spenser were . . . spoken only by people of the lowest condition"[79] and were thus incompatible with an otherwise courtly and humanist work.

Protestant allegory serves a critical purpose similar to that of language, pointing to religious rifts within the supposed unity of the Elizabethan settlement. This is especially evident in "Maye," where allegory not only undermines pastoral unity but insists on a reformation of pastoral itself. Like "Februarie," "Maye" features a debate between two shepherds, Piers and Palinode. "Maye" is, in fact, a careful reworking of "Februarie," and like its model it is also about some of the cultural contradictions that make pastoral impossible as a poetic form.

"Februarie" opens with Cuddie's complaints about the unendurable winter's cold. Old Thenot responds that this is only the way of the world, which always goes from good to bad and back again. He himself has learned stoic forbearance, enduring heat and cold without complaining or abandoning his duty: "And ever my flocke was my chiefe care, / Winter or Sommer they mought well fare" (23–24). "Maye" begins with a related but different problem, for now it is the pleasures of the season that threaten the business of shepherding. Palinode opens the eclogue by complaining:

> Is not thilke the mery moneth of May,
> When love lads masken in fresh aray?
> How falles it then, we no merrier bene,
> Ylike as others, girt in gawdy greene?
> Our bloncket liveryes bene all to sadde,
> For thilke same season, when all is ycladd
> With pleasaunce: the grownd with grasse, the Wods [woods]
> With greene leaves, the bushes with bloosming Buds.
> Yougthes folke now flocken in every where,
> To gather may buskets and smelling brere:
> And home they hasten the postes to dight,
> And all the Kirke pillours eare day light,
> With Hawthorne buds, and swete Eglantine,
> And girlonds of roses, and Sopps in wine.
> Such merimake holy Saints doth queme,
> But we here sytten as drownd in a dreme.
>
> (1–16)

To this Piers sternly replies that "For Younkers *Palinode* such follies fit, / But we tway bene men of elder witt" (17–18), thus establishing himself as the counterpart of the elderly Thenot, just as Palinode voices the youthful concerns of Cuddie.

E. K. informs us in the argument to "Maye" that "under the persons of two shepheards Piers and Palinodie, be represented two formes of pastoures or Ministers, or the protestant and the Catholique: whose chiefe talke standeth in reasoning, whether the life of the one must be like the other" (p. 46). Palinode certainly demonstrates the relatively greater tolerance of the Catholic church for May games and other popular festivities; his belief that "merimake holy Saints doth queme," and his delight in seeing church pillars festooned with mayflowers suggests the loose or "colonial" form of ideological rule characteristic of the medieval church. Indeed, the image of the ancient church pillar "dight . . . with Hawthorne buds, and swete Eglantine" seems calculated to recall the tale of the oak and the briar in "Februarie," as does Palinode's mention of "smelling brere" (10). Even more directly than did the oak, the church pillar represents the narrative tolerance of the church to parasitical or alien cultural forms. (The vines and flowers decking the pillars are analogous to the figures of medieval romance who were also allotted a physical space in the church.) This tolerance is reproduced in Palinode himself who, despite his disagreement with Piers, hopes that "conteck soone by concord mought be ended" (163). But the Protestant Piers does not believe in peaceful coexistence: "what concord han light and darke sam?" (168). Like the briar in "Februarie," Piers cannot endure the presence of a rival. And just as a humanist poetic could not tolerate a prehumanist one in the earlier eclogue, so Protestantism cannot endure Catholic religious practices here.

Piers's differences from Palinode are reflected in his mode of understanding pastoral and his role in it. Responding to Palinode's argument that shepherds should enjoy the good that God sends them, he proclaims:

> Ah *Palinodie*, thou art a worldes childe:
> Who touches Pitch mought needes be defilde.
> But shepheards (as Algrind used to say,)
> Mought not live ylike, as men of the laye.
>
> (73–76)

Piers and Palinode don't so much argue *with* as *past* one another, for Palinode's remarks concern real shepherds, but Piers's concern ministers, spiritual shepherds of their flocks. Palinode, that is, accepts the pastoral world literally, at face value, but Piers reads it as an allegorical or figurative signifier of spiritual meanings. Like E. K., though from a different perspective, he *interprets* pastoral and thus converts it into an object of knowledge. And as with

E. K., this activity alienates him from pastoral, renders him external to it, as signified by his refusal to join the season's festivities.

Piers defends his insistence on the need for interpretive suspicion by telling an Aesopian fable of the kid and the fox. In the tale, a mother goat who must leave home warns her kid to beware of wild beasts who will try to entrap him, and especially the treacherous fox. After her tearful farewell the dam departs, and the fox, disguised as a peddler, comes to the door "Bearing a trusse of tryfles at hys backe, / As bells, and babes, and glasses in hys packe" (239–40). The kid, not recognizing the fox and enticed by the knickknacks he carries, is snatched up in the fox's pack and carried off, leaving his mother to grieve his loss. "Such end had the Kidde, for he nould warned be / Of craft, coloured with simplicitie" (302–3).

Piers's Aesopian tale clearly corresponds to Thenot's in "Februarie," and like Thenot's, it describes the harmful effects of a guileful or sophistical rhetoric. And yet the story of the kid and the goat substitutes an essential enmity for the tale of parasitism or failed coexistence in "Februarie." The tale is clearly a religious allegory. E. K. interprets the fox as representing Roman Catholic priests with their vestments, bells, incense, relics, and other "knacks" used to allure and deceive innocent Christians, but Anthea Hume argues rather convincingly that the fox represents High Church Anglicans who are really Catholics in disguise.[80] In either case the tale asserts the need for suspicion and watchfulness, and in particular for reading beyond appearances to arrive at spiritual truths. It is thus an allegory about allegory, or about the imperative for allegorical reading. In this respect Palinode's reaction to the fable is telling:

> Now, I pray thee, lette me thy tale borrowe
> For our sir John, to say to morrowe
> At the Kerke, when it is holliday:
> For well he meanes, but little can say.
>
> (308–11)

Palinode, who completely misses the point of the fable, views it as an amusing *narrative* with which his unlearned priest can regale the congregation. His impulse is thus to assimilate it, uncomprehendingly, to his own beliefs, to graft it onto the narrative apparatuses of the church and thus undo Piers's double insistence on interpretation and discrimination.

Allegorical reading of the kind that Piers enjoins fundamentally disarticulates the pastoral fiction, or at least one version of it. For one thing, it transforms the pastoral landscape from arcadia or idyll to allegorical signifier; pastoral is thus no longer something one escapes *to*, but something one transcends or moves beyond. As Thomalin states in "Julye":

> The hylls, where dwelled holy saints,
>     I reverence and adore:
> Not for themselfe, but for the sayncts,
>     which han be dead of yore.
> And nowe they bene to heaven forewent,
>     theyr good is with them goe:
> Theyr sample onely to us lent,
>     that als we mought doe soe.
>
>                           (113–20)

By destroying the immanence of pastoral, Spenser's Protestant allegory looks forward to the kind of transcendental pastoral represented by Milton's *Lycidas*.[81]

But this formal or generic disarticulation entails a political and social one as well. In "Maye," allegorical interpretation is a way of constituting or identifying the body of the spiritual elect, a body that is no longer coterminous with that of the nation-state. In this sense "Maye" is less a reworking of "Februarie" than it is a riposte to "Aprill." The vision of England as pastoral or garden, unified politically and theologically, gives way to a sense of competing and incompatible understandings of church doctrine and discipline. Religious wisdom is no longer invested in Queen Elizabeth as figural Solomon and thence distributed to the nation as a whole. Rather, the elect must set themselves off from the profane and ungodly in their midst, must find their way by means of their own powers of interpretation in a world where deception and idolatry have infected even the official church. Unlike narrative knowledge, which is transmitted and legitimated by an existing social body, Protestant interpretation constitutes and legitimates the body of the elect, which it sets against traditional or customary social bodies.

In this context it is useful to recall one of the events that exerted an important influence on *The Shepheardes Calender*: the sequestration of Archbishop Edmund Grindal in 1577 over the issue of "prophesyings." This incident is directly addressed in "Julye," where Grindal is represented anagramatically as the shepherd Algrind, but I believe that his significance for Spenser's work is more global than this. Grindal was, in a sense, the last hope for the Elizabethan settlement. While he shared many of the Puritans' reformist interests, he also attacked nonconformity and tried "to make presbyterianism unnecessary by reforming the church."[82] His efforts to avoid sectarianism and to preserve the unity of church and state foundered, however, on the crisis of prophesyings in 1576–1577. Despite their charismatic name, prophesyings were actually gatherings of clergy and members of their congregations for the purpose of reading and interpreting biblical passages "outside of the context of the authorized homilies and licensed sermons permitted in Sunday services."[83] It has been argued that some conservative bishops represented these gatherings to the queen as being more subversive than they in fact were, though some prophesyings, especially those in the Midlands, were associated with the more radical Puritans.[84] In any case, the queen eventually ordered their suppression, Grindal wrote her an eloquent but impolitic letter in which he declined to transmit her order to the clergy, and after some unsuccessful attempts at negotiation he was eventually sequestered. The incident thus opened a breach between state and ecclesiastical authority while hindering attempts to keep potential sectarians within the fold of the established church. In every way it strained the supposed unities and harmonies of the Elizabethan settlement.

It is telling that this crisis of authority expressed itself through conflicts of interpretation. The suppression of the prophesyings was clearly intended to limit readings of the Bible to those traditional forms and channels that could be monitored by the state. Not surprisingly, the queen's decision would later be defended on the grounds that prophesyings fell under the rubric of adiaphora, hence were not a necessary form of worship and could be banned by the state. Yet although the crown applied a doctrine that was traditionally used to define its prerogative, it violated the accepted limits of its jurisdiction. As one historian of the affair has noted, "There was no more arbitrary exercise of the royal supremacy in the history of the Church of England than this."[85] It was hardly the sort of action to confirm Elizabeth's role as a Solomon of the nation, and may help to explain why the naïvely celebratory ode of "Aprill" is set in an irrecoverable past.

On the other side, prophesyings challenged the legitimacy of traditional interpretive practices, for biblical texts were now evaluated before the judgment and perhaps even with the participation of lay persons:

> After the appointed speakers had finished, the moderator would ask any learned man who might be present in the auditory to confirm or confute the doctrine delivered. . . . Meanwhile the godly would sit with their Geneva Bibles open on their laps, searching for the texts cited by the preachers. According to one observer, as soon as the public conference was over, the people would hotly discuss what they had heard amongst themselves, "all of them, men and women, boys and girls, workmen and simpletons."[86]

The royal letter of 7 May 1577 which ordered the suppression spoke of "assemblies of great numbers of people, out of their ordinary parishes and from places far distant, and that also of our subjects of good calling (though therein not well advised), to be hearers of their disputations and new devised opinions upon points of divinity, far unmeet for vulgar people."[87] This was a far cry from the aesthetic of courtly pastoral, in which base and rural elements subordinate themselves "so that more excellency may accrue to the principall." It was also a far cry from the narrativized, "colonial" culture of the medieval church. We don't know exactly what Spenser thought of the decision to suppress the prophesyings and sequester Grindal, though Leicester attended prophesyings when he was in the vicinity.[88] In "Julye," at any rate, both Morrel and Thomalin, the "High" and "Low" Church figures, agree on respecting Algrind and on little else. It is clear at least that Grindal represented for Spenser a chance to save the unity of the established church.

Whatever else they signified, the events of 1576–1577 posed a legitimation crisis for the modes of interpretation endorsed by the Church of England—or rather by the Tudor state. Religious knowledge becomes contested, and is now subject to explicitly posed questions of authority, reliability, and method. It is, in other words, "scientific"—not in any positive way but simply in the sense that there is no longer any traditional body that can legitimate religious knowledge primarily through its processes of social transmission. This transformation in religious knowledge and ideology is what renders interpretation "anxious" not only in *The Shepheardes Calender* but in book 1 of *The Faerie Queene* as well; it energizes and makes serious the problems of legitimation that were more playfully explored through E.K.'s humanist commentary.

Within Spenser's moral eclogues, this problem of legitimation is registered in a nagging inconclusiveness to all the religious dialogues. In "Maye" and "Julye" none of the debating shepherds is convinced of his own error, and the dialogical form of the eclogues makes it difficult to say with any certainty which positions Spenser himself endorses. What these eclogues stage, finally, is the absence of any normalizing framework that could decide contested issues. Isolated pairs of shepherds simply dispute in the countryside without any overarching authority or community to impose even a common mode of discourse. I do not claim that these theological debates are a displaced image of prophesying; nevertheless, they raise similar problems, for the pastoral melancholy that afflicts the moral eclogues attests to the absence of a narrative pragmatics that could stabilize and legitimize religious knowledge.

In 1641 Milton would quote approvingly from "Maye" as "a presage of these reforming times."[89] But the prophetic strain in this and the other moral eclogues is always intermittent, and never victorious. Unlike the staged debates that mark all of Milton's major poems, Spenser's never lead to any decisive resolution; the contending shepherds merely voice their opinions and, at day's end, lead their flocks home, often together. Lacking the conviction needed to found a church of one, the moral eclogues reject the customary framework of High Anglicanism, yet search in vain for another social body that can legitimate religious knowledge. Having kicked away the supports of a narrative pragmatics, they find themselves perched uncomfortably in midair, hearing perhaps the wistful exclamation of Samuel Beckett's Hamm: "Ah the old questions, the old answers, there's nothing like them!"

# CHAPTER SIX

# Historica Passio:
# King Lear's
# Fall into Feudalism

In act 2, scene 4, of *King Lear*, the sight of Kent bound in the stocks gives the king his first real taste of madness: "O! How this mother swells up toward my heart; / *Historica passio!* down, thou climbing sorrow! / Thy element's below. Where is this daughter?"[1] When the "mother" rises up through Lear's body it seems to affect his Latin as well as his reason, for in the Quarto and the first three editions of the Folio he diagnoses himself as suffering from the hitherto unheard-of disease *historica passio*.[2] By 1685, the year of the fourth Folio edition of the plays, Lear has apparently had time to bethink himself, for he now utters the "correct" and canonical phrase *hysterica passio*.

This small textual crux, lost perhaps in a play that has since been riven by such cruxes, nevertheless points nicely to a conflict of interpretive choices. What *does* Lear suffer from: hysteria or historia? Is the play to be read in a psychoanalytic, ethical, and personal register or in a political and historical one? (The term *passio* may be taken to invoke a third, bankrupt but nevertheless tenacious strain of readings: the religious or theological.)[3] Both approaches are partially satisfactory, neither fully so; both leave a residue that resists critical totalization. Like hysterica / historica, two terms fighting for the same textual space, each mode of reading has a certain claim to legitimacy, and neither manages fully to supplant or eradicate the other. This situation does not admit of happy pluralisms, however; as in Lear's kingdom, or as in his self-imagined anatomy, a sequence of painful displacements occurs as something is always trying to rise to the top.

One of the most insistent of the historical readings of *King Lear* was sketched out, though not quite filled in, by John Danby, who argued in 1952 that the play is poised uneasily between a "medieval vision" of society and "that of nascent capitalism." For Danby, the historical malady that afflicts both Lear and the fictional world he inhabits derives from a conflict of historically specific values. Characters such as Kent and Cordelia embody the old "feudal" virtues of loyalty and honor, while Goneril, Regan, and above all Edmund are prototypes of the capitalist "New Man" [sic]. Theirs is a society "based on unfettered competition, and the war of all against all. Lear's is the feudal state in decomposition."[4] The general outlines of Danby's reading have been taken up and argued for the most part by Marxist or Marxist-influenced critics.[5] Yet Danby himself was no Marxist, and his reading has appeared plausible to critics of a fairly wide range of ideological positions, in part because it responds to some salient aspects of the play. *King Lear* openly enunciates, at various points, an apparent nostalgia for a lost ideal of social order, an order represented largely by the "feudal" ideals of loyalty, generosity, and military honor embodied in Kent and betrayed in various ways by Goneril, Regan, and Edmund. Yet the appeal of Danby's reading owes more than a little to its vagueness, which allows multiple and possibly contradictory constructions of such terms as *feudalism* and *new man*.

It nevertheless seems clear that *King Lear* is at least partly "about" the transition from feudalism to capitalism, though critics might argue about the relative weight of this issue compared with others in the play. Yet even in its most general and therefore most intuitively appealing formulation, the transitional thesis enfolds a number of implicit assumptions, many of them contestable. John Turner, for instance, has recently challenged the notion that Edmund represents a protocapitalist "type." For Turner, in fact, "the true subject of *King Lear* . . . is not an old order succumbing to a new but an old order succumbing to its own internal contradictions."[6] According to this account *Lear* employs a utopianized and idealized image of feudalism to critique the contemporary social order but also sets strict limits to its utopian current, thus undercutting the nostalgia of the play's wistful old men, Gloucester, Kent, and Lear.

Turner's reading raises—and to a large extent answers—a number of questions about this "old order." To what extent was the word or concept of "feudalism" available to Shakespeare? To what degree does he imagine the feudal past as a sociocultural unity distinct from, yet related to that of his own day? What relation does this conception of the past bear to that of contemporary chroniclers and other historians? And in what ways does the "feudalism" depicted in the great tragedies—*King Lear, Hamlet, Macbeth*—differ from that depicted in the history plays?

Turner's reading of *Lear* attempts to relocate the play's arena of social and ideological struggle, situating it largely within feudalism rather than between two social formations. But whereas this strategy problematizes earlier "transitionalist" readings, it shares with them certain assumptions about history and dramatic form, in particular the Lukácsian idea that dramatic agon among characters is a privileged or inherently fitting way of representing struggles among historical classes.[7] Walter Cohen's brilliant reading of the play explicitly adopts this Lukácsian assumption and then drives it to its limit. Cohen sees *Lear* as a coherent analogical rehearsal of the class contradictions that would lead to the English Revolution—a revolution that "at the level of social structure . . . reenacts the three-sided conflict of Shakespeare's tragedy."[8] I shall return to this issue later to argue that there are some limitations to this "agonistic" model both for understanding Shakespeare's experience of the historical situation of 1605–1610 and for tracing its representation in the play.

The agonistic model or assumption is, in fact, only one answer to a larger question: how can drama, which by its nature focuses on persons rather than transpersonal institutions, possibly represent historical processes (either as the conscious goal of authorial design or as the unwitting effect of ideological and literary practices)? One might reasonably contend that Shakespeare's Edmund is in some respects a "capitalist" or "proto-capitalist" character, but certainly no one would think to argue that *King Lear* portrays capitalism or proto-capitalism. Likewise, the play contains traces of feudal institutions but in no way aspires (or could aspire) to represent feudalism as a social and institutional totality. Rather, we speak of Kent as embodying certain feudal "values," by which we mean that his expressed beliefs, his actions, his manner of expression and quite possibly his costume recall those of the feudal knightly class. What drama has at its disposal as a means of historical representation is primarily a repertoire of such gestural manifestations of value.[9] And insofar as drama manages to embody a historical vision of some sort, it does so largely by substituting these gestural *manifestations* for the social *production* of value. Historical and cultural formations exist through or are signified by dramatic persons; historical actants—collective or impersonal—designate themselves through dramatic agents, generally in an overdetermined fashion. *Historica passio*, the bearing or enduring or manifestation of historical force through one's person and one's body, is thus a fundamental precondition of dramatic art. What Lear feels rising up within him, overcoming him, is that conversion hysteria which constitutes him as a dramatic character and invests his every gesture with a richness of historical signification. Lear experiences his dramatic birth in a particularly traumatic way, whose intensity illuminates the process more generally, just as dramatic representation itself offers a dense and revealing image of our own constitution as social agents.

Dramatic agon, or confrontation, is one means by which a collision of social forces can be dramatically represented; it is one gestural embodiment of social values in conflict. But it does not exhaust the grammar of such gestures. This essay will situate the dramatic conflict of *Lear* within a larger framework of the gestural manifestation of value; and for *Lear* at least, agon is not necessarily the most important of these gestures. *King Lear* is indeed an explicitly "transitional" play, but it represents the tension between feudal and proto-capitalist cultures in ways that circle around and even evade the play's dramatic conflicts.


## Romance, Materialism, and the Space of Critique

It is Lear himself who begins the dissolution of the "feudal" order in the play by means of one sweeping gesture: division of the kingdom. None of Shakespeare's other plays, not even *The Winter's Tale*, gives the same impression of having been set in inexorable motion by one impulsive act. Here it is not only particular dramatic persons but, one feels, an entire social structure that is shattered by the king's decision: a case of *historica passio* in reverse, though it is clear that Lear's abdication merely unleashes tensions that predate it.

The term *abdication* is inexact, however. Lear doesn't resign from or hand down the kingship; he disestablishes it by dividing the kingdom, and thus momentarily distinguishes *King Lear* from the history plays, in which the transmission or capture of the crown is at stake. By so clearly violating the political rationality of the history plays and by incorporating so many mythic or folkloric elements, the division of the kingdom signals the play's generic allegiance to the "timeless" realm of romance—an allegiance suggested as well by the setting, at once medieval and pre-Roman and indeterminately "long ago."[10] At the same time, however, the division of the kingdom initiates a politically coherent examination of the problem of kingship and, more specifically, of the absolutist pretensions of King James I. *King Lear* is studded with references to James's policies and predilections and was clearly composed with a court performance in mind. The play is thus at once timeless and contemporary, ahistorical and politically cogent; its peculiar literary texture results from an apparent tension between the generic characteristics of romance and an embedded set of more-or-less "materialist" discourses that I shall describe.[11]

Insofar as *Lear* responds to or invokes a particular political occasion, it is clearly the "Union Controversy" raging from 1604–1608.[12] During this period James vigorously but unsuccessfully sought Parliament's aid in granting full political and legal force to what he had already accomplished genealogically and symbolically: the union of England and Scotland. As part of this campaign he repeatedly invoked the misfortunes that had befallen early Britain as the result of Brutus's division of his kingdom into three parts, a theme he had broached in the *Basilikon doron* even before ascending the English throne:

> And in case it please God to provide you to all these kingdomes [he writes to Prince Henry], make your eldest sonne *Isaac*, leaving him all your kingdoms; and provide the rest with private possessions: Otherwayes by deviding your kingdoms, yee shall leave the seed of division and discord among your posteritie; as befel to this Ile, by the division and assignement thereof, to the three sonnes of *Brutus, Locrine, Albanact*, and *Camber*."[13]

The tale of Lear thus had an obvious relevance to James's campaign to unite Britain (James, as it happened, had three children at the time *Lear* was written, one of whom was duke of Albany and another duke of Cornwall).[14] Paradoxically, then, what is perhaps the most "mythic" part of the Lear story had a quite pointed political reference.

Pointed, but nonetheless puzzling. Whereas some critics see *Lear* as a cautionary tale supporting James's cause (Shakespeare's keeping a royal performance and his company's status as the King's Men in mind), others are less sure.[15] In any case, I believe the play invokes this issue not to engage in polemic on either side but because the Union Controversy located a crucial fault line within English absolutism: that between absolutist theory and the real political power of the English crown. Unifying Great Britain would have given royal authority a reach known only in the mythical reign of Brutus. As a symbolic act, at least, it would significantly have bolstered James's absolutist ambitions. Yet Parliament remained unmoved by the king's repeated pleas, and the legal "unification" of the isle had ultimately to be effected through the back door, as it were, of the Court of the Exchequer.[16] Marie Axton's account of the controversy stresses "the flat contradiction of iconographic propaganda by the hard facts of continuing debate."[17] More globally, this incident marks the contradiction between absolutism as a cultural sign system and the economic and administrative weaknesses that placed structural limits on royal power during both the Tudor and the Stuart eras and kept the crown dependent on parliamentary and local authority.[18] King Lear, I think, is largely about the divorce between the signs and the material realities of royal power; the contemporary resonance of the Lear story is a first way of engaging this problem.

And so, for that matter, is the play's "feudal" setting, for the concept of feudalism was just emerging in debates about royal and parliamentary power. The feudal constitution of Scotland had informed James's absolutist conception of kingship even before he inherited the English throne; in 1603, moreover, the year of James's accession, Sir Thomas Craig published his Jus feudale and dedicated it to England's new king. Drawing on French studies of feudal law, Craig's book contends that the laws of both England and Scotland are feudal in character, and it "exhorts James VI and I to make full use of feudal principles in his government of each."[19] It is impossible to say whether Shakespeare read or knew of Craig's work, which was the first British attempt to explicate feudalism as a legal and historical concept. But he almost certainly knew of the king's own habit of invoking and reformulating feudal precedent to define his royal powers. In his introduction to James's political writings, C. H. McIlwain observes:

> In all these theories of the king with respect to the relations of the governor and the governed there are many traces of feudalism, particularly with the doctrine of hereditary right; but there is one aspect of the feudal relation that is conspicuous by its absence in James' politics. Of the reciprocal duties of *dominus* and *homo,* so prominent in the medieval conception of English kingship there remains not a

trace: it has been replaced entirely by the Roman conception of the king *legibus solutus*, placed so immeasurably above his *subditi* that he can in no way be bound by earthly law to the performance of any duties to them.[20]

McIlwain's remarks raise some interesting questions; principal among them is why James would invoke a feudal conception of kingship at all, inasmuch as such reciprocal notions of royal power were precisely those that absolutism sought to shake off. It is worth pursuing this point, for it allows us both to specify James's innovation in the theory of absolutist kingship and to see how this might be relevant to *King Lear*.

In fact, James's use of feudal precedent focused far less on medieval theories of royal power than on feudal property law. Against the "contract" theory of mutual obligations, under which possession of the crown is dependent on observance of the coronation oath, James asserted that the crown was a piece of inherited property: "For as hee [the king] is their heritable over-lord, and so by birth, not by any right in the coronation, commeth to the crown: it is alike unlawful (the crown ever standing full) to displace him that succeedeth thereto, as to eject the former." Not only the crown but, in James's mind, the entire kingdom and its inhabitants ultimately belonged to him as landlord; and it is this *property* relation that secured his political authority: "And as ye see it is manifest that the king is over-lord of the whole land: so he is master over every person that inhabiteth the same, having the power over the life and death of every one of them." James even used the conception of king as landlord to attack the powers of Parliament:

> And to proove this my assertion more clearly, it is evident by the rolles of our chancellory (which contain our eldest and fundamental lawes) that the king is *Dominus omnium bonorum* and *Dominus directus totius Dominii*, the whole subjects being but his vassals, and from him holding all their lands as their over-lord, who according to good services done unto him, chaungeth their holdings from tacke to few, from ward to blanch, erecteth new Baronies, and uniteth olde, without advice or authoritie of either Parliament or any other subalterin judiciall seate.[21]

Although Roman law may well have influenced James's conception of absolutist rule, it was feudal land law that he generally cited in defense of his privileges, thus turning kingship from a political into a property relation.

This feudal argument is only one strand in James's defense of royal prerogative, but it is, I think, his major innovation on the absolutist claims of the Tudors.[22] Its significance may become clear by comparing it with the theory of the "king's two bodies," which played a major role in medieval conceptions of kingship and in the Tudor succession controversies.[23] This theory relies on a divine conception of *political* authority, which is mystically passed from the body of the ruling king to his successor; it regards the monarch as the political representative of God and therefore invests the office of kingship with certain unique qualities. The "feudal" theory, by contrast, envisions not a mysterious transmission of power but a legal transmission of property, with the king as little more than a particularly privileged landlord. Political authority derives not from divine sanction but from the prerogatives of property ownership, and is conterminous with it. To vary James's own aphorism, "No Land, No King."

This is, of course, a bit of wisdom that King Lear has to learn the hard way. When the king gives away his land, he seems to expect some residue of the royal office to adhere to him: "the name and addition of king" (1.1.135). What he discovers, however, is that in giving away his land he has given away all, for the kingship is nothing more than the power that accrued to him from owning the kingdom. In this sense *Lear* is perhaps the most demystifying, indeed materialist, of Shakespeare's meditations on kingship, which the play refuses to hedge about with even a hint of divinity. Of course, James's arguments have to do only with the legitimacy of absolutist rule; *Lear* pushes these arguments one step farther, arriving at a kind of proto-Harringtonian insight that kingly authority is not only legitimated but constituted by landownership.

In the earlier history plays, Shakespeare clearly displays a sense of feudalism as a cultural order, embracing certain military-aristocratic ideals of honor, loyalty, and generosity. But in *King Lear* these ideals, and the notion of kingship itself, become strongly implicated with issues of property and landownership, largely, I think, in response to arguments put forth by James and possibly Craig. I am not arguing that *Lear* is a dramatic commentary on James's political writings; I am simply claiming that the king's defense of his prerogatives by means of feudal property law helped to inspire both *Lear*'s mise-en-scène and its relatively materialist conception of kingship. Thus the "feudal" setting of the play is of a vaguer historical character than those of the history plays—more the landscape of romance—and at the same time the play is, if anything, more pitilessly insistent on the real constituents of political power.

King James's defense of absolutist principles was not a mere expression of personal vanity and ambition; it was directed against the growing political and legislative powers of the Commons, powers already evident in the later years of Elizabeth's reign, and which to James's embarrassment manifested themselves in the refusal to ratify his royal proclamation unifying the kingdom. This ideological battle between crown and Parliament also took place partly on feudal terrain, where the historical priority of each institution was debated. In 1603, the same year in which Craig's *Jus feudale* was published, the first of Sir Edward Coke's writings also appeared, introducing the "common-law" interpretation of history whose significance has been so expertly traced by J. G. A. Pocock.[24] Coke, as is now well known, contended that the principles of common law were of immemorial origin, deriving from an "ancient constitution" that predated the institution of monarchy and was therefore immune from royal prerogative.[25] Coke further maintained that all the institutions mentioned by the present law—even Parliament and the Commons—predated the Norman period and that Parliament could be "proven" to have existed in the reign of King Arthur. Early historians of feudalism, such as Craig and Henry Spelman, argued, by contrast, that Parliament was of post-Norman provenance and thus subject to royal authority. Hence, as Pocock shows, the new historical studies of feudalism inevitably took on—or at least lent themselves to—royalist politics. James himself had already put forth a feudalist-royalist line in the *Trew Law:*

> The kings therefore in *Scotland* were before any estates or ranks of men within the same, before any Parliaments were holden, or lawes made: and by them was the land distributed (which at the first was whole theirs) states erected and discerned, and formes of government devised and established: And so it follows of necessitie, that the kings were authors and makers of the Lawes, and not the Lawes of the kings.[26]

The early historians of feudalism, suffering from what Pocock calls the "apparently universal delusion that 'feudal law' was an hierarchical system imposed from above as a matter of state policy,"[27] also invested feudalism with a fully absolutist character.

In addressing a myth of national origins, it is inevitable that *King Lear* should also engage, if only indirectly, the highly charged debate over the provenance of political authority in England, as John Turner has shown.[28] The Lear story, of course, originates neither in the pages of the common law nor in the antiquarian records used by seventeenth-century historians but in the mythic tales of early chronicle history. Yet this chronicle material implicitly supports the feudalist-royalist conception by depicting an early Britain ruled by kings without Parliament. In what John Turner has called the "early feudal" setting of *Lear, Macbeth, and Hamlet*, "Shakespeare has imagined worlds of kings and barons, without legal, ecclesiastical or parliamentary structures, without merchants, artisans, or labourers—without all those classes of people whom he imagined for the chronicle histories or the Venetian plays."[29] There is, of course, one "labourer"in *Lear*—Gloucester's faithful and nameless tenant who surfaces briefly in act 4, scene 1—but his appearance only reinforces our sense of a fully agararianized feudalism at whose summit sat the king. What we might call the "romance reduction" of society in *Lear* is predominantly an effect of literary genre, not local polemic, but it accords with the vision of early Britain promulgated by James.

The political import of this vision is, nevertheless, ambiguous. James undoubtedly enjoyed the spectacle of an early Britain without hated parliaments; whether he enjoyed a tale of disaster wrought by unfettered royal authority is less clear. In any case, even if Shakespeare's tragedies carry out a skeptical critique of absolutist rule—as is argued by Jonathan Dollimore, Franco Moretti, and others—this critique is scrupulously negative and disembodied.[30] Nowhere in *Lear*, certainly, does anything like a proparliamentary ideology emerge, even in the most displaced or disguised form. If the play undercuts some of the pretensions of absolutism, then, it nevertheless shows no interest in siding with the only political institution capable of challenging royal authority. *Lear*'s critique of absolutism is, in the main, economic rather than political—taking *political* in its most restricted sense—for Shakespeare is less interested in institutional battles for control of the state apparatus than he is in the ultimate constituents of class power. *Lear*'s romance version of feudalism accepts and totalizes the royalist conception of Britain's past in order to interrogate the relations among property, wealth, and military and political power within the postfeudal ruling classes, and it does so by "purifying" its feudal world of most alien elements. Romance as genre works here to construct a society composed entirely of royalty, nobility, servants, retainers, and tenants: an imagined "laboratory" of feudalism in which Shakespeare conducts his thought experiments. It is a paradox of *Lear* that romance itself takes on a materialist force even as it fends off all concrete historical events. The romance world of the play is nevertheless shot through with contemporary references, most of them provided by Edgar and the Fool. Edgar's portrayal of "Poor Tom" delineates the well-known figure of the Bedlam beggar and engages a running controversy about exorcism, while the Fool's references to James may have aroused the interest of the state censors. Both of these strains of contemporary reference, I believe, are fully congruent with the materialist bent of the play and thus with the political import of its romance elements.

Edgar's portrayal of "Tom o' Bedlam" has attracted a good deal of historical commentary and criticism. For example, the depiction and language of Tom's demonic "possession," it is now generally recognized, is largely inspired by a Protestant polemic published in 1603, Samuel Harsnett's *Declaration of Egregious Popish Imposters*. Harsnett's book describes and attempts to debunk a series of exorcisms performed by Roman Catholic priests in the south of England in the 1580s. These rites apparently converted a number of onlookers to the Catholic faith and were also darkly connected with the so-called Babington Plot to assassinate Elizabeth and install Mary Stuart as queen.[31] Harsnett clearly saw fit to invoke them in the atmosphere of Catholic plots, real and imagined, that gathered around the death of Elizabeth and the accession of James.

Harsnett's book is relevant here primarily for its rationalist and materialist bent: it demystifies seemingly spiritual or supernatural events by revealing them to be the effects of political machination and theatrical illusion. Edgar's dramatic *simulation* of demonic possession in *Lear*, his sometimes moving, sometimes comic pretense of being pursued by the devils Hoppidance and Flibbertigibet, seems to confirm Harsnett's view of possession as mere fakery. Edgar's pose as a Bedlam beggar or "Abraham man" was also associated with theatrical posturing, for the Elizabethan literature of roguery claimed that such men merely feigned madness to extort money from gullible citizens—sometimes going so far as to wound or scar themselves or to create hideous rashes by applying certain herbs to their skin.[32] Edgar's performance as madman is thus doubly hedged about by "debunking" discourses that attempted to provide social explanations for apparently spiritual or psychological phenomena.

Lear's more genuine madness engages the same tradition, for the diagnosis of *historica passio* or "suffocation of the mother" may have been inspired by a reference in Harsnett.[33] Or it may have been prompted by yet another treatise published in 1603, Edmund Jorden's *Brief Discourse of a Disease Called the Suffocation of the Mother*... [34] Jorden's book, like Harsnett's, is intended to debunk the supernatural. Growing out of the author's involvement in a 1602 witchcraft trial, it argues that many apparent cases of demonic possession, popularly attributed to the work of witches, could be more rationally explained as the symptoms of hysteria, resulting from wombs that wandered or released noxious vapors. Jorden's book represents the tradition of humanist medicine which derived madness from physiological and psychological, not supernatural causes; likewise, Lear's breakdown is always discussed in rational terms by other characters in the play, who attribute it to grief, anger, lack of sleep, and physical exposure to the elements. Lear's madness differs from Edgar's not only because it is genuine, then, but because its discursive framework derives from the traditions of humanist medicine. Edgar's "possession," by contrast, originates in traditions of religious and popular belief that were increasingly exposed to materialist critique.[35] *Lear*, in fact, is a play that constantly demystifies or debunks the supernatural: Edmund skeptically rejects astrology, while his brother Edgar fakes not only his own possession but also his father's "miraculous" salvation from Dover cliff and the fiend with a "thousand noses." Even the Fool's prophecy has been read as a parodic send-up of the popular apocalyptic prophecies that flourished around the time of Elizabeth's death and James's accession.[36]

The denial of transcendent or supernatural experience is, of course, crucial to *Lear*'s tragic effect, for it forecloses all possibilities of spiritual salvation.[37] This denial is most insistent at the end, when Lear's last, desperate belief that he sees the dead Cordelia breathing turns out to be just as false as Gloucester's revival was earlier. But the play's rationalist strain may well have had more topical applications. King James was, of course, himself an amateur demonologist and a man of a frequently rationalist bent. As Joseph Wittreich notes,

Various attitudes in the play—its interest in magic, demonology, and astronomy, together with its supposed distrust, and occasional deprecations, of prophecies and visions—have been cited as evidence of the extent to which the plays were now catering to James' pet atti-

tudes and of the extent, too, to which playwrights like Shakespeare
were inclined to represent James' interests, especially his opposition
to superstitious excesses.[38]

"Catering" may be the wrong word here, as Wittreich goes on to
say; but *Lear*'s rationalism is clearly influenced by the intellectual
tone and interests of the early Jacobean establishment. As Stephen
Greenblatt suggests, Harsnett's debunking of demonic possession
supported the desire of the Anglican church to establish a monopoly on charismatic experience and thus repress the political
unpredictability of popular magical-religious practices. "Spiritual
*potentia*", writes Greenblatt, "will henceforth be distributed with
greater moderation and control through the whole of the Anglican
hierarchy, at whose pinnacle sits the sole legitimate possessor of
absolute charismatic authority, the monarch, the Supreme Head of
the Church in England."[39] Even this formulation, however, suggests a conception of kingship rather different from that held by
James, who not only was spectacularly deficient in personal "cha-
risma" but also resisted participating in traditional practices of
charismatic monarchy, such as curing the King's Evil.[40]

James insisted, to be sure, on the divine authority of kingship, as
had his Tudor predecessors, but here again he put a personal spin
on older absolutist claims. In fact, the frequency and energy with
which he defended the divine right of kings may well obscure his
highly abstract, almost "deist" conception of this right. For James,
it was really the office of kingship rather than the king himself
that was girded by divine authority; he did not regard the king as
someone invested with charismatic powers or granted special communication or guidance. The king, in his view, was God's lieuten-
ant, not his confidant or prophet. If James denied that any secular
political bodies had power over the king, he also denied that the
king had any direct link to God's will other than that provided by
his own conscience, which was as other men's.[41] And if a king
therefore rules badly, he argued, the people have no recourse but to
bear their yoke and pray patiently for his removal, something that
James by no means assures them will occur.[42] For James, the divine right of kings is thus an almost purely virtual phenomenon.
It invests the king with an unimpeachable political authority but
provides no material means for safeguarding it and no spiritual
means for ensuring that it will be exercised wisely. By so attenuating the divinity of the royal office, it paradoxically enables a relatively secular conception of kingship. In this sense his treatment

of divine and feudal right are of a piece, in that both fend off "mystical" conceptions of royal power in order to substitute more juridical ones.

As James's own use of them suggests, the critical thrust of materialist discourses could be used to reformulate and to reinforce, rather than to demystify, the claims of royal power. Yet as Michael MacDonald points out, "Theologians and learned laymen were quick to see that materialist arguments denying the powers of demons and witches could easily be extended to question the potency of God and his angels."[43] Likewise, James's rationalist revision of the divine right of kings *might* be pushed far enough to question the concept altogether. At issue was whether the demystifying force of materialism could be limited to certain selected targets or whether it could be turned back against the ruling ideologies.

*King Lear* engages this materialist strain in certain Jacobean discourses and then totalizes it so as to render it politically ambiguous. The rationalist elements in the play can certainly be read as a nod to James's own intellectual preoccupations, but the play then mobilizes them and drives them to the point where they take on a potentially critical charge. In particular, it takes the Jacobean habit of rationalizing and attenuating the conception of divine efficacy and uses it to banish divinity altogether. Here the play's allusions to the materialists Harsnett and (possibly) Jorden combine with its pre-Christian setting to produce a totally secularized milieu in which gods as well as devils fall silent. *King Lear* is thus that paradoxical thing, an antitranscendental romance.

By removing the concept of divine intervention or restraint, the play both completes and unhinges the principles of royal absolutism. James had justified his claims to an authority unimpeded by Parliament by insisting, first, that kings ruled and even owned Britain before there were parliaments and, second, that kings were answerable only to God. Absolutist theory dispensed with the notion of political restraint exercised by the estates of the realm and substituted for it the notion of moral restraint exercised by the king's conscience alone in voluntary obedience to divine law. *Lear* takes this argument one step farther by creating a world in which royal will is restrained neither by Parliament nor by God and thus relies on nothing but its own faculties of prudence—faculties that fail disastrously in the opening scene. *Lear* depicts the divine right of kings as Pascal's wager in reverse: if there *is* a God, then the king's absolute authority can be justified and possibly controlled from above, and if there is not, then it is merely a human form of tyranny.

Lear's division of his kingdom is central to the play's imaginative attempt to "absolutize" the claims of royal absolutism. If all had gone according to his plan, Lear would have become the last king of Britain, a realm thenceforth divided forever into independent dukedoms. This may seem a peculiar way of manifesting royal power, but in fact it is fully consistent with King James's theories of absolutism, in which the power of the throne over the kingdom is almost always conceived of as depending on what restraints, if any, the kingdom or God can legitimately exert over the throne. Paradoxically, destroying the kingship is the truest demonstration that the office is the king's to do with as he pleases, hence that it is not established by social "contract" with the realm. Nor is it a divine institution that mystically and inevitably passes on to a successor. Rather, it is a piece of property—one that can be given away, like Lear's land, or simply consumed by royal fiat. By removing all sense of divine restraint, the play thus totalizes the absolutist conception of the kingship—and kingdom—as royal property.

In their different ways, then, the play's implicit references to the Union Controversy, its interest in feudal property, its pre-Christian and preparliamentary setting, and its materialist rejection of divine and spiritual phenomena all point to contemporary issues of royal power. More specifically, they brush aside the theological underpinnings of absolutism in order to focus on more material relations between property and authority. This critical labor is then extended by a second and even more explicitly political line of materialist discourse. Not surprisingly, the most dangerously direct references connecting Lear and King James come from the Fool, that figure of official licence, whose prophecy in act 3, scene 2, openly announces his function as a bearer of anachronistic meanings. As usual, the figure of the Fool draws on traditions of popular inversion; he is the focus of the theme of "handy-dandy" which critiques established authority in the play.[44] The Fool's popular-critical function is nevertheless partially blunted by having his bitterest and most trenchant remarks directed not at authority per se but at Lear's foolishness in abandoning it; he thus joins Kent as a nostalgic supporter of the old order. Still, his gibes at Lear point so directly to contemporary abuses that some of his remarks, particularly a set of exchanges in act 1, scene 4, were probably censored by the Master of the Revels.[45] This passage cuts to the heart of issues I have been discussing up to now, and so I shall quote it at some length:

> *Fool.* Dost thou know the difference, my boy, between a bitter Fool and a sweet one?
> *Lear.* No, lad; teach me.
> *Fool.* That lord that counsell'd thee
> To give away thy land,
> Come place him here by me,
> Do thou for him stand:
> The sweet and bitter fool
> Will presently appear;
> The one in motley here,
> The other found out there.
> *Lear.* Dost thou call me fool, boy?
> *Fool.* All thy other titles thou hast given away; that thou wast born with.
> *Kent.* This is not altogether Fool, my Lord.
> *Fool.* No, faith, lords and great men will not let me; if I had a monopoly out, they would have part on't: and ladies, too, they will not let me have all the fool to myself; they'll be snatching.
> (1.4.134–52)

It has long been recognized that the Fool's mention of "monopolies" probably glances at James's unpopular habit of granting them to needy courtiers. But as Gary Taylor has pointed out, the Folio omission, probably the result of censorship, includes much more than these few lines; he discovers in this passage a web of references to the king's prodigality and to the gluttony, promiscuity, and greediness of his court. Among these, the line "All thy other titles thou hast given away," probably points to James's "wholesale dispensation of titles" in the first months after assuming the English crown.[46] (This issue is raised again later when Kent calls Oswald a "hundred-pound" gentleman [2.2.14–15].)[47] Like his granting of monopolies, James's creation of titles came under intense parliamentary scrutiny. The king began apologizing for this initial burst of liberality as early as 1603, and he was still at it in 1609, when, begging a skeptical Parliament for supplementary revenues, he assured it that "the vastness of my expense is past, which I used at the first two or three years after my coming hither."[48] On the one hand, James's vast *creatio ex nihilo* of dukedoms and knighthoods was an audacious exercise of royal power; on the other, it was intended as bribery to secure what the king initially felt to be a weak political position. Moreover, it was a form of trade which got him into hot water as he became increasingly dependent on Parliament for revenues. Like the Union Controversy, then, the mass issuing of titles points to the difference between absolutism's strength as a sign system and its weakness in real economic and political power.

The Fool's line about giving away titles is especially interesting in that it connects James's practice of creating knighthoods with Lear's division of the kingdom and thus further enriches the political significance of Lear's gesture. If in one sense Lear is James's opposite, sundering Britain as James sought to unite it, there is another sense in which the two are alike, for James's profligacy was widely regarded as a foolish waste of national and royal resources. Lear carves up his patrimony in one bold if misguided stroke, whereas James fritters his away through conspicuous consumption and the inflation of honors. But James's is a "division of the kingdom" nonetheless, which contrasts ironically with his attempts to forge a unified nation.

In any case, the divisions of the real and fictional kingdoms create surprisingly similar results. Lear, having given all to his daughters, finds himself engaged in humiliating negotiations over the size and costs of his retinue. King James, having created his band of "hundred-pound" knights, finds himself explaining his personal expenses to a Commons in which more than a few of those knights may have sat. Lear bemoans the degradation of having to scrape before his daughters:

> Ask her forgiveness?
> Do you but mark how this becomes the house:
> "Dear daughter, I confess that I am old;
> Age is unnecessary: on my knees I beg
> That you'll vouchsafe me raiment, bed, and food."
> (2.4.149–53)

King James in a 1609 address to Parliament employs a similar brand of angry domestic pathos:

> For him that denies a good Law, I will not spare to quarrell: But for denying money, it is an effect of love: And therefore for the point of my necessities, I onely desire that I be not refused in that which of duety I ought to have.... For the king that is *Parens Patriae*, tells you his wants.... I confesse it is farre against my nature to be

burthensome to my people: for it cannot but grieve me to crave of others, that was born to be begged of.[49]

This speech was made too late to have affected the composition of *Lear*, but it is not impossible that James himself harked back to Shakespeare's play for his own rhetoric. Immediately before the passage just quoted, the king questions Parliament's insistence on economy with the same skepticism that Lear turns on his daughters:

> But as upon one side, I doe not desire you should yeeld to that extreame, in giving me more than (as I said formerly) upon such necessary occasions are fit for good and loving subjects to yeeld: . . . So on the other side, I hope you will not make vain pretences of wants, out of careless apprehensions, or idle excuses, neither cloake your own humours (when yourselves be unwilling) by alledging the povertie of the people.[50]

"O reason not the need!" he might well have added.

I adduce these parallels not in order to advance an absurd reading of *Lear* as a political *pièce à clef* (Goneril and Regan as recalcitrant M.P.'s and so forth), but to insist on the general relevance of royal finances to the play's consideration of kingship. For it was the crown's economic insufficiency that, in large part, rendered it increasingly subject to parliamentary will. As James himself admitted in his 1609 speech, he had the right to insist on laws but could only ask for money. This situation was nothing new, of course; the financial shortfalls created in large part by foreign wars were the main structural weakness of the English crown during the Tudor period, and James found himself saddled with Elizabeth's enormous war debt when he assumed the English throne.[51] It was because of this larger structural problem that James's personal expenditures were controversial at all or that he was driven to the creation of debased titles as a revenue-raising measure. Royal consumption, though extravagant by personal standards, became a national issue only because it capped a more extensive financial crisis. In a certain sense, James's vulnerability on this point was the obverse of his own absolutist theories; if he could claim that all the kingdom's law and authority rested on the royal will, no wonder if the kingdom's economic problems could be traced back to his royal appetites and caprices.

Shakespeare had already addressed the problem of royal finances rather directly—perhaps too directly—in *Richard II*, in which

Richard's venality and war debts force him to lease out much of the kingdom. John of Gaunt's famous speech on England ends with the darkly prophetic charge:

> This land of such dear souls, this dear dear land—
> Dear for her reputation through the world—
> Is now leased out—I die pronouncing it—
> Like to a tenement or pelting farm.
>
> (2.1.57–60)

And Gaunt then mocks Richard: "Landlord of England art thou now, not king" (2.1.113). Subsequent events probably taught Shakespeare that such explicit political commentary was unwise. *Lear* engages similar issues, I believe, but in a more displaced and mythicized form. In any case, the issue of royal consumption was even trickier in 1605, when James's largess had drawn parliamentary criticism and when Shakespeare's own company profited from it. As Walter Cohen remarks, "The accession of James brought with it a sharp rise in the frequency of court dramatic performances as compared with the late Elizabethan period, an economic windfall from which Shakespeare's company, now renamed the King's Men, benefited disproportionately."[52] *Lear* is thus directly implicated in the royal economy upon which it meditates; in its court performance it formed part of James's notorious excess.

For whatever reason, the play's attitude toward kingship—a few of the fool's more cutting remarks aside—is not so much critical as it is coolly analytical. It doesn't construct even an implicit polemic against James or his policies; it simply illustrates the impossibility of dividing authority from revenue. Lear's division of the kingdom is a wager of sorts, or even an experiment, to see if the signs of royal power can outlast their material base:

> Only we shall retain
> The name and all th'addition to a king; the sway,
> Revenue, execution of the rest,
> Beloved sons, be yours: which to confirm,
> This coronet part between you.
>
> (1.1.134–38)

The hopeless idealism of this gesture may be measured by the fact that, as Rosalie Colie points out, even Lear's palace seems mysteriously to disappear once he has renounced his power.[53]

Lear's failed wager, I state one last time, is also the wager of Stuart absolutism. For James's early battles with Parliament evinced precisely the same split between the signs and the realities of power: between a royal proclamation announcing the union of the kingdom and the failure to get it ratified, between an initial burst of sign production in the form of royal pageants and an inability to pay for them, between an increasingly elaborate theory of unencumbered royal authority and the reality of legislative and financial dependence on Parliament. This split was of course relative rather than absolute, but it was obviously widening, and it was symbolized by the king's pursuit of royal pleasures to the detriment of the daily government of the realm. As the Venetian ambassador reported in June 1607, James's subjects were highly displeased by his addiction to hunting, for the sake of which "he throws off all business, which he leaves to his Council and to his Ministers. *And so one may say that he is Sovereign in name and in appearance rather than in substance and effect.*"[54] This complaint disconcertingly parallels Lear's decision to abdicate all real power and retain only the name and addition of king. Conversely, Lear's self-demotion from king to player-king, from substance to sign, reflects upon a very real political crisis. *King Lear's* materialism creates the space for considering this crisis by banishing all transcendental elements and laying the basis for a rigorous, if symbolic, consideration of both the sign systems and the material economies of social power.

### The Order-Word and the Consumption-Sign

When Kent first objects to Lear's decision to disinherit Cordelia, the king accuses him of having

> sought to make us break our vow,
> Which we durst never yet, and with strain'd pride
> To come betwixt our sentence and our power,
> Which nor our nature nor our place can bear.
> (1.1.167–70)

Among the multiple ironies of these lines is that by dividing his kingdom, Lear himself effects a permanent divorce between his "sentence" and his "power." In the very next scene, Gloucester exclaims of the king: "prescrib'd his power! / Confined to exhibition!" (1.2.24–25). *Exhibition* here means an economic allowance, but it seems also to suggest that Lear has been reduced to a kind of spectacle, bearing only the visible signs of kingship without its authority. While the play clearly distinguishes the political or cultural signs of power from their material base of support, it is also true that in its consideration of kingship it elaborates two very different kinds of sign systems. One of these establishes signs as the effect and medium of (political) power—the "sentence" of power—and for this I shall borrow the term *order-word*.[55] The other designates those signs created by the consumption or destruction of wealth.[56] These constitute the exhibition value of the king, and they are mostly what Lear tries to reserve for himself after his abdication, along with some empty titles of respect, themselves voided of political authority and thus converted into other consumption-signs. These two sign systems are, of course, mutually reinforcing and mutually imbricated in practice, but they are distinguishable in principle, and Lear's abdication of power does in fact divorce them from each other.

Both are fully integrated, however, during the ceremony of the play's opening scene, where Lear's grandiose "expenditure" of his landed wealth and his absolutist deployment of political authority go hand in hand. "Know," he says, "that we have divided in three our kingdom" (1.1.36). Here the very act of hearing or apprehension is formulated as a command ("Know"); but the order-word is more at home in the form of the *announcement*, where it is no longer even subject to the vagaries of execution but simply given as fact ("that we have divided our kingdom"). The order-word completes itself not in the imperative mood but in the perfect tense, where it has begun to sediment into the "neutral" realm of description because utterance is already material reality. The whole opening ceremony, in fact, testifies to the peculiar belatedness of the order-word. "Tell me, my daughters," Lear commands,

> Which of us shall we say does love us most?
> That we our largest bounty may extend
> Where nature doth with merit challenge.
> (1.1.47, 50–52)

Lear suggests that his daughters are to conduct a kind of rhetorical tournament, with the prize piece of land going to the winner. But the play's opening lines reveal that this division has already been made and, moreover, that it is the relative valuation of Albany or

Cornwall, not of the daughters, that decides the portions. When Goneril, obliging her father, responds "I love you more than word can wield the matter" (1.1.54), she indirectly announces not only the moral hollowness of her discourse—the breach between "words" and "deeds" (1.1.183–85)—but also its political impotence. Goneril's word can "wield" nothing (for the moment), all decisions about her future already having been made by Lear's absolute authority. "Such," to quote Bolingbroke in *Richard II*, "is the breath of kings."

In dividing the kingdom, Lear divests himself of both military power and economic resources, and thus begins to dismantle both the order-word and the consumption-sign. Goneril's and Regan's attempt to accelerate this process centers naturally enough on the issue of Lear's retainers, for these underpin both systems of signs. As Rosalie Colie remarks, "retainers were not only a sign of an aristocrat's prestige but a defense of his prerogatives."[57] Goneril's first complaints against Lear's retinue thus focus on issues of expense and consumption: the knights are "disordered" and "deboshed," and they promote "epicureanism and lust" (1.4.238–49). When they finally strip their father of his retainers, Goneril and Regan argue the unnecessary waste of doubled servants, thereby provoking Lear's famous "reason not the need" speech in defense of the superfluous (2.4.258–84). Yet at other moments Goneril seems more greatly to fear the *military* power of her father's retainers, which "enguard his dotage with their power, / And hold our lives in mercy" (1.4.325–26). The retainers thus offer a conspicuous intersection of the order-word and the consumption-sign, revealing both their difference and their mutual implication.

The latter stages of the play largely concern Lear's attempt to reconstruct, in displaced and simulated forms, the royal prerogatives he has lost. In place of the order-word he substitutes an empty rhetoric of command whose impotence is balanced by its grandiosity, being directed not at political subjects but at nature itself: "Blow winds, and crack your cheeks! rage! blow! / You cataracts and hurricanoes, spout / Till you have drench'd our steeples, drown'd the cocks!" (3.2.1–3). To compensate for the loss of the consumption-sign he engages in symbolic forms of *dépense*, or destructive expenditure, to which I shall return in the final section of this essay.

As I have said, Lear's willful dismantling of the order-word parallels that effected by the contradictions of Jacobean absolutism, in which an increasingly hollow rhetoric of power and a growing dependence on consumption signs progressively substituted for real political efficacy. But this same process was also played out, and more globally, for the aristocracy as a whole. The topical relevance for *Lear* of the "crisis of the aristocracy" has been convincingly demonstrated by Rosalie Colie.[58] Here I wish only to recall some of the more general features of this crisis: first, the demilitarization of the aristocratic class carried out by the Tudors, which to a large extent eroded its independent political authority.[59] (This process, significantly, involved the forced disbanding of armed retainers.) Second, the aristocracy's increasing reliance on consumption and expenditure, along with formal education and administrative authority, as compensation for its loss of political-military power. Third, the economic difficulties wrought by rising expenses, coupled with a crisis of surplus extraction whose roots stretched back to the fourteenth century. The aristocracy as a whole thus faced the same general problems afflicting the throne: an erosion of political authority and a compensating turn toward conspicuous expenditure at the same time that its financial position was also weakening. What Gloucester says of Lear might thus also be applied to aristocrats in general: they were increasingly "confined to exhibition," their power having been "prescribed."[60]

Lavish consumption had, of course, always been a mark of aristocratic style, but its nature and structural position were changing. The older mode of consumption, based in the countryside, was strongly connected with the principle of hospitality; it thus helped to reinforce the economic and ideological structures of manorial production and hence of surplus extraction. It was, in the end, a kind of productive expenditure. The new mode was centered in London and thus divorced from any role in reproducing agrarian relations of production. Indeed, as Lawrence Stone points out, "In the effort to maintain status many families overreached themselves, fell heavily into debt, and eventually sold their patrimony and disappeared. At some stage along this dismal road they would be forced to violate another of the conventions of their class and oppress the tenantry in order to find the money to maintain expenditures."[61] The consumption-sign really came into its own in the urban environment of London, where it not only achieved an unprecedented intensity but decisively detached itself from economic production and hence from its own reproduction. Many Elizabethen and Stuart courtiers consumed their economic resources as stars consume their own fuel, throwing off a brilliant light of consumption-signs as they slowly collapsed from within.

The king's role in this process was ambiguous. By 1616 James was urging the nobility and gentry to return to the countryside and keep hospitality, complaining that "now in *England*, all the countrey is gotten into *London*," with the result that "the poore want reliefe for fault of the Gentlemens hospitalitie at home" and "the Gentlemen lose their own thrift, for lacke of their presence, in seeing to their business at home."[62] On the other hand, the king himself was the biggest and most profligate spender of all, the realm's self-appointed paragon of aristocratic privilege and consumption. Never was he more so than in the first years of his reign, which was inaugurated with a burst of extravagance. As he declared in his 1609 speech to Parliament:

> It is trew I have spent much; but yet if I had spared any of these things which caused a great part of my expense, I should have dishonoured the kingdome, my selfe, and the late Queene. Should I have spared the funerall of the late Queene? or the solemnitie of mine and my wife's entrie into this Kingdome, in some honourable sort? or should I have spared our entrie into *London*, or our Coronation? And when most of the Monarches, and great Princes in Christendome sent their Ambassadours to congratulate my comming hither, and some of them came in person, was I not bound, both for my owne honour, and the honour of the kingdome, to give them good entertainment?[63]

Faced with the need to raise funds for this expense, and lacking the educational opportunities offered by a night out on the heath, James was even able to imagine that "every good Subject would rather chuse to live more sparingly upon his owne, then that his kings state should be in want."[64] In other words, the king was willing to engage in a generalized version of the same "rent-racking" that his more profligate nobles carried out on their estates. The king thus concentrated within his person the contradictions of the aristocratic consumption-sign, which was increasingly divorced both from the order-word and from its own economic reproduction.

Lear reenacts these same contradictions symbolically by dismantling the kingship. But in *Lear* the divorce of authority from expense is of more than thematic interest, for it touches upon the very fabric—literal and figurative—of dramatic representation. The Elizabethan and Stuart theaters often relied upon aristocratic expenditure for their stage properties, especially costumes. As

Thomas Platter wrote in 1599, it was "the English usage for emmi-
nent lords or knights at their decease to bequeath and leave almost
the best of their clothes to their serving men, which it is unseemly
for the latter to wear, so that they offer them for a small sum to
the actors."[65] Aside from illustrating the paradoxes of trying to
"shake the superflux" (3.4.35), this practice quite directly impli-
cates the theater in the aristocratic economy of the consumption-
sign. Of course, the spectacle of players appearing in noblemen's
dress lent itself to humanist critiques of royal authority by revealing the king to be an ordinary man vested with the ceremonies
and trappings of power. (*Lear* makes use of this humanist critique
in its theme of "handy-dandy" and in Lear's putting off his kingly
robes to become "unaccommodated man.") But what the reduction
of aristocratic dress to stage property represented more particularly
was the complete divorce of the consumption-sign from the order-
word. By peopling itself with "noble" characters who bore the
signs of aristocratic expense but none of the accompanying social
or political authority, the Renaissance stage *produced* in a daz-
zlingly clear form the structural transformation of the aristocracy
from a politico-military ruling class to a consuming one. Conversely, the political powerlessness of the theater's own system of
representation was mirrored in the situation of a nobility "confined to exhibition." Faced with the absence of the order-word, the
English Renaissance theater could either produce an empty rhetoric of power, as Lear does on the heath, or it could try to make do
with an array of consumption-signs, using them to mimic political
efficacy.

In *Lear*, then, the dismantling of political authority is not only a
theme but also a material condition of dramatic form, and thus it
gives rise to frequent metadramatic reflection. One of the richest
examples is the so-called "mad trial" conducted by Lear, the Fool,
and Tom O' Bedlam in act 3, scene 6, of the Quarto text. Here
Lear's formal "prosecution" of an illusory Goneril and Regan measures the distance he has fallen since the parallel ceremony of the
play's opening scene:

> *Lear.* Arraign her first; 'tis Goneril. I here take my oath before this
>   honorable assembly, she kicked the poor King her father.
> *Fool.* Come, honorable mistress. Is your name Goneril?
> *Lear.* She cannot deny it.
> *Fool.* Cry your mercy, I took you for a joint-stool.
> *Lear.* And here's another, whose warp'd looks proclaim
>   What store her heart is made on. Stop her there!

Arms, arms, sword, fire! Corruption in the place!
False justicer, why hast thou let her 'scape?

(3.6.46–55)

Gary Taylor remarks perceptively on Lear's mistaking a joint-stool for his daughter: "Does the joint-stool represent a political victim condemned in absentia by a court the plaintiff himself appoints, or does it represent instead a pathetic substitute, the closest political impotence can get to punishing its oppressors?"[66] The first of these possibilities engages the absolutist conception of the order-word in which the king himself, being the basis of all law, bears unlimited power over life and property. The second represents the emptying out of this power in dramatic representation, where a simulated order-word can act only upon fictive or imagined substitutes for real subjects. By invoking both possibilities, the mad trial quite accurately gauges the impotence of dramatic representation, for which Lear's own powerlessness offers a compelling symbol.

*Lear*, I contend, constructs a highly complex and symbolic discourse about fundamental transformations in the nature of class power, and does so in ways that also reflect upon the political possibilities of theater itself. It is, thus, a play that quite explicitly engages the transition to capitalism, though limiting its focus almost entirely to the ruling groups. I might specify the nature of its "transitional" argument more precisely by criticizing John Danby's influential reading of the play as class allegory.

Danby's approach to *Lear* establishes a stark contrast between characters such as Kent and Cordelia, who obey the old "feudal" values of loyalty, honor, and custom, and characters such as Goneril, Regan, and Edmund, who represent proto-capitalist values of greed, ambition, and economic rationality. Edmund, above all, is for Danby the embodiment of the new man in all his ambiguous, iconoclastic grandeur. Rosalie Colie endorses this view, dubbing Edmund "a natural machiavel, a new man, outside the customary values"; he is "the natural talent unsupported by background who makes his way into the chancy world of Renaissance opportunity."[67] John Turner has recently challenged this view, arguing that Edmund is "the Bastard, the Unwanted, the Marginalized," who "emblematizes all the injustices of the history that we have inherited out of Lear's Britain."[68] Edmund is thus, according to Turner, the destructive return of the repressed who visits the contradictions of the feudal "order" back upon it. Both of these readings have something to be said for them—Edmund is, after all, overdetermined, as are all literary constructs—but both share the assumption that Edmund's role in the play is essentially to bring down an imagined version of feudalism. The Danby/Colie reading relies on the implicit neo-Smithian assumption that feudalism was dissolved from without by the unleashing of market forces, here associated with Edmund; Turner's reading proceeds by means of the more orthodox Marxist assumption that feudalism was the victim of its own internal contradictions.[69]

Edmund's class identification is largely defined by his first soliloquy in act 1, scene 2:

> Thou, Nature, art my goddess; to thy law
> My services are bound. Wherefore should I
> Stand in the plague of custom, and permit
> The curiosity of nations to deprive me,
> For that I am some twelve or fourteen moonshines
> Lag of a brother? Why bastard? Wherefore base?
>
> (1.2.1–6)

By choosing nature over custom, and by being a "base" social upstart who employs craftiness, intelligence, and personal ambition to "top th' legitimate," Edmund indeed recalls certain aspects of the merchant and gentry classes of the sixteenth century. This identification seems sealed by his last lines in the scene: "Let me, if not by birth, have lands by wit: / All with me's meet that I can fashion fit" (1.1.180–81). If the second of these lines proclaims a ruthless machiavellianism, the first reflects the gentry's view of its own success. It also recalls that Shakespeare himself won lands and a title by wit, and Danby has argued that the sympathetic aspects of Edmund's characterization result in part from his embodiment of elements of Shakespeare's own class wish.[70]

Edmund's role as a dissolving agent in the play is further enhanced by the somewhat anarchic qualities of his personal energy. In his first soliloquy he asks:

> Why brand they us
> With base? with baseness? with bastardy? base, base?
> Who in the lusty stealth of nature take
> More composition and fierce quality
> Than doth, within a dull, stale, tired, bed,
> Go to th'creating a whole tribe of fops,
> Got 'tween asleep and wake?
>
> (1.2.9–15)

Edmund is associated from the first with dissemination as against biological and social reproduction; and with a sexual force that refuses to be canalized along the lines of inheritance and property law. His "fierce quality" strains against the constraints of custom, which he portrays not as an idealized source of loyalty and honor but rather as a degenerate and ennervating routine. Such views might well reinforce Edmund's association with the anarchic force of the capitalist market, snapping the bonds of feudal custom. On the other hand, the phrase "fierce quality" has a military rather than a commercial ring to it, and Edmund's contempt for "fops" strongly foreshadows Kent's reaction to the new-style courtier Oswald. Here it might be recalled that Edmund's opening lines ("Thou, Nature, art my goddess; to thy law / My services are bound") strongly allude to the language of knightly enfeoffment and courtly love; that his illegitimate affair with Goneril, herself married off as part of a property settlement, puts him squarely in the position of the feudal courtly lover; and that he turns out, in the end, to be no mean soldier and even attains in his last moments to something like a knightly sense of honor as he tries vainly to undo his own plot against Cordelia.

It might equally be argued, then, that Edmund represents certain aspects of feudal ideology. At least it should be registered as a paradox that this supposedly proto-capitalist character drives the society of the play not forward into some postfeudal condition but *backward* into a fully feudalized mode. The play opens in the context of an absolutist, ceremonial, apparently demilitarized court; and it devolves, by the combined actions of Lear, Edmund, Goneril, and Regan, into a decentralized and fully militarized set of competing baronies. One of the weaknesses of many historical readings of *Lear* is that they equate the collapse of the play's social order with the collapse of feudalism, whereas in fact the play collapses *back into* feudalism. Kent and Gloucester, the play's old men, may complain about the decay of knightly values, but it is Edmund who at least half-wittingly reconstitutes a society in which these values can again have meaning. Edmund's dominant role in the play, then, is not to be midwife to capitalism; rather, it is to reintroduce the feudal war machine and thus fully reconstitute a baronial culture that had degenerated into ceremony and property rights. By the end of the play kingship is thus "won" by military prowess, not inherited along with land.

Edmund the "bastard" is thus the child of two very different ideological formations. If, on the one hand, he points forward to certain proto-capitalist values, on the other, he points backward to a more fully feudal conception of aristocratic rule and culture which predates the politico-military consolidation of absolutism. His structural role in the play is that of the donor who restores to the aristocracy its lost order-word, which had been confiscated and monopolized by the monarchy. In this sense *Lear* is to the history plays what an antiparticle is to a particle: sharing the same characteristics but "inverting" them by moving backward in time. If the history plays celebrate, however ambivalently, the consolidation of absolutism, *Lear* registers the decay of knightly values which results from the state's monopoly on military force, and the consequent transformation of an armigerous nobility into a class wielding only consumption-signs.

If Edmund evokes the Renaissance new man, then, he does so only for the purpose of driving it back to a culturally anterior form. He cannot simply by opposed to Kent, for he is the efficient cause that realizes Kent's nostalgia. There *is* a new man in *King Lear*, however, and his name is Oswald. Oswald's symbolic importance may very well be underestimated because his dramatic role is relatively small. But this is precisely the point: he is clearly wheeled in solely as a foil to Kent, and his very existence is conjured up only to complete the play's set of social "types." As his very name suggests, Oswald is spiritual kin to *Hamlet*'s Osric: he is that favorite butt of Shakespearean ridicule, the finical, flattering courtier. The mere sight of him provokes a kind of instinctive revulsion in Kent, who delights in beating him and burying him under piles of verbal abuse:

> A knave, a rascal, an eater of broken meats; a base, proud, shallow, beggarly, three-suited, hundred-pound, filthy worsted-stocking knave; a lily-livered, action-taking, whoreson, glass-glazing, super-serviceable, finical rogue; one-trunk-inheriting slave; one that wouldst be a bawd in way of good service, and art nothing but the composition of a knave, beggar, coward, pandar, and the son and heir of a mongrel bitch: one whom I will beat into clamorous whining if thou deni'st the least syllable of thy addition. (2.2.13–23)

Despite his contempt, Kent clearly needs Oswald to underpin his own existence: Oswald's artificiality secures Kent's authenticity; his effeminacy secures Kent's masculinity; his weakness and cowardice secure Kent's heroic valor; his social pretension secures Kent's venerable aristocracy. In short, his status as the "new man" of the court secures Kent's status as the "old man" of feudalism.

Kent's insults revolve around two conceptual centers: simulation and hybridization. The first of these pertains to Oswald's artificiality in general and to his pretensions to the status of gentleman in particular. Lacking a distinguished lineage, landed wealth, or military prowess, Oswald can only adopt the manners, gestures, bearing, and clothing of a gentleman: in short, the *consumption-signs* of aristocracy. (Kent here calls him a "filthy worsted-stocking knave," but then later insists that "a tailor made thee" [2.2.53].) He thus represents the end term of the transformation of the old baronial class to a new courtly one. Kent's taunts, intended to demonstrate Oswald's status as pure consumption-sign, nevertheless acknowledge the power of such signs to counterfeit aristocracy. In the real world, William Harrison complained that anyone who

> can live without manuel labour, and thereto is able and will bear the port, charge, and countenance of a gentleman, he shall for monie have a cote and armes bestowed upon him by heralds (who in the charter of the same doo of custome pretend antiquitie and service, and many gaie things) and thereunto being made so good cheape be called master, which is the title that men give to esquires and gentlemen, and reputed for gentlemen ever after.[71]

The reduction of nobility to a set of consumption-signs contributed, of course, to the debasing or "inflation" of honors described by Lawrence Stone.[72] Shakespeare himself, though certainly no Oswald, was nevertheless a "counterfeit" gentleman, as his heraldic motto—"Non sans droit"—anxiously attests. Perhaps Kent's haughty disdain expresses the other side of Shakespeare's own class wish.

Related to the problem of class simulation, though of even wider reach, is Kent's assault on Oswald as a class and sexual *hybrid*. Oswald is, in Kent's rant, "*the composition* of a knave, beggar, coward, pandar," and "the son and heir of a mongrel bitch" (Lear too refers to Oswald as a "mongrel" [1.4.48]); these insults attest to Oswald's mixture of masculine and feminine, common and gentlemanly traits. Although Oswald is perhaps the most explicitly and thoroughly hybridized character, however, he is hardly the only one. Edmund, of course, is a bastard, and Lear charges Goneril with being a "degenerate bastard" as well. Both Goneril and Regan take on monstrously "masculine" qualities in the latter stages of the play, and early on Goneril mocks Albany's "milky gentleness"

(1.4.340). And Lear, famously, expresses his own horror of female sexuality by describing women as "centaurs" (4.6.121–30). Hybridized or mixed beings define and inhabit the play's realm of the sexually abject, and contribute strongly to *Lear*'s "image of that horror"—in direct contrast to the early comedies, which tended to extol sexual androgyny. But they also add to the play's confusions of social class. Lear as the beggar-king, Edgar playing Tom o' Bedlam, and Kent in the stocks are only three of the play's more prominent and grotesque class hybrids. Oswald thus concentrates a more global phenomenon in the play: the collapse of sexual and class boundaries. When Kent threatens, "I'll teach you differences" (1.4.87), he attempts to secure the solidity of class and gender categories that Oswald disrupts.

Hybridization and simulation together represent the means of upward class mobility available to the gentry and merchant classes, who could assume only the consumption-signs of aristocracy. For their part, nobles did what they could to secure the system of class difference through sumptuary laws and other such means, but they could not quite stem the encroaching tide of parvenus represented in *Lear* by Oswald. Even Oswald's effeminacy or sexual hybridism impinges on this problem, for the aristocracy felt emasculated by conversion from a militarized to a consuming class. Thus Kent's formidable masculinity constitutes part of his class nostalgia, a last bulwark of heroic "authenticity" which resists the simulating and hybridizing capacities of the consumption-sign. The order-word is traditionally masculine.

Class struggle can assume a variety of social and cultural forms, sometimes involving open antagonism and opposition, sometimes involving assimilation and appropriation. In the *beginning* of the seventeenth century, before middle-class and Puritan cultural formations developed into clearly defined oppositional currents, some of the strongest challenges to the traditional privileges of aristocracy involved the appropriation of aristocratic consumption-signs by the gentry. The dominance of aristocratic culture was threatened not by a clearly antagonistic alternative but by the rearticulation of its own hegemony in such a way as to favor emergent bourgeois strata. While the proliferation of hybrids corroded the boundaries of the aristocratic signifier, the multiplying effects of simulacra "inflated" it and debased its value.

In *King Lear*, as well, the strongest challenge to feudal values does not come from Edmund, who hates the current order; it comes from Oswald, who loves it in such a way as to debase it terminally. This is why the Lukácsian thesis fails for *Lear:* dramatic agon does not represent class struggle. In this play the heralds of bourgeois culture refuse to fight; they are, indeed, defined by the absence of military prowess or heroic pride. Their mode of assault is friendly, marked by hybridism and the simulating capacities of the consumption-sign. As a courtier, Oswald represents the limit of this assimilationist tendency; his dramatic function is to empty out the formal aspects of aristocratic class culture without offering anything in the way of a distinctively or aggressively bourgeois alternative. In this respect he is the symbolic antipode to a Shakespearean character such as Shylock. Oswald may be said to represent the degree to which *Lear* is *not* the product of a directly prerevolutionary era—that is to say, the degree to which the social aspirations of the prebourgeois classes could still be defined within the bounds of aristocratic hegemony. The play does not offer presentiments of civil war; rather, it foretells a continuing debasement or dilution of ruling values in such characters as Oswald and "the dukes of wat 'rish Burgundy" (1.1.257).

Edmund occupies an ambiguous slot within the play's figurations of culture, for he cannot simply be opposed to Oswald. He is, after all, a bastard whom Albany addresses as "half-blooded fellow" (5.3.82). He is a simulator who insinuates himself into an alien system of values. His aggressive upward mobility and desperate desire for aristocratic legitimation invoke the class wishes of a wide range of parvenus. The difference is that Edmund joins this configuration solely to drive it backward by assimilating it to the feudal war machine. His historical trajectory puts him in the roles of courtly lover, military commander, and finally, losing but valiant contender in a chivalric battle with his brother Edgar. That Edmund is in the end willing to dispense with his formal class privileges and "answer an unknown opposite" (5.3.151–52) to defend his honor signals his choice of military or heroic prestige over mere titles of nobility. His effect on the world of the play is thus fully atavistic; he latches on to Lear's division of the kingdom and the subsequent decentralization of power to reestablish the hegemony of the aristocratic order-word. The fact and manner of his death attest to success in this project, not failure.

Edmund's role within the play embodies the tightly dialectical relation between kingship and social class and, more precisely, illustrates that the disintegration of the absolutist court with which the play begins is a necessary precondition for the remilitarization and reempowerment of the aristocracy. Historically, if the economic difficulties of the English throne enabled it to mirror in certain respects the situation of the aristocracy and even to substitute for it dramatically, it is also true that the politico-military consolidation of absolutist rule was accomplished at the expense of baronial power, and to this extent crown and nobility were directly in conflict. A shared crisis in the realm of the consumption-sign was predicated on the king's aggressive monopolization of the order-word. Hence in *Lear*, the kings' fall can both represent a general crisis of ruling-class values and point to a possible way beyond them by allowing a redistribution of political power: a redistribution for which Edmund serves as a catalyst or instigator.

This is not to deny that Edmund is, in the end, a villain, or at least a character of ambiguous energies. But he is a necessary agent in the constitution of the play's surviving "heroes," Edgar and Albany. For his part, Albany is good-hearted but weak for most of the play: "full of alteration, / And self-reproving" (5.1.3–4). Albany's "milky gentleness" renders him politically impotent, his honor and courage at odds. "Where I could not be honest," he moans, "I never yet was valiant" (5.1.23–24). Edmund enables Albany to remilitarize his virtue and thus reconstitute the unity of chivalric ideology. Edgar, too, displays the virtues of a (highly ambivalent) loyalty to his father, but is, like his brother, given to deception and dramatic simulation. His final defeat of Edmund reestablishes the authenticity of his genealogical and class identity while also demonstrating his military valor. In a sense, Edmund, Albany, and Edgar provide one another with complementary lessons in how to be a feudal aristocrat: the first learns from the other two at least a rudimentary and tragically belated sense of knightly honor, while they depend on him to hone their heroic valor. The combined actions of all the characters effect a cataclysmic shift from the opening mise-en-scène, an absolutist court rich with ceremony but paralysed by royal monopoly of the order-word, to a "gor'd state" (5.5.319) stripped of all consumption-signs but ruled by a newly remilitarized aristocracy. *Lear*, that is to say, narrates the transition to capitalism through the perspective of ruling-class ideology and, moreover, narrates it "backward." The play is, in effect, a fantastic but nonetheless coherent account of the transition from capitalism to feudalism.

This reading of *Lear* is of course a strongly masculinizing one. Not only does it focus on male characters rather exclusively as the bearers of class positions, but it argues that the play's "nostalgia" for a remilitarized aristocracy entails a corollary repression of the feminine. More generally, the dominance of the consumption-sign is associated with effeminacy, and the dominance of the order-word with masculinity. Yet this is also a play about daughters, good as well as bad, who participate in the problem of transition. Danby's approach joins Goneril and Regan with Edmund as competitive, greedy, and thus supposedly "capitalist" characters; the cost-cutting measures of the Regan administration bespeak a cruel economic rationality that contrasts with the old "feudal" virtues of generosity and hospitality. Cordelia, by contrast, offers a strongly domestic equivalent to Kent's values of honesty, loyalty, and plain speaking. For John Turner, Cordelia and Kent together serve to measure the increasingly unbridgeable chasm between feudal idealism and the real contradictions of the play's political order. Cordelia, of course, famously loves her father according to her *bond*, "the feudal equivalent of Roman *pietas*," as Turner puts it. The failure of Cordelia's and Kent's love and honesty at the beginning of the play reveals the venality and corruption of Lear's court, whereas "in Cordelia's [final] lament before her frenzied father, as in Lear's lament at her death, we see emblems of how the feudal pieties of pity, love, and service, idealized as they have become, can do no more than contemplate the unjust world which they have been compelled to vacate."[73]

There is much to recommend this view of Cordelia as a utopian figure of idealized but impotent goodness. Cordelia certainly offers an affirmative vision of the feminine to counterbalance that of Goneril and Regan, and even if her redemptive virtues are ultimately powerless, still they manage to carry over to some of the male characters.[74] Yet this reading, I believe, carries out two complementary reductions. On the one hand, it idealizes Cordelia's character and her relationship with her father; and on the other, it suppresses the ambiguities of the play's ending, which seems to fantasize historical gain (the revival of the aristocratic order-word) even as it portrays personal loss.

Cordelia is, to be sure, aligned strategically and symbolically with Kent in the opening scene. But if Kent's feudal nostalgia complicates his seeming opposition to the "villain" Edmund, Cordelia has more than a little in common with the play's villainous characters, including her sisters. In act 1, scene 1, she at least shares with Goneril and Regan an apparent helplessness in the face of her father's authority. Her sisters, of course, make a virtue of necessity and humor Lear in the knowledge that they will thus collect the material basis for their own power. Their insincerity foreshadows

Edmund's in the next scene, which establishes the villainous "grouping" of three. Cordelia, however, responds with her well-known but ill-fated honesty, insisting that she has "nothing" to say and that she loves her father only according to her bond. Cordelia's full heart and empty tongue clearly contrast with her sisters' false rhetoric in the ethical register of the play just as her improvident frankness contrasts with their calculations of gain. Yet Cordelia's response is more than honest; it is at least a little cruel, and thus presages her sister's more serious revenges later. Indeed, her wounding "economy" of words foreshadows Goneril's and Regan's cruelly rational system of household management ("Nothing" is what will be left of Lear's retinue if he submits to his daughters). It can of course be maintained that these parallels only establish a more fundamental contrast, but this argument reduces the ambivalence of Cordelia's feelings and reactions, which are fully coherent if understood as an assault on Lear's absolutist order-word.

What makes Cordelia's response especially powerful (in the dramatic as well as political sense) is precisely that it could not be *foreseen*. The whole opening ceremony, as I have said, is constructed according to the temporality of the order-word, which fulfills itself in the perfect tense. Ceremony, by its nature, is always performed as an invariable repetition. But by refusing to play her part and by impeding her father's ability to dispose of his property as he had wished, Cordelia disrupts the perfection of the order-word by reinjecting it with the contingency of the present (it is Lear's foolishness not to have understood the meaning of this gesture as a critique of his plan to divide the kingdom). This is not to say that Cordelia does not love her father; it is only to say that what she does poses a fundamental *challenge* to his authority and, moreover, means to do so.

Lear's power in the opening scene is doubly constituted, first, by the ceremonial coherence of his order-word and, second, by the grandiose gesture of dividing the kingdom, an act of aggressive generosity that cannot be matched, which reduces everyone else to the inferior and passive position of recipient (the ambivalence of the gift as described by Marcel Mauss if fully evident here).[75] Lear's double monopoly, of land and political authority, ensures that no one else has a countermove and that his ceremony cannot therefore become a *game*. Or so he thinks. For Cordelia responds with the only possible means of trumping her father: an act of self-divestiture, of aristocratic *dépense*, as powerful and extravagant as his own. Simply, she redoubles his own gesture by depriving herself of a kingdom—improves it, in fact, by leaving herself immediately and fully destitute. It is this, the powerfully aggressive *nobility* of her gesture, that takes the King of France with an unanticipated desire:

> Gods, gods! 'tis strange that from their cold'st neglect
> My love should kindle to inflam'd respect.
> Thy dowerless daughter, King, thrown to my chance,
> Is Queen of us, of ours, and our fair France.
>
> (1.1.253–56)

France's gaming metaphor ("thrown to my chance") is telling here—especially since it is Cordelia who throws *herself* down.

What Cordelia does in act 1, scene 1, is break the monopoly of the absolutist order-word and thereby release an aristocratic game of challenge and counterchallenge, expense and counterexpense. The first to respond to her gesture is Kent, who boldly criticizes Lear and, when threatened with death, answers, "My life I never held but as a pawn / To wage against thy enemies; nor fear to lose it / Thy safety being motive" (1.1.154–56). The game is now under way and will be pursued with increasing seriousness as the play unfolds.

The notion of a feudal "bond" in *King Lear*, as in much of chivalric ideology, is entirely misunderstood if it is regarded as a stable and positive relation. Enfeoffment is a dynamic involving an incomplete and volatile subordination of one independent power to another; its ties of loyalty and honor are not sentimental but rather fully ambivalent, charged with the counterchallenge that inheres in sacrifice. When Cordelia says that she loves her father "according to her bond," she thus initiates a specifically aristocratic game of expense. Later in the play she actually becomes a feudal military commander and leads a campaign to restore her now-helpless father to his throne. But even when she loses this she still wins the contest of expenditure, telling Lear, "For thee, oppressed King, I am cast down" (5.3.5). Cordelia's motives, or apparent motives, should not be allowed to conceal the actual result of her actions: she wins a total victory over her father, who by the end of the play is reduced to groveling and self-abasement. "No, Sir," she can say at the delicious moment of emotional triumph, "you must not kneel" (4.7.58).

This is not to deny that Cordelia and Kent love Lear but only to define the nature and effects of their love, which in the end differ very little from the nature and effects of the hatred of Lear's enemies. Cordelia, in particular, begins more and more to resemble Edmund: like him, she challenges paternal and political authority, and like him, she ultimately becomes a military commander. Her role too is to reintroduce the feudal war machine, to break the monopoly of the absolutist order-word, to unleash an atavistic movement in which the values of a militarized aristocracy are revived, even if in tragic form. But this is also the role of Kent, of Goneril, of Regan, and not least of Lear himself, whose division of the kingdom is the necessary precondition for the acts of all the others. Beneath the personal conflicts of the play, then, there is a surprising unanimity of social purpose; or rather, the revival of antagonism is itself a shared purpose. That this entails tragic destruction may, in the end, be seen not only as a drawback but also as a strange compensation.

## Tragedy and the Economies of the Zero Sum

Lear's first exchange with Cordelia, during the division of the kingdom, establishes a principle that is essential to tragedy as a genre. Goneril and Regan have already made their flattering speeches, and Lear bestows Regan's inheritance before turning to Cordelia, his third and favorite daughter:

> *Lear.* To thee and thine, [Regan,] hereditary ever,
> Remain this ample third of our fair kingdom,
> No less in space, validity, and pleasure,
> Than that conferr'd on Goneril. Now, our joy,
> Although our last, and least; to whose young love
> The vines of France and milk of Burgundy
> Strive to be interess'd; what can you say to draw
> A third more opulent than your sisters? Speak.
> *Cor.* Nothing.
> *Lear.* Nothing?
> *Cor.* Nothing.
> *Lear.* Nothing will come of nothing: speak again.
> *Cor.* Unhappy that I am, I cannot heave
> My heart into my mouth: I love your Majesty
> According to my bond; no more nor less.
> *Lear.* How, how, Cordelia! Mend your speech a little,
> Lest you may mar your fortunes.

*Cor.* Good my lord,
You have begot me, bred me, lov'd me: I
Return those duties back as are right fit,
Obey you, love you, and most honour you.
Why have my sisters husbands, if they say
They love you all? Happily, when I shall wed,
That lord whose hand must take my plight shall carry
Half my love with him, half my care and duty:
Sure I shall never marry like my sisters,
To love my father all.

(1.1.78–103)

Perhaps the most striking effect of Cordelia's reticence, at least initially, is the way it collapses Lear's own rhetoric of abundance. As he distributes each parcel of his kingdom, Lear gives speeches that metaphorically equate the natural fecundity of the land itself with his own royal magnificence, so that he, like the earth, becomes a seemingly magical and endless source of wealth. Even Cordelia, the "last, and least" (according to the Folio), is invested with a "more opulent" third as a sign of the king's power to amplify and increase as he wills. To this cornucopian rhetoric Cordelia responds with her curt and enigmatic "nothing," and it is as if the word itself empties out all that had preceded it, substituting a zero-sum economy for the illusion of inexhaustible riches. Lear, offended, ratifies this new regime of dearth when he replies: "Nothing will come of nothing: speak again." And Cordelia does speak, but only to insist even more strongly on the principle of limits: she loves her father exactly according to her bond, no more, no less. Her love merely repays benefits received, with no surplus remaining, and when she marries, she will transfer half of that to her husband.

What this exchange between Lear and Cordelia turns on, in part, are the figural economies of dramatic genre. Shakespeare's early romance comedies almost invariably require the production of a supplement of some sort in order to resolve plot difficulties. As often as not this takes the form of a literal or figurative doubling of characters which enables a series of marriages to take place. Lear's pastoral rhetoric of abundance recalls the green world of the early comedies, just as the multiple marrying off of daughters invokes earlier modes of plot resolution. The late romances likewise rely on a kind of redemptive surplus, typically the unexpected or miraculous return of a lost wife or daughter. The banishing of Cordelia invokes a set of romance expectations that will later be disappointed. Tragedy assumes the absence of any miraculous supplement to overcome loss. It is predicated on the economy of the zero sum.

In this respect *Lear* resembles all other tragedies. What distinguishes it is the thoroughness and explicitness with which it works out the economies of its genre. Within the play, the master figure for the zero-sum economy is, of course, land—Lear's kingdom itself. For despite the rhetoric of endless copia which accompanies its parceling out, it is clear that the kingdom can be divided only once, after which nothing remains. The ensuing struggles attempt to appropriate or reconstitute this initial sum, and all battles are fought out over a strictly delimited territory. Landed property, which by its nature can be divided or reapportioned but not increased, makes an appropriate figure for a bounded or inflexible economy. Perry Anderson's remarks on the role of war in the feudal mode of production are illuminating for *Lear* as well:

> The normal medium of inter-capitalist competition is economic, and its structure is typically additive: rival parties may both expand and prosper—although unequally—throughout a single confrontation, because the production of manufactured commodities is inherently unlimited. The typical medium of inter-feudal rivalry, by contrast, was military and its structure was always potentially the zero-sum conflict of the battlefield, by which fixed quantities of ground were won or lost. For land is a natural monopoly: it cannot be indefinitely extended, only redivided.

The very structure of feudal production ensured that "the nobility was a landowning class whose profession was war: its social vocation was not an external accretion but an intrinsic function of its economic position."[76] The rival parties in Shakespeare's play also wage war over a fixed sum of land, which forms the paradigm for the figurative economies of the play.

Lear's delusions about kingship can be understood as a failure to acknowledge the limits of the zero-sum economy, for Lear holds to the idealist belief that even if he gives away all his lands and power, some mystical residue of kingship will somehow remain with him. It is the task of the Fool, above all, to rid him of this tragic misconception:

*Fool.* Sirrah, I'll teach thee a speech.
*Lear.* Do.

*Fool.* Mark it, Nuncle:
Have more than thou showest,
Speak less than thou knowest,
Lend less than thou owest,
Ride more than thou goest,
Learn more than thou trowest,
Set less than thou throwest;
Leave thy drink and thy whore,
And keep in-a-door,
And thou shalt have more
Than two tens to a score.
*Lear.* This is nothing, Fool.
*Fool.* Then 'tis like the breath of an unfee'd lawyer; you gave me
nothing for't. Can you make no use of nothing, Nuncle?
*Lear.* Why, no, boy; nothing can be made out of nothing.
*Fool.* [*to Kent*] Prithee, tell him, so much the rent of his land comes
to: he will not believe a Fool. (1.4.113–32)

The prudential wisdom of the Fool's verses, which counsel retaining a surplus in all exchanges, is "nothing" to Lear, who has given all. Lear's line "nothing can be made out of nothing" ironically recalls his earlier advice to Cordelia, and the Fool's response only makes literal and explicit the relation between this economy and the nature of landed property. As the Fool tells Lear a few lines later, "now thou art an O without a figure" (1.4.189–90).

The just-quoted passage introduces the censored references to James's royal expenses and dispensation of titles, discussed in the first section of this chapter. And it thereby suggests the social basis for Shakespeare's meditation on the zero-sum economy. In one sense this is nothing other than the crisis of royal finances which erupted in the early years of King James's rule, leading to an economic tug-of-war between crown and Parliament. The contradiction between absolutist rhetoric and economic reality which afflicted the Stuart kingship took the form of an attempt to "create" titles and revenues out of nothing—a policy that ran up against the unexpandable limits of actual resources. Lear's illusion that a mysterious supplement will adhere to the kingship after everything has been spent resembles James's belief that the crown's economic woes could be solved by royal fiat.

The crown's financial embarrassment was, however, conditioned by a more widespread structural problem: the crisis of revenues afflicting the feudal landowning class as a whole. Feudal landed property was increasingly appearing as an unexpandable zero sum, and not only, or even primarily, because land cannot be physically augmented. The feudal mode of production itself inhibited the development of productive forces and hence of increased levels of surplus extraction.[77] Capitalist farming would expand both the extensive and intensive exploitation of agricultural labor, but for the feudal landowning class the seemingly insuperable limits to surplus extraction resulted in a persistent, if relative, financial squeeze. An understanding of social and economic causes was by no means necessary, of course, to an intuitive grasp of the fact that landed wealth was divisible but not expandable. It is suggestive, in any case, that *King Lear* employs the parceling of landed property as its founding emblem for the zero-sum economy.

Clearly, the play is "about" things other than property, but the point is that it portrays all other human or spiritual realms as similarly bounded. Isn't this, after all, the point of Cordelia's warning to Lear about a daughter's affections? Finding a husband doesn't create new love; it simply divides the original fund between two objects. Even the bearing of children, perhaps the closest thing to a "miraculous" creation of something from nothing, becomes a nightmare vision in which children and parents cannibalize each other. When Lear disclaims his paternity in Cordelia, he vows:

> The barbarous Scythian,
> Or he that makes his generation messes
> To gorge his appetite, shall to my bosom
> Be as well neighbour'd, pitied, and reliev'd,
> As thou my sometime daughter.
>
> (1.1.115–19)

Later, Lear asks the gods to "dry up" Goneril's "organs of increase" or else

> Create her child of spleen, that it may live
> And be a thwart disnatur'd torment to her!
> Let it stamp wrinkles in her brow of youth,
> With cadent tears fret channels in her cheeks,
> Turn all her mother's pains and benefits
> To laughter and contempt, that she may feel
> How sharper than a serpent's tooth it is
> To have a thankless child!
>
> (1.4.280–87)

The bodies of parent and child become, in this play, oedipal territories fought over as fiercely and brutally as landed properties. As

Edmund, contemplating the theft of his father's property, puts it, "the younger rises when the old doth fall" (3.3.25). What I earlier called the materialist and antitranscendental strain in *Lear* prevents the access of any divine or genuinely supernatural supplement to the play's original portion; and the nature of domestic relations, quite brutally implicated with and modeled on property relations, forecloses the possibility of an emotional or affective supplement as well. In every realm, the play becomes a scramble for strictly delimited resources.

The zero sum is not present in *Lear* as a thing or character but as a pervasive horizon or limitation on things and characters. If, on the one hand, it is felt as a generic tension between romance and tragedy—that is to say, between a literary world infused with the supplement and one that lacks it—on the other hand, it points to a historical contradiction: specifically, between increasing aristocratic expenditure and limited financial means. If *Lear* is, in some fundamental way, an extended meditation on the transformation of the aristocracy to a consuming class, if it conceives of the crisis of that class (and with it Shakespeare's own class wish) as in part its relegation to the realm of the consumption-sign, then the tragic portrayal of aristocratic values is completed by fears that even the consumption-sign may flicker and fail, a victim of economic insufficiency. The economy of the zero sum is the symbolic representation of this crisis *within* consumption, and it thus complements the political crisis of the aristocratic order-word.

To establish the zero sum as a kind of ultimate horizon for the play's economies, however, is not to describe the possible effects and practices within this global limit. What, to paraphrase Robert Frost, is one to make of a diminished thing? In fact, *Lear* contemplates three possibilities: inflation, rational apportionment or conservation, and *dépense* or destructive expenditure. These three alternatives project three possible futures or subsequent histories for aristocratic values and culture. And the play (if I may be permitted another physics metaphor) calculates something like a "sum over histories," assuming that *every* possible historical path is taken and averaging out the results.[78]

An inflationary economy, the first of the three paths, results from the attempt to make something come of nothing, or at least to expand a fixed sum by debasing, diluting, or dividing it. This seems to be the subject of one the Fool's gibes at Lear:

*Fool.* Nuncle, give me an egg, and I'll give thee two crowns.
*Lear.* What two crowns shall they be?

*Fool.* Why, after I have cut the egg i' th' middle and eat up the meat, the two crowns of the egg. When thou clovest thy crown i' th' middle, and gav'st away both parts, thou bor'st thine ass on thy back o'er the dirt: thou hadst little wit in thy bald crown when thou gav'st thy golden one away. (1.4.152–60)

Here the Fool's inflationary offer (two crowns would have been an absurdly high price to pay for an egg) introduces a densely symbolic discourse on the debasement of values.[79] For the Fool's inflated payment seems at first to offer Lear a miraculous profit on his egg—the creation of something from nothing. But this magical supplement disappears when the two "crowns" are revealed to be only the two evacuated halves of the egg, all that remains once the "meat"—the really valuable part—has been consumed. In a kind of allegory of inflation, what at first seemed increase or multiplication turns out in fact to be division or debasement. Such, implies the Fool, is the result of Lear's division of the kingdom: the expectation that a magical "supplement" of kingship would remain once the crown was divided has turned out to be false, and the only result is the debasing of the office. The egg, which completes the Fool's double pun on "crown," may be also taken as a symbol of natural fecundity, the apparently miraculous creative powers of the maternal, which also fail here, leading only to the image of the two ungrateful daughters. Every source of increase thus dries up, leaving only division and debasement: in short, inflation.

It is striking, I think, that this complex joke immediately follows the Fool's censored references to King James's profligate granting of titles and monopolies and forms a part of the same verbal exchange. It is as if the Fool has discovered, *avant la lettre,* the so-called "inflation of honors" described and named by Lawrence Stone.[80] Certainly, James's attempts to create value out of nothing by inventing new titles resembles Lear's baseless faith in the creative powers of the king. Inflation, in both instances, is the ruse that underlies the deceptive elasticity of the real; it is the toll exacted by an inflexible economy on the workings of the absolutist order-word. Oswald, the phony courtier, represents the outermost curve of this inflationary spiral, leading to complete dilution and debasement of aristocratic status.[81]

The problem of inflation in its directly economic sense may well inspire one of Lear's more provocative ravings on the heath. When he cries, "No, they cannot touch me for coining; I am the king himself" (4.6.83–84), Lear probably harks back to the Fool's pun on "crowns" as coins, and thus to the idea that in making two crowns out of one, he has in effect "coined" or created money. By recalling that coining was a royal prerogative, Lear tries to master the paranoid delusion that he may be arrested for counterfeiting. But here again the historical background is suggestive, for royal abuses of coining had been notorious for some time. The Tudors frequently manipulated English currency as a way of supplementing royal income; this practice reached a pitch in the 1540s, when major debasements of the currency, made in large part to cover massive war debts, contributed to a general economic crisis and soaring prices.[82] As Whitney R. D. Jones puts it, "the immense and direct influence of the monarch" was "the key to the first phase of the price inflation in England,"[83] and contemporaries understood that it was. In *A Shorte Treatise of Politicke Power* (1556), John Ponet blamed the crown for raising prices by debasing the currency. Ponet alludes to "evil governors and rulers . . . that contrary to all laws . . . counterfeit the coin that is ordained to run between man and man, turning the substance from gold to copper, from silver to worse than pewter, and advancing and diminishing the price at their pleasure."[84] Despite Lear's hopes, then, the king *could* be accused of counterfeiting, or "coining," though not prosecuted for it.

The debasement of English currency was halted, for a time, by royal proclamation in 1560. King James, however, wrought havoc with the Scots economy through continual manipulation of the coinage, once again in an attempt to repair "the wretched state of the king's private exchequer."[85] A 1593 paper explained this tampering as "necessarily for the sustening of his majesties hous and clothing."[86] It is difficult to know whether James's reputation as a "coiner" followed him to England, and thus whether the reference in *Lear* would have any immediate topical value.[87] But it seems clear at least that Lear's words would evoke the venerable habits of debasement practiced by Tudor monarchs. Price inflation was the inevitable and repeated result of this practice, thus demonstrating the resistance of economic "substance" to changes in "sign" and the intractability of economic law to the insistence of the royal order-word.[88]

Inflation in *Lear* occupies the crossroads of history and romance, where the romantic dream of a magical supplement collides with the historical nightmare of dearth. It evacuates romance by means of an inverted alchemy that transforms golden crowns into eggs. But this generic trajectory is also that of the aristocratic class, whose ideological values become mired in economic insufficiency and which sees in the troubles of the crown a specular image of its own contradictions. The play thus seeks to avoid the end terms of this history—bankrupt Lears and proliferating Oswalds, contracting means and diluted class identities—by exploring the two alternative economies of the zero sum, which produce alternative histories as well.

The first of these possible alternatives—rational apportionment or conservation—invokes the notion of need as a brake on lavish display or excess, and argues for a more prudent or charitable distribution of inherently limited means. This ideology of need is in fact doubly articulated in the play. The first, "false" version is presented by Goneril and Regan as they attempt to reduce Lear's retinue by claiming that a doubling of servants creates unnecessary expenses and leads to dangerous conflicts of authority. Their arguments provoke Lear's memorable defense of excess:

> *Gon.* Why might you not, my Lord, receive attendance
> From those that she calls servants, or from mine?
> *Reg.* Why not, my Lord? If then they chanc'd to slack ye
> We could control them. If you will come to me,
> For now I spy a danger, I entreat you
> To bring but five and twenty; to no more
> Will I give place or notice.
> *Lear.* I gave you all. . . .
> *Gon.*                                       Hear me, my Lord.
> What need you five-and-twenty, ten, or five,
> To follow in a house where twice so many
> Have a command to tend you?
> *Reg.*                                       What need one?
> *Lear.* O! reason not the need; our basest beggars
> Are in the poorest thing superfluous:
> Allow not nature more than nature needs,
> Man's life is cheap as beast's. Thou art a lady;
> If only to go warm were gorgeous,
> Why, nature needs not what thou gorgeous wear'st,
> Which scarcely keeps thee warm. But, for true need,—
> You Heavens, give me that patience, patience I need!—
>                              (2.4.241–48, 258–69)

Several contemporary issues float up vaguely through the daughters' rhetoric. One is the Tudor campaign to reduce the bands of armed retainers kept by noblemen. Another is a growing interest in rational estate management and limitation of expenses as a way of warding off economic ruin for aristocratic houses. Here the notion of rational expenditure, though opposed in principle to aristocratic consumption, actually attempts to conserve it from ruin in the context of a zero-sum economy.[89]

Lear's rejoinder, in any case, fully defends an aristocratic privilege of expense against the daughters' cost-cutting measures. More, it extends the principle of excess to all social classes and mounts what is, in fact, a theoretically cogent refutation of the ideology of need. Need, Lear argues correctly, does not come before superfluity; rather, it always includes and is predicated upon the superfluous. The king's insistence that even "basest beggars" retain a surplus cuts against the illusion of the bare biological minimum in a way that strongly recalls Thomas More's *Utopia*. It even, I think, helps to explain the effectiveness of this scene, or at least why a nonaristocratic audience might find pathos in the stripping of the king's retinue.[90]

Lear's invocation of "basest beggars" proves prophetic, of course. For in the course of his coming night on the heath he will meet "unaccommodated man" in the person of Tom o' Bedlam; and he will himself come to know, amid the rain and lightning and howling winds, a hitherto unexperienced intensity of need. It is hard not to feel that the famous "poor naked wretches" speech is in some way an answer to the earlier "reason not the need," and that Lear has achieved a broader vision of human community by learning that there really *is* in fact a thing called "need":

> Poor naked wretches, whereso'er you are,
> That bide the pelting of this pitiless storm,
> How shall your houseless heads and unfed sides,
> Your loop'd and window'd raggedness, defend you
> From seasons such as these? O! I have ta'en
> Too little care of this. Take physic, Pomp;
> Expose thyself to feel what wretches feel,
> That thou mayst shake the superflux to them,
> And show the Heavens more just.
>
> (3.4.28–36)

This, it might be argued, is the "true" version of rational apportionment, which serves as a rejoinder to Goneril's and Regan's false economizing. Lear's discovery of need does not merely conserve aristocratic resources so as to extend the life of the consumption-sign; rather, it seems to move beyond class interest altogether to envision a utopian and egalitarian redistribution of social goods. Lear has discovered, in a sense, that the zero sum enfolds the whole social body; and unlike King James, he has sense enough to see that most people would *not* rather tighten their own belts in order to keep the king living in a high style. And just in case anyone in the audience has dozed off and missed this edifying moment, Shakespeare provides us with an almost perfect reprise later on, through the person of Gloucester:

> Let the superfluous and lust-dieted man,
> That slaves [heaven's] ordinance, that will not see
> Because he does not feel, feel your power quickly;
> So distribution will undo excess,
> And each man have enough.
>
> (4.1.66–70)

This is moving stuff, and yet in the end it comes to nothing. The utopian strain, like the lightning that is its counterpoint, flashes briefly in the night of the play and is then swallowed up—along, one assumes, with the concept of need that founded it.

Even at first, though, there is something awry in the two pleas for rational or equitable distribution of wealth. "Shake the super-flux" has a decidedly aristocratic cachet of largess and, further-more, depends on a concept of superfluity or unnecessary excess which Lear has already made problematic. "Take physic, Pomp!" sounds less like a call to reason than like a violent bodily purge, and indeed, Lear's insight is an immediate prelude to madness. As for Gloucester, his idea of "rational" distribution is to hand his purse to a beggar and then fling himself from a cliff. The very expression of reasoned or moderate consumption is thus shot through with a frenzied excess, as if it can only be glimpsed too late.

In the Folio this interplay of reason and madness is represented by the immediate answer to Lear's "poor naked wretches" speech by the voice of Tom o' Bedlam crying "Fathom and half, fathom and half! Poor Tom!" (3.4.37–38). In his role as poor Tom, Edgar embodies precisely the image of need Lear has just invoked; he is "unaccommodated man," reduced to the bare biological minimum of existence, wandering in the heath, which is the landscape of natural lack. Tom and the heath form an ideological couplet, the personification and landscape of dearth, the zero sum reduced to the zero degree. At least, so Lear reads Tom:

> Thou wert better in a grave than to answer with thy uncover'd body this extremity of the skies. Is man no more than this? Consider him

well. Thou ow'st the worm no silk, the beast no hide, the sheep no
wool, the cat no perfume. Ha! There's three on's are sophisticated;
thou art the thing itself; unaccommodated man is no more but such
a poor, bare, forked animal as thou art. Off, off, you lendings! Come;
unbutton here. (3.4.99–107)

Here Lear seems directly to renounce his earlier view that "basest
beggars are in the poorest things superfluous." A humanist reading
of the play might wish to insist that Lear's confrontation with real
poverty has led him beyond his former, merely aristocratic insistence on excess to a broader understanding of human need. Unfortunately, the beginning of this new vision coincides exactly with
the onset of Lear's madness and is not so much ruined by as
founded upon that madness. Lear ends his "unaccommodated
man" speech by tearing off his own clothes, an unmistakable sign
of madness in Shakespeare's day.[91]

Then too, poor Tom is actually quite "sophisticated," in fact not
a beggar at all but a nobleman in disguise. Although Lear is apparently taken in by Edgar's act, others seem to suspect that this
beggar *does* hold something in reserve. Gloucester remarks,
"He has some reason, else he could not beg" (4.1.30), and the
Fool—responding to Lear's cry "Couldst thou save nothing?"—
quips: "Nay, he reserv'd a blanket, else we had all been sham'd"
(3.4.63–65).

The figure of the Bedlam beggar, in fact, cut to the heart of the
concepts of need and economic rationality. From one point of view
he was the "Abraham man," merely playing at madness to excite
sympathy and extort charitable contributions from passersby. The
appearance of insanity thus covered a calculated pursuit of economic gain. Edgar-as-poor-Tom played on contemporary suspicions
that most apparently mad beggars were only cleverly profiteering
actors.[92] Yet these same men were feared as genuine lunatics, rendered all the more frightening by their complete lack of economic
self-interest, as Michael MacDonald notes: "English laymen
thought that the stark, Bedlam madman was dangerous, inclined
to murder and assault, arson and vandalism. Unlike a criminal,
however, he could reap no conceivable benefit from his violence,
because he threatened and attacked people and property that were
essential aspects of his own social identity."[93]

As MacDonald has shown, the legal definition and disposition of
madness during the Renaissance depended heavily on the notion
of a specifically economic rationality, largely because the state's

sole interest in insanity involved protecting families and property from its financial consequences. The central question for juries in establishing insanity was whether the person in question "could perform the necessary economic chores to preserve the family property," and "the chief concern of the crown's policy toward insane landowners was to preserve the integrity of their estates so that their lineages would not be obliterated by the economic consequences of their madness"—a notion of some relevance to *Lear*.[94]

At the other end of the social scale, the Tudor and Stuart state included mad paupers among the classes of "deserving poor" whose families merited charitable assistance. And here too, the definition of insanity often rested on acts of economic madness such as window breaking or, significantly, the destruction of clothing: "Men and women who destroyed their own clothing were irrationally wasteful and socially self-defacing. Clothing was valuable property, which was very expensive to replace, for clothes cost ordinary villagers far more time and trouble than they do today."[95] This kind of economic destruction was classed quite easily with acts of physical self-mutilation and abuse, such as finger cutting and tongue biting, in that it contradicted a rational interest in self-preservation. It is important to note, however, that the forms of expenditure judged insane were not entirely unrelated to perfectly acceptable patterns of aristocratic expense. Was the nobleman who madly ruined or abandoned his property all that different from those who frittered theirs away in lavish living? The line between improvidence and mental unfitness seems to have depended at least a little on whether the destruction of value reaped the ephemeral benefit of consumption-signs. Likewise, poor madmen who tore their clothes indulged in an unacceptably aristocratic form of extravagance, demonstrating that even the little they had could be treated as "superflux" rather than according to the logic of need. One wonders whether the tendency to see such characters as calculating rogues was less an effect of cynicism than an attempt to inject a reassuring motive of economic rationality into this frightening display of *dépense*.

It is in this economic context, I think, that the relation between Lear and poor Tom takes on its fullest meaning. Lear begins the play with a "madly" improvident disposition of his own property in which aristocratic consumption begins to lose contact with economic and social reality. The self-deposed king is then treated, unsurprisingly, as a slightly mad dotard by his scheming daughters.

When confronted with their "rational" system of housekeeping, which will dispel his "needless' retainers, Lear responds with his "reason not the need" speech, and thereby explains his own impending madness: he rejects reason *in order to reject need,* in order, that is, to escape the cruelly logical system of conservation and apportionment imposed by his daughters. If the "poor naked wretches" speech signals a newly expanded social awareness, it is based not on an adherence to rational principles of need but rather on a universal insistence on the right to "superflux" or excess.

It is appropriate in this context that Lear's final guide down the road to madness should be poor Tom, a figure who, in the end, represents the triumph of superfluity over need, and who actually embodies a kind of negative cornucopia. Consider, for instance, his pretended diet: "Poor Tom; that eats the swimming frog, the toad, the todpole, the wall-newt, and the water; that in the fury of his heart, when the foul fiend rages, eats cow-dung for sallets; swallows the old rat and the ditch-dog; drinks the green mantle of the standing pool." (3.4.126–31). Whereas some of this menu reflects the real exigencies of vagrant life, Tom's description surpasses the realm of need and establishes him as a gourmet of the abject. His very malady—"possession"—harks back punningly to his prosperous past when he had "three suits to his back, six shirts to his body" (3.4.133), and the company of devils which inhabits him endows him with the paradoxical "fulness" of a black festivity. Poor Tom invokes the concept of need, but in the end shows that basest beggars *are* in the poorest things superfluous.[96]

Between them, Lear and poor Tom thus reject rational conservation or apportionment, opting instead for maddened or symbolic forms of luxury. It is perhaps understandable why Renaissance theater, itself a frivolous or unnecessary form of expense, would find it difficult to embrace an ideology of need. In any case, Lear and Tom point to the third possible economy of the zero sum, and the one apparently "chosen" by the play: *dépense* or destructive expenditure. *Dépense* resembles aristocratic expense but perfects it, in a sense, by refusing to recoup its losses through the cultural capital of the consumption sign.[97] It moves beyond mere luxury or display to the realm of the gamble, the challenge, suicide, madness; and hence it has available to it not only material wealth but a wider range of symbolic materials, including life itself. In this realm the zero-sum economy is not, for once, a limitation but an enabling resource, for it is not the magnitude of the display but the intensity of loss that counts. To "give all," as Lear puts it, to spend without reserve, is a gesture that operates at the boundaries of the possible: a flexible or magical economy of the supplement would empty it out. "The art of our necessities is strange, / And can make vile things precious" (3.2.70–71): lack actually extends the realm of symbolic expense by enabling it to operate with strictly limited means. Any scale will do, as long as it admits of total depletion.

The various economies I have invoked here will necessarily recall those at work in More's *Utopia*. Indeed, the parallels between these two works are quite striking: both are concerned with the problems of vagrancy and penury, both formulate a failed utopian response to this problem, both interrogate the notion of "need" though a counterlogic of *dépense*, or destructive expenditure. Curiously, however, *Utopia* is never really haunted by the notion of a zero-sum economy; instead, it imagines a potentially limitless social production of goods. I say "curiously" because *Lear* was written almost a century later, when capitalist agriculture was really beginning to create the material possibility of "endlessly" increasing production. Yet it is in *Lear* and not *Utopia* that the limits of the zero sum seem most insistent. This paradox can be explained in part by the class focus of the two works. More totalizes certain aspects of petty-producing culture, and Shakespeare addresses the crisis of the *aristocracy*, not the state of the Jacobean economy at large. Hence *Utopia* imagines a process of endless accumulation, but *Lear* is founded on the problem of distributing or consuming a fixed sum of wealth. Such considerations are not meant to substitute for more properly literary problems of genre, however; *Lear's* status as tragedy is not annulled but enhanced by its strategic response to the economic limits of aristocracy.

The logic of destructive expenditure is clearly visible in the division of the kingdom that opens the play. I have already discussed the references to King James's inflationary creation of titles; yet there is another, quite contradictory sense in which Lear's gesture differs from James's. Lear's is not a dribbling away or slow dilution of royal power but a grandiose and somewhat "mad" destruction of it. The division of the kingdom is therefore more than allusion, however displaced, to the limitations placed on absolutism by the realities of a zero-sum economy. The division surpasses these limitations not by evading them but by embracing them in the proper way. If inflation points toward an inevitable and degrading erosion of royal power, and particularly of royal consumption, then *dépense* offers the tragic but ennobling alternative of disposing of it all at once, in a grand, if suicidal gesture.

This option is what remains to Lear even after his material resources have been depleted. Reacting with "noble anger" to the conservative regime of his daughters, Lear declares:

> No, I'll not weep:
> I have full cause of weeping, but this heart
> Shall break into a hundred thousand flaws
> Or ere I'll weep.
>
> (2.4.281–85)

Weeping is a self-emasculating response and thus impossible for reasons already discussed; it is also an act of slow dilution fully consonant with the daughters' piecemeal reduction of Lear's royal power. Against this Lear can sill mount the challenge of violent and sudden self-destruction, which he pursues in his wanderings on the heath. Thus Lear in the storm "bids what will take all" (3.1.14). When nothing else is left to spend, he can spend himself, his heart, his reason. This is why stormy nature, the realm of lack into which he flings himself to be consumed, also appears to be a source of destructive copia, and why Lear's sufferings are all tinged with a strange voluptuary pleasure:

> Blow, winds, and crack your cheeks! rage! blow!
> You cataracts and hurricanoes, spout
> Till you have drench'd our steeples, drown'd the cocks!
> You sulph'rous and thought-executing fires,
> Vaunt-couriers of oak-cleaving thunderbolts,
> Singe my white head! And thou, all-shaking thunder,
> Strike flat the thick rotundity of the world!
> Crack Nature's moulds, all germens spill at once
> That makes ungrateful man!
>
> (3.2.1–9)

This apocalyptic strain totalizes the logic of expenditure: "all germens spill at once" in an act that is both universally orgasmic and universally self-destructive.

If Lear seems to be at his most kingly when challenging the skies, it is because he displays a conception of noble or aristocratic behavior that is largely founded on *dépense.* The very notion of feudal loyalty, which plays so central a role in the play's system of values, entails a self-destructiveness embodied in Kent's boast to Lear that "my life I never held but as a pawn / To wage against thine enemies" (1.1.154–55). The Fool, also commenting on the nature of loyalty, quips: "Let go thy hold when a great wheel runs down a hill, lest it break thy neck with following" (2.4.69–71). In this play the conception of "beautiful" behavior requires holding on and breaking one's neck; aristocratic virtue appears only when the king has fallen, thus enabling Kent, Cordelia, and others to demonstrate a suicidal loyalty whose "irrational" abandonment of the law of self-preservation recalls the madness of poor Tom. The subsequent militarizing of the play, which enables the reconstitution of the order-word, also sets the stage for a spectacle of destruction in the form of heroic self-sacrifice.

*King Lear*'s three economies of the zero sum—inflation, conservation, and *dépense*—are all imaginary responses to the crisis of aristocratic consumption. In particular, they respond to a contradiction between cultural value and material means: the increased reliance on economic consumption as a class marker during a period of decreasing or at least stable revenues. Of the three, inflation and conservation seem to point forward historically—the first toward a slow debasement of aristocratic values, the second toward more rational and bourgeois conceptions of expense. But the third, *dépense*, participates in the play's regress towards a fantasized rebirth of feudal values. Or rather, it signals both the completion and the impossibility of this project. If *Lear*'s retrograde movement attempts to "rescue" the aristocracy from its reliance on consumption and to reestablish its old position as a politico-military ruling class—in short, to revive the aristocratic order-word—it also tries to redeem the consumption-sign itself. *Dépense* moves consumption beyond mere economic display to a more heroic form of expense fraught with madness, suicide, nobility, the risks of battle. It takes the consumption-sign away from Oswald and refits it as a part of the feudal war machine.

But this cultural redemption entails a complex relation with the material economies of consumption. *Dépense* is enabled rather than curtailed by a zero-sum economy; moreover, it is able to feed on the destruction of a wide range of symbolic values, not all of them forms of material wealth. And yet it does not aim at self-reproduction or prolongation, for its very basis is a suicidal exhaustion of value. *Dépense* cannot extend or transcend the limits of its material; it simply reverses course and rushes toward implosion rather than conserve or dilute itself. Turning loss into a positive value, it chooses a catastrophic and tragic end over slow depletion. *King Lear's* "revival" of feudal values isn't miraculous or comic; it is predicated on disaster and must soon snuff itself out. Indeed, the play's values are *produced* by this consumption, as a flame is produced by the consumption of fuel; they exist only in departing.

Of all the gestures of self-spending in *King Lear* the richest may well be Gloucester's attempted suicide by leaping from Dover cliff. Edgar's portrayal of the abyss provides a kind of global emblem or figure for the play's axis of loss:

> Come on, sir; here's the place: stand still. How fearful
> And dizzy 'tis to cast one's eyes so low!
> The crows and coughs that wing the midway air
> Show scarce so gross as beetles; half way down
> Hangs one that gathers samphire, dreadful trade!
> Methinks he seems no bigger than his head.
> The fishermen that walk along the beach
> Appear like mice, and yond tall anchoring bark
> Diminish'd to her cock, her cock a buoy
> Almost too small for sight. The murmuring surge,
> That on th'unnumber'd idle pebble chafes,
> Cannot be heard so high. I'll look no more,
> Lest my brain turn, and the deficient sight
> Topple down headlong.
>
> (4.6.11–24)

Among other things, this imaginary landscape organizes and empowers the figures of height and depth scattered throughout the play. When Edgar says "I'll look no more, / Lest my brain turn, and the deficient sight / Topple down headlong," he clearly recalls Lear's "fall" into madness. The image of a height so great that it stills the roar of the sea powerfully figures consciousness perched above the abyss of unconscious desire—an image reinforced by Edgar's fear of the cliff's vertiginous allure. (Compare Lear's hysterical portrayal of sexuality as "the sulpherous pit" [4.6.127].) But Dover cliff also figures the social heights from which the king and others have fallen: in jumping from the edge Gloucester literalizes the notion of *de casibus* tragedy and the "fall of the great."

Indeed, Dover cliff may be read as a metadramatic image of *King Lear* itself as tragedy. It is, at least, a striking condensation of the play's attempts to create or manifest value through its destruction. Dover cliff represents loss as a positive strategy: not a slow and uncontrollable erosion of things but a throwing-over-the-edge. It is, in a sense, a machine for producing sublimity, a purely imaginative construct whose height allows doomed cultural values to flare out one last time as they are cast over the brink. Edgar's deception of his father cannot change anything, but it can create the momentary illusion that a magical supplement has intervened. "Thy life's a miracle," he tells Gloucester, who arises, briefly rejuvenated by this fiction.

To say that *Lear* attempts to revive the values of the feudal aristocracy, and that to this end it narrates in reverse a certain version of the transition to capitalist society, may create the false impression that it is a nostalgic play and that its tragic vision results from a consciousness of the impossibility of its historical project. But this is to mistake the matter entirely. The play does not passively watch the collapse of a social order which it portrays. It throws this order—or its declining values—over the edge, consumes it in a massive act of *dépense*. It thus reconstitutes through destruction. *King Lear* is, then, no more nostalgic for what is lost than someone watching a waterfall is nostalgic for the lake above. The destruction of the characters in increasingly costly warfare means not that a social structure is being torn apart but that it is being reconstituted in a tragic form. To be thrown over the edge is not, after all, the same as being rent asunder: it is, rather, to achieve a perfect but momentary state of equipoise, as even the force of gravity seems to be canceled in the seconds before impact. Albany's advice to "Fall and cease" (5.3.263) holds good for the whole play, which ends in smashing. "Break, heart; I prithee, break!" pleads Kent in the final moments (5.3.310), recalling Lear's promise that "this heart / Shall break into a hundred thousand flaws / Or ere I'll weep" (2.4.282–85).[98] This is at once a comment on the nature of tragic affect and a delineation of the play's imaginary response to history, the two converging here so as to illuminate, perhaps, what is meant by that enigmatic phrase *historica passio*.

# Notes

## Introduction

1. Various assaults on this metanarrative can be found in *The New Historicism*, a collection of essays edited by H. Aram Veeser (New York: Routledge, 1989). A post-Marxist variant of the new-historical critique appears in Ernesto Laclau and Chantal Mouffe, *Hegemony and Socialist Strategy* (London: Verso, 1985).

2. Althusser's most powerful methodological statements are "Contradiction and Overdetermination," in *For Marx*, trans. Ben Brewster (London: Verso, 1979), pp. 87–128, and his contributions to Althusser and Etienne Balibar, *Reading Capital*, trans. Ben Brewster (London: Verso, 1979). I think that Foucault's (admittedly conflicted) indebtedness to Althusser has not been sufficiently admitted, either by Foucault himself or by others who employ his work to attack Marxism. Fredric Jameson's most sustained argument for a Marxist hermeneutics is, of course, *The Political Unconscious: Narrative as a Socially Symbolic Act* (Ithaca: Cornell University Press, 1981), esp. chap. 1, "On Interpretation."

3. The Veeser volume attests both to the diversity of new-historical practice and to the fact that this need not impede either theorization or response.

4. See, for instance, Stephen Orgel, *The Illusion of Power: Political Theater in the English Renaissance* (Berkeley: University of California Press, 1975); Daniel Javitch, *Poetry and Courtliness in Renaissance England* (Princeton: Princeton University Press, 1978); Stephen Greenblatt, *Renaissance Self-Fashioning from More to Shakespeare* (Chicago: University of Chicago Press, 1980), esp. chaps. on More and Wyatt; Jonathan Goldberg, *James I and the Politics of Literature: Jonson, Shakespeare, Donne, and Their Contemporaries* (Baltimore: Johns Hopkins University Press, 1983); Leonard Tennenhouse, *Power on Display: The Politics of*

*Shakespeare's Genres* (New York: Methuen, 1986). Orgel's and Javitch's books predate the new historicism as a loosely defined critical school but clearly influenced it, especially during its early phase.

5. Karl Marx, *Capital*, vol. 1, trans. Ben Fowkes (New York: Vintage, 1977), p. 280.

6. The discourse of political economy obviously works to conceal economic domination; this is its ideological role. Yet Marx's critique of political economy should not be read as implying that it alone renders such domination "invisible."

7. Michel Foucault, *The History of Sexuality*, Vol. 1: *An Introduction*, ed. Robert Hurley (New York: Vintage, 1980), pp. 82, 87–91. "We must . . . conceive of sex without the law, and power without the king" (p. 91).

8. Michel Foucault, *Discipline and Punish*, trans. Alan Sheridan (New York: Vintage, 1979), p. 187.

9. Foucault, *History of Sexuality* 1:107.

10. Foucault, *Discipline and Punish*, p. 219.

11. Ibid.

12. Ibid., pp. 220–21.

13. See Frank Lentricchia, *Ariel and the Police: Michel Foucault, William James, Wallace Stevens* (Madison: University of Wisconsin Press, 1988), chap. 1. Peter Dews, "Power and Subjectivity in Foucault," *New Left Review* 144 (March–April 1984), 72–95, is less compromising but notes some similarities between Foucault's work and that of the Frankfurt School.

14. I retain the gender-specific meaning of this term, since Tudor grammar schools were institutions designed exclusively for adolescent males.

15. See Althusser, *Reading Capital*, pp. 94–99; Jameson, *Political Unconscious*, pp. 27–28.

16. Nicos Poulantzas, *Political Power and Social Classes*, trans. Timothy O'Hagan et al. (London: Verso, 1978), pp. 123, 44–45, 54, 56. This does not mean, of course, that the capitalist state never intervenes in the economic mechanism, employs violence, or exerts direct political domination over subaltern classes. Poulantzas's purpose here is to theorize what distinguishes the capitalist state from other kinds and to establish a framework within which its various interventions may be understood.

17. Ibid., pp. 190, 256.

18. Foucault, *History of Sexuality* 1:95, 94.

19. Ibid., 15–49.

20. Among the more distinguished examples of this trend are Greenblatt, "Invisible Bullets," chap. 2 of *Shakespearean Negotiations: The Circulation of Social Energy in Renaissance England* (Berkeley: University of California Press, 1988); Steven Mullaney, "The Rehearsal of Cultures," chap. 3 of *The Place of the Stage: License, Play, and Power in the English Renaissance* (Chicago: University of Chicago Press, 1988); Jonathan Dollimore, "Transgression and Surveillance in *Measure for Measure*," in *Political Shakespeare: New Essays in Cultural Materialism*, ed. Jonathan Dollimore and Alan Sinfield (Ithaca: Cornell University Press, 1985), pp. 72–87. See also the introduction to *Political Shakespeare*, pp. 10–15.

Needless to say, even those critics who argue for the successful subversion of such strategies are working within the same general problematic.

21. Poulantzas, *Political Power*, pp. 160, 166.

22. In this respect Poulantzas's analysis strikes me as preferable to Perry Anderson's, which holds that absolutism represented the interests of the late feudal nobility. For Poulantzas, the issue is not which class exercises political hegemony over the state apparatus but rather the internal articulation of the state itself and its characteristic modes of operation. The absolutist state is a transitional state not because the aristocratic and bourgeois classes exerted equal control over it (as Marx and Engels argued) but precisely because its relative autonomy allowed it to function in part as a capitalist state does. Bourgeois political hegemony over the state (or even "split" hegemony) is not, in this view, a necessary precondition for a capitalist state.

23. Poulantzas distinguishes between a "transitional situation," in which the birth of capitalism is merely possible, and a "transitional situation in the strict sense," which occurs after the break that institutes capitalist production (p. 158n). His analysis of absolutism concerns the transitional situation in the strict sense, and hence he assumes that capitalist property in its juridical form (though not in its economic form) is already entrenched. For Poulantzas, it is the firm establishment of private property that allows the absolutist state to assume its capitalist characteristics. His argument, thus, is not directly teleological; yet a teleological causality has been attributed to it simply because he says nothing about the prior "transitional situation" and therefore nothing about the origins of juridical private property or of absolutism. The problem is not that Poulantzas makes a faulty answer to the question of origins but that he ventures none at all.

24. Foucault, *History of Sexuality* 1:107.

25. This genealogical emphasis may partly explain, if not quite justify, a decentering of focus in the book. My purpose is not to trace a linear or progressive development but to locate dispersed elements. In writing a prehistory I do not claim to exempt myself from the theoretical and thematic coherence required of history, but I admit to having loosened the requirement a bit.

26. Stephen Greenblatt, *Shakespearean Negotiations*, esp. chap. 1, "The Circulation of Social Energy"; Greenblatt, "Toward a Poetics of Culture," in Veeser, *New Historicism*, pp. 1–14.

27. Lawrence Stone, *The Crisis of the Aristocracy, 1558–1641* (Oxford: Oxford University Press, 1965).

28. Only Jean-François Lyotard's book *The Postmodern Condition: A Report on Knowledge*, which I make use of in my chapter on Spenser, is unambiguously anti-Marxist. My use of Lyotard is purely local and tactical, and I assimilate his concepts of narrative and scientific "pragmatics" of knowledge to a framework he would disavow. Lyotard brooks no accommodation at all with the so-called *grand récit* of Marxism. Yet his own scheme of narrative, scientific, and postmodern "stages" looks peculiarly like such a grand narrative itself, and it owes more to the Marxist concepts of precapitalist, capitalist, and late-capitalist (or postindustrial) formations than it cares to admit.

## Chapter 1. A Mint of Phrases

1. Francis Bacon, *Advancement of Learning*, in *The Works of Francis Bacon*, ed. James Spedding et al. (1870; rpt. New York: Garrett Press, 1968), 3:283–84.
2. Richard Lanham, *The Motives of Eloquence: Literary Rhetoric in the Renaissance* (New Haven: Yale University Press, 1976), p. 33.
3. Gabriel Harvey, *Ciceronianus* (1577), rpt. with translation by Clarence A. Forbes, University of Nebraska Studies in the Humanities, 4 (Lincoln: University of Nebraska, 1945), p. 69.
4. Bacon's famous estimate of Ascham—and, by extension, of humanism in general—has been challenged by Thomas M. Greene, "Roger Ascham: The Perfect End of Shooting," *ELH* 36 (1969), 612. His views are seconded by Alvin Vos, " 'Good Matter and Good Utterance': The Character of English Ciceronianism," *Studies in English Literature, 1500–1900* 19 (1979), 3–18. Yet the relatively balanced educational program described by humanist writers seems often to have been given a formalist and stylistic inflection in practice.
5. Richard Mulcaster, *Positions* (1581; rpt. London, 1887), p. 268.
6. Ibid., p. 244.
7. New statistical evidence suggests that the explosive "take-off" of English elementary and grammar schools occurred not with the English Reformation, as was previously thought, but earlier, at the beginning of the sixteenth century. See Jo Ann Hoeppner Moran, *The Growth of English Schooling, 1340–1548* (Princeton: Princeton University Press, 1985), esp. pp. 92–122. Moran's study is limited to York diocese, but it shows that in the north of England at least, the major increase in the number of schools preceded both the Reformation and the influence of humanism. While one cannot extrapolate with certainty from regional studies, the patterns documented by Moran are so striking as to cast severe doubt on previous timetables. Humanist educational reforms, which began to take hold around 1510–1512 (John Colet took over St. Paul's School around 1510, and Erasmus published his massively influential *De copia* for Colet and St. Paul's in 1512), thus found an already burgeoning institutional base in the Tudor grammar schools.
8. On the role of schools in social reproduction, see Louis Althusser, "Ideology and the Ideological State Apparatus," in *Lenin and Philosophy*, trans. Ben Brewster (New York: Monthly Review Press, 1971), pp. 127–86; Pierre Bourdieu and Jean-Claude Passaron, *Reproduction in Education, Society, and Culture*, trans. Richard Nice (Beverly Hills, Calif.: Sage, 1977).
9. Marchamount Needham, *A Discourse concerning Schools* (1663), excerpted in David Cressy, *Education in Tudor England* (London: Edward Arnold, 1975), p. 23.
10. Quoted in Moran, *Growth of English Schools*, p. 45.
11. Anthony Grafton and Lisa Jardine, *From Humanism to the Humanities: Education and the Liberal Arts in Fifteenth- and Sixteenth-Century Europe* (London: Gerald Duckworth, 1986). The role of humanism in the religious controversies of Henry VIII's reign is described in detail by Maria Dowling, *Humanism in the Age of Henry VIII* (London: Croom Helm, 1986), pp. 1–74.

12. This movement "away" from religious ideology was, I should again stress, only relative. Colet, for instance, prescribed a number of postclassical Christian authors for the curriculum of St. Paul's and set aside part of the day for devotion and prayers (Dowling, *Humanism*, 113–14).

13. For merchant and middle-class endowments of grammar schools, see Louis B. Wright, *Middle-Class Culture in Elizabethan England* (Chapel Hill: University of North Carolina Press, 1935), pp. 43–80. For aristocratic endowment see Dowling, *Humanism*, pp. 123–31. Moran (*Growth of English Schools*, pp. 162–71) emphasizes the wide range of social classes that contributed financially to the building of village schools.

14. Mulcaster, *Positions*, p. 194.

15. John Lawson and Harold Silver, *A Social History of Education in England* (London: Methuen, 1973), p. 103.

16. Christopher Wase, *Considerations concerning Free Schools* (1678), excerpted in Cressy, *Education in Tudor England*, p. 19.

17. John Brinsley, *Ludus literarius* (1612; facs. rpt. Menston, England: Scolar Press, 1968), sigs. D2v–D3r, E1r. This work is especially useful for its frank discussions of many of the complaints leveled against common grammar schools by the parents of the humbler classes of students.

18. George Snell, *The Right Teaching Of Useful Knowledg, to fit Scholars for som honest Profession* (1649), quoted in Wright, *Middle-Class Culture*, p. 70.

19. Quoted in Wright, *Middle-Class Culture*, p. 67.

20. Lawson and Silver, *Social History of Education*, p. 45. Lawrence Stone develops the appropriation thesis in *The Crisis of the Aristocracy, 1558–1641* (Oxford: Oxford University Press, 1965), pp. 672–92.

21. In *The Second Part of the Anatomie of Abuses* (1583; facs. rpt. New York: Garland, 1973), Philip Stubbes complains that free schools are beginning to be "abused and perverted" by admitting rich children instead of poor (sig. D3r).

22. On humanist attempts to reform or suppress popular culture, see Peter Burke, *Popular Culture in Early Modern Europe* (London: Temple Smith, 1978), pp. 207–22.

23. Erasmus, *De pueris instituendis*, in William Harrison Woodward, *Desiderius Erasmus concerning the Aim and Method of Education*, Classics in Education Series, 19 (New York: Teacher's College, Columbia University, 1964), p. 214. Woodward's book includes complete translations of the *De ratione studii* and the *De pueris instituendis*, subsequently cited by title of Erasmus's work and page number in Woodward. It is suggestive that for Erasmus, *female* servants are the ones who threaten young boys with popular and susperstitious materials. This is not just a double threat of class and gender but a threat of class embedded in or mediated through gender; to produce a male subjectivity in schools is thus both an object in itself and an element in the production of class subjects.

24. Cressy, *Education in Tudor England*, p. 84.

25. Erasmus, *De pueris instituendis*, p. 202.

26. Mulcaster, *Positions*, p. 140, and see p. 139: "The *riche* not to have to much, the *poore* not to lacke to much, the one by overplus breadeth a loose and dissolute braine: the other by under minus a base and servile conceit."

27. Keith Thomas, *Rule and Misrule in the Schools of Early Modern England* (Reading, England: University of Reading, 1976), p. 6.

28. See Michel Foucault, *Discipline and Punish*, trans. Alan Sheridan (New York: Vintage, 1979), esp. pp. 170–94.

29. Erasmus, *De pueris instituendis*, pp. 204, 207.

30. Mulcaster, *Positions*, p. 273. Mulcaster also casts some unintended light on the sexual dynamics of punishment, referring to his rod as "my lady *birchely*" and, on at least one occasion, announcing a whipping as if it were a marriage ceremony between his "lady" and the boy's bottom (*Positions*, p. 274). See Foster Watson, *Richard Mulcaster and His "Elementarie"* (London, 1893), p. 5.

31. See Thomas, *Rule and Misrule*, pp. 16–31.

32. Walter Ong, "Latin Language Study as a Renaissance Puberty Rite," *Studies in Philology* 56 (1959), 103–24.

33. Mulcaster, *Positions*, pp. 150–51.

34. C. John Sommerville, "The Distinction between Indoctrination and Education in England, 1541–1719," *Journal of the History of Ideas* 44 (1983), 387.

35. Roger Ascham, *The Scholemaster* (1570), in William Aldis Wright, ed., *English Works* (Cambridge: Cambridge University Press, 1904), p. 176.

36. Mulcaster, *Positions*, p. 278.

37. Vives, *On Education: A Translation of the "De Tradendis Disciplinis" of Juan Luis Vives*, trans. and ed. Foster Watson (Cambridge: Cambridge University Press, 1913), p. 133.

38. In *The Education of Children in Learning* (1588), facs. rpt. in Robert D. Pepper, ed., *Four Tudor Books on Education* (Gainesville, Fla.: Scholars' Facsimiles and Reprints, 1966), William Kempe outlines a clear sequence of rewards, encouragements, and disciplinary actions:

> The good then he [the schoolmaster] shall encourage, first with words, praising them for their well doing, declaring what great commoditie ensueth thereof, and exhorting them to go forward. . . . Then he shall encourage them with rewards, for a good Schoolemaister is like a good Captaine . . . as sometimes to give trifles and gay things to such as shewe any token of forwardnes, diligence, and wittines, and to such as are victors in virtue, . . . sometimes to reward their painfull studie with libertie to recreate themselves by rest, honest disport, and walking abroad. . . . Let the unthriftie then, and those that do amisse, be reformed and corrected by admonition, rebuking and punishing, according to the qualitie of the fault. . . . First therefore let him be admonished, then rebuked: herein the cause shall be thoroughly sifted, paciently heard, by equitie judged, and last of all soundly reproved, that the conscience of the offender may be touched by the fault: if this will not serve, . . . ad also punishment. (sigs. H1v–H2r)

39. Mulcaster, *Positions*, p. 278.

40. Vives, *De ratione studii*, quoted in Dowling, *Humanism*, p. 181. In *De fructu qui ex doctrina percipitur*, Richard Pace praises Colet for appointing William Lily as the first headmaster of St. Paul's School:

You've chosen a virtuous and at the same time a skillful man to teach the boys and young men. In this you've imitated Isocrates, who wisely thought (as usual) that boys should be educated only by someone whose virtuous way of life went hand in hand with a sufficient amount of learning. That way, when they give themselves over to the imitation of their teachers, they'll absorb not only a certain amount of learning, but also good character. (Quoted in Dowling, pp. 114–15)

41. For a more thoroughly Lacanian reading of Tudor pedagogy, see William Kerrigan, "The Articulation of the Ego in the English Renaissance," in Joseph H. Smith, ed., *The Literary Freud: Mechanisms of Defense and the Poetic Will* (New Haven: Yale University Press, 1980), pp. 261–308.

42. Althusser, "Ideology," pp. 133, 152, 156.

43. Erasmus, *De pueris instituendis*, p. 198. Cf. Mulcaster: "In the litle young soules, first we finde, a capacitie to perceive that which is taught them, and to imitate the foregoer" (*Positions*, p. 127).

44. Erasmus, *De pueris instituendis*, p. 189.

45. Brinsley, *Ludus literarius*, sig. A4r. For more on humanist theories of teaching, see Gerald Strauss, "The State of Pedagogical Theory c. 1530: What Protestant Reformers Knew about Education," in Lawrence Stone, ed., *Schooling and Society: Studies in the History of Education* (Baltimore: Johns Hopkins University Press, 1976), pp. 69–94.

46. Brinsley, *Ludus literarius*, sig. H4r. William Kempe, *Education of Children*, sig. F4r, writes that when first teaching Latin the teacher must act "as a painfull nurse" who "cheweth it all to small peeces, and thrusteth it into the childes mouth."

47. T. W. Baldwin, *William Shakspere's Small Latine and Lesse Greeke* (Urbana: University of Illinois Press, 1944), 1:101. Erasmus's *De copia*, first published in London in 1512, enjoyed wide currency as a grammar school text, and his educational theories and methods had considerable influence on the major Tudor humanists.

48. Erasmus, *De pueris instituendis*, p. 199.

49. Erasmus, *De ratione studii*, p. 164. Compare Brinsley, *Ludus literarius:* "For the right learning of these [Latin] authors doth not so much consist in the construing and parsing them, as in getting by them the matter, phrase and style of the Author" (sig. J3r).

50. Any sharp distinction between "the practices of civil society" and the "law," if we conceive of the latter as an abstractly codified system, will be complicated for sixteenth-century England because common law, the dominant legal tradition at this time, relied primarily on custom and precedent and resisted codification. Civil law, which began to influence English jurisprudence in the early seventeenth century and which was more closely tied to the theory of absolutism than was the common law, is somewhat closer to the concept of law I have in mind here. See Brian P. Levack, "Law and Ideology: The Civil Law and Theories of Absolutism in Elizabethan and Jacobean England," in Heather Dubrow and Richard Streir, eds., *The Historical Renaissance: New Essays on Tudor and Stuart Literature and Culture* (Chicago: University of Chicago Press, 1988), pp. 220–41.

51. Joan Simon, *Education and Society in Tudor England* (Cambridge: Cambridge University Press, 1966), pp. 89–90.

52. See Richard Foster Jones, *The Triumph of the English Language* (Stanford: Stanford University Press, 1953), esp. chaps. 1–4.

53. See Kerrigan, "Articulation of the Ego," pp. 286–88.

54. Erasmus, *De civilitate morum puerilium* (1530), trans. Robert Whittington (London, 1534), sigs. A2r, A2v.

55. Kempe writes that the father and schoolmaster must join to "prescribe unto [the child] a good order for manners and behaviour, for repairing home, for attendance, for diet, for apparell, for exercise in learning, that his behaviour be godly and honest, in serving God, in keeping his Church, in humilitie towards his superiors, in humanitie towards all men" (sig. F1r). The humanist grammarian William Lily also wrote a tract on manners for the boys of St. Paul's titled *Carmen de moribus*, "comprising some eighty Latin verses setting out rules of conduct" (Simon, *Education and Society*, p. 79).

56. Erasmus, *De civilitate*, sig. A2v.

57. Norbert Elias, *The History of Manners*, trans. Edmund Jephcott (New York: Pantheon, 1978), pp. 77–78.

58. See Baldwin, *Shakspere's Small Latine* 1:454, 458–59.

59. Terence Cave, *The Cornucopian Text: Problems of Writing in the French Renaissance* (New York: Oxford University Press, 1979), p. 26.

60. Vives, *On Education*, p. 196.

61. *The Colloquies of Erasmus*, trans. Craig R. Thompson (Chicago: University of Chicago Press, 1965), pp. 3, 625. Kempe, following Erasmus, writes that "because Children learne first to talke familiarly with their fellowes or others, Dialogs are most easie for their capacitie" (sig. F4r).

62. Compare Thomas Wilson, *Arte of Rhetorique* (1560; rpt. Oxford: Clarendon Press, 1909): "Now, before we use either to write, or speake eloquently, wee must dedicate our myndes wholy, to followe the most wise and learned men, and seek to fashion *as wel their speache and gesturing, as their witte or endyting*. The which when we earnestly mind to doe, we can not but in time appere somewhat like them" (p. 5, my emphasis). Gesture was, of course, an important part of classical oratory; what is striking is that northern humanism should retain this requirement even though its emphasis is on writing, not public speaking.

63. See Quentin Skinner, *The Foundations of Modern Political Thought*, vol. 1: *The Renaissance* (Cambridge: Cambridge University Press, 1978).

64. Lawrence Stone, *The Family, Sex, and Marriage in England, 1500–1800* (London: Weidenfeld and Nicolson, 1977), p. 166.

65. Dowling, *Humanism*, pp. 112–39, shows that humanist curricula found their way even into schools in the west country and into free schools. And in a study of local village schools in Cambridgeshire, 1574–1604, Margaret Spufford found that "the general quality of the masters teaching in them was extraordinarily high." *Contrasting Communities: English Villages in the Sixteenth and Seventeenth Centuries* (Cambridge: Cambridge University Press, 1974), p. 189. Spufford's research into village education leads her to conclude that "it is impossible to believe either in the reliability of the records or in any interpretation of sixteenth-century

local schooling which rests on a rigid typology of schools according to class" (p. 189).

66. Mulcaster, *Positions*, p. 284.

67. Ibid., p. 278. When Brinsley writes of "that extreame sharpnes used ordinarily in schools amongst the poore children" (*Ludus literarius*, sig. ¶3 r and v), he seems to suggest that wealthier children enjoyed the benefits of at least relative leniency. Stone's contention that corporal punishment in schools was "a standard practice applied to rich and poor, young and old, regardless of rank" (*Family*, p. 163), though true, obscures probable differences in the severity and frequency of such punishment.

68. Mulcaster, *Positions*, p. 300.

69. Ascham, *The Scholemaster*, pp. 243–44.

70. For an excellent discussion of Erasmus's historical arguments, see G. W. Pigman III, "Imitation and the Renaissance Sense of the Past: The Reception of Erasmus' *Ciceronianus*," *Journal of Medieval and Renaissance Studies* 9.2 (1979), 155–77.

71. Erasmus, *The Ciceronian: A Dialogue on the Ideal Latin Style*, trans. Betty I. Knott, vol. 28 of *The Collected Works of Erasmus*, ed. Craig R. Thompson, 66 vols. (Toronto: University of Toronto Press, 1986), pp. 396–97, 402.

72. Thomas Nashe, *Strange News* (1592), excerpted in G. Gregory Smith, *Elizabethan Critical Essays*, 2 vols. (Oxford University Press, 1904), 2:243. Here Nashe denies only that he follows any English models; he doesn't repudiate classical models, though it can hardly be said that he follows any either.

73. Gabriel Harvey, *Pierce's Supererogation* (1593), excerpted in Smith, *Elizabethan Essays* 2:277.

74. Stephen Gosson, *The School of Abuse* (1579; rpt. London: The Shakespeare Society, 1841), p. 18.

75. Erasmus, *The Ciceronian*, p. 350.

76. See Jacques Lacan, "Aggressivity in Psychoanalysis," in *Ecrits: A Selection*, trans. Alan Sheridan (New York: Norton, 1977), pp. 8–25.

77. Erasmus, *Copia: Foundations of the Abundant Style*, trans. Betty I. Knott, vol. 24 of *Collected Works* (Toronto: University of Toronto Press, 1978), p. 306.

78. See Frances Elizabeth Baldwin, *Sumptuary Legislation and Personal Regulation in England* (Baltimore: Johns Hopkins University Press, 1926), passim; Frank Whigham, *Ambition and Privilege: The Social Tropes of Elizabethan Courtesy Theory* (Berkeley: University of California Press, 1984), pp. 155–69.

79. Philip Stubbes, *The Anatomy of Abuses* (1583; rpt. New York: Garland, 1973), sig. Ciiv.

80. William Harrison, "The Description of Britaine," in *Holinshed's Chronicles*, 6 vols. (1586; rpt. England, 1807–8), 1:289.

81. Erasmus, *Colloquies*, pp. 210–16.

82. See Roland Barthes, *The Fashion System*, trans. Matthew Ward and Richard Howard (New York: Hill and Wang, 1983).

83. Thomas Dekker, *The Seven Deadly Sins of London*, in *The Nondramatic Works of Thomas Dekker*, ed. Alexander B. Grosart (London: Privately printed, 1885), 2:58–59.

84. Ibid., 59–60.
85. Ibid., 57–58.
86. Etienne Dolet, *De imitatione ciceroniana* (1535), quoted in Cave, *Cornucopian Text*, p. 50.
87. Erasmus, *De ratione studii*, p. 164.
88. Ludwig Wittgenstein, *Philosophical Investigations: The English Text of the Third Edition*, trans. G. E. M. Anscombe (New York: Macmillan, 1958), sec. 67.
89. See Stephen S. Hilliard, *The Singularity of Thomas Nashe* (Lincoln: University of Nebraska Press, 1986).
90. Patricia Parker and David Quint, *Literary Theory/Renaissance Texts* (Baltimore: Johns Hopkins University Press, 1986), p. 3.
91. Jean Baudrillard, *Simulations*, trans. Paul Foss, Paul Patton, and Philip Beitchman (New York: Semiotext(e), 1983). My point here is not that the imitation becomes indistinguishable from the model—quite the contrary—but that criteria of exactness or accuracy give way to those of performativity.
92. Baldwin, *Shakspere's Small Latine* 2:386.
93. Ascham, *Scholemaster*, p. 287.
94. Vives, *On Education*, p. 136, my emphasis.
95. Cawdry, quoted from Baldwin, *Shakspere's Small Latine* 1:116. The passage, lifted from Plutarch, appears slightly altered in Francis Meres's *Palladis tamia* (Smith, *Elizabethan Essays* 2:311).
96. Vives, *On Education*, p. 128.
97. *Petrarch's Letters to Classical Authors*, ed. Mario Emilio Cosenza (Chicago: University of Chicago Press, 1910), pp. 84–85.
98. Vives, *On Education*, p. 129.
99. Stone, *Crisis*, p. 673.
100. Althusser, "Ideology," pp. 133, 152, 156.
101. See Simon, *Education and Society*, pp. 316–32.
102. Ibid., p. 316: "Castellion's *Dialogues Sacrés* (1543) were based entirely on the bible—'the subject-matter thus precisely met the puritan demand for scripture-knowledge' while the book also 'satisfied the classical schoolmaster by its sound Latinity.' Cordier's *Colloquorum Scholasticorum* (1564) depicted the doings of boys in and out of school, notably sons of farmers and tradesmen, and were pervaded by Geneva outlook."
103. Cave, *Cornucopian Text*, pp. 3–34.
104. Joan Simon vigorously maintains (*Education and Society*, chap. 3) that Erasmus's educational theory does *not* elevate style over content and that Vives is closer to the founders of empirical science than he is to verbal formalists. Her arguments offer a useful counterpoint to Cave's and my own. Yet I insist that when converted into actual classroom practice, humanist pedagogical theory was shifted in a formalist, stylistic direction.
105. Bacon, *De augmentis scientiarum*, in *Works* 4:472. Erasmus outlined this procedure in *Copia*, pp. 635–48.
106. Walter S. Ong, S. J., "Tudor Writings on Rhetoric, Poetic, and Literary Theory," in *Rhetoric, Romance, and Technology: Studies in the Interaction of Expression and Culture* (Ithaca: Cornell University Press, 1971), pp. 48–103.
107. Besides the material in Baldwin, *Shakspere's Small Latine*, and

Donald L. Clark, *John Milton at St. Paul's School: A Study of Ancient Rhetoric in English Renaissance Education* (New York: Columbia University Press, 1948), there is a good discussion of the Aphthonian theme in Joel B. Altman, *The Tudor Play of Mind: Rhetorical Inquiry and the Development* of *Elizabethan Drama* (Berkeley: University of California Press, 1978), pp. 31–63.

108. Zachary S. Schiffman, "Montaigne and the Rise of Skepticism in Early Modern Europe: A Reappraisal," *Journal of the History of Ideas* 45 (1984), 499–516.

109. John Marston, *What You Will*, 2.2.151–55, in *The Works of John Marston*, ed. A. H. Bullen, 3 vols. (London, 1887).

110. Aristotle and Plato, quoted in Donald L. Clark, *Rhetoric in Greco-Roman Education* (New York: Columbia University Press, 1957), pp. 44, 61.

111. See John Morgan, *Godly Learning: Puritan Attitudes towards Reason, Learning, and Education, 1560–1640* (Cambridge: Cambridge University Press, 1986), chap. 9, esp. pp. 178–80.

112. William Webbe, *Discourse of English Poetry*, in Smith, *Elizabethan Essays* 1:228, 227.

113. Ibid., 1:231.

114. George Puttenham, *The Arte of English Poesie* (1589; rpt. Kent State, Ohio: Kent State University Press, 1970), p. 24.

115. Ascham, *Scholemaster*, p. 189.

116. Mulcaster, *Positions*, p. 270.

117. For poetics as an academic science in Italy, see Bernard Weinberg, *A History of Literary Criticism in the Italian Renaissance*, 2 vols. (Chicago: University of Chicago Press, 1961), 1:1–37.

118. Bacon, *De augmentis scientiarum* 4:292, 315.

119. Pierre de La Primaudaye, *The Second Part of the French Academie*, trans. T. B. (London, 1594), p. 155, quoted in William Rossky, "Imagination in the English Renaissance: Psychology and Poetic," *Studies in the Renaissance* 5 (1958), 58.

120. Indeed, the "unlawful matching and divorcing" of things in sixteenth-century theories of poetic imagination seems strikingly to foreshadow the labors of condensation and displacement that constitute the so-called primary processes in Freud's writings on the dream work. And it may be useful in this context to recall that rhetorical decoding, like the dream work, served as a means of ideological censorship.

121. Puttenham, *Arte of Poesie*, p. 160.

122. "The ancient primary school was almost the exact equivalent of the Elizabethan petty school and the first and second forms of the grammar school" (Clark, *Rhetoric*, p. 61).

123. Bacon, *De augmentis scientiarum* 4:443–44.

124. Sir Philip Sidney, *An Apology for Poetry* (1595; rpt. Indianapolis: Bobbs-Merrill, 1970), p. 14.

125. See Ovid, *Metamorphoses* 2:78–83, 193–209. For an excellent discussion of poetic imagination and its role as usurper, see John Guillory, *Poetic Authority: Spenser, Milton, and Literary History* (New York: Columbia University Press, 1983), esp. chap. 1, "The Genealogy of Imagination."

126. Bacon, *De augmentis scientiarum* 4:314.
127. Puttenham, *Arte of Poesie*, p. 89.
128. Webbe, *Discourse of English Poetry*, Smith 1:234.
129. Francis Clement, *The Petie Schole with an English Orthographie* (London, 1587), in Pepper, *Four Tudor Books*, pp. 45–46.

Chapter 2. Breeding Capital

1. Christopher Caudwell, *Illusion and Reality: A Study of the Sources of Poetry* (London: Macmillan, 1937), chap. 4, sec. 1, "Primitive Accumulation."
2. Barry Hindess and Paul Q. Hirst, *Pre-capitalist Modes of Production* (London: Routledge and Kegan Paul, 1975), p. 228.
3. Karl Marx, *Capital*, vol. 1., trans. Ben Fowkes (New York: Vintage, 1977), p. 875. Chaps. 20 and 36 in vol. 3 give historical material on the role of merchant's and usurer's capital, partly to show how they laid the foundations for capitalist production and partly to show how their dominance is structurally incompatible with it. In chap. 47 of vol. 3 Marx also lays out crucial differences between feudal and capitalist ground rent.
4. Ibid., 1:873.
5. Ibid., 1:874–75.
6. Ibid., 1:873–940.
7. Ibid., 1:895.
8. Louis Althusser and Etienne Balibar, *Reading Capital*, trans. Ben Brewster (London: Verso, 1979), p. 279.
9. Not without being transformed in the process, however, which is what keeps Marx's analysis from generating a mere "combinatory" of invariant elements. The point is that the elements that constitute a structure are always dialectically informed by that structure itself. See Althusser and Balibar, *Reading Capital*, pp. 176, 216, 226, 241.
10. Ibid., p. 279.
11. Walter Benjamin, "Theses on the Philosophy of History," in *Illuminations*, trans. Harry Zohn (New York: Schocken, 1969), p. 263.
12. Althusser and Balibar, *Reading Capital*, p. 280.
13. Hindess and Hirst, *Pre-capitalist Modes*, p. 222.
14. Adam Smith, *An Inquiry into the Nature and Causes of the Wealth of Nations*, ed. R. H. Campbell and A. S. Skinner, 2 vols. (Oxford: Clarendon Press, 1976), pp. 277, 337.
15. Marx, *Capital* 1:873.
16. Karl Marx, *Grundrisse: Foundations of Political Economy*, trans. Martin Nicolaus (New York: Random House, 1973), p. 459.
17. Marx, *Capital*, vol. 3, trans. David Fernbach (New York: Random House, 1981), pp. 445, 452–53.
18. The first "wave" of historical debate was inspired by the publication of Maurice Dobb's book *Studies in the Development of Capitalism* (New York: International, 1947) and is largely compiled in Rodney Hilton et al., eds., *The Transition from Feudalism to Capitalism* (London: Verso, 1978). In *Genealogies of Capitalism* (London: Macmillan, 1981), pp. 1–34, Keith Tribe provides a useful political context for understanding the work of Dobb and the other members of the British Historians Group in the

1940s. The second "wave" was provoked by Robert Brenner's essays in the 1970s and is collected in T. H. Ashton and C. H. E. Philpin, eds., *The Brenner Debate: Agrarian Class Structure and Economic Development in Preindustrial Europe* (Cambridge: Cambridge University Press, 1983).

19. Hindess and Hirst, *Pre-capitalist Modes*, p. 15.

20. William Lazonick, "Karl Marx and Enclosures in England," *Review of Radical Political Economics* 6.2 (1974), 4.

21. Marx, *Capital* 1:876, 878 (my emphasis).

22. Marx, quoted in Althusser and Balibar, *Reading Capital*, p. 236.

23. Ibid., p. 236.

24. See Hindess and Hirst, *Pre-capitalist Modes*: "The formal subsumption of labour under capital . . . must not be confused with the mere appearance of the wage-labour relation in connection with commodity production. Whether or not manufacturing is capitalist depends not on the form of organization of the labour process but on its articulation within the system of social production as a whole." Wage labor as such can appear under feudalism and other modes of production. Thus more is at stake than a simple "recombination" of two elements of production, even under new forms of ownership. The rearticulation of the labor-process within the system of social production requires a series of other developments that contribute to the chronological dislocation of stages.

25. When I speak of structural "necessity" I mean this in an explanatory or descriptive, rather than a causal sense. Capitalism was in no sense historically "necessary." Yet once can say that, given the existence of a certain mode of production and its structural features, certain things were necessary in order for it to achieve its present form.

26. Althusser and Balibar, *Reading Capital*, pp. 99–101.

27. Dobb, *Studies*, pp. 178–86.

28. See A. L. Beier, *Masterless Men: The Vagrancy Problem in England, 1560–1640* (London: Methuen, 1985), p. 172. When I speak of a "terminus" here, I do not mean to suggest that the process of primitive accumulation ceases or even slows. Rather, manufacture and capitalist agriculture begin at this point to absorb some of the expropriated. The numbers of vagrant unemployed may even continue to rise, but they make up a smaller percentage of the total population than they did in the sixteenth century.

29. See John E. Martin, *Feudalism to Capitalism: Peasant and Landlord in English Agrarian Development* (Atlantic Highlands, N.J.: Humanities Press, 1983), pp. 117–27.

30. See George Unwin, *Industrial Organization in the Sixteenth and Early Seventeenth Centuries* (1904; rpt. London: Cass, 1957), esp. chaps. 3–5.

31. Gilles Deleuze and Félix Guattari, *Anti-Oedipus: Capitalism and Schizophrenia*, trans. Robert Hurley, Mark Seem, and Helen R. Lane (New York: Viking Press, 1957), p. 227.

32. Marx, *Capital* 3:453.

33. Ibid., 1:875.

34. Martin, *Feudalism to Capitalism*, pp. 118, 120.

35. Subsequent debates have questioned the extent and timing of the enclosure movement as well as its role in creating a landless proletariat.

For an attack on the Marxist view of enclosure, see J. D. Chambers, "Enclosure and the Labor Supply in the Industrial Revolution," *Economic History Review*, 2d ser., 5 (1953), 319–43. Replies include John Saville, "Primitive Accumulation and Early Industrialization in Britain," *Socialist Register* (1969), pp. 247–71, and Lazonick, "Marx and Enclosures." On the timing of enclosure, see J. R. Wordie, "The Chronology of English Enclosure, 1500–1914," in *Economic History Review*, 2d ser., 36 (1983), 483–505, as well as the exchange between Wordie and John Chapman in vol. 37 (1984) of the same journal, pp. 557–62. John E. Martin offers extensive discussion of enclosure and its effects in the Midlands. Regional studies now seem to confirm that enclosure peaked during the fifteenth and seventeenth centuries; only 2 percent of the total county area in England was enclosed during the sixteenth century, though this figure may be misleading because the percentage of *cultivated* land was much higher and because enclosure was highly (roughly 80 percent) concentrated in the Midlands. See Martin, *Feudalism to Capitalism*, pp. 132–40. Martin's estimate that roughly 20 percent of cultivated land in the Midlands was enclosed during the sixteenth century still seems high; Wordie's estimate of 10 percent is probably closer to the truth, though any figure involves a good deal of guesswork and the existing documents almost certainly fail to record the full extent of enclosure.

36. This is not to insist that manorial lords necessarily played the leading role in the engrossment of holdings or to ignore the role of land purchases by substantial copyholders. See Patricia Croot and David Parker, "Agrarian Class Structure and the Development of Capitalism: France and England Compared," in Ashton and Philpin, *Brenner Debate*, pp. 82–83, 85; and Robert Brenner's response in "The Agrarian Roots of European Capitalism," *Brenner Debate*, pp. 295–301.

37. Quoted in Dobb, *Studies*, p. 227.

38. Marx, *Capital* 1:874.

39. Ibid., 1:916.

40. See J. Thomas Kelly, *Thorns on the Tudor Rose: Monks, Rogues, Vagabonds, and Sturdy Beggars* (Jackson: University Press of Mississippi, 1977); Beier, *Masterless Men*.

41. Accurate statistics for the total numbers of vagabonds are unavailable, however, and Beier admits that "we are unlikely ever to possess [them]" (Beier, *Masterless Men*, p. 15).

42. Ibid., pp. 73–74.

43. Ibid., pp. 75–76.

44. J. L. Vives, *On Assistance to the Poor*, trans. Sister Alice Tobriner, in *A Sixteenth-Century Urban Report* (Chicago: University of Chicago, 1971), p. 36.

45. When I speak of the vagrant poor as being "decoded" I do not mean that they lacked any organized social life, only that this life and its structures were largely detached from the ruling ones.

46. Smith, *Wealth of Nations*, pp. 151, 157.

47. See Joan Simon, *Education and Society in Tudor England* (Cambridge: Cambridge University Press, 1966), pp. 179–244.

48. See George Unwin, "Medieval Guilds and Education," in R. H. Tawney, ed., *Studies in Economic History* (London: Macmillan, 1927), pp. 92–99.

49. John Lawson and Harold Silver, *A Social History of Education in England* (London: Methuen, 1973), p. 74.

50. Ibid., p. 48.

51. Vives, who was an exception, "recommended training in the 'inferiour' arts of husbandry, architecture, transportation and politics, and also stressed the empirical value of the skilled workman." John Morgan, *Godly Learning: Puritan Attitudes towards Reason, Learning, and Education, 1560–1640* (Cambridge: Cambridge University Press, 1986), p. 178.

52. Beier, *Masterless Men*, pp. 10, 44.

53. Thomas Cromwell, Royal Injunction, excerpted in David Cressy, *Education in Tudor England* (London: Edward Arnold, 1975), p. 17.

54. Hugh Latimer, quoted in Simon, *Education and Society*, p. 220.

55. Richard Morison, *A Remedy for Sedition* (1536), rpt. in David Sandler Berkowitz, *Humanist Scholarship and Public Order* (Washington, D.C., Folger Shakespeare Library, 1984), p. 128.

56. Vives, *On Assistance to the Poor*, p. 43.

57. See Beier, *Masterless Men*, pp. 164–69, on the bridewell as a "proto-penal institution that failed."

58. See Simon, *Education and Society*, pp. 369–75.

59. Richard Mulcaster, *Positions* (1581, rpt. London, 1887), p. 18.

60. John Brinsley, *Ludus literarius* (1612; facs. rpt. Menston, England: Scholar Press, 1968), sig. H1v.

61. This section was completed before I could benefit from the publication of Jonathan Goldberg's excellent book, *Writing Matter: From the Hands of the English Renaissance* (Stanford: Stanford University Press, 1990).

62. Brinsley, *Ludus literarius*, sig. E2v.

63. Francis W. Steer, *A History of the Worshipful Company of Scriveners of London* (London: Phillimore, 1973), p. 10.

64. Erasmus, *De recta graeci et latini sermonis pronunciatione*, quoted in A. S. Osley, *Scribes and Sources: Handbook of the Chancery Hand in the Sixteenth Century* (Boston: Faber & Faber, 1980), p. 29.

65. Brinsley, *Ludus literarius*, sig. F3v.

66. See Osley, *Scribes and Sources*, p. 36.

67. Peter Bales, *The Writing Schoolmaster* (1590), sig. R2v.

68. See Giles E. Dawson and Laetitia Kennedy-Skipton, *Elizabethan Handwriting, 1500–1650: A Manual* (New York: Norton, 1966), p. 8.

69. See Goldberg, *Writing Matter*, pp. 91–98.

70. Brinsley, *Ludus literarius*, sigs. E3v, F2v, E4v.

71. My vocabulary of "smooth" and "striated" spaces and of nomadic and sedentary regimes is borrowed from Gilles Deleuze and Félix Guattari, *A Thousand Plateaus*, trans. Brian Massumi (Minneapolis: University of Minnesota Press, 1987), esp. chap. 12.

72. See Goldberg, *Writing Matter*, pp. 66–68, on the career of the writing master John Bales.

73. Brinsley, *Ludus literarius*, sig. F3v.

74. S. H. Steinberg, "Mediaeval Writing-Masters," *Library: Transactions of the Bibliographical Society*, ser. 4, 22 (1941), 1–24.

75. John Awdelay, *The Fraternitye of Vacabondes* (1575; rpt. London: Early English Text Society, 1869), p. 5.

76. Beier, *Masterless Men*, p. 102.

77. Ibid., pp. 143–44.
78. R. H. Tawney and Eileen Power, eds., *Tudor Economic Documents*, 3 vols. (New York: Longmans, Green, 1924), 2:328.
79. Brinsley, *Ludus literarius*, sigs. F4v, F3v.
80. I am speaking of its virtual regimes, described in Chapter 1. But popular poetry, at least, was also hawked by itinerant peddlers, whose most famous literary representative is Shakespeare's Autolycus.
81. The discrepancies between Smith's actual views and Marx's depiction of them can be traced by dissecting the phrase "diligent, intelligent, and above all frugal elite," which Marx employs in summarizing Smith's supposedly ethical account of the origins of capitalism. As to diligence or industry, Smith clearly states that it is the product rather than the cause of capital: "The proportion [of social wealth] between capital and revenue, therefore, seems everywhere to regulate the proportion between industry and idleness. Wherever capital predominates, industry prevails: wherever revenue, idleness" (Smith, *Wealth of Nations*, p. 337). The industry of the working classes, moreover, is determined by the level of wages: "Where wages are high, . . . we shall always find the workmen more active, diligent, and industrious, than where they are low" (p. 99). Smith insists that "the idleness, so much and so loudly complained of" when workers are discussed really results from overwork, and that the whole system of wage labor discourages industry as compared to self-employment (pp. 101, 100). As to intelligence,

> the difference of natural talents in different men is, in reality, much less than we are aware of; and the very different genius which appears to distinguish men of different professions, when grown up to maturity, *is not upon many occasions so much the cause, as the effect of the division of labour*. The difference between the most dissimilar characters, between a philosopher and a common street porter, for example, seems to arise not so much from nature, as from habit, custom, and education. (Pp. 28–29, my emphasis)

Finally, Smith holds that necessity generally makes the poor *more* frugal and parsimonious than the rich, unless their economy is infected by the "disorders" of the latter (p. 98).
82. Smith does tell one tale of an Edenic fall, but this results from the appropriation of land and thus foreshadows Marx's understanding of primitive accumulation:

> In that original state of things, which precedes both the appropriation of land and the accumulation of stock, the whole produce of labour belongs to the labourer. He has neither landlord nor master to share with him. . . . But this original state of things, in which the labourer enjoyed the whole produce of his own labour, could not last beyond the first introduction of the appropriation of land and the accumulation of stock. It was at an end, therefore, long before the most considerable improvements were made in the productive power of labour, and it would be to no purpose to trace farther what might have been its effects upon the recompense or wages of labour. (Smith, *Wealth of Nations*, p. 82)

83. "No society can be flourishing and happy," he writes, "of which the far greater part of the members are poor and miserable. It is but equity, besides, that they who feed, cloath and lodge the whole body of the people, should have such a share of the produce of their own labour as to be themselves tolerably well fed, cloathed, and lodged" (Smith, *Wealth of Nations*, p. 96). Smith stops short of demanding that the working classes possess *all* the wealth they produce. It is necessary only that they be "tolerably" well fed, clothed, and housed—that is, that their labor power be reproduced. Still, these views are a far cry from those Marx attributes to Smith.

84. Marx, *Capital* 1:179.

85. Lawrence Stone, "Social Mobility in England, 1500–1700," *Past and Present* 33 (1966), 16–55.

86. See Louis B. Wright, *Middle-Class Culture in Elizabethan England* (Chapel Hill: University of North Carolina Press, 1935), pp. 170–200. See also Michael McKeon, *The Origins of the English Novel, 1600–1704* (Baltimore: Johns Hopkins University Press, 1987), chap. 6, "Stories of Virtue."

87. Stone, "Mobility," p. 26.

88. Beier, *Masterless Men*, p. 127.

89. Ibid., p. 86.

90. William Harrison, quoted ibid., p. 10.

91. Vives, *On Assistance to the Poor*, p. 52.

92. Kelly, *Thorns*, esp. chaps. 3 and 4.

93. Stone, "Mobility," p. 46.

94. Thomas Cranmer, quoted in Maria Dowling, *Humanism in the Age of Henry VIII* (London: Croom Helm, 1986), p. 125.

95. Brinsley, *A Consolation for our Grammar Schooles* (1622; facs. rpt. New York: Da Capo, 1969), sigs. D3v, C3, C2v. At the same time, he hopes that the gentry will "excell all others therein, according to their places and degrees."

96. Edmund Coote, *The English Schoole-Maister* (1596; rpt. Menston, England: Scolar Press, 1968), sig. A4r.

97. Brinsley, *Ludus literarius*, sig. H1v.

98. Thomas Wilson, *Arte of Rhetorique* (1560; rpt. Oxford: Clarendon Press, 1909), p. 209.

99. Erasmus, *Copia: Foundations of an Abundant Style*, trans. Betty I. Knott, vol. 24 of *Collected Works of Erasmus*, ed. Craig R. Thompson (Toronto: University of Toronto Press, 1978), p. 572.

100. Mulcaster, *Positions*, p. 25. The concept of native capacity plays a role in the educational theories of Isocrates, Quintilian, and other classical writers, where it assumes a wide range of ideological functions. See Donald Clark, *Rhetoric in Greco-Roman Education* (New York: Columbia University Press, 1957), chap. 1.

101. Brinsley, *Ludus literarius*, sig. Rr2r.

102. Brinsley, *A Consolation*, sig. C1v.

103. Erasmus, *De pueris instituendis*, in William Harrison Woodward, *Desiderius Erasmus concerning the Aim and Method of Education*, Classics in Education Series, 19 (New York: Teacher's College, Columbia University, 1964), p. 209.

104. Mulcaster, *Positions*, p. 154. Yet he adds that the schoolmaster "is no absolute potentate in our common weale, to dispose of wittes, and to sorte mens children, as he liketh best" (p. 155). Rather, he must counsel parents about the best course for their child.

105. Mulcaster, *Positions*, p. 137.

106. Brinsley, *Ludus literarius*, sig. Pp4r–v.

107. Tawney and Power, *Tudor Economic Documents* 2:308.

108. Bernard Mandeville, *The Fable of the Bees; or, Private Vices, Publick Benefits* (1723), ed. F. B. Kaye, 2 vols. (Oxford: Clarendon Press, 1924), 1:43–44. Mandeville clearly refers to the ideals of civic humanism extolled in the Italian Renaissance, for which see Quentin Skinner, *The Foundations of Modern Political Thought*, vol. 1: *The Renaissance* (Cambridge: Cambridge University Press, 1978). Charles Lamb's essay "The Two Races of Men" divides mankind into lenders and borrowers.

109. Thomas Hobbes, *Leviathan*, in *The English Works of Thomas Hobbes*, ed. Sir William Molesworth, 11 vols. (London, 1839; rpt. Darmstadt: Scientia Verlag Aulen, 1966), 3:110; John Locke, *Some Thoughts concerning Human Education* (1693), in *The Educational Writings of John Locke*, ed. James L. Axtell (Cambridge: Cambridge University Press, 1968), p. 114.

110. See Joyce Oldham Appleby, *Economic Thought and Ideology in Seventeenth-Century England* (Princeton: Princeton University Press, 1978), pp. 145–47.

111. John Locke, *The Second Treatise on Government*, ed. Thomas P. Peardon (New York: Liberal Arts Press, 1952), chap. 5, para. 48. The Reverend Joseph Priestley, a disciple of Locke, describes "a difference in industry" as introducing and legitimating inequalities of property, "so that in time some will become rich and others poor." *Lectures on History and General Policy* (1788). Adam Ferguson, *An Essay on the History of Civil Society* (1767; rpt. New York: Garland, 1971), p. 282, actually lists "a difference of natural talents and dispositions" as only one ground of social difference, along with education and "the unequal division of property."

112. See Appleby, *Economic Thought*, pp. 129–57.

113. *Proposals for the better management of the poor* [1681], quoted ibid., p. 155.

114. Joseph Harris, *An Essay upon Money and Coins* (1758), p. 15.

115. Mandeville, *Fable of the Bees* 1:193–94.

116. Harris, *Essay upon Money*, p. 11.

117. Mandeville, *Fable of the Bees* 1:288.

118. Smith, *Wealth of Nations*, pp. 139–40, 146, 148–50.

119. Stephen Penton, *The Guardian's Instructions* (1688), quoted in Locke, *Some Thoughts*, p. 168n.

120. Locke, *Some Thoughts*, pp. 164, 166–68.

121. Ibid., pp. 157–59, 164, 182, 190–92.

122. Ibid., pp. 195–96, 197.

Chapter 3. The Twittering Machine

1. *Merrie Tales . . . by Master John Skelton* (1567), in *Shakespeare Jest-Books*, ed. W. Carew Hazlitt (1864; rpt. New York: Burt Franklin, [196?]), 2:1–36.

2. In a letter to Allan Cunningham, 23 November 1823, quoted by Arthur B. Kinney in *John Skelton, Priest as Poet: Seasons of Discovery* (Chapel Hill: University of North Carolina Press, 1987), p. 206.

3. C. S. Lewis, *English Literature in the Sixteenth Century* (New York: Oxford University Press, 1954), p. 143.

4. In a fine discussion of Skelton's place in literary history, A. C. Spearing maintains that "Skelton is the only English poet . . . [of his age who] wants something more than to *be* Chaucer" and that this larger desire paradoxically enables him to develop Chaucer's work. *Medieval to Renaissance in English Poetry* (Cambridge: Cambridge University Press, 1985), p. 234. For an argument that the dullness of fifteenth-century poetry was a consciously adopted literary and political strategy, see David Lawton, "Dulness and the Fifteenth Century," *ELH* 54 (1987), 761–99.

5. For a description of the Grammarians' War see William Nelson, *John Skelton, Laureate* (New York: Columbia University Press, 1939), pp. 148–58.

6. All quotations of Skelton's poetry are taken from *John Skelton: The Complete English Poems*, ed. John Scattergood (New Haven: Yale University Press, 1983).

7. Greg Walker, *John Skelton and the Politics of the 1520s* (Cambridge: Cambridge University Press, 1988), p. 48.

8. Ian A. Gordon, *John Skelton: Poet Laureate* (Melbourne, Aus.: Melbourne University Press, 1943), pp. 9, 45.

9. Stanley Fish, *John Skelton's Poetry* (New Haven: Yale University Press, 1965), p. 249.

10. Spearing, *Medieval to Renaissance*, pp. 229, 265. Spearing's very suggestive reading of the transition from medieval to Renaissance poetics is based on a similar structure of anticipation. Briefly, Spearing argues that Chaucer really became the first "Renaissance" poet as a result of influences he picked up on his travels to Italy. His English successors then re-medievalized what they found in Chaucer, so that the literary history of the fifteenth century progresses, in a sense, backward.

11. F. L. Brownlow, "*The Boke of Phyllyp Sparowe* and the Liturgy," *English Literary Renaissance* 9 (1979), 5–20; Kinney, *John Skelton*.

12. Walker, *John Skelton*.

13. See Perry Anderson, *Lineages of the Absolutist State* (London: New Left Books, 1974), pp. 15–17.

14. Ibid., p. 19.

15. Ibid., pp. 20–24.

16. Ibid., p. 119.

17. John E. Martin, *Feudalism to Capitalism: Peasant and Landlord in English Agrarian Development* (Atlantic Highlands, N.J.: Humanities Press, 1983), p. 109.

18. "In England the religious foundations made extensive use of labour-rent and demesne production, they tended to persist with labour-services longer, to manage their estates more carefully and to supervise production more thoroughly, and to defend their rights of labour-service more tenaciously, than any other type of feudal landlord." Barry Hindess and Paul Q. Hirst, *Pre-capitalist Modes of Production* (London: Routledge and Kegan Paul, 1975), p. 253. Also see G. R. Elton, *England under the Tudors* (2d ed.; London: Methuen, 1974), p. 103.

19. J. Thomas Kelly, *Thorns on the Tudor Rose: Monks, Rogues, Vagabonds, and Sturdy Beggars* (Jackson: University Press of Mississippi, 1977), p. 3.
20. Isabel D. Thornley, "The Destruction of Sanctuary," in R. W. Seton-Watson, ed., *Tudor Studies* (London: Longmans, 1924), pp. 183–84.
21. Elton, *England under the Tudors*, pp. 21–22.
22. Walker, *John Skelton*, p. 5.
23. Kinney, in particular, argues this line *(John Skelton)*.
24. Walker, *John Skelton*, p. 88.
25. Ibid., chap. 1.
26. Ibid., p. 42.
27. Ibid., p. 151.
28. Ibid., chap. 6.
29. Ibid., p. 190.
30. Ibid., pp. 53–100.
31.

> Evangelia
> Concha et conchelia,
> Accipiter et sonalia,
> Et bruta animalia,
> Cetera quoque talia
> Tibi sunt equalia
> (311–16)

The Gospels, vessels and vestments, a hawk with its bells and unreasoning animals and other such things are all the same to you. (Scattergood trans.)

32. Fish, *Skelton's Poetry*, p. 89.
33. Ibid., pp. 89–98.
34. Kinney, *John Skelton*, p. 83.
35. Lewis, *English Literature*, p. 138.
36. Cf. Spearing, *Medieval to Renaissance*, p. 242: "It seems to me . . . that the structure of a Skelton poem is combinatory rather than organic, and that the persona is one means among others of bringing together the various elements of which it is made up."
37. See H. L. R. Edwards, *Skelton: The Life and Times of an Early Tudor Poet* (London: Jonathan Cape, 1949), pp. 24–25.
38. Lewis, *English Literature*, p. 139.
39. This, at least, is the opinion of Fish *(Skelton's Poetry* pp. 102–3) and of Brownlow *("Boke of Phyllyp Sparrowe,"* esp. pp. 9–10). Gordon insists that the poem is parodic, in the spirit of the goliards, but even he wavers on this point *(John Skelton*, pp. 132–33), and in any case, Brownlow makes a much stronger argument.
40. Brownlow, who has done the most careful study of liturgical influences on *Phyllyp Sparowe*, writes that "the liturgical frame gives the poem an objective, external form, but it does not have the internal, organic unity of form we are trained to recognize. . . . The wholeness of the

poem is like the wholeness of the liturgy it imitates, being a wholeness of tone and purpose rather than of form" ("*Boke of Phyllyp Sparrowe*," p. 6). I would go one step farther and claim that the liturgy does not even provide a consistent external form.

Taking another tack, Stanley Fish analyzes the form of the poem not in terms of the liturgy but in terms of Ciceronian and medieval rhetoric. While he isolates certain local rhetorical structures, though, he fails to elevate any rhetorical schema into an overarching master code (*Skelton's Poetry*, pp. 98–125).

41. For the most detailed account of Jane Scrope, see Edwards, *Skelton*, pp. 102–14.

42. But see also the following:

> My byrde so fayre,
> . . . was wont to repayre,
> And go in at my spayre [opening or slit in a gown],
> And crepe in at my gore [part of a skirt]
> Of my gowne before,
> Flyckerynge with his wynges!
> 　　. . . . . .
> How pretely it wolde syt
> Many tymes and ofte,
> Upon my finger alofte!
> I played with him tytell-tattyll,
> And fed him with my spattyl,
> With his byll betwene my lippes,
> It was my pretty Phyppes!
> Many a prety kusse
> Had I of his swete musse.
> 　　　　　　(343–48, 354–62)

43. Fish, *Skelton's Poetry*, pp. 111–12.

44. The phrase ends the original poem, not counting the "addicyon" that was tacked on after 1509.

45. R. W. McConchie says that the poem "develops the bawdy possibilities of Phillip, especially the phallic ones, through the innocent voice of Jane herself. . . . Clearly Phillip is a kind of sexual surrogate, and more particularly a phallic symbol." "Phyllyp Sparowe," *Parergon* 24 (1979), 31–35. This is a masterful bit of oedipal ideology: since Phyllyp gives erotic pleasure, he must be a "surrogate" or "symbol" for the phallus. In other words, all sexuality is phallic.

Interestingly, some of the contemporary texts that McConchie cites to prove his case actually refute it. For instance, a madrigal by Gascoigne clearly refers back to Skelton's poem, but here Phyllyp is female:

> She never wanders far abroad,
> 　But is at home when I do call.
> If I command she lays on load
> 　With lips, with teeth, with tongue and all.
> 　　　　　　(17–20)

E. H. Fellowes, *English Madrigal Verse, 1588–1632,* 3d ed. (New York: Oxford University Press, 1967), pp. 358–59. In *Magnyfycence,* Skelton himself used the phrase "Phylyp Sparowe" to refer to a woman (1562). Thus the tradition sometimes portrays Phyllyp as feminine and as a "symbol" of oral, not phallic sexuality. Or rather, the conjunction of name and attributes tends to confuse sexual difference.

Phyllyp's sexual ambiguities help to lay bare the real mechanisms of jealousy behind the Catullan sparrow tradition. If the sparrow were really only a sexual surrogate or phallic symbol, then the male poet could easily displace it (being the bearer of the "real thing"). But it is the bird's non-phallic characteristics—its wanderings, its gentle oral stimulations—which make it potentially more satisfying to women than men are. The male poet's (or critic's) tendency to read the sparrow as a phallic rival thus exemplifies the very thing whose absence makes the sparrow such a dangerous rival in the first place. The interpretive fixations of the Oedipus merely reproduce the genital fixations of "normal" male sexuality; despite the surface despair that it generates, to see the sparrow as a phallic rival is actually comforting to the male, because it opens up a possible line of identification and displacement *via* the reductive teleology of the Oedipus. This is not to say that Phyllyp *never* assumes a phallic role, but merely that the poem never privileges this particular symbolization over others.

46. Interestingly, Skelton claimed to have translated from French into English "Of Mannes Lyfe the Peregrination."

47. Gilles Deleuze and Félix Guattari, *Anti-Oedipus: Capitalism and Schizophrenia,* trans. Robert Hurley, Mark Seem, and Helen R. Lane (New York: Viking Press, 1957), p. 78.

48. I do not mean, of course, to identify Jane with these libidinal flows. She is also a speaking subject and, in this capacity, an often acute reader of texts. See Susan Schibanoff, "Taking Jane's Cue: *Phyllyp Sparowe* as a Primer for Women Readers," *PMLA* 101 (1986), 832–47.

49. Chaucer's castrated (?) Pardoner carries a compensatory "walet . . . in his lappe, / Bretful of pardoun, comen from Rome al hoot" ("General Prologue" 686–87), and this wallet is referred to a few lines later as his "male."

50. "In the second part of the poem, Vespers being ended, Skelton speaks in his own voice. Using the same book of devotions he 'commends,' not the departed soul into the hands of God, but the living person of Jane Scrope." Brownlow, *"Boke of Phyllyp Sparowe,"* p. 10.

51. See Fish, *Skelton's Poetry,* pp. 114–17.

52. Ibid., pp. 112–16.

53. Cf. *Phyllyp Sparowe* 182: "With his wanton eye."

54. Compare *Phyllyp Sparowe* 175–76—"Phyllyp had leve to go / To pyke my lytell too"—with *Speke Parott* 107—"With my beke I can pyke my lyttel praty too."

55. See Fish, *Skelton's Poetry,* p. 146; and F. L. Brownlow, "The Boke Compiled by Maister Skelton, Poet Laureate, Called Speake Parrot," *English Literary Renaissance* 1 (1971), 21.

56. Spearing, *Medieval to Renaissance,* p. 269.

57. Cf. also 124–25: "And *assilum, whilom refugium miserorum, /*

*Non phanum, sed prophanum*, standyth in lytyll sted [And asylum, formerly the refuge of wretches, is not a sanctuary but is to be made secular]" (Scattergood trans.).

58. Walker, *John Skelton*, pp. 85–86, 132.
59. Sebastian Giustiani, quoted ibid., p. 162.
60. Kinney, *John Skelton*, pp. 133–34.
61. "Whence I bring forth arguments in a sacred school of poets" (Scattergood trans.).
62. Walker, *John Skelton*, p. 91, says that the poem's obscurities baffled its original readers.
63. Ibid., pp. 79–80.
64. Quoted ibid., p. 173.
65. Ibid., pp. 73–78, 80–89.
66. The headless arrow also has another, more specific reference. During the negotiations at Calais the emperor Charles asked Henry to send six thousand English archers in fulfillment of his treaty obligations. Henry and Wolsey disagreed over whether the archers should be sent at all while the negotiations were still proceeding, and they then quarreled bitterly over who should "head" them. See J. J. Scarisbrick, *Henry VIII* (Berkeley: University of California Press, 1968), p. 86. The issue of the archers marked the first serious breach between Henry and his negotiator and raised the issue of which of the two was the other's "head." Thus I read the image of the arrow as referring both to the specific subject of the quarrel and to Wolsey in his role as delegate.
67. Nelson, *John Skelton*, p. 182.
68. Fish, *Skelton's Poetry*, p. 135.
69. Walker, *John Skelton*, p. 93.

## Chapter 4. Rational Kernel, Mystical Shell

1. Frederick Engels, *Socialism: Utopian and Scientific*, trans. Edward Aveling (New York: International, 1978), p. 36.
2. Engels is mainly interested in the utopian thinkers of the nineteenth century. He does not even mention Thomas More by name, but he does refer to "utopian pictures of ideal social conditions" which appeared in the sixteenth and seventeenth centuries; moreover, he classes these among the "theoretical enunciations corresponding with . . . [the] revolutionary uprisings of a class not yet developed [i.e., the proletariat]" (p. 33), and thus he inserts them in the evolutionary line that leads to utopian and thence to scientific socialism. Karl Kautsky's book, *Thomas More and His World* (1888), uses Engels's framework to situate More.
3. Quoted from Louis Althusser, "Contradiction and Overdetermination," in *For Marx*, trans. Ben Brewster (London: Verso, 1979), p. 89.
4. Ibid., p. 93. His reading of this figure is highly instructive.
5. A useful summary and discussion of Marin's book is provided by Fredric Jameson in his review article "Of Islands and Trenches: Naturalization [*sic*] and the Production of Utopian Discourse," *Diacritics* (June 1977), 2–21. "Naturalization " in the printed title should read "Neutralization." Christopher Kendrick's fine essay "More's *Utopia* and Uneven

Development," *boundary 2* 13.2–3 (1985), 233–66, also develops Marin's reading while specifying the historical determinants that make possible the utopian "plays of space."

6. Louis Marin, *Utopiques: Jeux d'espaces* (Paris: Minuit, 1973), p. 249. For quotations from Marin's "Theses on Ideology and Utopia" (chap. 9 of his book), I use Fredric Jameson's translation in *Minnesota Review* 6 (Spring 1976), 71–75. Page references will be to Marin's book, however. Translations from chapters other than this one are my own.

Marin's concept of utopia as an ideological critique of ideology derives in part from Louis Althusser, "A Letter on Art in Reply to André Daspré," in *Lenin and Philosophy*, trans. Ben Brewster (London: New Left Books, 1971), pp. 203–8, and the elaboration of Althusser's approach by Pierre Macherey in *A Theory of Literary Production*, trans. Geoffrey Wall (London: Routledge and Kegan Paul, 1978).

7. Marin, *Utopiques*, 250, 253 (my emphasis).

8. Beginning from very different premises and a very different conception of science, George M. Logan also views *Utopia* as a step on the way to "scientific" political thought. See George M. Logan, *The Meaning of More's "Utopia"* (Princeton: Princeton University Press, 1983), esp. p. 105.

9. Marin, *Utopiques*, p. 250.

10. Jameson, "Of Islands," p. 6.

11. Marin, *Utopiques*, pp. 10, 199.

12. See Sigmund Freud, *The Interpretation of Dreams*, trans. James Strachey (New York: Avon, 1965), chaps. 6 and 7.

13. "For a few weeks, historical time was suspended, the totality of the institution and of the law was placed in question in and by discourse. . . . A liberating explosion, an extratemporal moment of 'overturning,' May 1968 was also the moment of the seizure of speech [la prise de la parole]" (Marin, *Utopiques*, p. 15).

14. C. S. Lewis, *English Literature in the Sixteenth Century* (New York: Oxford University Press, 1954), p. 169. On the critical tradition that views *Utopia* as *jeu d'esprit*, see Logan, *Meaning*, p. 5.

15. Lewis, *English Literature*, p. 168.

16. J. H. Hexter, *The Vision of Politics on the Eve of the Reformation: More, Machiavelli, and Seyssel* (New York: Basic Books, 1973), p. 125n, quoted in Logan, *Meaning*, p. 8.

17. Thomas More, *Utopia*, ed. Edward Surtz and J. H. Hexter. Vol. 4 of *The Complete Works of St. Thomas More* (New Haven: Yale University Press, 1965), pp. 219–21. There is one additional restriction on speech, which does not, however, apply to Utopia's ordinary citizens: elected officials are forbidden, under penalty of death, to discuss matters of public policy outside of the senate or public assembly (*Utopia*, p. 325). The point of this law is not to limit free expression, however, but to prevent conspiracies among officials which might oppress the people or overturn the Utopian form of government. Even elected officials may say whatever they wish, so long as they conduct their public duties in public.

18. Kautsky is surely correct when he writes of More: "Had he not written *Utopia* his name would scarcely be better known to-day than that of his friend who shared his fate, Bishop Fisher of Rochester. His socialism made him immortal." *More and His World*, p. 159.

19. See Fredric Jameson, "Reification and Utopia in Mass Culture," *Social Text* 1 (1979), 130–48. See also Jameson, "The Dialectic of Utopia and Ideology," chap. 6 of *The Political Unconscious* (Ithaca: Cornell University Press, 1981), pp. 281–99.

20. Thomas More, *Utopia*, trans. Paul Turner (Harmondsworth, Eng.: Penguin, 1965).

21. Quotation and translation from the Loeb edition.

22. The Yale edition similarly interprets the name of the mythical Polylerites to mean "the People of Much Nonsense." *Leros* does mean "nonsense, garbage, frippery." In the *Protagoras* (347d), Socrates compares an ongoing discussion of poetry to the wine parties held by common loungers in the marketplace, who, because they lack education, find their own voices and thoughts insufficient to carry on a conversation. Hence they "put a premium on flute-girls by hiring the extraneous (*lerou*) voice of the flute at a high price, and carry on their intercourse by means of its utterance." Trans. W. R. H. Lamb (London: Heinemann, 1924). Here *leros* describes "speech" that is both pleasurable and lacking in intellectual content. Note that *hythlos* and *leros* are both associated with demotic or marginalized groups: old wives, flute girls, common marketfolk. Hence Utopia takes as its own the language of the excluded, which always appears as "nonsense" to those in power.

23. Stephen Greenblatt, *Renaissance Self-Fashioning from More to Shakespeare* (Chicago: University of Chicago Press, 1980), pp. 40–41.

24. Ibid., p. 40.

25. Jameson, "Of Islands," p. 7.

26. To my reading it may be objected that Hythlodaeus gives reasons for Utopian travel other than the desire to see new places—i.e., to visit friends in other cities and to avoid work. But the same problems remain. Everything in Utopia works to assure the economic and social self-sufficiency of each city and to isolate it from the others. Hence acquaintances across city lines are difficult to imagine. And if evading work were the only motivation for travel, then presumably the Utopian officials would never grant permission for it.

27. Lewis, *English Literature*, pp. 169–70.

28. Vespucci was impressed by the indifference the indigenous peoples of South America displayed toward gold. See the references in the Yale edition of *Utopia*, p. 428.

29. Karl Marx, *Capital*, vol. 1, trans. Ben Fowkes (New York: Vintage, 1977), pp. 164–65.

30. Ibid., 1:167.

31. Greenblatt, *Renaissance Self-Fashioning*, p. 41.

32. Elizabeth McCutcheon, "Denying the Contrary: More's Use of Litotes in the *Utopia*," in R. S. Sylvester and G. P. Marc'hadour, eds., *Essential Articles for the Study of Thomas More* (Hamden, Conn.: Archon, 1977), pp. 263–74.

33. Marin, *Utopiques*, pp. 226–32. As elsewhere, because of space limitations, my summary of Marin's complex arguments must be both reductive and partial.

34. Marin, *Utopiques*, p. 81: "The short and fragmentary stories rip apart the representational description, tearing a hole in the canvas on

which the image of a better government was imprinted and revealing within Utopia the work of a utopian practice, its meaning, its relation to history and to the sociohistorical conditions of its production."

35. Indeed, so stinging is More's analysis of class and state domination that some critics have tried to blunt its force by foregrounding the rhetorical irony focused on the speaking persona of Hythlodaeus. The most maddening of these attempts is Robbin Johnson's book More's "Utopia": Ideal and Illusion (New Haven: Yale University Press, 1969). For a more "measured" approach, see Richard S. Sylvester, " 'Si Hythlodaeo Credimus': Vision and Revision in More's Utopia," in Sylvester and Marc'hadour, Essential Articles, pp. 290–301. The argument of such studies can be reduced to the following: since Hythlodaeus is such an "un-Utopian" character (egotistical, antisocial, domineering), his discourses on Utopia and contemporary England are therefore rendered more or less ironic. More undercuts the viewpoint of this extremist and radical persona in order to endorse a more moderate, humanist vision of reform.

Several points need to be made here. The first is that the reformist persona of More is subjected to an irony at least as intense as that directed against Hythlodaeus (an irony to which critics of Hythlodaeus seem relatively blind). Indeed, the liberal reformist reading of Utopia is probably the least defensible of all possible readings, even on purely literary grounds. Second, Hythlodaeus is under no obligation to embody as well as to describe a Utopian "ethic," even according to the standards of humanist ideology. Defending his decision not to counsel kings, he says: "Plato was right in seeing that if kings themselves did not turn to philosophy, they would never approve of the advice of real philosophers because they have been from their youth saturated and infected with the wrong ideas" (p. 67). And earlier, on the subject of thievery, he excoriates the hypocrisy of "allow[ing] your youths to be badly brought up and their characters, even from their early years, to become more and more corrupt, [and then] to be punished, of course, when, as grown-up men, they commit the crimes which from boyhood they have shown every prospect of committing" (p. 71). Given this emphasis on education, is it then surprising that Hythlodaeus, whose "character, even from its earliest years, has become more and more corrupt" through contact with class society, has developed as he has? A flawless Hythlodaeus would actually contradict his own contention that ethical perfection can arise only in a utopian polity.

36. See Marin, Utopiques, pp. 185–211, on how this section of the text is structured by a scission between ethicotheological and sociohistorical modes of discourse.

37. Cf. Gilles Deleuze and Félix Guattari on oedipalization: "The law tells us: You will not marry your mother, and you will not kill your father. And we docile subjects say to ourselves: so that's what I wanted! Will it ever be suspected that the law discredits—and has an interest in discrediting and disgracing—the person it presumes to be guilty and wants to be made to feel guilty? One acts as if it were possible to conclude directly from psychic repression the nature of the repressed, and from prohibition the nature of the prohibited. . . . [But] what really takes place is that the law prohibits something that is perfectly fictitious in the order of desire or of the 'instincts,' so as to persuade its subjects that they had the intention

corresponding to this fiction. This is indeed the only way the law has of getting a grip on intention, of making the unconscious guilty." *Anti-Oedipus: Capitalism and Schizophrenia,* trans. Robert Hurley, Mark Seem, and Helen R. Lane (New York: Viking Press, 1957), pp. 114–15.

38. A materialist critique of ethical ideology is enabled by the humanist rhetoricity that allows More to "suspend" his own theological training for the length of the Utopian game. In Hythlodaeus's reported discourse, this suspension is figured in the person of Cardinal Morton, who acts as a framing agent. As lord chancellor, More's Morton embodies a disinterested administrative rationality that allows him to regulate the debaters at his table while refusing to impose his own political will. But Morton's relative nonintervention as a political authority is paired with his absolute nonintervention as a religious authority. The deafening silence of Morton the archbishop, his refusal to impose a theological framework on the debate over thieves (despite some subtle prompting from Hythlodaeus), provides a secular "enclosure" within which the creation and critique of the ethical subject can proceed. In this, Morton figures the more global suspension of theology which allows the utopian project as a whole to take form.

39. In his chapters on primitive accumulation Marx twice quotes from Hythlodaeus's speech on cannibalistic sheep and the ravages of enclosure. *Capital* 1:880, 898.

40. The lawyer completes this pun by his suggested means for dealing with vagrants: executing them, that is, eliminating them, sending them to "nowhere."

41. See James Holstun, *A Rational Millennium: Puritan Utopias of Seventeenth-Century England and America* (Oxford: Oxford University Press, 1987), pp. 34–37. Holstun's excellent book shows how the strategy of using displaced and disorganized populations as its raw material marks not only the utopia as a literary genre but its incarnation in actual projects of utopian reform and colonization.

42. Jameson coined the term *ideologeme* to denote "the smallest intelligible unit of the essentially antagonistic collective discourses of social classes." *The Political Unconscious: Narrative as a Socially Symbolic Act* (Ithaca: Cornell University Press, 1981), p. 76.

43. See Nicos Poulantzas, *Political Power and Social Classes,* trans. Timothy O'Hagan et al. (London: Verso, 1978), pp. 210–28, on the juridico-political as the dominant ideological "region" within the capitalist mode of production.

44. Cf. Aristotle, *Politics,* 1257b, on the limitlessness of the art of acquiring wealth.

45. In the introduction to the Yale edition of *Utopia,* J. H. Hexter writes: "More's interest was not in the most effective organization of economic resources for the satisfaction of human wants because he was not concerned with the best economy or with the satisfaction of wants, and probably he had no clear conception of an economy distinct from the other relations of men in a community" (p. cxii). I can only respond that I find this position almost entirely mistaken and, moreover, self-evidently so.

46. As Marin points out, the Utopian "map" allows no space for the

governor or his congress in Amaurotum. *Utopiques,* pp. 169–70. The Utopian polity answers tit for tat, leaving "no room for politics" among its philosophical citizens.

47. Poem quoted from *The Oxford Book of Medieval English Verse,* ed. Celia Sisam and Kenneth Sisam (Oxford: Oxford University Press, 1970).

48. Jean Baudrillard, "The Ideological Genesis of Needs," in *For a Critique of the Political Economy of the Sign,* trans. Charles Levin (St. Louis: Telos Press, 1981), p. 80.

49. Ibid., pp. 80–81.

50. Georges Bataille, "The Notion of Expenditure," in *Visions of Excess: Selected Writings, 1927–1939,* trans. Allan Stoekl (Minneapolis: University of Minnesota Press, 1985), pp. 105–16, 118.

51. "The consumption of excess of energy by a determined class is not the destructive consuming of meaning, but the significative appropriation of a surplus value within the space of restricted economy." Jacques Derrida, "A Hegelianism without Reserve: A Reading of Georges Bataille," in *Writing and Difference,* trans. Alan Bass (Chicago: University of Chicago Press, 1978), p. 337.

52. Christopher Kendrick has argued that Utopia embodies a "petty wish," i.e., the desires of a class of feudal petty producers which for determinate reasons has no historical future and thus cannot formulate a class project. "More's *Utopia,*" pp. 245–46, 250–52. As will become clear, the term "petty wish" seems problematic to me; I see Utopia as perfecting petty production, but this alone cannot constitute a class wish.

53. See Marin, *Utopiques,* pp. 65–85.

54. More read Vespucci's 1504 letter to Piero Soderini in the Latin translation that was appended to the *Cosmographiae introductio* of Martin Waldseemueller (1507). A facsimile and translation of the entire volume was published by the United States Catholic Historical Society in 1907. Since Vespucci's letter is annoyingly bowdlerized by the English translator at key points, I quote from George Tyler Northrup's edition, Amerigo Vespucci, *Letter to Piero Soderini,* Vespucci Reprints, Texts, and Studies, 4 (Princeton: Princeton University Press, 1916).

55. Vespucci, *Letter,* pp. 10, 4–5, 26, 35–36.

56. Johnson, *More's "Utopia,"* p. 72: "The point of this anecdote is that haste and enthusiasm may turn well-intentioned and benevolent gestures into corrupting gifts. . . . May not More be uttering a similar general warning to the reader when he suggests 'that what was thought likely to be a great benefit to them may, through their own imprudence, cause them great mischief'?"

57. See Bataille, *Visions of Excess,* p. 119: "In various competitive games, loss in general is produced under complex conditions. . . . As much energy as possible is squandered in order to produce a feeling of stupefaction—in any case with an intensity infinitely greater than in productive enterprises. The danger of death is not avoided; on the contrary, it is the object of a strong unconscious attraction."

58. Baudrillard discusses an incident in which a radical group in the United States occupies and "liberates" a department store. To the group's surprise, people take only a few inconsequential items from the store. Baudrillard's remarks on this event are instructive. "Concerning

the Fulfillment of Desire in Exchange Value," in *For a Critique,* pp. 204–12.

59. See Logan, *Meaning,* p. 169–72, for classical sources of this philosophy.

60. I borrow this expression, with some trepidation, from Deleuze and Guattari, who in turn derive it from Antonin Artaud. In *Anti-Oedipus,* the body without organs is a "dead thing" (p. 20) at "zero intensity" (p. 19) with a "smooth, slippery, opaque, taut surface" (p. 9). "The full body without organs is the unproductive, the sterile, the unengendered, the unconsumable" (p. 8). It is an antiproductive recording surface on which the workings of the desiring machines are inscribed.

61. "The positive . . . is only designated by the modification of a letter from the 'negative' name. The omicron of negation becomes the epsilon of happiness." Marin, *Utopiques,* p. 123.

62. Trans. R. Hackforth, in *The Collected Dialogues of Plato,* ed. Edith Hamilton and Huntington Cairns (Princeton: Princeton University Press, 1961). On the influence of the *Philebus,* first noticed by Ernst Cassirer, see Judith P. Jones, "The *Philebus* and the Philosophy of Pleasure in Thomas More's *Utopia,*" *Moreana* 31–32 (1971), 61–69. On the influence of Epicurean *voluptas* see Logan, *Meaning,* pp. 144–81.

63. See Marin, *Utopiques,* pp. 222–23.

64. "As dreadful as it is, human poverty has never had a strong enough hold on human societies to cause the concern for conservation—which gives production the appearance of an end—to dominate the concern for unproductive expenditure." Bataille, *Visions of Excess,* p. 120. Also see Baudrillard, "Ideological Genesis of Needs," p. 81; and Marshall Sahlins, *Stone Age Economics* (New York: Aldine, 1972), chap. 1, "The Original Affluent Society."

65. For a discussion of the Aristotelian ideal of social "autarchy" and its influence on More, see Thomas I. White, "Aristotle and Utopia," *Renaissance Quarterly* 29 (1976), 635–75. Also see Logan, *Meaning,* p. 87.

66. Guy Debord, *Society of the Spectacle* (Detroit: Black and Red Press, 1970), sec. 38 (my emphasis).

Chapter 5. Margins and Modernity

1. For a detailed discussion of the typographical formats of *The Shepheardes Calender* and humanist editions of Virgil, see Ruth Samson Luborsky, "The Allusive Presentation of *The Shepheardes Calender,*" *Spenser Studies* 1 (1980), 42–53. See also Bruce R. Smith, "On Reading *The Shepheardes Calender,*" *Spenser Studies* 2 (1981), 69–93. Luborsky locates other possible sources for Spenser's layout in certain editions of Ronsard and such emblem books as Alciati's.

2. William Nelson, *The Poetry of Edmund Spenser: A Study* (New York: Columbia University Press, 1963), p. 33, quoted by Luborsky, "Allusive Presentation," p. 29.

3. See Luborsky, "Allusive Presentation," p. 30; Smith, "On Reading," p. 79.

4. Sir Philip Sidney, *An Apology for Poetry* (1595; rpt. Indianapolis: Bobbs-Merrill, 1970), p. 74.

5. Edmund Spenser, *The Minor Poems*, vol. 1 of *The Works of Edmund Spenser: A Variorum Edition*, ed. Edwin Greenlaw et al., 11 vols. (Baltimore: Johns Hopkins University Press, 1932–57), p. 8. Henceforth all excerpts from E. K.'s prefatory materials will be cited by page number in this volume; excerpts from the poems will be cited by month and line number; and E. K.'s critical glosses will be cited by the line numbers to which they refer—all citations to be given in my text.

6. In *Spenser's "Shepheardes Calender": A Study in Elizabethan Allegory* (Notre Dame, Ind.: Notre Dame University Press, 1961), Paul McLane argues that at the time he wrote the *Calender*, Spenser was an orthodox and even conservative Anglican on matters of theology and church government and that his anti-Catholic sentiments were largely nationalist, sparked by the queen's marriage negotiations with the French duke of Alençon. In "Spenser, Puritanism, and the 'Maye' Eclogue," *Review of English Studies*, n.s. 20 (1969), pp. 155–67, and later in *Edmund Spenser: Puritan Poet* (Cambridge: Cambridge University Press, 1984), Anthea Hume insists that Spenser was in fact of strongly Puritan sympathies. What McLane sees as attacks on the Roman Catholic church, Hume regards as veiled criticisms of high-church Anglicans. Her views are basically seconded by David Norbrook in *Poetry and Politics in the English Renaissance* (London: Routledge and Kegan Paul, 1984), chap. 3, where he describes Spenser as a "moderate Puritan" (p. 36). In his article "Was Spenser a Puritan?" *Spenser Studies* 6 (1986), 1–31, John N. King takes issue with Hume and Norbrook, though his disagreements focus more on the use of the term *Puritan* than on Spenser's theological position. King prefers the phrase "progressive Protestant" (p. 1). King also insists that the dialogical structure of the eclogues resists reduction to one-sided theological arguments or satires.

7. Norbrook, *Poetry and Politics*, p. 75.

8. See Smith, "On Reading," pp. 87–89.

9. Michael McCanles, "*The Shepheardes Calender* as Document and Monument," *Studies in English Literature* 22 (1982), 5.

10. Henry V. S. Ogden and Margaret S. Ogden, *English Taste in Landscape in the Seventeenth Century* (Ann Arbor: University of Michigan Press, 1955), p. 1.

11. "A Short Treatise of Perspective," sixteenth-century manuscript quoted ibid., p. 1.

12. Henry Peacham, *The Art of Drawing with the Pen* (1606; facs. rpt. New York: Da Capo Press, 1970), sigs. E2v–E3r.

13. In his discussion of Kant's *Critique of Aesthetic Judgement*, Jacques Derrida has argued that such uncertainties are endemic to the very concept of the parergon: "That which constitutes things as *parerga* is not simply their exteriority as surplus; it is their internal structural relation which binds them to a lack at the interior of the *ergon*. And this lack is constitutive of the very unity of the *ergon*. Without this lack, the *ergon* would have no need of the *parergon*." Jacques Derrida, *La vérité en peinture* (Paris: Flammarion, 1978), p. 69.

14. Victoria Kahn, *Rhetoric, Prudence, and Skepticism in the Renaissance* (Ithaca: Cornell University Press, 1985), pp. 25–26.

15. Barbara J. Shapiro, *Probability and Certainty in Seventeenth-Century England: A Study of the Relationships between Natural Science, Religion, Law, and Literature* (Princeton: Princeton University Press, 1983), p. 121.

16. Valla, *Antidoti in Poggium*, IV (I, 387), quoted in Donald R. Kelley, *Foundations of Modern Historical Scholarship* (New York: Columbia University Press, 1970), p. 33.

17. Aldo Scaglione, "The Humanist as Scholar and Politian's Conception of the *Grammaticus*," *Studies in the Renaissance* 8 (1961), 69–70: "For Politian the words of the texts must be pinned down in their original, individual, unequivocally precise, historically concrete meaning, so as to be made intelligible with absolute, scientific certainty, as an empirical unitary fact endowed with a relative, well-delimited value." E. J. Kenney argues that philology became scientific only when it began to engage in *conjectural* emendation. "The Character of Humanist Philology," in R. R. Bolgar, ed., *Classical Influences on European Culture, A.D. 500–1500* (Cambridge: Cambridge University Press, 1971), pp. 119–28. Kenney contends that the philological achievements of the early humanists have been somewhat exaggerated by modern scholars.

18. See Joseph M. Levine, *Humanism and History: Origins of Modern English Historiography* (Ithaca: Cornell University Press, 1987), pp. 69, 71, 99.

19. Shapiro, *Probability and Certainty*, p. 61.

20. Ibid., pp. 30, 62–63, 269–70.

21. Ibid., pp. 75–76.

22. Ibid., pp. 30, 74–118.

23. R. R. Bolgar, *The Classical Heritage and Its Beneficiaries* (Cambridge: Cambridge University Press, 1954), pp. 297–98.

24. Hugh G. Dick, "Thomas Blundeville's *The True Order and Method of Wryting and Reading Hystories* (1574)," *Huntington Library Quarterly* 3.2 (1940), 152–53.

25. Norbrook, *Poetry and Politics*, p. 79. See also G. C. Moore Smith, ed., *Gabriel Harvey's Marginalia* (Stratford-upon-Avon: Shakespeare Head Press, 1913), p. 121.

26. Compare Blundeville in Dick, "Blundeville's *True Order*," p. 164.

27. Spenser, *Works* 10:84–85.

28. McCanles, "*Calender* as Document," p. 5.

29. Jean-François Lyotard, *The Postmodern Condition: A Report on Knowledge*, trans. Geoff Bennington and Brian Massumi (Minneapolis: University of Minnesota Press, 1984).

30. The outlines of what Lyotard calls "narrative knowledge" have already been set down in part by Eric Havelock in his *Preface to Plato* (Cambridge, Mass.: Harvard University Press, 1963). For Lyotard, however, the pragmatics of narrative knowledge cannot be fully defined by the context of oral transmission, as they are for Havelock.

31. Lyotard, *Postmodern Condition*, pp. 19 (my emphasis), 27.

32. Ibid., p. 25. Obviously, some criteria are needed to distinguish sci-

entific statements from other denotative utterances. Lyotard offers the principles that the object of a scientific utterance must be available to repeated access and that "it must be possible to decide whether or not a given statement pertains to the language judged relevant by the experts" (p. 18).

33. The term *scientific*, as used here, cannot be taken in any positivistic sense. Scientific knowledge is defined for Lyotard not by a stricter adherence to the "real" but by its social procedures of transmission, its rules as a language game. (Lyotard wishes to criticize Enlightenment mythologies of science, not to reproduce them). Still less should the concepts of narrative and scientific knowledge be reduced to the commonplace notions of "faith" and "reason"—a particular danger given humanist treatments of the historical conjuncture being discussed here. Faith and reason are concepts derived from a psychology of faculties, and hence from a problematic utterly alien both to Lyotard and to Marxism. What is at issue is not the mental "stance" of individual subjects but the different social-discursive practices that produce these subjective effects.

34. In his introductory essay to *The Postmodern Condition*, Fredric Jameson attempts to make this connection more explicit. See esp. p. xi.

35. See McCanles, "*Calender* as Document."

36. See G. R. Evans, *The Language and Logic of the Bible: The Earlier Middle Ages* (Cambridge: Cambridge University Press, 1984).

37. On the narrative reduction effected by figural readings of the Bible, see (from two rather different perspectives) Hans Frei, *The Eclipse of Biblical Narrative* (New Haven: Yale University Press, 1974), pp. 1–7; and Fredric Jameson, *The Political Unconscious: Narrative as a Socially Symbolic Act* (Ithaca: Cornell University Press, 1981), pp. 29–32. R. R. Bolgar argues that medieval logic performed a similar narrative reduction: "Logic was used first to explain contradictions in patristic teaching and secondly to reinforce the edifice of dogma by establishing rhetorical connections between its several parts" (*Classical Heritage*, p. 206).

38. Frei, *Eclipse*, pp. 1–7.

39. See Jameson, *Political Unconscious*, pp. 29–32.

40. On this guild structure, see Walter J. Ong, S. J., *Ramus: Method and the Decay of Dialogue* (Cambridge, Mass.: Harvard University Press, 1958; rpt. New York: Octagon, 1979), pp. 54, 132–36, 153, and references there.

41. Ibid., pp. 59–63.

42. For the case of Pecock, see Levine, *Humanism and History*, pp. 54–66. Pecock was accused of heresy for maintaining that the "doom of reason" offered a separate and legitimate source of knowledge about matters of divine truth. He claimed that syllogistic logic gave true results "though all the angels in heaven should say and hold that conclusion were not true" (quoted by Levine, p. 57).

43. Lyotard, *Postmodern Condition*, p. 27.

44. Levine, *Humanism and History*, p. 29.

45. Ibid., pp. 29, 30–31.

46. Judson Boyce Allen, *The Friar as Critic: Literary Attitudes in the Later Middle Ages* (Nashville: Vanderbilt University Press, 1971), p. 102.

47. Kenneth Sisam, ed., *Fourteenth-Century Verse and Prose* (Oxford:

Oxford University Press, 1921), p. xiii, quoted by Levine, *Humanism and History*, p. 28.

48. *The Kalendar of Shepherdes*, ed. H. Oscar Sommer, 3 vols. (London: Kegan Paul, 1892), 1:33.

49. *Kalendar* 3:9. Volume 3 is a reprint of R. Pynson's edition of 1506. In *Society and Culture in Early Modern France* (Stanford: Stanford University Press, 1973), Natalie Zemon Davis writes that the Kalendars "appear a cross between a folklorist's recording and a pastoral, a shaped version of the peasant world for country gentlemen and city people and a way for such readers to identify themselves with the simple wisdom of 'the great shepherd of the mountain' " (pp. 197–98). In fact, however, there is very little about the *Kalendar* that is pastoral or even "shaped." The volume is not a romanticized or idealized depiction of country life but a frequently dry and even technical compilation of useful facts and charts that would seem to hold little interest for the kind of audience she describes. In any case, it seems unlikely that this kind of pastoral nostalgia would exist in France or England in the late fifteenth and early sixteenth centuries. Ruth Luborsky feels that the crude depictive woodcuts used in the *Kalendar* are a sign that it was directed at a "semi-literate audience" (Luborsky, "Allusive Presentation," p. 55).

50. For the assimilation of human "seasons" to those of the year—a conceit that Spenser will borrow for *The Shepheardes Calender*—see *Kalendar* 3:10–12.

51. Keith Thomas, *Religion and the Decline of Magic* (New York: Charles Scribner's Sons, 1971), chap. 2, "The Magic of the Medieval Church."

52. Ibid., pp. 63–65.

53. Joseph Levine notes that prehumanist writers "understood that a true story was not an invention, that history was not a fiction," but they don't "seem to have had any idea how practically to distinguish among them—nor, when all is said and done, any strong motive to do so." *Humanism and History*, p. 39.

54. Luborsky, "Allusive Presentation," p. 55.

55. See Louis Montrose, "Interpreting Spenser's February Eclogue: Some Contexts and Implications," *Spenser Studies* 2 (1981), 67–74.

56. Phrase taken from Smith, "On Reading," p. 83, where he uses it to describe a German illustration of Virgil's works.

57. Samuel Johnson, *Selected Poetry and Prose*, ed. Frank Brady and William K. Wimsatt (Berkeley: University of California Press, 1977), p. 172.

58. See Montrose, "Interpreting." Also see Roland B. Bond, "Supplantation in the Elizabethan Court: The Theme of Spenser's February Eclogue," *Spenser Studies* 2 (1981), 55–65; and McLane, *Spenser's "Shepheardes Calender*," pp. 61–76.

59. See Edwin A. Greenlaw, "*The Shepheards Calender*," *PMLA* 26 (1911), 421.

60. Theodore Bathurst, *The shepherds calendar* (1653), sig. A3v. The Latin—"inductus . . . Romana toga"—is perhaps more suggestive than it means to be. The verb *induco* can mean "to dress or clothe in" but also "to erase writing" or "to draw a line through." The phrase thus suggests both a recasting and an erasure of the original.

61. Ibid., sig. A4r.

62. Abraham Fraunce, *The Lawyer's Logic* (1588; rpt. Menston, England: Scolar Press, 1969), sig. q2r.

63. Ibid., sig. Biiiv.

64. Ibid., sigs. Ciiv–Ciiir.

65. Ibid., sig. Biiiv.

66. Ibid., sig. qq3r.

67. In *Intellectual Origins of the English Revolution* (Oxford: Oxford University Press, 1965), Christopher Hill describes Fraunce as "a noted Cambridge Ramist and Puritan" (p. 134). The only direct evidence he gives for Fraunce's Puritanism, however, is a passing reference in *The Countess of Pembroke's Emanuell* comparing Caiaphas to a prelate. As H. R. Trevor-Roper has shown in a review, Hill's book is sometimes a bit hasty in describing various figures as Puritans (*History and Theory* 5 [1966], 61–82). Fraunce's cultural tastes and social circle suggest at least moderate Puritan leanings, but Fraunce generally kept his exact religious allegiances out of print, and in the absence of much biographical information about him, any label is bound to be speculative.

68. See Anthea Hume, "Spenser, Puritanism, and the 'Maye' Eclogue," *Review of English Studies*, n.s. 20 (1969), 155–67.

69. For details and background, see McLane, *Spenser's "Shepheardes Calender,"* pp. 13–26. Norbrook criticizes some of McLane's allegorical readings but doesn't deny the general relevance of the Alençon affair.

70. See Mary Parmenter, "Spenser's *Twelve Aeglogues Proportionable to the Twelve Monthes,"* ELH 3 (1936), 190–217.

71. For a discussion of adiaphorism and the Anglican church, see Arthur B. Ferguson, *Clio Unbound: Perception of the Social and Cultural Past in Renaissance England* (Durham, N.C.: Duke University Press, 1979), pp. 172–82.

72. Ibid., p. 171.

73. Shapiro, *Probability and Certainty*, p. 78.

74. See L. Staley Johnson, "Elizabeth, Bride and Queen: A Study of Spenser's April Eclogue and the Metaphors of English Protestantism," *Spenser Studies* 2 (1981), 75–89.

75. On Elizabeth as Solomon, see ibid. In a poem that directly imitates the "Aprill" ode, the poet Thomas Blenerhasset expresses a similar idea by pairing Pallas, who represents *prudentia*, or worldly rulership, with Minerva (Elizabeth), who represents *sapientia*, or heavenly wisdom. See *A Celebration of the True Minerva* (1582), ed. Josephine Waters Bennett (New York: Scholars' Facsimiles and Reprints, 1941), sig. A2 r–v.

76. Writing of the reigns of William the Conquerer and his successors, William Camden noted that the Normans "would have yoked the English under their tongue, as they did under their command" (quoted by Arthur Ferguson, *Clio Unbound*, p. 317).

77. For a rich discussion of the political contradictions in defenses of literary and linguistic nationalism in the Renaissance, see Margaret W. Ferguson's reading of Du Bellay's *Deffence et illustration de la langue françoyse* in *Trials of Desire: Renaissance Defenses of Poetry* (New Haven: Yale University Press, 1983), pp. 18–53.

78. Thomas Wilson, *The Arte of Rhetoricke* (1560; rpt. Oxford: Clarendon Press, 1909), p. 164.

79. Quoted in Spenser, *Works* 8:571.
80. See Hume, "Spenser, Puritanism, and the 'Maye' Eclogue."
81. See Joseph Wittreich, *Visionary Poetics: Milton's Tradition and His Legacy* (San Marino, Calif.: Huntington Library, 1979), pp. 105–16.
82. King, "Was Spenser a Puritan?" p. 2.
83. Ibid., p. 17.
84. Patrick Collinson, *Archbishop Grindal, 1519–1583: The Struggle for a Reformed Church* (Berkeley: University of California Press, 1979), pp. 234–36.
85. Ibid., p. 249.
86. Patrick Collinson, *The Elizabethan Puritan Movement* (London: Methuen, 1967), p. 175.
87. Quoted in Collinson, *Archbishop Grindal*, p. 248.
88. Collinson, *Puritan Movement*, p. 176.
89. John Milton, *Animadversions upon the Remonstrants Defence against Smectymnuus*, in *Complete Prose Works of John Milton*, ed. Don M. Wolfe, 8 vols. (New Haven: Yale University Press, 1953), 1:722–23.

Chapter 6. *Historica Passio*

1. All quotations of the text are from the Arden edition of the play, edited by Kenneth Muir (London: Methuen, 1972). I will identify discrepancies between Folio and Quarto readings where appropriate, but I believe that it is perfectly defensible to employ a conflated text of *Lear* for most critical purposes, including those of this chapter.
2. *Historica* is the reading of Q, F1, and F2. F3 gives the hybrid form *Hystorica*. For a discussion of Renaissance theories of "the mother" and their relevance to the play, see Coppélia Kahn, "The Absent Mother in *King Lear*," in Margaret W. Ferguson, Maureen Quilligan, and Nancy J. Vickers, eds., *Rewriting the Renaissance: The Discourses of Sexual Difference in Early Modern Europe* (Chicago: University of Chicago Press, 1986), pp. 33–49.
3. It is clear that the play refers to contemporary theological controversies, including those pertaining to demonic possession, but does so mainly as part of a political argument. See, e.g., Stephen Greenblatt, "Shakespeare and the Exorcists," in his *Shakespearean Negotiations: The Circulation of Social Energy in Renaissance England* (Berkeley: University of California Press, 1988), pp. 94–128; John L. Murphy, *Darkness and Devils: Exorcism and "King Lear"* (Athens: Ohio University Press, 1984); Joseph Wittreich, *"Image of that Horror": History, Prophecy, and Apocalypse in King Lear* (San Marino, Calif.: Huntington Library, 1984). Wittreich's book, however, makes the further and, I think, totally unwarranted assertion that religious or Christian "meanings" play a significant role in *Lear*.
4. John Danby, *Shakespeare's Doctrine of Nature: A Study of "King Lear"* (London: Faber and Faber, 1951), pp. 52, 138.
5. See, e.g., Paul Delaney, "*King Lear* and the Decline of Feudalism," *PMLA* 92 (1977), 429–440; Paul Siegel, *Shakespearean Tragedy and the Elizabethan Compromise* (New York: New York University Press, 1957), pp. 161–88; Walter Cohen, *Drama of a Nation: Public Theater in Renais-*

sance *England and Spain* (Ithaca: Cornell University Press, 1985), pp. 327–56; John Turner, "The Tragic Romances of Feudalism," in Graham Holderness, Nick Potter, and John Turner, eds., *Shakespeare: The Play of History* (Iowa City: University of Iowa Press, 1987), pp. 85–118.

6. Turner, "Tragic Romances," p. 101.

7. Georg Lukács, *The Historical Novel*, trans. Hannah Mitchell and Stanley Mitchell (London: Merlin Press, 1962), p. 150.

8. Cohen, *Drama of a Nation*, p. 352.

9. See David Bevington, *Action Is Eloquence: Shakespeare's Language of Gesture* (Cambridge, Mass.: Harvard University Press, 1984). What I describe here as representation or manifestation might well be seen as an exchange or appropriation of value along the lines argued by Stephen Greenblatt in *Shakespearean Negotiations: The Circulation of Social Energy in Renaissance England* (Berkeley: University of California Press, 1988), esp. chap. 1. I focus less on the acquisition than on the consumption or destructive expenditure of social value.

10. See Turner, "Tragic Romances," pp. 89–90 and passim. On the play's romance elements see Maynard Mack, *"King Lear" in Our Time* (London: Methuen, 1966). The next few paragraphs cover issues also discussed by Turner and are at various points indebted to his analysis.

11. Mack speaks of *Lear's* "combination of parable and parable situations with acute realism" as one of the play's "distinctive features" (p. 56).

12. See, principally, John Draper, "The Occasion of *King Lear*," *Studies in Philology* 34 (1937), 176–85; Marie Axton, "*King Lear* and the Union Controversy," in Axton, *The Queen's Two Bodies: Drama and the Elizabethan Succession* (London: Royal Historical Society, 1977), pp. 131–43.

13. James I, *Basilikon doron*, in *The Political Works of King James I*, ed. Charles Howard McIlwain (Cambridge, Mass.: Harvard University Press, 1918), p. 37.

14. See Axton, "*Lear* and the Union Controversy," p. 136.

15. See Turner, "Tragic Romances," p. 97; Axton, "*Lear* and the Union Controversy," p. 136.

16. Axton, "*Lear* and the Union Controversy," p. 145.

17. Ibid., p. 136.

18. On absolutism as a cultural sign system, see Jonathan Goldberg, *James I and the Politics of Literature* (Baltimore: Johns Hopkins University Press, 1983). On the structural limitations to royal authority in the Tudor and Stuart eras, see Perry Anderson, *Lineages of the Absolutist State* (London: New Left Books, 1974; Verso, 1979), pp. 113–42; Lawrence Stone, *The Causes of the English Revolution, 1529–1642* (New York: Harper and Row, 1972), pp. 60–67.

19. J. G. A. Pocock, *The Ancient Constitution and the Feudal Law: English Historical Thought in the Seventeenth Century* (Cambridge: Cambridge University Press, 1957), p. 87.

20. McIlwain, *Political Works of James I*, p. xiii.

21. James I, *Trew Law*, in *Political Works*, pp. 69, 63, 62. McIlwain writes: "For [James] the king's right to his crown is heritable precisely as was the right of the eldest son of a tenant of a *foedum militare* under feudal law" (p. xxxvii).

22. In this respect I must disagree with Lawrence Stone's assertion

that James's views on kingship, "although more extravagantly phrased and more insistently repeated, did not differ in any significant respect from those of Queen Elizabeth" (*Causes of the Revolution*, p. 94).

23. See Axton, "*Lear* and the Union Controversy," passim; Ernst Hartwig Kantorowitz, *The King's Two Bodies: A Study in Mediaeval Political Theology* (Princeton: Princeton University Press, 1957).

24. Pocock, *Ancient Constitution*.

25. Ibid., pp. 30–55. Coke's argument was, of course, somewhat more complex than this. As Pocock shows, arguments about historical priority alone marked the simplified version of common-law history used in pre- and postrevolutionary polemic.

26. James I, *Trew Law*, p. 62.

27. Pocock, *Ancient Constitution*, p. 97.

28. Turner, "Tragic Romances," pp. 85–94 and passim.

29. Ibid., p. 87.

30. Jonathan Dollimore, *Radical Tragedy: Religion, Ideology, and Power in the Age of Shakespeare* (Brighton, Sussex: Harvester Press, 1984); Franco Moretti, "The Great Eclipse: Tragic Form as the Deconsecration of Sovereignty," in his *Signs Taken for Wonders: Essays in the Sociology of Literary Forms*, trans. Susan Fischer, David Forgues, and David Miller (London: New Left Books, 1983), pp. 42–82. Walter Cohen also maintains, correctly in my view, that Shakespeare's "tragic period is the climactic dramatic representation of the failings of absolutism." *Drama of a Nation*, p. 306. That this position is not universally self-evident, however, is made clear by John Murphy's reading. "In *King Lear*, as elsewhere," Murphy states, "Shakespeare is an impassioned Royalist and the most profound apologist for hierarchy and degree as answering to the deepest needs of humanity as one can find in English literature." *Darkness and Devils*, p. 87.

31. Murphy, *Darkness and Devils*, pp. 15–69, provides the most detailed historical account of the exorcisms and the plot. See also Greenblatt, *Shakespearean Negotiations*.

32. See William C. Carroll, " 'The Base Shall Top th'Legitimate': The Bedlam Beggar and the Role of Edgar in *King Lear*," *Shakespeare Quarterly* (Winter 1987), 426–41.

33. See appendix 7 to the Arden edition of the play, p. 239.

34. For a discussion of Jorden's work, see Ilza Veith, *Hysteria: The History of a Disease* (Chicago: University of Chicago Press, 1965), chap. 7.

35. Michael MacDonald, *Mystical Bedlam: Madness, Anxiety, and Healing in Seventeenth-Century England* (Cambridge: Cambridge University Press, 1981), discusses these two traditions.

36. Wittreich, "*Image*," pp. 31, 47.

37. See Greenblatt, *Shakespearean Negotiations*, pp. 123–25.

38. Wittreich, "*Image*," p. 26.

39. Greenblatt, *Shakespearean Negotiations*, p. 97. On popular magico-religious practices during the early modern period, see, of course, Keith Thomas, *Religion and the Decline of Magic* (New York: Charles Scribner's Sons, 1971).

40. Thomas, *Religion*, p. 153.

41. "For albeit it be trew that I have at length prooved, that the king is

above the law, as both the author and giver of strength thereto; yet a good king will not onely delight to rule his subjects by the lawe, but even wil conforme himselfe in his owne actions thereunto, alwaies keeping that ground, that the health of the common-wealth be his chief lawe." James I, *Trew Law*, p. 63.

42. Ibid., p. 57, 66–67.

43. MacDonald, *Mystical Bedlam*, p. 208.

44. For a brilliant exposition of the theme of "handy-dandy" and the role of the Fool in *Lear*, see Danby, *Shakespeare's Doctrine*, pt. 2, chap. 2.

45. The following remarks are based on Gary Taylor, "Monopolies, Show Trials, Disaster, and Invasion: *King Lear* and Censorship," in Gary Taylor and Michael Warren, eds., *The Division of the Kingdoms: Shakespeare's Two Versions of King Lear* (Oxford: Clarendon Press, 1983), pp. 75–119. Taylor's carefully argued piece uses political censorship of the Folio edition to argue that the Quarto text was derived from Shakespeare's foul papers.

46. Taylor, "Monopolies," pp. 102–3.

47. See the note in the Arden edition.

48. James I, Speeches to Parliament (1603 and 1609), pp. 279, 320.

49. Ibid., 1609, pp. 318–19.

50. Ibid., p. 318.

51. See Stone, *Causes of the Revolution*; Anderson, *Lineages*.

52. Cohen, *Drama of a Nation*, p. 266.

53. Rosalie Colie, "Reason and Need: *King Lear* and the 'Crisis' of the Aristocracy," in R. L. Colie and F. T. Flahiff, eds., *Some Facets of King Lear: Essays in Prismatic Criticism* (Toronto: University of Toronto Press, 1974), pp. 191–92.

54. Ambassador quoted and emphasis added by Taylor, "Monopolies," p. 103.

55. See Gilles Deleuze and Félix Guattari, "November 20, 1923: Postulates of Linguistics," in *A Thousand Plateaus*, trans. Brian Massumi (Minneapolis: University of Minnesota Press, 1987), pp. 75–110. For Deleuze and Guattari, the term *mot d'ordre* suggests "order" both as "command" and as "arrangement" or "ordering"; it clearly invokes the etymology of the Greek *logos* as well as the first words of God in the book of Genesis, where he structures the world by divine command. The *mot d'ordre* does not isolate the command as a particular form of utterance, however; rather, it reveals that the most "neutral" linguistic conception of language as a signifying system entails certain operations of power. Even in its blandest designative or signifying functions, language acts as a command.

56. See Jean Baudrillard, *For a Political Economy of the Sign*, trans. Charles Levin (St. Louis: Telos Press, 1981). For Baudrillard, linguistic difference (and hence signification) is bound up with the "invidious difference" created by consumption, the two participating in a more general economy of signs. Baudrillard's, like Deleuze and Guattari's, is a social critique of language as a system of domination and of linguistics as a "science" that colludes with and reinforces this domination. The two critiques are incompatible in certain respects, however, and I am using them here to designate different terrains or effects within cultural sign systems.

In general (at least as far as I am aware), Baudrillard and Deleuze and Guattari maintain a peculiar silence with respect to each other.

57. Colie, "Reason and Need," p. 199.

58. Colie, "Reason and Need."

59. This erosion was only relative, of course. As Lawrence Stone puts it, "If the gentry were the ruling, the aristocracy were the governing class." *The Crisis of the Aristocracy, 1558–1641* (Oxford: Clarendon Press, 1965), p. 55. But the conditions and institutions of class governance were, of course, decisively altered by the politicomiltary consolidation of Tudor absolutism.

60. See Stone, *Crisis.*

61. Ibid., p. 44.

62. James I, Speech in Star Chamber (1616), in *Political Writings*, pp. 343–44.

63. James I, Speech to Parliament (1609), in *Political Writings*, p. 319.

64. Ibid., p. 321.

65. *Thomas Platter's Travels in England, 1599*, trans. Clare Williams (London: Jonathan Cape, 1937), p. 167, quoted in Bevington, *Action Is Eloquence*, p. 36.

66. Taylor, "Monopolies," p. 92.

67. Colie, "Reason and Need," p. 205, 206.

68. Turner, "Tragic Romances," p. 111.

69. It should be said, though, that Turner's reading explicitly turns away from a historical totalization of the play's meaning, and that he accounts for Edmund's, Goneril's, and Regan's roles in the play (unsatisfactorily, in my view) by means of the concept of perversion.

70. Danby, *Shakespeare's Doctrine*, p. 48.

71. William Harrison, "A Description of England," in *Holinshead's Chronicles of England, Scotland, and Ireland . . .*, 6 vols. (London, 1807–8), 1:273.

72. Stone, *Crisis*, pp. 65–128.

73. Turner, "Tragic Romances," p. 105.

74. When asked by Albany, "How have you known the miseries of your father?" Edgar responds, "By *nursing* them, my lord" (5.3.179–80). Edgar's "good" androgyny clearly contrasts with Oswald's "bad," partly because of his figurative association with Cordelia as opposed to Goneril. Albany's aforementioned "milky gentleness" serves a similar purpose.

75. Marcel Mauss, *The Gift: Forms and Functions of Exchange in Archaic Societies*, trans. Ian Cunnison (New York: Norton, 1967).

76. Anderson, *Lineages*, p. 31. It is, of course, an exaggeration to claim that "the production of manufactured commodities is inherently unlimited," but this production is certainly flexible, and Anderson's larger point is valid.

77. See Robert Brenner, "The Origins of Capitalist Development: A Critique of Neo-Smithian Marxism," *New Left Review* 104 (1977), 25–92.

78. For the "sum over histories," see Richard P. Feynman, *QED: The Strange Theory of Light and Matter* (Princeton: Princeton University Press, 1985).

79. See Taylor's commentary: "Eggs were also, proverbially, dirt cheap; in 1605 a hundred of them sold for as little as 3 shillings 10 pence.

The Fool's offer to pay Lear two crowns—ten shillings—for a single egg is, therefore, an action entirely appropriate for an idiot" ("Monopolies," pp. 107–8).

80. Stone, *Crisis*, pp. 65–128.

81. William Harrison's reflections on gavelkind are suggestive for *Lear's* division of the kingdom and the problem of inflation:

> Customarie law consisteth of certeine laudable customes used in some privat countrie, intended first to begin upon good and reasonable considerations, as gavell kind, which is all the male children equallie to inherit, and continued to this daie in Kent: wher it is onelie to my knowledge reteined, and no wher else in England. It was at the first devised by the Romans, as appeareth by Caesar in his commentaries, wherein I find, that to breake and daunt the force of the rebellious Germans, they made a law that all the male children (or females for want of males which holdeth still in England) should have their father's inheritance equallie divided amongst them. By this meanes also it came to passe, that whereas before time for the space of sixtie yeares, they had put the Romans to great and manifold troubles, within the space of thirtie yeares after this lawe made, their power did waxe so feeble, and such discord fell out amongst themselves, thet they were not able to mainteine warres with the Romans, nor raise anie juste armie against them. For as a river runing with one streame is swift and more plentifull of water than whan it is drained or drawne into manie branches: so the lands and goods of the ancestors being dispersed amongst their issue males, of one strong their were raised sundrie weake, whereby the originall or generall strength to resist the adversarie, became enfeebled and brought almost to nothing. ("Description of England," p. 303)

The name of Shakespeare's Kent (who is significantly childless) may well have been intended to evoke the one county in England where the practice of gavelkind continued. Harrison's oblique defense of primogeniture seems a response in part to recent encroachments against it. As Rosalie Colie writes: "In spite of marked deference shown parents by their children in England, it is clear that over the century and a half of the Renaissance, fathers lost their unquestioned authority in the disposition of their children's lives and fortunes. Legal requirements came to protect, particularly, daughters. . . . often too, fathers provided so generously for daughters and younger sons (in some cases, for bastards as well) that support for entailed estates was severely jeopardized." "Reason and Need," p. 189.

82. See Whitney R. D. Jones, *The Tudor Commonwealth, 1529–1559* (London: Athelone Press, 1970), pp. 133–34. Jones cites a proclamation of 1551, which frankly admits that "the late king of famous memory . . . considering at the beginning of his last wars that great and notable sums of money were requisite . . . for the maintenance . . . of the same, did therefore devise to abase and diminish the goodness of the coin." *Proclamations* no. 372 (30 April 1551), cited by Jones, p. 134–35. Might this connection between war costs and debasement of the coinage help explain why Lear's mad ravings move directly from "coining" to "press-money"?

83. Jones, *Tudor Commonwealth*, p. 134.

84. John Ponet, *A Shorte Treatise of Politicke Power* (1556), sigs. Fii–Fiii, cited by Jones, *Tudor Commonwealth*, p. 140.

85. S. G. E. Lythe, "The Economy of Scotland under James VI and I," in Alan G. R. Smith, ed., *The Reign of King James VI and I* (New York: St. Martin's Press, 193), p. 67.

86. "Anent the reforming of the Cunye" (1593), quoted in Edward Burns, *The Coinage of Scotland*, 3 vols. (Edinburgh, 1887), 2:411.

87. It is worth noting that Folio gives the nonsensical "crying" in place of "coining." Could this be another example of the kind of censorship described by Taylor? Coining pertains to the problem of royal expense, the one topic that, as Taylor has argued, was probably censored in *Lear*. It would be necessary to show, of course, that James's abuse of the Scots currency was known in England in 1605 and that it was considered a possible source of embarrassment.

88. Jones (*Tudor Commonwealth*, p. 142) quotes an instructive exchange from *A Discourse of the Common Weale of this Realm of England* (1549), cast as a colloquy among several characters. One of these, the Knight, asks whether, since "the coin is but a token to go from man to man . . . stricken with the King's seal to be current," it matters "what metal it be of, yea though it be but leather or paper?" To this the Doctor replies "that the substance and the quantity is esteemed in coin and not the name" and that "we may not set the price of things at our pleasure but follow the price of the universal market of all the world."

89. By mouthing principles of economic rationality, Goneril and Regan secure their credentials as two of the play's "proto-bourgeois" characters. But of course this is all a mere pretense to strip the king of his powers, as Lear himself recognizes. The daughters' historical trajectory, like Edmund's, leads backward.

90. Compare James H. Kavanagh's discussion of this speech in "Shakespeare in Ideology," in John Drakakis, ed., *Alternative Shakespeares* (London: Methuen, 1985), pp. 158–60.

91. See MacDonald, *Mystical Bedlam*, p. 130.

92. See Carroll, " 'The Base Shall Top.' "

93. MacDonald, *Mystical Bedlam*, p. 42.

94. Ibid., pp. 5–6. As MacDonald also points out, children often tried to prove mental unfitness as a way of wresting estates from aging parents: "There were good reasons for old people's reluctance to relinquish control of their property. An elderly man or woman who had not reserved some part of his estate to himself had to rely upon his children's concern and willingness to pay all of his expenses, including the charges to obtain medical treatment. The fact that mortal sickness and mental decay were considered the natural companions of old age may have made the younger persons who controlled the purse reluctant to part with their money" (p. 46). Maynard Mack suggests that *Lear* may have been directly inspired by the case of Sir Brian Annesley:

Annesley, a gentleman pensioner to Queen Elizabeth, had three daughters, the elder two married; the youngest, unmarried, was named Cordell. In late 1603, a year or two before the composition of

Shakespeare's play, Annesley's eldest daughter and her husband seem to have taken steps to have him declared incompetent, and to lay hands on his possessions. Cordell resisted the move, persuaded Robert Cecil by a letter that her father deserved a better reward for his late services to the Queen "than at his last gasp to be recorded and registered a Lunatic," and succeeded in sequestering his estate even when, on his death soon after, the eldest daughter contested the will. (Mack, *"Lear" in Our Time*, pp. 45–46)

95. MacDonald, *Mystical Bedlam*, p. 130.

96. I am not arguing, of course, that beggars are less "needy" than they appear, but rather that the whole metaphysics of need has at best a merely sentimental value and at worst a quite reactionary one, however much it might be voiced in popular or progressive contexts. It is one of the theoretical virtues of Marxism to have recognized from the very beginning that the class struggle is always a struggle over *surplus*, and that the levels of "need" which define the reproduction of labor power, for example, are always calculated from what remains after surplus value is subtracted. A recent and spectacular example of the dominance of *dépense* over need was provided by Joyce Brown, the New York streetperson who resisted Mayor Edward Koch's attempts to force her into a shelter and who frequently astonished passersby when she burned paper money donated to her. See *New York Times*, 13 November 1987, A1, B2. A similar blend of excess and resistance was sometimes reported of beggars in the early modern period. The *Regulations for Relief of the Poor at Norwich* (1570) recorded shock that beggars offered food did not eat for nourishment but seemed rather to engage in destructive acts of feasting: "Moreover, those that daielie wente abowt pretendinge to satisfye their hunger, were not onelye contented to take at mens doores that [which] suffized them, but being overgorged they caste foorthe the reste into the streete, so that they might be followed by the sight therof in pottage, breade, meate, and drinke which they spoiled very voluptuously." Quoted in R. H. Tawney and Eileen Power, eds., *Tudor Economic Documents*, 3 vols. (New York: Longmans, Green, 1924), 2:317. These vomiting vagrants are, in a sense, lowerclass parodies of Gloucester's "superfluous and lust-dieted man." It is possible that what the author of these regulations attributes to excess results in fact from illness or stomachs unused to food. It is likely too that vagrants intentionally overate whenever they were offered food because they never knew when their next meal might come. Yet at the same time their actions suggest a craving for surplus which is stronger than biological need. This is a case in which distribution does *not* undo excess. A similar logic causes these beggars to reject shelter if it means accepting the debasements of charity:

Agayne, these crewes in their contynuall beggynge respected no worke to prepare them lodginge, but used churche porshes, mens seller[s], doores, barnes and haye chambers, and other backe corners to bestowe themselves, and such as had howses did not worke for lodginge other than that they laye upon the colde grounde. So cared they not for apparrell, though the colde strooke so deepe into them, that what with diseases and wante of shyftenge their Fleshe was eaton with vermyne and corrupte diseases grew upon them so faste and so grevouslye as they were past remedye. (ibid.)

With this one should compare Lear's refusal of shelter and stripping off of his garments. In all these cases a social insistence on surplus overrides the biological demands of need.

97. Jacques Derrida, "A Hegelianism without Reserve: A Reading of Georges Bataille," in *Writing and Difference*, trans. Alan Bass (Chicago: University of Chicago Press, 1978).

98. Compare James I, *A Defense of the Rights of Kings*, in *Political Works*, p. 245: "Let a cat be throwen from a high roofe to the bottom of a cellour or vault, she lighteth on her feet, and runneth away without taking any harme. A king is not like a cat, howsoever a cat may looke upon a king: he cannot fall from the loftie pinacle of Royaltie, to light on his feet upon the hard pavement of a private state, without crushing all his bones to pieces."

# Index

Library of Congress Cataloging-in-Publication Data

Halpern, Richard.
  The poetics of primitive accumulation : English Renaissance culture and the genealogy of capital / Richard Halpern.
     p.  cm.
  ISBN 0–8014–2539–5 (alk. paper).—ISBN 0–8014–9772–8 (pbk. : alk. paper)
     1. English literature—Early modern. 1500–1700—History and criticism. 2. Capitalism and literature—England—History—16th century. 3. Great Britain—Economic conditions—16th century. 4. Economics in literature. 5. Marxist criticism. I. Title.
  PR428.C25H35   1991
  820.9′003—dc20                                                     90–55757